METROPOLITAN OPERA ANNALS

ANNALS

SECOND SUPPLEMENT: 1957-1966

AUDITORIUM OF THE OLD METROPOLITAN OPERA HOUSE, 1883-1966

Photo: Alexandre Georges

METROPOLITAN OPERA ANNALS

SECOND SUPPLEMENT: 1957-1966

A Chronicle of Artists and Performances

Compiled by
WILLIAM H. SELTSAM

With a Foreword by
FRANCIS ROBINSON
Assistant Manager
Metropolitan Opera Association, Inc.

NEW YORK
THE H. W. WILSON COMPANY

In Association with
THE METROPOLITAN OPERA GUILD, INC.
NINETEEN HUNDRED SIXTY-EIGHT

To
MARY ELLIS PELTZ
with gratitude and affection
W.H.S.

FOREWORD

"There are people who will read about music and nothing else," Bernard Shaw says on the flyleaf of his collected music reviews. "To them dead prima donnas are more interesting than saints, and extinct tenors than mighty conquerors. They are presumably the only people who will dream of reading these volumes. If my wisdom is to be of any use to them it must come to them in this form. And so I let it go to them for what it is worth."

It would be easy to say Mr. Shaw's *envoi* applies to the three volumes of METROPOLITAN OPERA ANNALS, but it would not be quite the truth. In far less than the eight decades since the first Metropolitan Opera House threw open its doors, opera has passed from luxury to necessity.

When Rudolf Bing became manager of the Metropolitan in 1950, the season was eighteen weeks. He promptly extended it to twenty-two, and the first season in the new house is thirty-one. The number of subscription series has tripled. The number of subscribers has more than doubled, and they come from all walks of life and all levels of society. Far and wide they transcend Mr. Shaw's rarefied classification.

Any volume of METROPOLITAN OPERA ANNALS is of consequence. This one is particularly so, since it marks the end of several glittering eras, the end of the old house. And how momentous these nine years just past have been. This volume will share the snares of its predecessors. It's like going to *Webster's Unabridged*. Rarely do you get off with only your original inquiry. Something catches your eye and fancy, and you may even forget what you went to look for in the first place. You become a retriever with an oversensitive nose. You would flunk the field trials, but if it's a winter evening and you are not on a deadline it's wonderful.

Just thumb through: the new productions of *Don Giovanni* and *Butterfly*, *Turandot* and *Falstaff*, the first production by the Metropolitan of *Wozzeck*, the debuts of Price, Nilsson, Sutherland and Corelli, the Martinelli gala, the farewell of Milanov, and the death of Leonard Warren. And what about the last season recorded here, which brought the debuts of Freni, Scotto and Caballé? Study the program of the Gala Farewell. It is not, Mr. Bing said on that emotion-packed last night, a troupe of guest artists passing through the city. It is the Metropolitan Opera *company*. And by some special grace the first performance in the new house, a Metropolitan Opera Guild Student Performance for some three thousand of "the audience of the future," was in the same week as the last performance in the old.

The author of the introduction to the first volume of METROPOLITAN OPERA ANNALS was Edward Johnson, the author of the foreword to the first supplement was Rudolf Bing. This does not imply I am to be the next general manager. Far from it. If for no other reason, by the time Mr. Bing fulfills his existing contract I shall be near the age to collect Social Security; but I am proud to have my name even in a small way on something so important and so lasting. I am reminded of what Sir Joshua Reynolds said as he signed his name to the great portrait of Mrs. Siddons as the Tragic Muse:

"Content, Madame," he said, "to go down in history on the hem of your garment."

FRANCIS ROBINSON
Assistant Manager, Metropolitan Opera

New York
April 1966

PREFACE

In 1957 we expressed appreciation that the widespread public interest in opera made possible the publication of the first supplement to the foundation volume of METROPOLITAN OPERA ANNALS. Today, with the added interest of opera-on-television (which we hope may soon be extended regularly to the Metropolitan performances) plus the growing popularity of Metropolitan Opera broadcasts by radio, we are again gratified that it is now possible to publish a second supplementary volume. The present volume extends from the performance of *Eugene Onegin* on October 28, 1957, to the final curtain at the historic theater for the Gala Performance of April 16, 1966.

The plan and arrangement remain identical with that of the foundation volume and the first supplement: only performances *in* the Metropolitan Opera House and *by* the resident company are included. A fascinating added feature is a valuable list of all artist-debuts (1883-1966), compiled by Gerald Fitzgerald and John W. Freeman of *Opera News* with the invaluable assistance of Marietta Fuller of the Metropolitan Opera Archives and Robert Textor, who confirmed the information.

The records of performances have been reproduced photographically from *Opera News* and Metropolitan Opera Annals of the Season through the courtesy of the publishers, The Metropolitan Opera Guild, Inc. Without such reproduction, publication of this supplement would not have been financially feasible.

While it is impossible to name all of those who have helped in bringing the record up to date, the compiler again wishes to cite Mrs. John DeWitt Peltz, Metropolitan Opera Archivist. Her immediate interest was aroused when the huge typescript of the foundation volume was first presented for her perusal. Though we have received many letters indicating gratitude for the METROPOLITAN OPERA ANNALS, Mary Ellis Peltz deserves far more thanks than this compiler for her unswerving faith and devotion to the project. To Gerald Fitzgerald our special thanks, for the many months he worked on this second supplement. Our admiration and gratitude are expressed inadequately in cold print.

For permission to quote from the criticism of their music editors, adding to the perspective and significance of this supplement, as before, grateful acknowledgments are made to the *Christian Science Monitor, Hartford Times, New York Daily News, New York Herald Tribune, New York Journal-American, New York Mirror, New York Post, New York Times, New York World-Telegram and Sun, New Yorker,* and *Saturday Review.*

W. H. S.

April 1966

CONTENTS

Foreword vii

Preface ix

List of Illustrations xiii

Metropolitan Opera Annals: 1957-1962 1

Portraits of Artists 55

Metropolitan Opera Annals: 1962-1966 59

List of Debuts 109

List of Errata in the First Printing of Metropolitan Opera
    Annals: First Supplement, 1947-1957 121

List of Omissions 121

Index 122

LIST OF ILLUSTRATIONS

PAGE

AUDITORIUM OF THE OLD METROPOLITAN OPERA HOUSE,
1883-1966 .... frontispiece

NICOLAI GEDDA as Faust 55

LEONIE RYSANEK as Abigaille in *Nabucco* 55

GIULIETTA SIMIONATO as Azucena in *Il Trovatore* 55

BARRY MORELL as Lt. B. F. Pinkerton in *Madama Butterfly* 55

CORNELL MACNEIL as Nabucco 55

ANNA MOFFO as Manon 55

BIRGIT NILSSON as Isolde 56

JON VICKERS as Florestan in *Fidelio* 56

ANSELMO COLZANI as Sir John Falstaff 56

GABRIELLA TUCCI as Alice Ford in *Falstaff* 56

EILEEN FARRELL as Alcestis 56

EZIO FLAGELLO as the Maharajah in *The Last Savage* 56

LEONTYNE PRICE as Leonora in *Il Trovatore* 57

FRANCO CORELLI as Calaf in *Turandot* 57

SÁNDOR KÓNYA as Walther von Stolzing in *Die Meistersinger* 57

JOAN SUTHERLAND as Lucia di Lammermoor 57

JUDITH RASKIN as Anne in *Falstaff* 57

JAMES MCCRACKEN as Otello 57

RÉGINE CRESPIN as the Marschallin in *Der Rosenkavalier* 58

JESS THOMAS as Lohengrin 58

GERAINT EVANS as Leporello in *Don Giovanni* 58

ELISABETH SCHWARZKOPF as Donna Elvira in *Don Giovanni* 58

MIRELLA FRENI as Adina in *L'Elisir d'Amore* 58

NICOLAI GHIAUROV as Méphistophélès in *Faust* 58

FINAL CURTAIN AT THE GALA FAREWELL, April 16, 1966 108

1957-1958 SEASON

PERSONNEL
Male Artists
Alvary, Lorenzo
Anthony, Charles
Baccaloni, Salvatore
Bardelli, Cesare
Barioni, Daniele
Baum, Kurt
Bergonzi, Carlo
Burke, Peter
Campora, Giuseppe
Carelli, Gabor
Cassel, Walter
Cehanovsky, George
Corena, Fernando
Crain, Jon
Da Costa, Albert
Davidson, Lawrence
Del Monaco, Mario
De Paolis, Alessio
Edelmann, Otto
Ernster, Dezso
Fernandi, Eugenio
Flagello, Ezio
Franke, Paul
Gari, Giulio
Gedda, Nicolai
Guarrera, Frank
Harrell, Mack
Harvuot, Clifford
Hawkins, Osie
Herbert, Ralph
Hines, Jerome
Keith, George
Kelley, Norman
Kullman, Charles
Labo, Flaviano
Lewis, William
London, George
Marsh, Calvin
Mayreder, Rudolf
Merrill, Robert
Moscona, Nicola
Nagy, Robert
Pechner, Gerhard
Peerce, Jan
Ritchard, Cyril
Scott, Norman
Sereni, Mario
Sgarro, Louis
Siepi, Cesare
Singher, Martial
Strasfogel, Andrew
Tozzi, Giorgio
Tucker, Richard
Uppman, Theodor
Valentino, Frank
Valletti, Cesare
Vinay, Ramon
Warren, Leonard
Wilderman, William
Zanasi, Mario

Female Artists
Albanese, Licia
Allen, Mildred
Amara, Lucine
Amparan, Belen
Borkh, Inge
Callas, Maria Meneghini
Chambers, Madelaine
Conner, Nadine
Cundari, Emilia
Curtis-Verna, Mary
Dalis, Irene
Davy, Gloria
Della Casa, Lisa
De Los Angeles, Victoria
Dobbs, Mattiwilda
Elias, Rosalind
Gueden, Hilde
Harshaw, Margaret
Hoffman, Grace
Holland, Florence
Hurley, Laurel
Krall, Heidi
Lansing, Gladys
Lewis, Brenda
Lind, Gloria
Lipton, Martha
Madeira, Jean
Melatti, Jean
Milanov, Zinka
Miller, Mildred
Moedl, Martha
Moll, Mariquita
Munsel, Patrice
Ordassy, Carlotta
Peters, Roberta
Pobbe, Marcella
Pons, Lily
Rankin, Nell
Resnik, Regina
Roggero, Margaret
Schech, Marianne
Shawn, Dorothy
Steber, Eleanor
Stella, Antonietta
Stevens, Risë
Thebom, Blanche
Vanni, Helen
Votipka, Thelma
Wilson, Dolores

Ballet Soloists
Ames, Suzanne
Andrew, Thomas
Bardin, Micheline
Black, Margaret
de Lavallade, Carmen
Etgen, Ann
Farrington, Hubert
Grishin, Natalie
Hayden, Melissa
Holder, Geoffrey
Jerrell, Edith

Keane, Audrey
King, Nancy
Markova, Alicia
Marks, Bruce
Martin, Donald
Maule, Michael
San Miguel, Lolita
Schoch, Jean Lee
Solov, Zachary (choreographer)
Warren, Marsha
Wiland, Steve

Conductors
Adler, Kurt
Boehm, Karl
Cimara, Pietro
Cleva, Fausto
Hagen, Walter
Leinsdorf, Erich
Mitropoulos, Dimitri
Morel, Jean
Rudolf, Max
Schippers, Thomas
Stiedry, Fritz

General Manager
Bing, Rudolf

October 28 (Opening Night)
EUGENE ONEGIN (Tchaikovsky)
Conductor: Mitropoulos
Larina ....Lipton
Tatyana ....Amara
Olga ....Elias
Onegin ....London
Lenski ....Tucker
Prince Gremin ....Tozzi
Filippyevna ....Amparan
Captain ....Sgarro
Zaretski ....Cehanovsky
Triquet ....De Paolis

October 31
DON GIOVANNI (Mozart)
Conductor: Boehm
Don Giovanni ....Siepi
Donna Anna ....Steber
Donna Elvira ....Della Casa
Zerlina ....Peters
Don Ottavio ....Valletti
Commendatore ....Tozzi
Leporello ....Corena
Masetto ....Uppman

November 1
FAUST (Gounod)
Conductor: Morel
Faust ....Gedda
Marguerite ....Gueden
Méphistophélès ....Hines
Valentin ....Guarrera
Siébel ....Miller
Marthe ....Votipka
Wagner ....Marsh

1

1957-58

November 2 (matinee)
Metropolitan Opera
Guild Student Preview
LA PERICHOLE (Offenbach)
Conductor: Morel

Don Andres	Ritchard
Don Pedro	Hawkins
Panatellas	Franke
Tarapote	Mayreder
Perichole	Hurley
Paquillo	Uppman
Guadalena	Cundari
Estrella	Chambers
Virginella	Elias
Notaries	Anthony, Marsh
Old Prisoner	De Paolis
Clown	Andrew
Ballerina	King
Jailer	Marsh
Ninetta	Melatti
Frasquinella	Holland
Brambilla	Shawn
Manuelita	Lansing

November 2
Benefit Mizrachi
Women's Organization
LA TRAVIATA (Verdi)
Conductor: Cleva

Violetta	De Los Angeles
Alfredo	Barioni
Germont	Warren
Flora	Vanni
Gastone	Carelli
Baron Douphol	Marsh
Marquis d'Obigny	Cehanovsky
Dr. Grenvil	Harvuot
Annina	Allen
Giuseppe	Nagy
Gardener	Hawkins

November 4
DON GIOVANNI (Mozart)
Same cast as October 31

November 6
LA PERICHOLE (Offenbach)
Same cast as November 2

November 7
FAUST (Gounod)
Same cast as November 1

November 8
EUGENE ONEGIN (Tchaikovsky)
Same cast as October 28 except:
Lenski .... Gari

November 9 (matinee)
TOSCA (Puccini)
Conductor: Mitropoulos

Tosca	Stella
Cavaradossi	Peerce
Scarpia	Warren
Angelotti	Harvuot
Sacristan	Pechner
Spoletta	Franke
Sciarrone	Marsh
Jailer	Flagello
Shepherd	Keith

November 9
ANDREA CHENIER (Giordano)
Conductor: Cleva

Andrea Chénier	Del Monaco
Maddalena	Milanov
Countess di Coigny	Lipton
Carlo Gérard	Sereni
Bersi	Elias
Fléville	Cehanovsky
Abbé	Carelli
Madelon	Amparan
Mathieu	Corena
Spy	De Paolis
Fouquier	Scott
Dumas	Hawkins
Roucher	Valentino
Schmidt	Marsh
Major domo	Sgarro

November 11
FAUST (Gounod)
Same cast as November 1 except:
Marguerite ...... De Los Angeles

November 12
TOSCA (Puccini)
Same cast as November 9 except:
Jailer .... Sgarro

November 13
DON GIOVANNI (Mozart)
Same cast as October 31 except:

Don Giovanni	London
Zerlina	Hurley
Don Ottavio	Gedda
Leporello	Flagello

November 14
IL BARBIERE DI SIVIGLIA
(Rossini)
Conductor: Rudolf

Almaviva	Valletti
Dr. Bartolo	Corena
Rosina	Peters
Figaro	Guarrera
Don Basilio	Siepi
Berta	Roggero
Fiorello	Cehanovsky
Sergeant	De Paolis
Ambrogio	Mayreder

November 15
ANDREA CHENIER (Giordano)
Same cast as November 9 except:
Mathieu .... Pechner
Spy .... Anthony

November 16 (matinee)
LA TRAVIATA (Verdi)
Same cast as November 2 except:
Alfredo .... Campora

November 16
LA PERICHOLE (Offenbach)
Same cast as November 2

November 18
ANDREA CHENIER (Giordano)
Same cast as November 9 except:
Spy .... Anthony

November 19
EUGENE ONEGIN (Tchaikovsky)
Same cast as October 28

November 20
LA TRAVIATA (Verdi)
Same cast as November 2 except:
Violetta .... Stella
Germont .... Merrill
Dr. Grenvil .... Sgarro

November 21
TOSCA (Puccini)
Same cast as November 9 except:
Cavaradossi .... Campora

November 22
DER ROSENKAVALIER (R. Strauss)
Conductor: Boehm

Princess von Werdenberg	Della Casa
Baron Ochs	Edelmann
Octavian	Stevens
Von Faninal	Herbert
Sophie	Gueden
Marianne	Votipka
Valzacchi	De Paolis
Annina	Lipton
Police Commissioner	Hawkins
Major domo of Princess	Nagy
Major domo of von Faninal	Anthony
Notary	Pechner
Innkeeper	Franke
Singer	Baum
Orphans	Chambers, Cundari, Vanni
Milliner	Allen
Hairdresser	Wiland
Leopold	Mayreder
Animal Vendor	Carelli
Blackamoor	Warren

November 23 (matinee)
LA PERICHOLE (Offenbach)
Same cast as November 2 except:
Ballerina .... Ames

November 23
Benefit Yeshiva Women's
Organization
IL BARBIERE DI SIVIGLIA
(Rossini)
Same cast as November 14

November 25
EUGENE ONEGIN (Tchaikovsky)
Same cast as October 28

November 26
DER ROSENKAVALIER (R. Strauss)
Same cast as November 22

November 27
FAUST (Gounod)
Same cast as November 1 except:
Faust .... Campora
Marguerite .... De Los Angeles
Méphistophélès .... Siepi

2

November 28
LA TRAVIATA (Verdi)
Same cast as November 2 except:
Violetta ....Stella
Germont ....Sereni

November 29
LA FORZA DEL DESTINO (Verdi)
Conductor: Stiedry
Marquis ....Scott
Leonora ....Milanov
Don Carlo ....Warren
Don Alvaro ....Labo
Padre Guardiano ....Hines
Fra Melitone ....Corena
Preziosilla ....Roggero
Curra ....Chambers
Trabucco ....Franke
Surgeon ....Marsh

November 30 (matinee)
AIDA (Verdi)
Conductor: Cleva
King ....Sgarro
Amneris ....Dalis
Aida ....Curtis-Verna
Radames ....Bergonzi
Amonasro ....Merrill
Ramfis ....Tozzi
Messenger ....Nagy
Priestess ....Vanni

November 30
Benefit Hartman Homecrest
LA PERICHOLE (Offenbach)
Same cast as November 2 except:
Don Pedro ....Herbert
Tarapote ....Alvary
Perichole ....Munsel
Virginella ....Vanni
Ballerina ....Ames

December 2
IL BARBIERE DI SIVIGLIA
(Rossini)
Same cast as November 14 except:
Rosina ....De Los Angeles
Fiorello ....Marsh

December 4
CARMEN (Bizet)
Conductor: Schippers
Carmen ....Stevens
Don José ....Tucker
Micaela ....Cundari
Escamillo ....Guarrera
Zuniga ....Scott
Morales ....Marsh
Frasquita ....Krall
Mercédès ....Roggero
Dancaire ....Cehanovsky
Remendado ....Franke

December 5
Benefit Bagby Music
Lovers' Foundation
TOSCA (Puccini)
Same cast as November 9 except:
Tosca ....Milanov
Cavaradossi ....Bergonzi
Sciarrone ....Hawkins

December 6
DON GIOVANNI (Mozart)
Same cast as October 31 except:
Don Ottavio ....Peerce
Commendatore ....Scott

December 7 (matinee)
EUGENE ONEGIN (Tchaikovsky)
Same cast as October 28

December 7
LA FORZA DEL DESTINO (Verdi)
Same cast as November 29

December 8
LA BOHEME (Puccini)
Conductor: Schippers
Rodolfo ....Bergonzi
Marcello ....Guarrera
Schaunard ....Cehanovsky
Colline ....Tozzi
Mimi ....De Los Angeles
Musetta ....Krall
Benoit ....Flagello
Parpignol ....Nagy
Alcindoro ....Alvary
Sergeant ....Marsh
Customs Officer ......Nagy

December 9
DER ROSENKAVALIER (R. Strauss)
Same cast as November 22 except:
Sophie ....Peters

December 10
FAUST (Gounod)
Same cast as November 1 except:
Faust ....Campora
Marguerite .....De Los Angeles
Méphistophélès ....Siepi

December 11
ANDREA CHENIER (Giordano)
Same cast as November 9 except:
Andrea Chénier ....Baum
Carlo Gérard ....Warren
Bersi ....Roggero
Mathieu ....Flagello
Spy ....Anthony

December 12
CARMEN (Bizet)
Same cast as December 4 except:
Carmen ....Madeira
Micaela ....Gueden
Escamillo ....London

December 13
IL BARBIERE DI SIVIGLIA
(Rossini)
Same cast as November 14 except:
Rosina ....De Los Angeles
Don Basilio ....Hines

December 14 (matinee)
DON GIOVANNI (Mozart)
Same cast as October 31 except:
Don Ottavio ....Peerce

December 14
AIDA (Verdi)
Same cast as November 30 except:
Ramfis ....Scott

December 16
ORFEO ED EURIDICE (Gluck)
Conductor: Rudolf
Orfeo ....Stevens
Euridice ....Gueden
Amore ....Cundari
Ombre Felici ......Allen, Vanni

December 18
TOSCA (Puccini)
Same cast as November 9 except:
Tosca ....Milanov
Cavaradossi ....Labo
Spoletta ....De Paolis
Sciarrone ....Cehanovsky

December 19
LE NOZZE DI FIGARO (Mozart)
Conductor: Leinsdorf
Almaviva ....London
Countess ....Della Casa
Susanna ....Hurley
Figaro ....Siepi
Cherubino ....Miller
Marcellina ....Resnik
Bartolo ....Corena
Basilio ....Kelley
Don Curzio ....Carelli
Antonio ....**Alvary**
Barbarina ....Allen
Peasant Girls ..Chambers, Vanni

December 20
AIDA (Verdi)
Same cast as November 30 except:
Amonasro ....Bardelli
Priestess ....Krall

December 21 (matinee)
IL BARBIERE DI SIVIGLIA
(Rossini)
Same cast as November 14 except:
Don Basilio ....Hines

December 21
LUCIA DI LAMMERMOOR
(Donizetti)
Conductor: Cleva
Lucia ....Dobbs
Enrico Ashton ....Sereni
Edgardo ....Tucker
Alisa ....Votipka
Raimondo ....Moscona
Arturo ....Anthony
Normanno ....Nagy

December 23
LA PERICHOLE (Offenbach)
Same cast as November 2 except:
Tarapote ....Alvary
Perichole ....Munsel
Guadalena ....Krall
Virginella ....Vanni
Ballerina ....Black

December 24
LA TRAVIATA (Verdi)
Same cast as November 2 except:
Germont ....Merrill
Dr. Grenvil ....Sgarro

3

December 25
LUCIA DI LAMMERMOOR
(Donizetti)
Same cast as December 21 except:
Lucia ....Peters

December 26
ORFEO ED EURIDICE (Gluck)
Same cast as December 16

December 27
DON GIOVANNI (Mozart)
Same cast as October 31 except:
Donna Anna ......Curtis-Verna
Donna Elvira ....Amara

December 28 (matinee)
ANDREA CHENIER (Giordano)
Same cast as November 9 except:
Andrea Chénier ....Tucker
Carlo Gérard ....Warren
Spy ....Anthony

December 28
LA BOHEME (Puccini)
Same cast as December 8 except:
Rodolfo ....Labo
Schaunard ....Harvuot
Colline ....Hines
Benoit ....Davidson
Sergeant ....Flagello

December 29
CARMEN (Bizet)
Same cast as December 4 except:
Don José ....Bergonzi
Micaela ....Amara
Escamillo ....Merrill
Morales ....Harvuot

December 30
TOSCA (Puccini)
Same cast as November 9 except:
Tosca ....Curtis-Verna
Cavaradossi ....Labo
Scarpia ....London
Sciarrone ....Cehanovsky

December 31
LA PERICHOLE (Offenbach)
Same cast as November 2 except:
Tarapote ....Alvary
Perichole ....Munsel
Guadalena ....Krall
Virginella ....Vanni
Ballerina ....Ames

January 1
IL BARBIERE DI SIVIGLIA
(Rossini)
Same cast as November 14 except:
Figaro ....Merrill
Don Basilio ....Hines

January 2
LA FORZA DEL DESTINO (Verdi)
Same cast as November 29 except:
Leonora ....Curtis-Verna
Padre Guardiano ....Tozzi
Fra Melitone ....Pechner
Preziosilla ....Amparan
Surgeon ....Cehanovsky

January 3
AIDA (Verdi)
Same cast as November 30 except:
Amonasro ....Warren
Ramfis ....Scott

January 4 (matinee)
FAUST (Gounod)
Same cast as November 1 except:
Valentin ....Merrill
Siébel ....Roggero

January 4
LE NOZZE DI FIGARO (Mozart)
Same cast as December 19 except:
Almaviva ....Singher
Susanna ....Peters
Cherubino ....Elias

January 6
LA BOHEME (Puccini)
Same cast as December 8 except:
Rodolfo ....Gari
Schaunard ....Harvuot
Colline ....Moscona
Mimi ....Albanese
Musetta ....Lewis
Benoit ....Davidson
Sergeant ....Flagello

January 8
LA FORZA DEL DESTINO (Verdi)
Same cast as November 29 except:
Marquis ....Sgarro
Leonora ....Curtis-Verna
Don Carlo ....Sereni
Don Alvaro ....Bergonzi
Padre Guardiano ....Wilderman
Preziosilla ....Amparan

January 9
DER ROSENKAVALIER (R. Strauss)
Same cast as November 22 except:
Octavian ....Miller
Sophie ....Hurley
Annina ....Roggero

January 10
ORFEO ED EURIDICE (Gluck)
Same cast as December 16 except:
Euridice ....Amara

January 11 (matinee)
LE NOZZE DI FIGARO (Mozart)
Same cast as December 19 except:
Susanna ....Gueden
Figaro ....Tozzi

January 11
LA TRAVIATA (Verdi)
Same cast as November 2 except:
Violetta ....Albanese
Alfredo ....Gari
Germont ....Sereni
Gastone ....Anthony
Dr. Grenvil ....Sgarro
Annina ....Cundari

January 13
LA FORZA DEL DESTINO (Verdi)
Same cast as November 29 except:
Conductor: In Act I Cimara was
replaced by Walter Hagen and
Adler; in Acts II & III by Stiedry.
Marquis ....Sgarro
Don Carlo ....Sereni
Don Alvaro ....Baum
Padre Guardiano ....Wilderman
Fra Melitone ....Pechner
Preziosilla ....Amparan
Trabucco ....De Paolis
Surgeon ....Cehanovsky

January 14
CARMEN (Bizet)
Same cast as December 4 except:
Don José ....Bergonzi
Micaela ....Amara
Frasquita ....Lind

January 15
World Premiere
VANESSA (Barber)
Conductor: Mitropoulos

Vanessa ....Steber
Erika ....Elias
Baroness ....Resnik
Anatol ....Gedda
Doctor ....Tozzi
Major domo ....Cehanovsky
Footman ....Nagy

January 16
LA BOHEME (Puccini)
Same cast as December 8 except:
Rodolfo ....Barioni
Schaunard ....Harvuot
Colline ....Moscona
Mimi ....Munsel
Musetta ....Lewis
Benoit ....Davidson
Sergeant ....Flagello

January 17
LA TRAVIATA (Verdi)
Same cast as November 2 except:
Violetta ....Albanese
Alfredo ....Labo
Germont ....Sereni
Gastone ....Anthony
Dr. Grenvil ....Sgarro

January 18 (matinee)
ORFEO ED EURIDICE (Gluck)
Same cast as December 16 except:
Euridice ....Amara

January 18
DER ROSENKAVALIER (R. Strauss)
Same cast as November 22 except:
Princess von Werdenberg. . Steber
Octavian .... Miller
Sophie .... Hurley
Annina .... Roggero
Singer .... Gedda

January 19
Benefit West Side
Institutional Synagogue
TOSCA (Puccini)
Same cast as November 9 except:
Conductor: Adler
Tosca .... Milanov
Cavaradossi .... Bergonzi
Scarpia .... Cassel
Angelotti .... Alvary
Sciarrone .... Hawkins

January 20
LUCIA DI LAMMERMOOR
(Donizetti)
Same cast as December 21 except:
Edgardo .... Labo

January 21
VANESSA (Barber)
Same cast as January 15

January 22
LA BOHEME (Puccini)
Same cast as December 8 except:
Rodolfo .... Barioni
Marcello .... Valentino
Colline .... Scott
Mimi .... Albanese
Musetta .... Lewis
Benoit .... Davidson
Sergeant .... Flagello

January 23
AIDA (Verdi)
Same cast as November 30 except:
Amneris .... Rankin
Amonasro .... Bardelli

January 24
GIANNI SCHICCHI (Puccini)
Conductor: Mitropoulos
Gianni Schicchi .... Corena
Lauretta .... Conner
La Vecchia .... Amparan
Rinuccio .... Carelli
Gherardo .... De Paolis
Nella .... Allen
Gherardino .... Strasfogel
Betto .... Cehanovsky
Simone .... Moscona
Marco .... Harvuot
La Ciesca .... Votipka
Spinelloccio .... Pechner
Ser Amantio di Nicolao. . Flagello
Pinellino .... Hawkins
Guccio .... Sgarro

SALOME (R. Strauss)
Conductor: Mitropoulos
Herod .... Kelley
Herodias .... Thebom
Salome .... Borkh
Jochanaan .... Harrell
Narraboth .... Crain
Page .... Roggero
First Nazarene ..... Wilderman
Second Nazarene ...... Marsh
First Jew .... Anthony
Second Jew .... Nagy
Third Jew .... De Paolis
Fourth Jew .... Franke
Fifth Jew .... Davidson
First Soldier .... Scott
Second Soldier .... Sgarro
Cappadocian .... Hawkins
Slave .... Allen

January 25 (matinee)
LA FORZA DEL DESTINO (Verdi)
Same cast as November 29 except:
Marquis .... Sgarro
Don Carlo .... Sereni
Padre Guardiano .... Siepi
Curra .... Votipka
Surgeon .... Cehanovsky

January 25
ORFEO ED EURIDICE (Gluck)
Same cast as December 16 except:
Amore .... Allen

January 27
CARMEN (Bizet)
Same cast as December 4 except:
Carmen .... Thebom
Don José .... Bergonzi
Micaela .... Conner
Morales .... Harvuot

January 28
LA PERICHOLE (Offenbach)
Same cast as November 2 except:
Tarapote .... Alvary
Perichole .... Munsel
Guadalena .... Krall
Virginella .... Vanni
Clown .... Wiland
Ballerina .... Black

January 29
GIANNI SCHICCHI (Puccini)
Same cast as January 24 except:
Rinuccio .... Anthony
Nella .... Chambers
Simone .... Alvary

SALOME (R. Strauss)
Same cast as January 24 except:
Narraboth .... Gari
First Jew .... Carelli

January 30
ANDREA CHENIER (Giordano)
Same cast as November 9 except:
Andrea Chénier .... Bergonzi
Bersi .... Roggero
Madelon .... Elias
Schmidt .... Davidson

January 31
LUCIA DI LAMMERMOOR
(Donizetti)
Same cast as December 21 except:
Enrico Ashton .... Valentino
Edgardo .... Peerce
Raimondo .... Wilderman

February 1 (matinee)
VANESSA (Barber)
Same cast as January 15

February 1
TRISTAN UND ISOLDE (Wagner)
Conductor: Stiedry
Tristan .... Vinay*
Isolde .... Moedl
King Marke .... Edelmann
Kurvenal .... Cassel
Brangäne .... Dalis
Melot .... Marsh
Steersman .... Sgarro
Shepherd .... Franke
Sailor's Voice .... Nagy
*Da Costa sang Tristan in Act 3

February 3
LE NOZZE DI FIGARO (Mozart)
Same cast as December 19 except:
Figaro .... Tozzi
Cherubino .... Elias
Bartolo .... Baccaloni

February 4
AIDA (Verdi)
Same cast as November 30 except:
Amneris .... Thebom
Aida .... Stella
Ramfis .... Scott

February 5
DIE WALKUERE (Wagner)
Conductor: Stiedry
Wotan .... Edelmann
Fricka .... Thebom
Brünnhilde .... Harshaw
Siegmund .... Vinay
Sieglinde .... Borkh
Hunding .... Wilderman
Helmwige .... Lind
Gerhilde .... Ordassy
Ortlinde .... Krall
Rossweisse .... Roggero
Grimgerde .... Lipton
Waltraute .... Moll
Siegrune .... Vanni
Schwertleite .... Amparan

February 6
Benefit Free Milk Fund for
Babies, Inc.
LA TRAVIATA (Verdi)
Same cast as November 2 except:
Violetta .... Callas
Germont .... Zanasi
Gastone .... Anthony
Dr. Grenvil .... Sgarro

5

February 7
LA BOHEME (Puccini)
Same cast as December 8 except:
Marcello ....Sereni
Schaunard ....Harvuot
Colline ....Scott
Mimi ....Albanese

February 8 (matinee)
GIANNI SCHICCHI (Puccini)
Same cast as January 24 except:
Lauretta ....Hurley
Rinuccio ....Anthony
Nella ....Chambers

SALOME (R. Strauss)
Same cast as January 24 except:
Herod ....Vinay
Narraboth ....Gari
First Jew ....Carelli

February 8
TOSCA (Puccini)
Same cast as November 9 except:
Conductor: Adler
Tosca ....Steber
Cavaradossi ....Campora
Angelotti ....Alvary
Sacristan ....Baccaloni
Sciarrone ....Hawkins

February 10
LA TRAVIATA (Verdi)
Same cast as November 2 except:
Violetta ....Callas
Alfredo ....Campora
Germont ....Zanasi
Dr. Grenvil ....Sgarro

February 12
AIDA (Verdi)
Same cast as November 30 except:
Aida ....Davy
Radames ....Baum
Amonasro ....Warren
Ramfis ....Wilderman

February 13
LUCIA DI LAMMERMOOR
(Donizetti)
Same cast as December 21 except:
Lucia ....Callas
Edgardo ....Bergonzi

February 14
DIE WALKUERE (Wagner)
Same cast as February 5 except:
Schwertleite ....Lansing

February 15 (matinee)
LA BOHEME (Puccini)
Same cast as December 8 except:
Marcello ....Sereni
Schaunard ....Harvuot
Colline ....Scott
Mimi ....Albanese
Musetta ....Hurley

February 15
VANESSA (Barber)
Same cast as January 15 except:
Vanessa ....Lewis

February 17
GIANNI SCHICCHI (Puccini)
Same cast as January 24 except:
Lauretta ....Cundari
Nella ....Chambers

SALOME (R. Strauss)
Same cast as January 24 except:
Herod ....Kullman
First Nazarene ....Ernster
Fifth Jew ....Pechner
First Soldier ....Flagello

February 18
TRISTAN UND ISOLDE (Wagner)
Same cast as February 1 except:
Steersman ....Hawkins

February 19
Benefit Sponsored by the
Metropolitan Opera Guild for the
Production Fund
MADAMA BUTTERFLY (Puccini)
Conductor: Mitropoulos
Cio-Cio-San ....Stella
B. F. Pinkerton ......Fernandi
Sharpless ....Zanasi
Suzuki ....Roggero
Kate Pinkerton ......Chambers
Goro ....De Paolis
Yamadori ....Cehanovsky
Uncle-Priest ....Flagello
Imperial Commissioner ..Marsh

February 20
LUCIA DI LAMMERMOOR
(Donizetti)
Same cast as December 21 except:
Lucia ....Callas
Edgardo ....Bergonzi
Raimondo ....Scott

February 21 (matinee)
95th Metropolitan Opera
Guild Student Performance
CARMEN (Bizet)
Same cast as December 4 except:
Conductor: Adler
Carmen ....Amparan
Don José ....Gari
Micaela ....Hurley
Escamillo ....Valentino
Zuniga ....Sgarro
Mercédès ....Vanni

February 21
VANESSA (Barber)
Same cast as January 15 except:
Doctor ....Harvuot

February 22 (matinee)
LA TRAVIATA (Verdi)
Same cast as November 2 except:
Alfredo ....Campora
Germont ....Merrill
Dr. Grenvil ....Sgarro

February 22
CARMEN (Bizet)
Same cast as December 4 except:
Conductor: Adler
Carmen ....Thebom
Don José ....Bergonzi
Micaela ....Hurley
Escamillo ....Zanasi
Morales ....Harvuot
Remendado ....De Paolis

February 24
AIDA (Verdi)
Same cast as November 30 except:
Conductor: Adler
Amneris ....Thebom
Aida ....Stella
Ramfis ....Wilderman
Priestess ....Krall

February 25
LUCIA DI LAMMERMOOR
(Donizetti)
Same cast as December 21 except:
Lucia ....Callas
Edgardo ....Fernandi
Raimondo ....Tozzi

February 26
DER ROSENKAVALIER (R. Strauss)
Same cast as November 22 except:
Conductor: Rudolf
Princess von Werdenberg..Steber
Sophie ....Hurley
Notary ....Flagello
Singer ....Gedda

February 27
OTELLO (Verdi)
Conductor: Cleva
Otello ....Del Monaco
Desdemona ....De Los Angeles
Iago ....Warren
Emilia ....Elias
Cassio ....Franke
Roderigo ....Anthony
Lodovico ....Moscona
Montano ....Harvuot
Herald ....Marsh

February 28 (matinee)
96th Metropolitan Opera
Guild Student Performance
CARMEN (Bizet)
Same cast as December 4 except:
Conductor: Adler
Carmen ....Amparan
Don José ....Gari
Escamillo ....Valentino
Zuniga ....Sgarro
Mercédès ....Vanni

February 28
TOSCA (Puccini)
Same cast as November 9 except:
Tosca ....Callas
Cavaradossi ....Tucker
Scarpia ....Cassel
Angelotti ....Scott
Sacristan ....Davidson
Spoletta ....De Paolis
Sciarrone ....Hawkins
Shepherd ....Burke

March 1 (matinee)
TRISTAN UND ISOLDE (Wagner)
Same cast as February 1 except:
Isolde ....Harshaw
Brangäne ....Thebom
Steersman ....Hawkins

March 1
GIANNI SCHICCHI (Puccini)
Same cast as January 24 except:
Conductor: Leinsdorf
Lauretta ....Hurley
Rinuccio ....Anthony
Nella ....Chambers
Spinellocchio ....Davidson

SALOME (R. Strauss)
Same cast as January 24 except:
Conductor: Leinsdorf
Herodias ....Resnik
Jochanaan ....Cassel
Narraboth ....Lewis
Page ....Vanni
First Jew ....Carelli

March 3
VANESSA (Barber)
Same cast as January 15

March 5
TOSCA (Puccini)
Same cast as November 9 except:
Tosca ....Callas
Cavaradossi ....Tucker
Scarpia ....London
Spoletta ....De Paolis
Sciarrone ....Hawkins
Shepherd ....Burke

March 6
DIE WALKUERE (Wagner)
Same cast as February 5 except:
Fricka ....Dalis
Brünnhilde ....Moedl
Siegmund ....Da Costa
Sieglinde ....Schech

March 7 (matinee)
97th Metropolitan Opera
Guild Student Performance
CARMEN (Bizet)
Same cast as December 4 except:
Conductor: Adler
Carmen ....Elias
Don José ....Crain
Micaela ....Krall
Escamillo ....Valentino
Zuniga ....Sgarro
Frasquita ....Lind
Mercédès ....Vanni
Remendado ....Anthony

March 7
MADAMA BUTTERFLY (Puccini)
Same cast as February 19

March 8 (matinee)
OTELLO (Verdi)
Same cast as February 27

March 8
Benefit Vassar Club
Scholarship Fund
LA BOHEME (Puccini)
Same cast as December 8 except:
Conductor: Adler
Colline ....Hines
Mimi ....Pobbe
Musetta ....Hurley
Benoit ....Davidson
Alcindoro ....De Paolis
Sergeant ....Flagello

March 10
DIE WALKUERE (Wagner)
Same cast as February 5 except:
Fricka ....Madeira
Siegmund ....Da Costa
Sieglinde ....Schech
Schwertleite ....Lansing

March 11
GIANNI SCHICCHI (Puccini)
Same cast as January 24 except:
Lauretta ....Cundari
Rinuccio ....Anthony
Nella ....Chambers

SALOME (R. Strauss)
Same cast as January 24 except:
Herod ....Vinay
Herodias ....Madeira
Jochanaan ....Cassel
Page ....Vanni
First Jew ....Carelli

March 12
MADAMA BUTTERFLY (Puccini)
Same cast as February 19

March 13
SAMSON ET DALILA (Saint-Saëns)
Conductor: Cleva
Dalila ....Stevens
Samson ....Del Monaco
High Priest ....Singher
Abimelech ....Scott
Old Hebrew ....Tozzi
Philistine Messenger ....Nagy
Philistines ....Carelli, Hawkins

March 14 (matinee)
98th Metropolitan Opera
Guild Student Performance
CARMEN (Bizet)
Same cast as December 4 except:
Conductor: Adler
Carmen ....Elias
Don José ....Crain
Micaela ....Ordassy
Escamillo ....Valentino
Zuniga ....Sgarro
Frasquita ....Chambers
Mercédès ....Vanni
Remendado ....De Paolis

March 14
TRISTAN UND ISOLDE (Wagner)
Same cast as February 1 except:
Tristan ....Da Costa
Isolde ....Harshaw
King Marke ....Hines
Brangäne ....Thebom
Steersman ....Hawkins

March 15 (matinee)
TOSCA (Puccini)
Same cast as November 9 except:
Cavaradossi ....Tucker
Angelotti ....Scott
Sacristan ....Baccaloni
Sciarrone ....Cehanovsky
Jailer ....Sgarro

March 15
IL BARBIERE DI SIVIGLIA
(Rossini)
Same cast as November 14 except:
Rosina ....Hurley
Don Basilio ....Tozzi
Fiorello ....Marsh

March 17
OTELLO (Verdi)
Same cast as February 27 except:
Desdemona ....Milanov

March 18
LA BOHEME (Puccini)
Same cast as December 8 except:
Conductor: Adler
Rodolfo ....Peerce
Marcello ....Zanasi
Mimi ....Pobbe
Benoit ....Davidson
Parpignol ....Anthony
Customs Officer ....Anthony

March 19
MADAMA BUTTERFLY (Puccini)
Same cast as February 19 except:
Sharpless ....Harvuot

March 20
PARSIFAL (Wagner)
Conductor: Stiedry
Amfortas ....Harrell
Titurel ....Wilderman
Gurnemanz ....Hines
Parsifal ....Vinay
Klingsor ....Pechner
Kundry ....Moedl
Voice ....Amparan
Knights ......Nagy, Hawkins
Esquires ....Chambers, Roggero,
Anthony, Carelli
Flower Maidens ..Hurley, Elias,
Vanni, Krall, Cundari, Roggero

7

1957-58

March 21 (matinee)
99th Metropolitan Opera
Guild Student Performance
CARMEN (Bizet)
Same cast as December 4 except:
Conductor: Adler

Carmen ....Resnik
Don José ....Gari
Micaela ....Ordassy
Escamillo ....Zanasi
Zuniga ....Sgarro
Frasquita ....Chambers
Mercédès ....Vanni

March 21
SAMSON ET DALILA (Saint-Saëns)
Same cast as March 13 except:
Dalila ....Thebom
High Priest ....Harvuot
Old Hebrew ....Wilderman

March 22 (matinee)
DER ROSENKAVALIER (R. Strauss)
Same cast as November 22 except:
Conductor: Rudolf
Princess von Werdenberg..Steber
Sophie ....Hurley
Blackamoor ....Grishin

March 22
EUGENE ONEGIN (Tchaikovsky)
Same cast as October 28

March 26
LE NOZZE DI FIGARO (Mozart)
Same cast as December 19 except:
Countess ....Amara
Susanna ....Wilson
Figaro ....Tozzi
Cherubino ....Elias
Marcellina ....Roggero
Bartolo ....Flagello
Basilio ....De Paolis

March 27
TRISTAN UND ISOLDE (Wagner)
Same cast as February 1 except:
Brangäne ....Hoffman

March 28 (matinee)
One Hundredth Metropolitan
Opera Guild Student
Performance
CARMEN (Bizet)
Same cast as December 4 except:
Conductor: Adler

Carmen ....Elias
Don José ....Gari
Micaela ....Krall
Escamillo ....Zanasi
Zuniga ....Sgarro
Frasquita ....Lind
Mercédès ....Vanni
Remendado ....De Paolis

March 28
OTELLO (Verdi)
Same cast as February 27 except:
Desdemona ....Milanov
Emilia ....Lipton
Lodovico ....Scott
Montano ....Hawkins

March 29 (matinee)
MADAMA BUTTERFLY (Puccini)
Same cast as February 19 except:
Sharpless ....Harvuot

March 29
FAUST (Gounod)
Same cast as November 1 except:
Faust ....Tucker
Marguerite ....Pobbe
Siébel ....Vanni
Wagner ....Sgarro

March 31
SAMSON ET DALILA (Saint-Saëns)
Same cast as March 13 except:
Old Hebrew ......Wilderman

April 2 (matinee)
101st Metropolitan Opera
Guild Student Performance
CARMEN (Bizet)
Same cast as December 4 except:
Conductor: Adler

Carmen ....Amparan
Don José ....Crain
Micaela ....Allen
Escamillo ....Valentino
Zuniga ....Hawkins
Frasquita ....Chambers
Mercédès ....Vanni

April 2
EUGENE ONEGIN (Tchaikovsky)
Same cast as October 28 except:
Prince Gremin ....Hines

April 3
MADAMA BUTTERFLY (Puccini)
Same cast as February 19 except:
Cio-Cio-San .....De Los Angeles
B. F. Pinkerton ......Bergonzi
Sharpless ....Guarrera
Uncle-Priest ....Scott

April 4 (matinee)
PARSIFAL (Wagner)
Same cast as March 20 except:
Amfortas ....London
Gurnemanz ....Edelmann
Klingsor ....Davidson
Kundry ....Harshaw

April 5 (matinee)
LUCIA DI LAMMERMOOR
(Donizetti)
Same cast as December 21 except:
Lucia ....Peters
Enrico Ashton ....Zanasi
Edgardo ....Peerce

April 5
DON GIOVANNI (Mozart)
Same cast as October 31 except:
Conductor: Stiedry
Don Giovanni ....London
Donna Elvira ....Amara
Zerlina ....Hurley
Commendatore ....Scott

April 7
MADAMA BUTTERFLY (Puccini)
Same cast as February 19 except:
B. F. Pinkerton ......Bergonzi
Suzuki ....Amparan
Kate Pinkerton ....Vanni
Goro ....Franke

April 8
DON GIOVANNI (Mozart)
Same cast as October 31 except:
Conductor: Stiedry
Don Giovanni ....London
Donna Elvira ....Amara
Commendatore ....Scott

April 9
OTELLO (Verdi)
Same cast as February 27

April 10
MADAMA BUTTERFLY (Puccini)
Same cast as February 19 except:
B. F. Pinkerton ......Bergonzi
Sharpless ....Guarrera
Kate Pinkerton ....Vanni
Goro ....Franke

April 11
CARMEN (Bizet)
Same cast as December 4 except:
Conductor: Adler

Carmen ....Madeira
Don José ....Baum
Micaela ....Amara
Escamillo ....London
Zuniga ....Alvary
Remendado ....De Paolis

April 12 (matinee)
SAMSON ET DALILA (Saint-Saëns)
Same cast as March 13

April 12
LUCIA DI LAMMERMOOR
(Donizetti)
Same cast as December 21 except:
Lucia ....Pons
Enrico Ashton ....Zanasi
Edgardo ....Peerce
Raimondo ....Wilderman

8

EXCERPTS FROM PRESS REVIEWS

NEW PRODUCTION of Tchaikovsky's *Eugene Onegin,* October 28, 1957

The opening production of *Eugene Onegin* ... was ... a triumph, but the triumph was scored by Rolf Gérard's scenery, Peter Brook's staging, Dimitri Mitropoulos' conducting, and the singing of an excellent cast in the face of certain difficulties presented by the work itself. It is no news that Tchaikovsky's most famous opera is a fairly weak thing from the dramatic standpoint, mainly owing to its tenuous story and to the negative and unimpassioned nature of its title role. It is weak in other respects, too—particularly in its lack of anything approaching real melodic power. . . . Even in intentionally grand moments as Tatyana's letter aria in the first act, and Lenski's soliloquy before the duel scene, the composer fails to rise above the level of mere prettiness. In order to strengthen the work, Mr. Mitropoulos added a number of entr'acte interludes based on material from the opera and put together by Julius Burger, and I must say I found them as effective as anything in it. The Metropolitan, however, spared no pains in converting *Onegin* into a lovely spectacle. The scenery was splendid, the ballet sequences were lively, and the cast, including George London, Lucine Amara, Richard Tucker, and Giorgio Tozzi, was absolutely unbeatable. —Winthrop Sargeant, *The New Yorker*

NEW PRODUCTION of Mozart's *Don Giovanni* and DEBUT OF KARL BOEHM, October 31, 1957.

Mozartians, rejoice. *Don Giovanni,* the master's grandest opera, returned to the Metropolitan Opera last night in a grand new production. The Met at its best adorned Mozart at his best. . . .
Karl Boehm, who was head of the Vienna Opera for a time, makes his New York debut as a conductor. His interpretation is in the Viennese tradition, which is Mozart's, after all. His tempos are a shade slower than those we are accustomed to, but at no point is he leaden-footed. And in a scene like the first-act finale he builds a climax of irresistible power. . . .

Because he adores Mozart, Mr. Boehm has a high regard for every nuance. He has seen to it that subtle touches for voice and orchestra have their proper attention. The result is a continuous flow, not merely an emphasis on the big set numbers. *Don Giovanni* emerges as it should—an integrated music drama.
Only a great opera house could assemble such a cast, and there are accomplished replacements. These are singers with first-rate voices. They have the experience and sensibility to sing Mozart glowingly. And every one can act. There is not a weak link in the chain.
Cesare Siepi's Don Giovanni has grown in magnetism and diablerie. His voice is smoother, mellower, more supple than ever. His Champagne Aria is headier than any product of the vine, and his Serenade is sensuous enough to melt any girl's heart.
Eleanor Steber . . . is a Donna Anna of blazing temperament; her "Or sai chi l'onore" is all intensity and fire, and everywhere she is a stylist. Lisa Della Casa's Donna Elvira is not a scold but an ill-used and loving woman, and her singing is pure, elegant and sensitive. Roberta Peters, who took time off last season to start a family, returns with voice immensely refreshed; her Zerlina catches in song the warmth and sensuousness of the cunning little baggage.
Cesare Valletti, always a Mozart specialist, sings with suavity and surprising vocal amplitude. Fernando Corena is a rare Leporello, one who sings every note and does not clown shamelessly. Theodor Uppman's Masetto is amusing and neatly sung. Giorgio Tozzi's rich bass gives the Commendatore unaccustomed stature.
Eugene Berman's costumes are handsome, and his sets have solidity and grandeur. The production has been designed so that the scene may change quickly despite the Met's antiquated stage. . . . Herbert Graf's staging is rooted in the tradition of the opera. At the same time it is flexible enough to adapt itself to the spaces and levels of this production. Zachary Solov's choreography adds color, especially to the ballroom scene.
With a *Don Giovanni* of this caliber the Met fulfills one of the functions of a major opera house: to be faithful custodian of the masterpieces of the lyric theater.— Howard Taubman, *New York Times*

DEBUT OF NICOLAI GEDDA as Faust, November 1, 1957

A slim, personable chap with a very engaging stage presence, young Gedda revealed a pretty lyric tenor that, while essentially light in substance, was able to carry nicely through the auditorium. Best of all, he obviously enjoys singing a great deal and does so with a pleasant ease, phrasing his material in a personal but entirely musical manner.—Douglas Watt, *New York Daily News*

DEBUT OF FLAVIANO LABO as Don Alvaro in *La Forza del Destino,* November 29, 1957

In his late twenties, the Italian newcomer made a triumphant debut . . . singing with a wealth of glowing tone and mature grasp of line and phrasing that belied his years. Mr. Labò is a little fellow, quite good-looking and extremely graceful in his action about the stage, and in *La Forza,* with its vendetta-haunted duels and pursuits, there is plenty of action. But more to the point was the voice— and the way he used it. The tones were easily and suavely produced. —Louis Biancolli, *New York World-Telegram and Sun*

WORLD PREMIERE of Samuel Barber's *Vanessa,* January 15, 1958

A crowded house of listeners gave a warm welcome to the world premiere performance of *Vanessa,* with music by Samuel Barber and text by Gian Carlo Menotti, at the Metropolitan Opera House last night. For his first presentation of a work by an American composer (and the first new full-length opera by an American to be seen at the Metropolitan since the thirties), Rudolf Bing put not only his best foot but also his best "hands" forward — these belonging to Cecil Beaton as scenic designer, Dimitri Mitropoulos as conductor and Mr. Menotti as stage director.
Though Mr. Barber's score does not break down into arias and set pieces in the old style, they are deftly woven into the fabric, and several times in the four acts the audience broke in to applaud the singing of one of its favorites. Opinion is likely to be unanimous that *Vanessa* is a rarity among first operas in quality, with a fourth-act quintet that has no equal among works of American origin (always excepting Gersh-

win) for sustained melodic flow and eloquence. This is no common feat among experienced operatic composers, and Mr. Barber deserves warm commendation for handling his climax so expertly. It should be a source of satisfaction for all that the end of *Vanessa* marks his beginning as a real theater composer.

Earlier, the composer seemed sometimes at odds with the libretto (which in many ways seemed more suitable to Mr. Menotti's compositional talents than Mr. Barber's). . . . On the technical level, Mr. Menotti's libretto is resourceful and recurrently marked by singable lines and scenes (such as the last one), but its lack of real substance or true characterization puts an enormous burden on the composer to involve the listener by the sheer power of his music. A conspicuous character, for example, is the Old Baroness (expertly played by Miss Resnik), who maintains a stony silence throughout, save for a scene or two with Erika. But we are left to guess why she has cut herself off from everyone, including her own daughter, Vanessa.

Principal honors among the uniformly superior cast went to young Miss Elias . . . whose fine voice and appealing presence made her Erika to the life, and Nicolai Gedda . . . who confounded all theories by singing the English text more clearly than any of the natives. Giorgio Tozzi . . . was close beside him in the role of a doctor and family friend, but very little could be understood of Miss Steber's part. Doubtless she will have it better under control soon, for it was yeoman work for her to learn it all in the six weeks since Sena Jurinac cabled regrets that she could not take part, as planned.—Irving Kolodin, *Hartford* (Connecticut) *Times*

DEBUT OF INGE BORKH as Salome, January 24, 1958

Mme. Borkh is a handsome figure of a woman. She's tall and lithe; she has curves that would make any Broadway musical comedy impresario seek to sign her to a contract. In a costume of pink, green and royal purple that was plenty revealing, she made a lot of eyes pop in last night's audience.

Fortunately, Mme. Borkh has a voice to match her looks. Salome is a part to tax any singer, and she met the vocal challenge beauti-

fully. If she was less than perfect in the lower register once in a while, her top notes were exciting. All things considered, we think Mme. Borkh's Salome as thrilling, pictorially and emotionally, as any we've ever caught.—Robert Coleman, *New York Daily Mirror*

MARIA CALLAS as Violetta and DEBUT OF MARIO ZANASI as Germont in *La Traviata,* February 6, 1958

Maria Meneghini Callas made history at the Metropolitan last night. Singing her first Violetta, she gave the finest performance she has ever given here. She also may have portrayed the character of Violetta more completely than any other singer in the long line of sopranos who have appeared in *La Traviata* at the Metropolitan.

Mme. Callas is that rare opera singer: a living stage personality. Admittedly her voice is not the most beautiful to be heard in this role. Violetta happens, however, to be one of the best roles for her voice. In it she can use her expressive power to the fullest extent. Since her capacity for dramatic inflection is extraordinary, she can draw an audience naturally into the story of the opera. Last night Violetta lived her part to the very moment of death.

To have recreated Violetta, not just to have sung the role, was Mme. Callas's achievement. This became the more evident in the framework of the performance of the remainder of the cast; they were wooden in comparison, both in voice and in action.

Making his Metropolitan debut as the elder Germont, Mario Zanasi revealed a good baritone voice. With only a stock gesture or two, he could hardly give substance to the character.—Miles Kastendieck, *New York Journal-American*

DEBUT OF GLORIA DAVY as Aida, February 12, 1958

Last night [Miss Davy] was always an appealing figure as the Ethiopian slave girl, and her voice, as she has shown here in other appearances, is one of exceptional beauty. One hopes, however, that this, her third major assignment in the role, will not make it a part in which she is permanently typecast. The truth is, it is not fully right for her, and when the Nile Scene came along, and she was onstage with such veteran singers as

Leonard Warren as Amonasro and Kurt Baum as Radames, she was understandably outmatched. Her voice does not have the full dramatic force needed for the part, nor as yet does she have the sort of emotional intensity it needs. Yet she is clearly an asset to the company, for she is an actress of grace and touching naturalness. — Ross Parmenter, *New York Times*

NEW PRODUCTION of Puccini's *Madama Butterfly* and DEBUT OF EUGENIO FERNANDI as Pinkerton, February 19, 1958

Puccini's *Madama Butterfly* has received the most thoroughgoing face lifting in its career at the Metropolitan Opera. Last night's performance was no ordinary "revival," with some new scenery and somewhat modernized stage business; it was a brand new production, with features that are as unusual as they are handsome.

The Met imported for this task native talent from Japan. Yoshio Aoyama assumed generalship over the stage, and Motohiro Nagasaka designed the sets and costumes, both of them assisted by Charles Elson and Ming Cho Lee—quite an international crew.

Much of the material was imported from Japan, and the Met was perfectly willing to bring over even cherry blossoms, but Mr. Nagasaka found that he could make them in Manhattan. The sets were indeed most artistic, delicate and evocative, the costumes authentic and fetching. The singers were patiently taught gestures and motions genuinely Japanese, and although their physique is palpably different from the Orientals they represent, they succeeded in creating the proper illusion.

The title role in *Madama Butterfly* is not just the principal role, it is practically the whole opera. Antonietta Stella, last night's Cio-Cio-San, lived up magnificently to the challenge. Singing with a rich and pliable voice, she produced the high tones effortlessly. . . . Her acting was imaginative, convincing and without any affectation. The applause given her was earned, every bit of it.

Eugenio Fernandi, the new tenor, is a man with a voice, a good voice. While it cannot be denied that his stage deportment leaves something to be desired, Mr. Fernandi, a mere youth, gave many indications that he is someone to be reckoned with.—Paul Henry Lang, *New York Herald Tribune*

1958-1959 SEASON

PERSONNEL

Male Artists
Alperstein, Max
Alvary, Lorenzo
Anthony, Charles
Arthur, Henry
Baccaloni, Salvatore
Backgren, Arthur
Bardelli, Cesare
Barioni, Daniele
Baum, Kurt
Bergonzi, Carlo
Burke, Peter
Campora, Giuseppe
Carelli, Gabor
Cassel, Walter
Cehanovsky, George
Corena, Fernando
Da Costa, Albert
Davidson, Lawrence
De Cesare, Luigi
D'Elia, Frank
Del Monaco, Mario
De Paolis, Alessio
Doench, Karl
Edelmann, Otto
Emanuel, Dawin
Feiersinger, Sebastian
Fernandi, Eugenio
Flagello, Ezio
Folmer, Joseph
Franke, Paul
Frydel, John
Gari, Giulio
Gedda, Nicolai
Ghazal, Edward
Gilford, Jack
Gobbi, Tito
Guarrera, Frank
Harvuot, Clifford
Hawkins, Osie
Hemmerly, Walter
Hines, Jerome
Knight, Arnold
Kuestner, Charles
Kullman, Charles
Lewis, William
Liebl, Karl
London, George
MacNeil, Cornell
Mandile, Frank
Marcella, Lou
Marsh, Calvin
Merrill, Robert
Mollica, Giulio
Morell, Barry
Moscona, Nicola
Nagy, Robert
Olvis, William
Pechner, Gerhard
Peerce, Jan
Powell, Thomas
Ringland, Earl
Roberts, Hal
Rothmuller, Marko
Scott, Norman
Sereni, Mario
Sgarro, Louis

Siepi, Cesare
Singher, Martial
Stanz, William
Starling, William
Sternberg, Harold
Sternberg, Sam
Strang, Lloyd
Sullivan, Brian
Tomanelli, Carlo
Tozzi, Giorgio
Trehy, John
Tucker, Richard
Uhde, Hermann
Uppman, Theodor
Uzunov, Dimiter
Valentino, Frank
Valletti, Cesare
Warren, Leonard
Wildermann, William
Zambruno, Primo
Zanasi, Mario

Female Artists
Albanese, Licia
Allen, Mildred
Amara, Lucine
Amparan, Belen
Arroyo, Martina
Chambers, Madelaine
Cundari, Emilia
Curtis-Verna, Mary
Davy, Gloria
Della Casa, Lisa
De Los Angeles, Victoria
Dobbs, Mattiwilda
Dunn, Mignon
Elias, Rosalind
Fenn, Jean
Gueden, Hilde
Harshaw, Margaret
Hurley, Laurel
Imai, Kunie
Krall, Heidi
Lewis, Brenda
Lind, Gloria
Lipton, Martha
Loevberg, Aase Nordmo
Madeira, Jean
Milanov, Zinka
Miller, Mildred
Ordassy, Carlotta
Peters, Roberta
Plotkin, Alice
Rankin, Nell
Resnik, Regina
Roggero, Margaret
Rysanek, Leonie
Steber, Eleanor
Stella, Antonietta
Stevens, Risë
Tebaldi, Renata
Thebom, Blanche
Vanni, Helen
Votipka, Thelma
Wilson, Dolores

Ballet Soloists
Ames, Suzanne
Andrew, Thomas
d'Amboise, Jacques

Douglas, Scott
Etgen, Ann
Gutierrez, Jose
Jerell, Edith
Kaye, Nora
Keane, Audrey
King, Nancy
Lee, Sondra
Linn, Bambi
Marks, Bruce
Martin, Donald
Murray, Ron
San Miguel, Lolita
Serrano, Lupe
Sibley, Louellen
Zybine, Alek

Conductors
Adler, Kurt
Boehm, Karl
Cleva, Fausto
Gniewek, Raymond
Leinsdorf, Erich
Mitropoulos, Dimitri
Morel, Jean
Rich, Martin
Schick, George
Schippers, Thomas
Strasfogel, Ignace
Taussig, Walter
Walter, Bruno

General Manager
Bing, Rudolf

October 27 (Opening Night)
TOSCA (Puccini)
Conductor: Mitropoulos

Tosca ....Tebaldi
Cavaradossi ....Del Monaco
Scarpia ....London
Angelotti ....Harvuot
Sacristan ....Corena
Spoletta ....De Paolis
Sciarrone ....Cehanovsky
Jailer ....Sgarro
Shepherd ....Burke

October 29
BORIS GODUNOV (Mussorgsky)
Conductor: Mitropoulos

Boris Godunov ....Siepi
Fyodor ....Roggero
Xenia ....Cundari
Nurse ....Dunn
Shuiski ....Kullman
Shchelkalov ....Marsh
Pimen ....Tozzi
Grigori ....Baum
Marina ....Rankin
Rangoni ....Harvuot
Varlaam ....Flagello
Missail ....Anthony
Innkeeper ....Lipton
Officer ....Hawkins
Simpleton ....Franke
Nikitich ....Davidson
Boyar ....Nagy
Woman ....Votipka
Mityukh ....Powell
Khrushchov ....Roberts

October 30
RIGOLETTO (Verdi)
    Conductor: Cleva
Duke ....Fernandi
Rigoletto ....Warren
Gilda ....Peters
Sparafucile ....Moscona
Maddalena ....Amparan
Giovanna ....Votipka
Monterone ....Scott
Marullo ....Marsh
Borsa ....Carelli
Ceprano ....Cehanovsky
Countess ....Chambers
Page ....Allen
Guard ....Sgarro

October 31
LES CONTES D'HOFFMANN
             (Offenbach)
    Conductor: Morel
Hoffmann ....Gedda
Olympia ....Dobbs
Giulietta ....Elias
Antonia ....Amara
Nicklausse ....Miller
Lindorf ....London
Coppélius ....London
Dappertutto ....London
Dr. Miracle ....London
Spalanzani ....Franke
Schlemil ....Harvuot
Crespel ....Scott
Voice ....Dunn
Andrès ....De Paolis
Cochenille ....De Paolis
Pitichinaccio ....De Paolis
Frantz ....De Paolis
Luther ....Davidson
Nathanael ....Nagy
Hermann ....Marsh
Stella ....King

November 1 (matinee)
MADAMA BUTTERFLY (Puccini)
    Conductor: Leinsdorf
Cio-Cio-San......De Los Angeles
B. F. Pinkerton.........Morell
Sharpless ....Zanasi
Suzuki ....Miller
Kate Pinkerton ....Chambers
Goro ....Franke
Yamadori ....Cehanovsky
Uncle-Priest ....Hawkins
Imperial Commissioner...Marsh
Registrar ....De Cesare

November 1
TOSCA (Puccini)
Same cast as October 27 except:
Cavaradossi ....Campora
Scarpia ....Bardelli
Sciarrone ....Hawkins

November 2
Benefit Yeshiva University
Women's Organization
LA TRAVIATA (Verdi)
    Conductor: Cleva
Violetta ....Albanese
Alfredo ....Valletti

Germont ....Sereni
Flora ....Vanni
Gastone ....Carelli
Baron Douphol ....Marsh
Marquis d'Obigny....Cehanovsky
Dr. Grenvil ....Sgarro
Annina ....Allen
Giuseppe ....Marcella
Gardener ....Trehy

November 3
RIGOLETTO (Verdi)
Same cast as October 30 except:
Rigoletto ....Merrill
Marullo ....Davidson

November 4
TOSCA (Puccini)
Same cast as October 27 except:
Cavaradossi ....Campora
Sciarrone ....Hawkins

November 5
LA TRAVIATA (Verdi)
Same cast as November 2 except:
Alfredo ....Morell
Germont ....Merrill

November 6
BORIS GODUNOV (Mussorgsky)
Same cast as October 29

November 7
CAVALLERIA RUSTICANA
             (Mascagni)
    Conductor: Mitropoulos
Santuzza ....Milanov
Lola ....Elias
Turiddu ....Zambruno
Alfio ....Bardelli
Lucia ....Votipka
PAGLIACCI (Leoncavallo)
    Conductor: Mitropoulos
Nedda ....Amara
Canio ....Del Monaco
Tonio ....Warren
Beppe ....Anthony
Silvio ....Sereni
Villagers ....Folmer, Starling

November 8 (matinee)
LA BOHÈME (Puccini)
    Conductor: Schippers
Rodolfo ....Campora
Marcello ....Zanasi
Schaunard ....Cehanovsky
Colline ....Siepi
Mimì..........De Los Angeles
Musetta ....Krall
Benoit ....Davidson
Parpignol ....Nagy
Alcindoro ....De Paolis
Sergeant ....Tomanelli
Customs Officer ....S. Sternberg

November 8
Benefit Bagby Music
Lover's Foundation
MADAMA BUTTERFLY (Puccini)
Same cast as November 1 except:
Cio-Cio-San ....Tebaldi
B. F. Pinkerton........Fernandi

November 10
CAVALLERIA RUSTICANA
             (Mascagni)
Same cast as November 7
PAGLIACCI (Leoncavallo)
Same cast as November 7 except:
Villagers ..Alperstein, Tomanelli

November 12
TOSCA (Puccini)
Same cast as October 27 except:
Tosca ....Curtis-Verna
Cavaradossi ....Fernandi
Angelotti ....Scott
Sacristan ....Davidson

November 13
LES CONTES D'HOFFMANN
             (Offenbach)
Same cast as October 31 except:
Olympia ....Hurley
Lindorf ....Singher
Coppélius ....Singher
Dappertutto ....Singher
Dr. Miracle ....Singher

November 14
LA TRAVIATA (Verdi)
Same cast as November 2 except:
Alfredo ....Campora
Germont ....Merrill

November 15 (matinee)
OTELLO (Verdi)
    Conductor: Cleva
Otello.............Del Monaco
Desdemona ....Tebaldi
Iago ....Warren
Emilia ....Lipton
Cassio ....Franke
Roderigo ....Anthony
Lodovico ....Moscona
Montano ....Harvuot
Herald ....Marsh

November 15
MADAMA BUTTERFLY (Puccini)
Same cast as November 1 except:
Cio-Cio-San ....Imai
Suzuki ....Roggero
Goro...............De Paolis

November 17
LA BOHÈME (Puccini)
Same cast as November 8 except:
Rodolfo ....Tucker

November 18
THE MAGIC FLUTE (Mozart)
    Conductor: Leinsdorf
Sarastro ....Tozzi
Tamino ....Gedda
High Priest ....Scott
Priest ....Olvis
Queen of the Night.......Peters
Pamina ....Davy
Ladies....Krall, Dunn, Amparan
Papageno ....Uppman
Papagena ....Allen
Monostatos ....Franke
Genii...Cundari, Vanni, Roggero
Guards ....Gari, Sgarro
Slaves....Arthur, Frydel, Roberts

November 19
MADAMA BUTTERFLY (Puccini)
Same cast as November 1 except:
Cio-Cio-San . . . . Tebaldi

November 20
CAVALLERIA RUSTICANA
(Mascagni)
Same cast as November 7
PAGLIACCI (Leoncavallo)
Same cast as November 7

November 21
CARMEN (Bizet)
Conductor: Morel
Carmen . . . . Stevens
Don José . . . . Tucker
Micaela . . . . Gueden
Escamillo . . . . Zanasi
Zuniga . . . . Sgarro
Morales . . . . Marsh
Frasquita . . . . Krall
Mercédès . . . . Roggero
Dancaire . . . . Cehanovsky
Remendado . . . . De Paolis

November 22 (matinee)
RIGOLETTO (Verdi)
Same cast as October 30 except:
Rigoletto . . . . Merrill
Gilda . . . . Dobbs

November 22
BORIS GODUNOV (Mussorgsky)
Same cast as October 29

November 24
OTELLO (Verdi)
Same cast as November 15

November 25
MADAMA BUTTERFLY (Puccini)
Same cast as November 1 except:
Sharpless . . . . Harvuot
Suzuki . . . . Roggero

November 26
LES CONTES D'HOFFMANN
(Offenbach)
Same cast as October 31 except:
Olympia . . . . Hurley

November 27
FLEDERMAUS (J. Strauss)
Conductor: Leinsdorf
Eisenstein . . . . Uppman
Rosalinda . . . . Gueden
Adele . . . . Peters
Ida . . . . King
Alfred . . . . Valletti
Orlofsky . . . . Thebom
Dr. Falke . . . . Guarrera
Frank . . . . Harvuot
Dr. Blind . . . . Franke
Frosch . . . . Gilford

November 28
CAVALLERIA RUSTICANA
(Mascagni)
Same cast as November 7 except:
Turiddu . . . . Barioni
PAGLIACCI (Leoncavallo)
Same cast as November 7 except:
Tonio . . . . Merrill
Villagers . . Alperstein, Tomanelli

November 29 (matinee)
CARMEN (Bizet)
Same cast as November 21

November 29
LA BOHÈME (Puccini)
Same cast as November 8 except:
Marcello . . . . Guarrera
Schaunard . . . . Harvuot
Colline . . . . Scott
Benoit . . . . Flagello
Alcindoro . . . . Davidson

December 1
MADAMA BUTTERFLY (Puccini)
Same cast as November 1 except:
Cio-Cio-San . . . . Albanese
B. F. Pinkerton . . . . Fernandi
Suzuki . . . . Roggero

December 3
MANON LESCAUT (Puccini)
Conductor: Cleva
Manon . . . . Tebaldi
Lescaut . . . . Guarrera
Des Grieux . . . . Tucker
Geronte . . . . Flagello
Edmondo . . . . Anthony
Ballet Master . . . . De Paolis
Innkeeper . . . . Cehanovsky
Musician . . . . Vanni
Sergeant . . . . Marsh
Lamplighter . . . . Nagy
Captain . . . . Hawkins

December 4
CARMEN (Bizet)
Same cast as November 21 except:
Carmen . . . . Thebom
Don José . . . . Baum
Morales . . . . Harvuot

December 5
BORIS GODUNOV (Mussorgsky)
Same cast as October 29 except:
Boris Godunov . . . . London
Fyodor . . . . Miller
Pimen . . . . Scott
Grigori . . . . Gari
Marina . . . . Elias
Varlaam . . . . Davidson
Nikitich . . . . Sgarro

December 6 (matinee)
THE MAGIC FLUTE (Mozart)
Same cast as November 18

December 6
TOSCA (Puccini)
Same cast as October 27 except:
Cavaradossi . . . . Fernandi
Scarpia . . . . Gobbi
Sacristan . . . . Davidson
Sciarrone . . . . Hawkins
Jailer . . . . Marsh

December 8
LES CONTES D'HOFFMANN
(Offenbach)
Same cast as October 31 except:
Olympia . . . . Hurley

December 9
150th Anniversary of
the House of Ricordi
Benefit Metropolitan Employees'
Welfare Fund and Casa Verdi
OTELLO (Verdi)
Same cast as November 15 except:
Iago . . . . Gobbi

December 10
CARMEN (Bizet)
Same cast as November 21 except:
Don José . . . . Uzunov
Micaela . . . . Krall
Escamillo . . . . Guarrera
Frasquita . . . . Chambers
Remendado . . . . Franke

December 11
LA GIOCONDA (Ponchielli)
Conductor: Cleva
La Gioconda . . . . Milanov
Laura Adorno . . . . Rankin
Alvise Badoero . . . . Tozzi
La Cieca . . . . Amparan
Enzo Grimaldo . . . . Tucker
Barnaba . . . . Merrill
Zuane . . . . Cehanovsky
Singers . . . . Marsh, Nagy
Isepo . . . . De Paolis
Monk . . . . Scott
Steersman . . . . Sgarro

December 12
LA BOHÈME (Puccini)
Same cast as November 8 except:
Rodolfo . . . . Fernandi
Colline . . . . Moscona
Mimì . . . . Tebaldi
Benoit . . . . Flagello
Parpignol . . . . D'Elia

December 13 (matinee)
FLEDERMAUS (J. Strauss)
Same cast as November 27 except:
Ida . . . . Ames

December 13
EUGENE ONEGIN (Tchaikovsky)
Conductor: Mitropoulos
Larina . . . . Lipton
Tatyana . . . . Amara
Olga . . . . Elias
Onegin . . . . London
Lenski . . . . Gedda
Prince Gremin . . . . Tozzi
Filippyevna . . . . Amparan
Captain . . . . Sgarro
Zaretski . . . . Cehanovsky
Triquet . . . . De Paolis

December 14
Benefit Mizrachi
Women's Organization
LUCIA DI LAMMERMOOR
(Donizetti)
Conductor: Cleva
Lucia . . . . Peters
Enrico Ashton . . . . Sereni
Edgardo . . . . Peerce
Alisa . . . . Votipka
Raimondo . . . . Wildermann
Arturo . . . . Anthony
Normanno . . . . Nagy

December 15
LA GIOCONDA (Ponchielli)
Same cast as December 11 except:
Enzo Grimaldo .... Baum

December 17
THE MAGIC FLUTE (Mozart)
Same cast as November 18

December 18
EUGENE ONEGIN (Tchaikovsky)
Same cast as December 13 except:
Lenski .... Tucker
Prince Gremin ..... Wildermann

December 19
RIGOLETTO (Verdi)
Same cast as October 30 except:
    Conductor: Adler
Rigoletto .... Merrill
Gilda .... Hurley
Sparafucile .... Wildermann
Maddalena .... Roggero
Monterone .... Sgarro
Marullo .... Harvuot
Guard .... Marsh

December 20 (matinee)
OTELLO (Verdi)
    Same cast as November 15

December 20
Benefit Hartman Homecrest
FLEDERMAUS (J. Strauss)
Same cast as November 27 except:
Ida .... Ames
Alfred .... Carelli

December 22
MANON LESCAUT (Puccini)
Same cast as December 3 except:
Cleva became ill in Act III and
was replaced by Gniewek and
Schick; Cleva returned for Act IV.
Geronte .... Baccaloni

December 23
CAVALLERIA RUSTICANA
                    (Mascagni)
Same cast as November 7 except:
Turiddu .... Barioni
Alfio .... Zanasi
PAGLIACCI (Leoncavallo)
Same cast as November 7 except:
Silvio .... Guarrera
Villagers .. Alperstein, Tomanelli

December 24
LA BOHEME (Puccini)
Same cast as November 8 except:
Rodolfo .... Peerce
Schaunard .... Harvuot
Colline .... Tozzi
Mimi .... Amara
Musetta .... Hurley
Benoit .... Flagello
Parpignol .... D'Elia

December 25
TOSCA (Puccini)
Same cast as October 27 except:
Cavaradossi .... Fernandi
Angelotti .... Scott
Sacristan .... Baccaloni
Spoletta .... Franke
Sciarrone .... Hawkins

December 26
LOHENGRIN (Wagner)
    Conductor: Schippers
King Henry .... Edelmann
Lohengrin .... Sullivan
Elsa .... Della Casa
Telramund .... Uhde
Ortrud .... Harshaw
Herald .... Sereni
Nobles .... Mollica, Knight,
        Backgren, Hemmerly

December 27 (matinee)
MADAMA BUTTERFLY (Puccini)
Same cast as November 1 except:
Cio-Cio-San .... Albanese
Sharpless .... Guarrera

December 27
LES CONTES D'HOFFMANN
                    (Offenbach)
Same cast as October 31 except:
Giulietta .... Amparan
Nicklausse .... Vanni
Lindorf .... Singher
Coppélius .... Singher
Dappertutto .... Singher
Dr. Miracle .... Singher
Luther .... Cehanovsky

December 28
OTELLO (Verdi)
    Same cast as November 15

December 29
BORIS GODUNOV (Mussorgsky)
Same cast as October 29 except:
Fyodor .... Miller
Grigori .... Gari
Marina .... Thebom
Rangoni .... Valentino
Nikitich .... Sgarro

December 30
EUGENE ONEGIN (Tchaikovsky)
Same cast as December 13 except:
Lenski .... Tucker

December 31
FLEDERMAUS (J. Strauss)
Same cast as November 27 except:
Orlofsky .... Resnik

January 1
LA BOHEME (Puccini)
Same cast as November 8 except:
Rodolfo .... Fernandi
Mimi .... Tebaldi
Parpignol .... D'Elia

January 2
UN BALLO IN MASCHERA (Verdi)
    Conductor: Schippers
Riccardo .... Tucker
Renato .... Merrill
Amelia .... Stella
Ulrica .... Madeira
Oscar .... Hurley
Silvano .... Marsh
Samuel .... Moscona
Tom .... Scott
Judge .... Olvis
Servant .... Nagy

January 3 (matinee)
CAVALLERIA RUSTICANA
                    (Mascagni)
Same cast as November 7 except:
Turiddu .... Barioni
Alfio .... Zanasi
PAGLIACCI (Leoncavallo)
    Same cast as November 7

January 3
AIDA (Verdi)
    Conductor: Cleva
King .... Flagello
Amneris .... Thebom
Aida .... Davy
Radames .... Uzunov
Amonasro .... Merrill
Ramfis .... Scott
Messenger .... Nagy
Priestess .... Vanni

January 5
TOSCA (Puccini)
Same cast as October 27 except:
Cavaradossi .... Fernandi
Scarpia .... Cassel
Sciarrone .... Marsh

January 6
LOHENGRIN (Wagner)
    Same cast as December 26

January 7
VANESSA (Barber)
    Conductor: Mitropoulos
Vanessa .... Steber
Erika .... Elias
Baroness .... Resnik
Anatol .... Gedda
Doctor .... Tozzi
Major domo .... Cehanovsky
Footman .... Nagy

January 8
AIDA (Verdi)
    Same cast as January 3 except:
Aida .... Stella
Radames (Scene 1 only) . Bergonzi
Amonasro .... Zanasi

January 9
THE MAGIC FLUTE (Mozart)
Same cast as November 18 except:
Tamino .... Valletti

January 10 (matinee)
LA GIOCONDA (Ponchielli)
Same cast as December 11 except:
Alvise Badoero .... Siepi

January 10
FLEDERMAUS (J. Strauss)
Same cast as November 27 except:
Rosalinda .... Lewis
Adele .... Hurley
Ida .... Ames
Orlofsky .... Resnik

January 12
CARMEN (Bizet)
Same cast as November 21 except:
Carmen .... Madeira
Don José .... Uzunov

Micaela ....Amara
Frasquita ....Chambers
Mercédès ....Vanni
Remendado ....Franke

January 14
LA BOHÈME (Puccini)
Same cast as November 8 except:
Rodolfo ....Morell
Marcello ....Sereni
Schaunard ....Harvuot
Colline ....Tozzi
Mimi ....Tebaldi
Benoit ....Pechner

January 15
DON GIOVANNI (Mozart)
Conductor: Boehm
Don Giovanni ....Siepi
Donna Anna ....Steber
Donna Elvira ....Della Casa
Zerlina ....Peters
Don Ottavio ....Valletti
Commendatore .....Wildermann
Leporello ....Corena
Masetto ....Uppman

January 16
TOSCA (Puccini)
Same cast as October 27 except:
Tosca ....Curtis-Verna
Cavaradossi ....Fernandi
Scarpia ....Warren
Angelotti ....Alvary
Sacristan ....Pechner
Spoletta ....Franke
Sciarrone ....Hawkins

January 17 (matinee)
MANON LESCAUT (Puccini)
Same cast as December 3 except:
Geronte ....Corena

January 17
UN BALLO IN MASCHERA (Verdi)
Same cast as January 2 except:
Riccardo ....Morell

January 18
Benefit West Side
Institutional Synagogue
AIDA (Verdi)
Same cast as January 3 except:
King ....Sgarro
Amonasro ....Zanasi
Ramfis ....Tozzi

January 19
THE MAGIC FLUTE (Mozart)
Same cast as November 18 except:
Sarastro ....Hines
Tamino ....Valletti
Pamina ....Amara
First Guard ....Da Costa
Third Slave ....D'Elia

January 20
LA BOHÈME (Puccini)
Same cast as November 8 except:
Rodolfo ....Bergonzi
Marcello ....Sereni
Schaunard ....Harvuot
Mimi ....Tebaldi
Benoit ....Corena

January 21
TOSCA (Puccini)
Same cast as October 27 except:
Tosca ....Stella
Cavaradossi ....Fernandi
Scarpia ....Cassel
Angelotti ....Scott

January 22
DIE MEISTERSINGER (Wagner)
Conductor: Boehm
Hans Sachs ....Edelmann
Pogner ....Tozzi
Eva ....Della Casa
Magdalene ....Resnik
Walther ....Feiersinger
Beckmesser ....Doench
Kothner ....Rothmuller
Vogelgesang ....Anthony
Nachtigall ....Marsh
Zorn ....Olvis
Eisslinger ....Nagy
Moser ....Carelli
Ortel ....Hawkins
Schwarz ....Flagello
Foltz ....Sgarro
David ....Franke
Night Watchman ......Harvuot

January 23
TOSCA (Puccini)
Same cast as October 27 except:
Conductor: Adler
Tosca ....Curtis-Verna
Cavaradossi ....Tucker
Scarpia ....Cassel
Angelotti ....Scott
Jailer ....Marsh
Shepherd ....Vanni

January 24 (matinee)
LA TRAVIATA (Verdi)
Same cast as November 2 except:
Conductor: Adler

January 24
OTELLO (Verdi)
Same cast as November 15 except:
Otello ....Uzunov
Desdemona ....Milanov
Lodovico ....Scott

January 26
EUGENE ONEGIN (Tchaikovsky)
Same cast as December 13 except:
Conductor: Strasfogel

January 27
UN BALLO IN MASCHERA (Verdi)
Same cast as January 2 except:
Riccardo ....Peerce
Tom ....Alvary

January 28
DON GIOVANNI (Mozart)
Same cast as January 15

January 29
MADAMA BUTTERFLY (Puccini)
Same cast as November 1 except:
Cio-Cio-San ....Stella
B. F. Pinkerton ....Fernandi
Suzuki ....Roggero

January 30
VANESSA (Barber)
Same cast as January 7 except:
Conductor: Strasfogel
Doctor ....Harvuot

January 31 (matinee)
LOHENGRIN (Wagner)
Same cast as December 26 except:
Telramund ....Cassel

January 31
LUCIA DI LAMMERMOOR
(Donizetti)
Same cast as December 14 except:
Lucia ....Dobbs
Enrico Ashton ....Zanasi

February 2
LA TRAVIATA (Verdi)
Same cast as November 2 except:
Violetta ....Stella
Alfredo ....Morell

February 3
CARMEN (Bizet)
Same cast as November 21 except:
Carmen ....Madeira
Micaela ....Amara
Escamillo ....London
Morales ....Harvuot

February 4
DIE MEISTERSINGER (Wagner)
Same cast as January 22 except:
Pogner ....Wildermann

February 5
Benefit Sponsored by the
Metropolitan Opera Guild for the
Production Fund
MACBETH (Verdi)
Conductor: Leinsdorf
Macbeth ....Warren
Lady Macbeth ....Rysanek
Banquo ....Hines
Macduff ....Bergonzi
Malcolm ....Olvis
Lady-in-Attendance .....Ordassy
Physician ....Pechner
Murderer ....Hawkins
Warrior ....Marsh
Bloody Child ....Cundari
Crowned Child ....Allen
Manservant ....H. Sternberg
King Duncan ....Hemmerly

February 6
MADAMA BUTTERFLY (Puccini)
Same cast as November 1 except:
Cio-Cio-San ....Stella
B. F. Pinkerton ....Fernandi
Sharpless ....Guarrera
Suzuki ....Amparan

February 7 (matinee)
LES CONTES D'HOFFMANN
(Offenbach)
Same cast as October 31 except:
Nicklausse ....Vanni
Luther ....Cehanovsky

15

February 7
DON GIOVANNI (Mozart)
Same cast as January 15 except:
Zerlina ....Hurley
Leporello ....Flagello

February 9
UN BALLO IN MASCHERA (Verdi)
Same cast as January 2 except:
Riccardo ....Peerce
Renato ....Sereni
Ulrica ....Amparan
Oscar ....Dobbs

February 10
MACBETH (Verdi)
Same cast as February 5

February 11
LOHENGRIN (Wagner)
Same cast as December 26 except:
Lohengrin ....Liebl
Elsa ....Nordmo-Loevberg
Telramund ....Cassel
Ortrud ....Rankin
Nobles ....Stanz, Mandile,
                    Strang, Emanuel

February 12
VANESSA (Barber)
Same cast as January 7 except:
Conductor: Strasfogel
Vanessa ....Lewis
Doctor ....Harvuot

February 13
LA BOHEME (Puccini)
Same cast as November 8 except:
Rodolfo ....Peerce
Marcello ....Guarrera
Schaunard ....Harvuot
Colline ....Hines
Mimi ....Albanese
Musetta ....Lewis
Benoit ....Pechner
Alcindoro ....Alvary

February 14 (matinee)
DON GIOVANNI (Mozart)
Same cast as January 15 except:
Don Giovanni ....London
Zerlina ....Hurley
Leporello ....Flagello

February 14
Benefit—Vassar Club
Scholarship Fund
MADAMA BUTTERFLY (Puccini)
Same cast as November 1 except:
Cio-Cio-San ....Stella
B. F. Pinkerton ....Fernandi
Suzuki ....Amparan
Goro ....De Paolis
Uncle-Priest ....Scott

February 16
FLEDERMAUS (J. Strauss)
Same cast as November 27 except:
Adele ....Hurley
Alfred ....Carelli
Orlofsky ....Resnik

February 17
LA TRAVIATA (Verdi)
Same cast as November 2 except:
Germont ....Zanasi
Giuseppe ....Kuestner

February 18
RIGOLETTO (Verdi)
Same cast as October 30 except:
Conductor: Schick
Duke ....Morell
Gilda ....Dobbs
Sparafucile ....Wildermann
Maddalena ....Roggero

February 19
LUCIA DI LAMMERMOOR
                    (Donizetti)
Same cast as December 14 except:
Edgardo ....Fernandi
Raimondo ....Scott

February 20
AIDA (Verdi)
Same cast as January 3 except:
Amneris ....Resnik
Aida ....Stella
Radames ....Baum
Amonasro ....Zanasi
Ramfis ....Wildermann

February 21 (matinee)
MACBETH (Verdi)
Same cast as February 5

February 21
DIE MEISTERSINGER (Wagner)
Same cast as January 22 except:
Vogelgesang ....Kuestner
David ....Anthony

February 23
VANESSA (Barber)
Same cast as January 7 except:
Conductor: Strasfogel
Doctor ....Harvuot

February 25
AIDA (Verdi)
Same cast as January 3 except:
Amneris ....Rankin
Aida ....Rysanek
Radames ....Bergonzi
Amonasro ....Warren
Ramfis ....Siepi

February 26
LA TRAVIATA (Verdi)
Same cast as November 2 except:
Alfredo ....Fernandi
Germont ....Guarrera
Giuseppe ....Kuestner

February 27
DON GIOVANNI (Mozart)
Same cast as January 15 except:
Donna Anna ....Curtis-Verna
Zerlina ....Hurley
Don Ottavio ....Gedda
Commendatore ....Tozzi
Leporello ....Flagello

February 28 (matinee)
UN BALLO IN MASCHERA (Verdi)
Same cast as January 2 except:
Riccardo ....Peerce
Silvano ....Cehanovsky

February 28
MACBETH (Verdi)
Same cast as February 5 except:
Lady-in-Attendance ....Lind

March 2
LOHENGRIN (Wagner)
Same cast as December 26 except:
Lohengrin ....Liebl
Elsa ....Nordmo-Loevberg
Telramund ....Cassel
Herald ....Marsh
Nobles ....Stanz, Mandile,
                    Strang, Emanuel

March 3
BORIS GODUNOV (Mussorgsky)
Same cast as October 29 except:
Conductor: Leinsdorf
Boris Godunov ....Hines
Grigori ....Gari
Missail ....Nagy
Simpleton ....Carelli
Nikitich ....Sgarro
Boyar ....Marcella

March 4
AIDA (Verdi)
Same cast as January 3 except:
King ....Sgarro
Amneris ....Madeira
Aida ....Curtis-Verna
Radames ....Bergonzi
Amonasro ....Zanasi
Ramfis ....Wildermann

March 5
Benefit Sponsored by the
Metropolitan Opera Guild for the
Production Fund
WOZZECK (Berg)
                    Conductor: Boehm
Wozzeck ....Uhde
Marie ....Steber
Margret ....Roggero
Captain ....Franke
Doctor ....Doench
Drum Major ....Baum
Andres ....Anthony
Fool ....De Paolis
First Apprentice ....Flagello
Second Apprentice ....Marsh
Soldier ....Ringland
Marie's Child ....Plotkin
Townsman ....Kuestner

March 6 (matinee)
102nd Metropolitan Opera
Guild Student Performance
LA BOHEME (Puccini)
                    Conductor: Rich
Rodolfo ....Gari
Marcello ....Harvuot
Schaunard ....Cehanovsky
Colline ....Sgarro
Mimi ....Curtis-Verna

16

Musetta ....Hurley
Benoit ....Alvary
Parpignol ....D'Elia
Alcindoro ....Hawkins
Sergeant ....Strang
Customs Officer ....Emanuel

March 6
MACBETH (Verdi)
Same cast as February 5 except:
Lady-in-Attendance ....Lind

March 7 (matinee)
DIE MEISTERSINGER (Wagner)
Same cast as January 22 except:
Eva ....Nordmo-Loevberg

March 7
CAVALLERIA RUSTICANA
(Mascagni)
Conductor: Adler
Santuzza ....Rankin
Lola ....Vanni
Turiddu ....Barioni
Alfio ....Zanasi
Lucia ....Dunn
PAGLIACCI (Leoncavallo)
Same cast as November 7 except:
Conductor: Adler
Nedda ....Davy
Canio ....Baum
Tonio ....Merrill
Silvio ....Guarrera

March 9
LUCIA DI LAMMERMOOR
(Donizetti)
Same cast as December 14 except:
Conductor: Adler
Lucia ....Wilson
Enrico Ashton ....Zanasi
Raimondo ....Scott

March 11 (matinee)
103rd Metropolitan Opera
Guild Student Performance
LA BOHEME (Puccini)
Same cast as March 6

March 11
CAVALLERIA RUSTICANA
(Mascagni)
Conductor: Adler
Santuzza ....Rankin
Lola ....Vanni
Turiddu ....Barioni
Alfio ....Zanasi
Lucia ....Dunn
PAGLIACCI (Leoncavallo)
Same cast as November 7 except:
Conductor: Adler
Nedda ....Davy
Canio ....Baum
Tonio ....Merrill
Silvio ....Guarrera
Villagers ..Alperstein, Tomanelli

March 12
TOSCA (Puccini)
Same cast as October 27 except:
Conductor: Adler
Tosca ....Steber
Cavaradossi ....Morell

Sacristan ....Alvary
Spoletta ....Franke
Sciarrone ....Hawkins

March 13
MANON LESCAUT (Puccini)
Same cast as December 3 except:
Manon ....Albanese
Lescaut ....Sereni
Des Grieux ....Bergonzi
Sergeant ....Sgarro

March 14 (matinee)
WOZZECK (Berg)
Same cast as March 5

March 14
DON CARLO (Verdi)
Conductor: Cleva
Philip II ....Siepi
Don Carlo ....Fernandi
Rodrigo ....Merrill
Grand Inquisitor ....Uhde
Elizabeth ....Rysanek
Princess Eboli ....Rankin
Theobald ....Chambers
Count Lerma ....Nagy
Friar ....Sgarro
Herald ....Olvis
Voice ....Arroyo
Countess Aremberg ......Keane

March 16
MACBETH (Verdi)
Same cast as February 5 except:
Macduff ....Morell
Lady-in-Attendance ....Lind
Warrior ....Sgarro

March 17 (matinee)
104th Metropolitan Opera
Guild Student Performance
LA BOHEME (Puccini)
Conductor: Strasfogel
Rodolfo ....Anthony
Marcello ....Valentino
Schaunard ....Marsh
Colline ....Wildermann
Mimi ....Krall
Musetta ....Lind
Benoit ....Pechner
Parpignol ....D'Elia
Alcindoro ....Alvary
Sergeant ....Strang
Customs Officer ....Emanuel

March 17
AIDA (Verdi)
Same cast as January 3 except:
Amneris ....Rankin
Radames ....Bergonzi
Amonasro ....Bardelli

March 18
LA GIOCONDA (Ponchielli)
Same cast as December 11 except:
Laura Adorno ....Elias
Alvise Badoero ....Siepi
La Cieca ....Dunn
Enzo Grimaldo ....Baum
First Singer ....Hawkins

March 19 (matinee)
105th Metropolitan Opera
Guild Student Performance
LA BOHEME (Puccini)
Same cast as March 17 except:
Rodolfo ....Carelli

March 19
UN BALLO IN MASCHERA (Verdi)
Same cast as January 2 except:
Conductor: Schick
Riccardo ....Morell
Renato ....Sereni
Amelia ....Curtis-Verna
Ulrica ....Resnik
Oscar ....Allen
Silvano ....Cehanovsky
Samuel ....Flagello

March 20
DIE MEISTERSINGER (Wagner)
Same cast as January 22 except:
Pogner ....Wildermann
Eva ....Nordmo-Loevberg
Walther ....Da Costa
Vogelgesang ....Kuestner
Schwarz ....Scott
David ....Anthony

March 21 (matinee)
BORIS GODUNOV (Mussorgsky)
Same cast as October 29 except:
Conductor: Leinsdorf
Grigori ....Gari
Varlaam ....Alvary
Innkeeper ....Vanni

March 21
RIGOLETTO (Verdi)
Same cast as October 30 except:
Duke ....Morell
Rigoletto ....MacNeil
Gilda ....Hurley
Sparafucile ......Wildermann
Maddalena ....Elias
Giovanna ....Dunn

March 22
FOUR NEW BALLETS
IN THE BEGINNING (Butler)
Symphony No. 1 ....Barber
Conductor: Strasfogel
Linn, Marks, Lee, Andrew
THE EXCHANGE (Ross)
Organ Concerto ....Poulenc
Organ Soloist: Shay
Conductor: Schick
Kaye, Douglas, Gutierrez
LES DIAMANTS (Danilova)
Scène de Ballet ....Bériot
Violin Soloist: Gniewek
Conductor: Taussig
Serrano, Marks
HAIL AND FAREWELL (Tudor)
Festival March,
Serenade,
Four Last Songs ......R. Strauss
Soprano Soloist: Steber
Conductor: Rich
Kaye, Serrano, Jerell, Keane

March 23
WOZZECK (Berg)
Same cast as March 5 except:
Marie .... Lewis

March 24
DON GIOVANNI (Mozart)
Same cast as January 15 except:
Don Giovanni .... London
Donna Anna ...... Curtis-Verna
Donna Elvira .... Amara
Zerlina .... Hurley
Don Ottavio .... Gedda

March 25 (matinee)
106th Metropolitan Opera
Guild Student Performance
LA BOHEME (Puccini)
Conductor: Adler
Rodolfo .... W. Lewis
Marcello .... Harvuot
Schaunard .... Marsh
Colline .... Scott
Mimi .... Cundari
Musetta .... B. Lewis
Benoit .... Pechner
Parpignol .... D'Elia
Alcindoro .... Alvary
Sergeant .... Ghazal
Customs Officer .... Emanuel

March 25
DON CARLO (Verdi)
Same cast as March 14 except:
Grand Inquisitor ... Wildermann
Princess Eboli .... Thebom

March 26
MANON LESCAUT (Puccini)
Same cast as December 3 except:
Manon .... Albanese
Lescaut .... Sereni

March 27 (matinee)
LA FORZA DEL DESTINO (Verdi)
Convent Scene
Conductor: Walter
Leonora .... Krall
Padre Guardiano .... Tozzi
MESSA DA REQUIEM (Verdi)
Conductor: Walter
Soloists .... Krall, Elias,
Bergonzi, Tozzi

March 28 (matinee)
RIGOLETTO (Verdi)
Same cast as October 30 except:
Sparafucile .... Wildermann
Maddalena .... Roggero

March 28
CARMEN (Bizet)
Same cast as November 21 except:
Micaela .... Hurley
Escamillo .... Sereni
Zuniga .... Alvary
Morales .... Harvuot
Frasquita .... Lind
Mercédès .... Vanni
Remendado .... Franke

March 29
LA FORZA DEL DESTINO (Verdi)
Convent Scene
Same cast as March 27 except:
Leonora .... Milanov
MESSA DA REQUIEM (Verdi)
Same soloists as March 27 except:
Milanov, who fainted following
the Dies Irae; Krall replaced her.

March 30
BORIS GODUNOV (Mussorgsky)
Same cast as October 29 except:
Conductor: Leinsdorf
Boris Godunov .... London
Fyodor .... Vanni
Shuiski .... Franke
Pimen .... Scott
Grigori .... Da Costa
Marina .... Elias
Varlaam .... Alvary
Simpleton .... Carelli
Nikitich .... Sgarro

April 1
WOZZECK (Berg)
Same cast as March 5 except:
Doctor .... Alvary
Drum Major .... Da Costa
Andres .... Lewis

April 2
GALA PERFORMANCE
LA BOHEME (ACT III) (Puccini)
Conductor: Strasfogel
Rodolfo .... Tucker
Marcello .... Zanasi
Mimi .... Amara
Musetta .... Lewis
Sergeant .... Ghazal
Customs Officer .... Emanuel
TOSCA (ACT II) (Puccini)
Conductor: Adler
Tosca .... Albanese
Cavaradossi .... Fernandi
Scarpia .... London
Spoletta .... Franke
Sciarrone .... Cehanovsky
HAIL AND FAREWELL (R. Strauss)
Same cast as March 22
AIDA (ACT III) (Verdi)
Conductor: Cleva
Amneris .... Dunn
Aida .... Rysanek
Radames .... Bergonzi
Amonasro .... Merrill
Ramfis .... Scott

April 3 (matinee)
107th Metropolitan Opera
Guild Student Performance
LA BOHEME (Puccini)
Same cast as March 25 except:
Conductor: Cleva
Mimi .... Hurley
Musetta .... Lind
Benoit .... Alvary
Alcindoro .... De Paolis

April 3
EUGENE ONEGIN (Tchaikovsky)
Same cast as December 13 except:
Conductor: Strasfogel
Prince Gremin ..... Wildermann
Filippyevna .... Dunn

April 4 (matinee)
DON CARLO (Verdi)
Same cast as March 14 except:
Philip II .... Hines
Don Carlo .... Gari
Princess Eboli .... Thebom

April 4
LA BOHEME (Puccini)
Same cast as March 25 except:
Rodolfo .... Tucker
Marcello .... Guarrera
Mimi .... Albanese
Musetta .... Fenn

April 8
FLEDERMAUS (J. Strauss)
Same cast as November 27 except:
Rosalinda .... Fenn
Adele .... Hurley
Ida .... Ames
Orlofsky .... Resnik

April 9
WOZZECK (Berg)
Same cast as March 5 except:
Doctor .... Alvary
Drum Major .... Da Costa
Andres .... Lewis

April 10 (matinee)
108th Metropolitan Opera
Guild Student Performance
LA BOHEME (Puccini)
Same cast as March 25 except:
Rodolfo .... Carelli
Mimi .... Hurley
Musetta .... Lind
Alcindoro .... Hawkins

April 10
DON CARLO (Verdi)
Same cast as March 14 except:
Philip II .... Tozzi
Don Carlo .... Gari
Rodrigo .... Sereni
Elizabeth .... Curtis-Verna

April 11 (matinee)
TOSCA (Puccini)
Same cast as October 27 except:
Conductor: Adler
Tosca .... Steber
Cavaradossi .... Bergonzi
Angelotti .... Alvary
Sacristan .... Pechner
Sciarrone .... Hawkins

April 11
LA GIOCONDA (Ponchielli)
Same cast as December 11 except:
Laura Adorno .... Resnik
Alvise Badoero ..... Wildermann
La Cieca .... Roggero

EXCERPTS FROM PRESS REVIEWS

DEBUT OF BARRY MORELL as Pinkerton in *Madama Butterfly*, November 1, 1958

Mr. Morell, young-looking and a reasonably good actor, sounds like a thoroughly dependable tenor. At the City Center . . . his voice did sound somewhat bigger than it does in the stretches of the Met. But his is a well-produced lyric voice, always on pitch, and he sings with taste. At the end of Act I, for example, he did not bawl out his "Vieni! Vieni!" but instead managed to get a tender quality into the phrase.—Harold C. Schonberg, *New York Times*

NEW PRODUCTIONS of Mascagni's *Cavalleria Rusticana* and Leoncavallo's *Pagliacci* and DEBUT OF PRIMO ZAMBRUNO as Turiddu, November 7, 1958

Last week the Metropolitan gave [*Pagliacci*] a new production under the stage direction of José Quintero, and . . . the result seemed . . . one of general manager Rudolf Bing's happier efforts to combine opera with the theatrical craftsmanship of Broadway. Mr. Quintero's practiced hand was continually in evidence in the livening up of dramatic detail and in the intensification of the realism of the spectacle. Nedda sang her first-act monologue lying lazily and voluptuously on her back against a staircase. Canio sang "Vesti la giubba" while daubing greasepaint on his face, with the pedestal of a truncated column serving as a dressing table. . . . The crowds followed the action of the principals with intense absorption, and the little *commedia dell' arte* play-within-a-play was charmingly stylized and formal, giving the final double murder an increased emotional voltage by contrast. The set, by Rolf Gérard, was simple and about as effective as any I have seen for this opera.

Though I have heard warmer, tenderer and more despairing Canios than . . . Mario Del Monaco, he sang throughout with uninhibited brilliance, and the rest of the cast was close to ideal. Leonard Warren demonstrated again that he is . . . the finest Tonio currently before the public. Some magic on Mr. Quintero's part had overcome Lucine Amara's customary placidity of temperament and turned her into a wild and passionate Nedda, and her voice . . . sounded wonderfully limpid and expressive. . . . Even the lesser roles, sung by Charles Anthony and Mario Sereni, were done with great polish, and Dimitri Mitropoulos conducted not only with his usual gusto but with taste as well. . . .

I have always found *Cavalleria Rusticana* a comparative bore, and had hoped that Mr. Quintero would manage to do something special with it, too. The staging was . . . as resourceful as possible, and this opera also had a new set by Mr. Gérard, which was handsome enough in its own right. But Zinka Milanov as Santuzza was not in her best vocal form, and a new tenor named Primo Zambruno proved pretty wooden as an actor . . . though he sang a few fairly glowing phrases.—Winthrop Sargeant, *The New Yorker*

RENATA TEBALDI as Cio-Cio-San in *Madama Butterfly*, November 8, 1958

There was a clear, strong note of affirmation in the coming of Renata Tebaldi in her first *Butterfly*, reminding us that the Met has old standards as well as new productions. The strong-voiced soprano gratified best hopes with a warmly colored, expertly shaded treatment of the vocal score, which attested not only to her capacity for artistic growth but also her response to the leadership of conductor Erich Leinsdorf and the suggestive stage direction of Yoshio Aoyama. From the one she derived an increased effectiveness of her powerful vocal means, from the other a heightened awareness of what can be accomplished by integrated action and gesture.—Irving Kolodin, *Saturday Review*

TITO GOBBI as Iago in *Otello*, December 9, 1958

He is not a sinister, sinuous Iago in action. He plays the part of Otello's ancient with a good deal of open-faced geniality. But this approach is permissible so long as the character is limned in all his bitter evil through the voice. Musically, Mr. Gobbi knows his business thoroughly. He phrases with subtlety of tone and rhythm. At times he fashions a pianissimo line that has an ominous velvetiness: one can understand that it would work on Otello like a diabolical torture weapon. Mr. Gobbi can also pour out his rage at a futile world in a rousing "Credo."

This is a good voice, if not a great one. It has some hollowness and a bit of wobble. But one is willing to overlook these things in an artist who has a grasp of style. He understands Verdi: he helps to communicate the tempestuous drama that the composer poured into *Otello*.—Howard Taubman, *New York Times*

DEBUTS OF SEBASTIAN FEIERSINGER, KARL DOENCH and MARKO ROTHMULLER in *Die Meistersinger*, January 22, 1959

Sebastian Feiersinger . . . made a tall, good-looking if too-well-fed Walther von Stolzing, and his vocalism was generally creditable. Though he had to strain for his top notes in the Quintet and in the Prize Song, he sang better than most Germanic tenors, while his voice was pleasant in quality and able-bodied. He also was above average in his acting.

Bass-baritone Karl Doench proved an excellent Beckmesser, matching a gift for humor with a droll-sounding voice which fitted the part admirably. His acting was restrained and yet humorous, though he became so engrossed with his singing in his second-act serenade that he forgot sometimes to play "at" his lute while the sounds were coming from below.

Marko Rothmuller, who made a quaint-looking Kothner, enhanced by spectacles . . . had a dry-sounding voice that also fitted his part. He was well in the picture, along with his fellow Meistersingers, a picturesque if stuffy lot.—Harriett Johnson, *New York Post*

METROPOLITAN PREMIERE of Verdi's *Macbeth* and DEBUT OF LEONIE RYSANEK, February 5, 1959

Though there are ghosts onstage and off, the Metropolitan Opera's new *Macbeth* is not haunted. It is, indeed, a handsome, moving production of the finest of Verdi's early operas.

The apparitions onstage, including that of Banquo, are handled so that they make their effect. . . . As for the ghost offstage, that of Maria Meneghini Callas, for whom this production . . . was originally planned, it was exorcised by the radiant new soprano, Leonie Rysanek.

As Miss Rysanek made her first

19

entrance, some well-bred gentleman shouted, "Brava Callas!" But the German soprano has been to the wars [and] has the courage to cope with adversity. It is possible to find fault with Miss Rysanek. Her voice is not harsh and edgy, as Verdi wished Lady Macbeth to be; on the contrary, it is beautifully schooled and controlled.

Miss Rysanek phrases with the intelligence and sensibility of a musician. Her soprano is securest and loveliest above the staff, where its texture is both delicate and brilliant. She can float a high pianissimo exquisitely. And her fortissimos soar above the massed ensemble at the end of the first act with proud refulgence.

Leonard Warren evokes the troubled, terrified Macbeth with subtle authority; as is his habit, he sings with subtle art. . . . Carlo Bergonzi . . . as Macduff . . . sings his aria . . . lyrically. Jerome Hines brings presence, resonance and feeling to Banquo. William Olvis and Carlotta Ordassy are effective in small roles.

Erich Leinsdorf, who took over as conductor less than a fortnight ago when Dimitri Mitropoulos was struck down by a heart attack, leads with meticulous discipline. He is not given to flights of feverish intensity . . . yet [he] gives momentum to a work that, because of its numerous scene changes, cannot avoid a certain amount of choppiness.

As significant for the Met's future as the arrival of Miss Rysanek is the collaboration of Carl Ebert, who staged this *Macbeth,* and Caspar Neher, who designed it. . . . In his handling of masses and individuals, [Ebert] shows that he is a theater man of a high order. He cannot make Verdi's abundance of witches . . . anything more than ingenuous, and the dancing in these scenes adds nothing to the illusion. Mr. Neher's profusion of masks doesn't help much either, but for the rest, his sets and costumes have imagination and flavor. Great Birnam Wood comes to Dunsinane Hill most amusingly.—Howard Taubman, *New York Times*

DEBUTS OF AASE NORDMO LOEVBERG and KARL LIEBL in *Lohengrin,* February 11, 1959

Of the two [newcomers] Miss Nordmo Loevberg [as Elsa] was much the more impressive, though neither of them proved exactly epoch-making. The voice sounded

strong and fresh enough, at its best in the upper register, where there were reminders of Mme. Flagstad. But the newcomer was somewhat ill-at-ease vocally. The pitch wasn't always certain, and lower notes tended to lose quality and steadiness. It is a voice of substance, however, and one awaits Miss Nordmo Loevberg's next role.

One also awaits Mr. Liebl's next role. His debut as Lohengrin was far from convincing, though here again the fundamental isn't at all bad. The fact is the singing seemed under stress. At times Mr. Liebl belted his tones. It is possible both artists were overawed by the implications of a Metropolitan debut.—Louis Biancolli, *New York World Telegram and Sun*

METROPOLITAN PREMIÈRE of Berg's *Wozzeck,* March 5, 1959

An event of extraordinary musical significance took place last night at the Met. One of the masterpieces of the modern opera stage finally reached the old boards of our celebrated theater when Alban Berg's *Wozzeck* was presented in a lavish, spacious, intensely moving and beautifully executed production. The opera was sung in English.

Wozzeck is not a glamorous operatic hero, nor is his girl a vivacious belle. This opera is the drama of unheroism, of senseless accident, the tragedy of a poor harassed private soldier who kills his girl and himself. The numerous changes in the opera chase one another like feverish apparitions until the last bloodcurdling scenes are reached, by which time the listener is limp and shaken. . . .

The stage director [Herbert Graf] was faced with a great handicap: the old Met has no revolving stage. It is to Mr. Graf's credit that he managed the many rapid changes of scene with a minimum of inconvenience, always maintaining the taut atmosphere and the continuity of the action. He was aided by Caspar Neher's imaginative scenery and costumes. . . .

Hermann Uhde played and sang the pathetic soldier with a gauche forlornness that was very moving. He was but a cog in the big reaper that gathers in the harvest for an unknown owner. His gradual deterioration culminated in the scene of his drowning—the house was hushed.

Paul Franke as the Captain was fidgety, half-hearted and sadistic, as

the role requires. The extremely difficult high notes and sudden falsettos which abound in his part were handled with remarkable ease.

Karl Doench's Doctor was a fine character performance in the German expressionistic style: eccentric and malevolent. When he listened to the moans of the drowning Wozzeck, his comments were chilling. Kurt Baum interpreted the vain and stupid Drum Major convincingly, while Charles Anthony, Alessio de Paolis, Ezio Flagello, Calvin Marsh and Earl Ringland completed the excellent male cast.

Eleanor Steber added another gold medal to her collection with her portrayal of Marie. She sang the cruel role with impressive musical security, never hesitating to let her voice soar. Her acting was very good, and at times, as when she read from the Bible, gripping. Margaret Roggero sang the brief role of Margret commendably, and the choral work was excellent. . . .

Both conductor [Karl Boehm] and the brilliant orchestra lived up to the highest demands. The applause they received before the third act was unusual in its warmth.—Paul Henry Lang, *New York Herald Tribune*

DEBUT OF CORNELL MACNEIL as Rigoletto, March 21, 1959

Sometimes an artist can plug along year in and year out without any breaks. Then, with a whoosh, he'll go right to the top. Cornell MacNeil, Minneapolis-born baritone, has just taken that dizzying ride. On March 5 the thirty-four-year-old singer made his successful European debut at La Scala in Milan, and Saturday night he made an unexpected but equally well received Metropolitan debut in the title role of Verdi's *Rigoletto.* . . .

Mr. MacNeil came through superbly. When he cut loose, the rafters trembled. But he did not forget to sing softly and lyrically. Only in the big scene in Act III, beginning "Cortigiani, vil razza dannata," were there any signs of strain or pushing.

At this point Mr. MacNeil's desire to produce an intense and moving dramatic moment led him to musical excess. Elsewhere the characterization was expressed with and within the music, the vocal and visual elements being effectively integrated. If this is not yet a great Rigoletto, it is certainly a very good one.—Eric Salzman, *New York Times*

1959-1960 SEASON

PERSONNEL

Male Artists
Alvary, Lorenzo
Anthony, Charles
Baccaloni, Salvatore
Bardelli, Cesare
Barioni, Daniele
Bastianini, Ettore
Baum, Kurt
Bergonzi, Carlo
Birlenbach, Erich
Bjoerling, Jussi
Borg, Kim
Cappuccilli, Piero
Carelli, Gabor
Cassel, Walter
Cehanovsky, George
Colzani, Anselmo
Corena, Fernando
Czerwenka, Oskar
Da Costa, Albert
Davidson, Lawrence
De Cesare, Luigi
De Paolis, Alessio
Ernster, Dezso
Fernandi, Eugenio
Flagello, Ezio
Folmer, Joseph
Franke, Paul
Gedda, Nicolai
Ghazal, Edward
Guarrera, Frank
Harvuot, Clifford
Hawkins, Osie
Hemmerly, Walter
Herbert, Ralph
Hines, Jerome
Kessler, Kurt
Kuestner, Charles
Kullman, Charles
Liebl, Karl
Lisitsian, Pavel
London, George
MacNeil, Cornell
Marcella, Lou
Marsh, Calvin
Mayreder, Rudolf
Merrill, Robert
Miles, Roland
Mollica, Giulio
Morell, Barry
Moscona, Nicola
Nagy, Robert
Olvis, William
Oppicelli, Aurelio
Pechner, Gerhard
Peerce, Jan
Reitan, Roald
Rothmuller, Marko
Ryan, George
Scott, Norman
Sereni, Mario
Sgarro, Louis
Siepi, Cesare
Slezak, Walter
Stanz, William
Starling, William
Strang, Lloyd
Tomanelli, Carlo

Tozzi, Giorgio
Trehy, John
Tucker, Richard
Uhde, Hermann
Uppman, Theodor
Uzunov, Dimiter
Valentino, Frank
Valletti, Cesare
Vickers, Jon
Vinay, Ramon
Warren, Leonard
Wildermann, William
Zanasi, Mario

Female Artists
Albanese, Licia
Allen, Mildred
Amara, Lucine
Amparan, Belen
Clark, Charleen
Conner, Nadine
Curtis-Verna, Mary
Dalis, Irene
Davy, Gloria
Della Casa, Lisa
De Los Angeles, Victoria
De Salvo, Dina
Dobbs, Mattiwilda
Dunn, Mignon
Elias, Rosalind
Fercana, Mary
Gueden, Hilde
Harshaw, Margaret
Hurley, Laurel
Jones, Lexi
Kirsten, Dorothy
Kirwan, Jane
Krall, Heidi
Lansing, Gladys
Lind, Gloria
Lipton, Martha
Loevberg, Aase Nordmo
Ludwig, Christa
Madeira, Jean
Milanov, Zinka
Miller, Mildred
Moedl, Martha
Moffo, Anna
Nache, Maria
Nelli, Herva
Nilsson, Birgit
Ordassy, Carlotta
Peters, Roberta
Rankin, Nell
Reep, Nancy
Resnik, Regina
Roggero, Margaret
Rysanek, Leonie
Savage, May
Shawn, Dorothy
Simionato, Giulietta
Soederstroem, Elisabeth
Steber, Eleanor
Stella, Antonietta
Stevens, Risë
Stratas, Teresa
Tebaldi, Renata
Vanni, Helen
Vicos, Athena
Votipka, Thelma

Wall, Joan
Yauger, Maria

Ballet Soloists
Ames, Suzanne
Andrew, Thomas
Burdick, William
Douglas, Scott
Farrington, Hubert
Hirschl, Ilona
Horn, Catherine
Jerell, Edith
Jones, Harry
Keane, Audrey
King, Nancy
Marks, Bruce
Martin, Donald
Murray, Ron
Piper, Frank
San Miguel, Lolita
Sibley, Louellen
Verdy, Violette
Warren, Marsha

Conductors
Adler, Kurt
Boehm, Karl
Cleva, Fausto
Leinsdorf, Erich
Mitropoulos, Dimitri
Morel, Jean
Rich, Martin
Schick, George
Schippers, Thomas
Strasfogel, Ignace
Taussig, Walter
Verchi, Nino

General Manager
Bing, Rudolf

October 26 (Opening Night)
IL TROVATORE (Verdi)
Conductor: Cleva
Leonora ....Stella
Manrico ....Bergonzi
Count Di Luna ....Warren
Azucena ....Simionato
Inez ....Vanni
Ferrando ....Wildermann
Ruiz ....Anthony
Gypsy ....Reitan
Messenger ....Nagy

October 28
MANON (Massenet)
Conductor: Morel
Manon ....De Los Angeles
Lescaut ....Herbert
Des Grieux ....Gedda
Count des Grieux ....Tozzi
Poussette ....Stratas
Javotte ....Vanni
Rosette ....Wall
Guillot ....De Paolis
Brétigny ....Cehanovsky
Innkeeper ....Marsh
Guards ....Kuestner, Strang
Servant ....Savage
Sergeant ....Mollica

21

1959-60

October 29
Tosca (Puccini)
Conductor: Mitropoulos
Tosca . . . . Milanov
Cavaradossi . . . . Fernandi
Scarpia . . . . Warren
Angelotti . . . . Scott
Sacristan . . . . Davidson
Spoletta . . . . Franke
Sciarrone . . . . Hawkins
Jailer . . . . Reitan
Shepherd . . . . Ryan

October 30
Benefit Sponsored by the
Metropolitan Opera Guild for the
Production Fund
Le Nozze Di Figaro (Mozart)
Conductor: Leinsdorf
Almaviva . . . . Borg
Countess . . . . Della Casa
Susanna . . . . Soederstroem
Figaro . . . . Siepi
Cherubino . . . . Miller
Marcellina . . . . Resnik
Bartolo . . . . Flagello
Basilio . . . . Kullman
Don Curzio . . . . Carelli
Antonio . . . . Davidson
Barbarina . . . . Allen
Peasant Girls . . . . . . Stratas, Wall

October 31 (matinee)
Cavalleria Rusticana
(Mascagni)
Conductor: Verchi
Santuzza . . . . Simionato
Lola . . . . Elias
Turiddu . . . . Peerce
Alfio . . . . Cassel
Lucia . . . . Votipka
Pagliacci (Leoncavallo)
Conductor: Verchi
Nedda . . . . Amara
Canio . . . . Uzunov
Tonio . . . . MacNeil
Beppe . . . . Anthony
Silvio . . . . Sereni
Villagers . . . . . . Folmer, Starling

October 31
Benefit Mizrachi
Women's Organization
Carmen (Bizet)
Conductor: Morel
Carmen . . . . Madeira
Don José . . . . Olvis
Micaela . . . . Nache
Escamillo . . . . Merrill
Zuniga . . . . Sgarro
Morales . . . . Harvuot
Frasquita . . . . Krall
Mercédès . . . . Roggero
Dancaire . . . . Cehanovsky
Remendado . . . . Franke

November 2
Tosca (Puccini)
Same cast as October 29 except:
Scarpia . . . . MacNeil

November 3
Il Trovatore (Verdi)
Same cast as October 26

November 4
La Traviata (Verdi)
Conductor: Verchi
Violetta . . . . De Los Angeles
Alfredo . . . . Valletti
Germont . . . . Sereni
Flora . . . . Vanni
Gastone . . . . Carelli
Baron Douphol . . . . Marsh
Marquis d'Obigny . . Cehanovsky
Dr. Grenvil . . . . Sgarro
Annina . . . . Stratas
Giuseppe . . . . Marcella
Gardener . . . . Trehy

November 5
Cavalleria Rusticana
(Mascagni)
Same cast as October 31
Pagliacci (Leoncavallo)
Same cast as October 31 except:
Nedda . . . . Davy
Canio . . . . Bergonzi

November 6
Le Nozze Di Figaro (Mozart)
Same cast as October 30

November 7 (matinee)
Carmen (Bizet)
Same cast as October 31 except:
Morales . . . . Marsh

November 7
Madama Butterfly (Puccini)
Conductor: Mitropoulos
Cio-Cio-San . . . . Stella
B. F. Pinkerton . . . . Morell
Sharpless . . . . Harvuot
Suzuki . . . . Roggero
Kate Pinkerton . . . . Wall
Goro . . . . Kullman
Yamadori . . . . Cehanovsky
Uncle-Priest . . . . Hawkins
Imperial Commissioner . . Marsh
Registrar . . . . De Cesare

November 9
Aida (Verdi)
Conductor: Cleva
King . . . . Sgarro
Amneris . . . . Rankin
Aida . . . . Amara
Radames . . . . Uzunov
Amonasro . . . . Merrill
Ramfis . . . . Siepi
Messenger . . . . Nagy
Priestess . . . . Krall

November 11
Le Nozze Di Figaro (Mozart)
Same cast as October 30 except:
Basilio . . . . Carelli
Don Curzio . . . . Nagy

November 12
Carmen (Bizet)
Same cast as October 31 except:
Carmen . . . . Stevens
Don José . . . . Uzunov
Micaela . . . . Krall
Escamillo . . . . Sereni
Zuniga . . . . Scott
Frasquita . . . . Stratas

November 13
Manon (Massenet)
Same cast as October 28 except:
Second Guard . . . . Tomanelli

November 14 (matinee)
La Traviata (Verdi)
Same cast as November 4 except:
Violetta . . . . Moffo
Germont . . . . MacNeil

November 14
Il Trovatore (Verdi)
Same cast as October 26

November 16
Cavalleria Rusticana
(Mascagni)
Same cast as October 31 except:
Turiddu . . . . Bjoerling
Pagliacci (Leoncavallo)
Same cast as October 31 except:
Nedda . . . . Davy

November 17
Madama Butterfly (Puccini)
Same cast as November 7

November 18
Carmen (Bizet)
Same cast as October 31 except:
Carmen . . . . Elias
Don José . . . . Baum
Micaela . . . . Krall
Escamillo . . . . Zanasi
Zuniga . . . . Scott
Frasquita . . . . Stratas
Remendado . . . . De Paolis

November 19
Benefit Bagby Music
Lovers' Foundation
La Traviata (Verdi)
Same cast as November 4 except:
Germont . . . . Merrill

November 20
Il Trovatore (Verdi)
Same cast as October 26 except:
Count Di Luna . . . . Sereni

November 21 (matinee)
Tosca (Puccini)
Same cast as October 29 except:
Tosca . . . . Curtis-Verna
Cavaradossi . . . . Bjoerling
Scarpia . . . . MacNeil

22

November 21
MANON (Massenet)
Same cast as October 28 except:
Manon .... Albanese
Des Grieux .... Valletti

November 22
Benefit Yeshiva University
Women's Organization
AIDA (Verdi)
Same cast as November 9 except:
Amonasro .... Warren
Ramfis .... Wildermann
Priestess .... Vanni

November 23
CARMEN (Bizet)
Same cast as October 31 except:
Carmen .... Stevens
Zuniga .... Scott
Frasquita .... Stratas
Mercédès .... Vanni
Remendado .... De Paolis

November 24
LA TRAVIATA (Verdi)
Same cast as November 4 except:
Violetta .... Albanese
Germont .... Zanasi

November 25
THE GYPSY BARON (J. Strauss)
Conductor: Leinsdorf
Emperor of Austria .. De Paolis
Count Homonay .... Reitan
Carnero .... Flagello
Barinkay .... Gedda
Saffi .... Della Casa
Szupán .... Slezak
Arsena .... Hurley
Mirabella .... Dunn
Czipra .... Resnik
Ottokar .... Franke
Mihaly .... Nagy
Pali .... Birlenbach
Imperial Chamberlain .. Mayreder
Sergeant .... Stanz
Peasant Girls .... Reep, DeSalvo

November 26
MADAMA BUTTERFLY (Puccini)
Same cast as November 7 except:
B. F. Pinkerton ...... Fernandi
Sharpless .... Zanasi

November 27
CAVALLERIA RUSTICANA
(Mascagni)
Same cast as October 31 except:
Santuzza .... Milanov
Turiddu .... Bjoerling
PAGLIACCI (Leoncavallo)
Same cast as October 31 except:
Nedda .... Davy
Canio .... Bergonzi

November 28 (matinee)
AIDA (Verdi)
Same cast as November 9 except:
Amonasro .... Warren
Ramfis .... Tozzi

November 28
LE NOZZE DI FIGARO (Mozart)
Same cast as October 30

November 30
LA TRAVIATA (Verdi)
Same cast as November 4 except:
Violetta .... Moffo
Alfredo .... Morell
Germont .... Warren

December 2
PELLEAS ET MELISANDE
(Debussy)
Conductor: Morel
Mélisande .... De Los Angeles
Arkel .... Tozzi
Pelléas .... Uppman
Golaud .... London
Geneviève .... Resnik
Yniold .... Allen
Physician .... Harvuot

December 3
IL TROVATORE (Verdi)
Same cast as October 26 except:
Azucena .... Madeira

December 4
MADAMA BUTTERFLY (Puccini)
Same cast as November 7 except:
Cio-Cio-San .... Albanese
B. F. Pinkerton .... Fernandi
Suzuki .... Elias
Imperial Commissioner .. Reitan

December 5 (matinee)
THE GYPSY BARON (J. Strauss)
Same cast as November 25

December 5
CAVALLERIA RUSTICANA
(Mascagni)
Same cast as October 31 except:
Santuzza .... Milanov
Lola .... Amparan
PAGLIACCI (Leoncavallo)
Same cast as October 31 except:
Nedda .... Nache
Tonio .... Sereni
Silvio .... Marsh
First Villager .... Miles

December 6
Benefit Order of Lafayette
and
American-French Foundation
CARMEN (Bizet)
Same cast as October 31 except:
Carmen .... Stevens
Micaela .... Krall
Zuniga .... Scott
Frasquita .... Stratas
Remendado .... De Paolis

December 7
IL TROVATORE (Verdi)
Same cast as October 26 except:
Azucena .... Dunn

December 8
FAUST (Gounod)
Conductor: Morel
Faust .... Bjoerling
Marguerite .... Soederstroem
Méphistophélès .... Siepi
Valentin .... Merrill
Siébel .... Miller
Marthe .... Votipka
Wagner .... Reitan

December 9
THE GYPSY BARON (J. Strauss)
Same cast as November 25

December 10
LE NOZZE DI FIGARO (Mozart)
Same cast as October 30 except:
Countess .... Amara
Figaro .... Tozzi
Cherubino .... Ludwig
Basilio .... De Paolis
Barbarina .... Stratas
Peasant Girls ..... Clark, Shawn

December 11
TOSCA (Puccini)
Same cast as October 29 except:
Cavaradossi .... Bjoerling
Sacristan .... Pechner

December 12 (matinee)
MANON (Massenet)
Same cast as October 28 except:
Second Guard .... Tomanelli

December 12
Benefit Hartman Homecrest
MADAMA BUTTERFLY (Puccini)
Same cast as November 7 except:
B. F. Pinkerton ...... Fernandi
Suzuki .... Elias
Kate Pinkerton .... Allen
Imperial Commissioner .. Reitan

December 14
PELLEAS ET MELISANDE
(Debussy)
Same cast as December 2

December 15
LE NOZZE DI FIGARO (Mozart)
Same cast as October 30 except:
Figaro .... Tozzi
Cherubino .... Ludwig
Basilio............... De Paolis
Barbarina .... Stratas
Peasant Girls ..... Clark, Shawn

December 16
TOSCA (Puccini)
Same cast as October 29 except:
Tosca .... Albanese
Cavaradossi .... Bjoerling

December 17
MANON (Massenet)
Same cast as October 28 except:
Count des Grieux .. Wildermann
Guillot .... Carelli
Second Guard .... Tomanelli

23

December 18
Benefit Sponsored by the
Metropolitan Opera Guild for the
Production Fund
TRISTAN UND ISOLDE (Wagner)
Conductor: Boehm
Tristan ....Liebl
Isolde ....Nilsson
King Marke ....Hines
Kurvenal ....Cassel
Brangäne ....Dalis
Melot ....Marsh
Steersman ....Sgarro
Shepherd ....Franke
Sailor's Voice ....Anthony

December 19 (matinee)
FAUST (Gounod)
Same cast as December 8

December 19
AIDA (Verdi)
Same cast as November 9 except:
Amneris ....Resnik
Aida ....Curtis-Verna
Amonasro ....MacNeil
Ramfis ....Wildermann
Priestess ....Vanni

December 21
LE NOZZE DI FIGARO (Mozart)
Same cast as October 30 except:
Susanna ....Hurley
Basilio ....Carelli
Don Curzio ....Nagy
Barbarina ....Stratas
Peasant Girls .....Clark, Shawn

December 22
CAVALLERIA RUSTICANA
(Mascagni)
Same cast as October 31 except:
Conductor: Mitropoulos
Santuzza ....Curtis-Verna
Lola ....Vanni
Turiddu ....Bjoerling
Alfio ....Bardelli
PAGLIACCI (Leoncavallo)
Same cast as October 31 except:
Conductor: Mitropoulos
Silvio ....Guarrera
Villagers ......Miles, Tomanelli

December 23
TRISTAN UND ISOLDE (Wagner)
Same cast as December 18 except:
Tristan ....Vinay

December 24
FAUST (Gounod)
Same cast as December 8 except:
Faust ....Gedda
Méphistophélès ....London
Siébel ....Elias

December 25
AIDA (Verdi)
Same cast as November 9 except:
King ....Flagello
Aida ....Rysanek
Radames ....Baum
Amonasro ....MacNeil
Priestess ....Vanni

December 26 (matinee)
DER ROSENKAVALIER (R. Strauss)
Conductor: Leinsdorf
Princess von Werdenberg
Della Casa
Baron Ochs ....Czerwenka
Octavian ....Ludwig
Faninal ....Herbert
Sophie ....Soederstroem
Marianne ....Votipka
Valzacchi ....De Paolis
Annina ....Amparan
Police Commissioner ......Scott
Major domo of Princess . .Carelli
Major domo of Faninal . .Anthony
Notary ....Hawkins
Innkeeper ....Franke
Singer ....Fernandi
Orphans .....Kirwan, L. Jones,
Shawn
Milliner ....Fercana
Hairdresser ....H. Jones
Leopold ....Farrington
Animal Vendor ....Kessler
Blackamoor ....M. Warren
Lackeys ....Folmer, Trehy,
Marcella, Ghazal

December 26
CARMEN (Bizet)
Same cast as October 31 except:
Don José ....Uzunov
Micaela ....Amara
Escamillo ....Guarrera
Frasquita ....Stratas

December 28
TRISTAN UND ISOLDE (Wagner)
Same cast as December 18 except:
Tristan (Act 1) ....Vinay
Tristan (Act 3) ......Da Costa

December 29
MANON (Massenet)
Same cast as October 28 except:
Poussette ....Allen
Guillot ....Carelli
First Guard ....Miles

December 30
MADAMA BUTTERFLY (Puccini)
Same cast as November 7 except:
Cio-Cio-San ....Albanese
Kate Pinkerton ....Allen
Goro ....Franke
Imperial Commissioner . .Reitan
Registrar ....Kessler

December 31
THE GYPSY BARON (J. Strauss)
Same cast as November 25

January 1
CARMEN (Bizet)
Same cast as October 31 except:
Carmen ....Amparan
Don José ....Uzunov
Micaela ....Amara
Escamillo ....Guarrera
Zuniga ....Scott
Frasquita ....Stratas
Mercédès ....Vanni

January 2 (matinee)
MACBETH (Verdi)
Conductor: Leinsdorf
Macbeth ....Warren
Lady Macbeth ....Rysanek
Banquo ....Hines
Macduff ....Barioni
Malcolm ....Olvis
Lady-in-Attendance .....Ordassy
Physician ....Pechner
Murderer ....Hawkins
Warrior ....Sgarro
Bloody Child ....Stratas
Crowned Child ....Allen
Manservant ....Tomanelli
King Duncan ....Hemmerly

January 2
PELLEAS ET MELISANDE
(Debussy)
Same cast as December 2 except:
Golaud ....Borg

January 4
DER ROSENKAVALIER (R. Strauss)
Same cast as December 26 except:
Singer ....Gedda

January 6
AIDA (Verdi)
Same cast as November 9 except:
King ....Flagello
Amneris ....Dalis
Amonasro ....Bardelli
Priestess ....Vanni

January 7
LA TRAVIATA (Verdi)
Same cast as November 4 except:
Conductor: Cleva
Violetta ....Curtis-Verna
Alfredo ....Gedda
Germont ....MacNeil
Flora ....Wall
Annina ....Allen

January 8
FAUST (Gounod)
Same cast as December 8 except:
Faust ....Fernandi
Valentin ....Guarrera
Siébel ....Roggero
Marthe ....Dunn
Wagner ....Marsh

24

January 9 (matinee)
TRISTAN UND ISOLDE (Wagner)
Same cast as December 18 except:
Tristan ....Vinay

January 9
THE GYPSY BARON (J. Strauss)
Same cast as November 25 except:
Szupán ....Herbert
Mirabella ....Votipka

January 11
MANON (Massenet)
Same cast as October 28 except:
Count des Grieux ..Wildermann
Poussette ....Allen

January 12
TRISTAN UND ISOLDE (Wagner)
Same cast as December 18 except:
Tristan ....Vinay

January 13
DER FLIEGENDE HOLLAENDER
(Wagner)
Conductor: Schippers
Daland ....Tozzi
Senta ....Rysanek
Erik ....Liebl
Mary ....Amparan
Steersman ....Olvis
Dutchman ....London

January 14
AIDA (Verdi)
Same cast as November 9 except:
King ....Flagello
Amneris ....Ludwig
Amonasro ....MacNeil
Ramfis ....Scott
Priestess ....Vanni

January 15
TRISTAN UND ISOLDE (Wagner)
Same cast as December 18 except:
Tristan ....Vinay

January 16 (matinee)
PELLEAS ET MELISANDE
(Debussy)
Same cast as December 2

January 16
DON GIOVANNI (Mozart)
Conductor: Boehm
Don Giovanni ....Siepi
Donna Anna ....Steber
Donna Elvira ....Della Casa
Zerlina ....Peters
Don Ottavio ....Valletti
Commendatore .....Wildermann
Leporello ....Corena
Masetto ....Uppman

January 17
Benefit West Side
Institutional Synagogue
CAVALLERIA RUSTICANA
(Mascagni)
Same cast as October 31 except:
Conductor: Adler
Santuzza ....Rankin
Lola ....Vanni
Turiddu ....Tucker
PAGLIACCI (Leoncavallo)
Same cast as October 31 except:
Conductor: Adler
Nedda ....Nache
Canio ....Vickers
Silvio ....Marsh

January 18
MACBETH (Verdi)
Same cast as January 2

January 19
THE GYPSY BARON (J. Strauss)
Same cast as November 25 except:
Mirabella ....Votipka
Peasant Girls ....Fercana, Shawn

January 20
DON GIOVANNI (Mozart)
Same cast as January 16 except:
Donna Elvira ....Amara
Zerlina ....Dobbs

January 21
TRISTAN UND ISOLDE (Wagner)
Same cast as December 18 except:
Brangäne ....Ludwig

January 22
PELLEAS ET MELISANDE
(Debussy)
Same cast as December 2

January 23 (matinee)
LE NOZZE DI FIGARO (Mozart)
Same cast as October 30

January 23
Benefit Vassar Club
Scholarship Fund
AIDA (Verdi)
Same cast as November 9 except:
Amneris ....Dalis
Radames ....Baum
Amonasro ....London
Ramfis ....Wildermann
Priestess ....Vanni

January 25
THE GYPSY BARON (J. Strauss)
Same cast as November 25 except:
Mirabella ....Votipka
Peasant Girls ....Fercana, Shawn

January 27
FAUST (Gounod)
Same cast as December 8 except:
Faust ....Morell
Méphistophélès ....Hines
Valentin ....Sereni
Siébel ....Vanni
Marthe ....Dunn

January 28
FIDELIO (Beethoven)
Conductor: Boehm
Don Fernando ....Siepi
Don Pizarro ....Uhde
Florestan ....Vickers
Leonore ....Loevberg
Rocco ....Czerwenka
Marzelline ....Hurley
Jacquino ....Anthony
First Prisoner ....Olvis
Second Prisoner ....Marsh

January 29
DON GIOVANNI (Mozart)
Same cast as January 16 except:
Don Giovanni ....London
Don Ottavio ....Gedda

January 30 (matinee)
CAVALLERIA RUSTICANA
(Mascagni)
Same cast as October 31 except:
Conductor: Mitropoulos
Santuzza ....Rankin
Lola ....Vanni
PAGLIACCI (Leoncavallo)
Same cast as October 31 except:
Conductor: Mitropoulos
Canio ....Baum
Tonio ....Merrill
Silvio ....Guarrera

January 30
TRISTAN UND ISOLDE (Wagner)
Same cast as December 18 except:
Tristan ....Vinay
King Marke ....Borg
Brangäne ....Ludwig

February 1
LA FORZA DEL DESTINO (Verdi)
Conductor: Schippers
Marquis ....Sgarro
Leonora ....Rysanek
Don Carlo ....Bastianini
Don Alvaro ....Tucker
Padre Guardiano ....Siepi
Fra Melitone ....Corena*
Preziosilla ....Dunn
Curra ....Ordassy
Trabucco ....Franke
Surgeon ....Reitan
*Pechner sang in Acts 2 and 3

February 2
FIDELIO (Beethoven)
Same cast as January 28 except:
Don Fernando ......Wildermann
First Prisoner ....Franke

February 3
MADAMA BUTTERFLY (Puccini)
Same cast as November 7 except:
Cio-Cio-San ....Albanese
B. F. Pinkerton ....Fernandi
Sharpless ....Sereni
Registrar ....Folmer

25

February 4
MACBETH (Verdi)
Same cast as January 2 except:
Lady Macbeth ....Dalis
Banquo ....Tozzi
Macduff ....Morell
Warrior ....Marsh

February 5
DER ROSENKAVALIER (R. Strauss)
Same cast as December 26 except:
Valzacchi ....Kullman
Notary ....Pechner
Singer ....Gedda

February 6 (matinee)
CARMEN (Bizet)
Same cast as October 31 except:
Carmen ....Stevens
Don José ....Tucker
Micaela ....Amara
Escamillo ....Guarrera
Zuniga ....Scott
Frasquita ....Stratas

February 6
DER FLIEGENDE HOLLAENDER
(Wagner)
Same cast as January 13

February 8
FAUST (Gounod)
Same cast as December 8 except:
Faust ....Fernandi
Méphistophélès ....London
Valentin ....Sereni
Siébel ....Vanni

February 9
DIE WALKUERE (Wagner)
Conductor: Boehm
Wotan ....Hines
Fricka ....Dalis
Brünnhilde ....Nilsson
Siegmund ....Vickers
Sieglinde ....Loevberg
Hunding ....Ernster
Helmwige ....Krall
Gerhilde ....Ordassy
Ortlinde ....Lind
Rossweisse ....Roggero
Grimgerde ....Lipton
Waltraute ....Dunn
Siegrune ....Vanni
Schwertleite ....Amparan

February 10
MACBETH (Verdi)
Same cast as January 2 except:
Banquo ....Tozzi
Macduff ....Morell
Malcolm ....Nagy

February 11
THE GYPSY BARON (J. Strauss)
Same cast as November 25 except:
Emperor of Austria ....Kullman
Barinkay ....Olvis
Mirabella ....Votipka
Czipra ....Amparan
Peasant Girls ...Fercana, Shawn

February 12
DER FLIEGENDE HOLLAENDER
(Wagner)
Same cast as January 13 except:
Daland ....Wildermann
Senta ....Harshaw

February 13 (matinee)
FIDELIO (Beethoven)
Same cast as January 28 except:
Don Fernando ....Tozzi
Leonore ....Nilsson

February 13
LA FORZA DEL DESTINO (Verdi)
Same cast as February 1 except:
Leonora ....Amara
Padre Guardiano ...Wildermann

February 15
DER FLIEGENDE HOLLAENDER
(Wagner)
Same cast as January 13 except:
Daland ....Wildermann
Senta ....Harshaw
Erik ....Da Costa
Mary ....Dunn

February 16
DON GIOVANNI (Mozart)
Same cast as January 16 except:
Donna Anna ......Curtis-Verna
Donna Elvira ....Amara
Zerlina ....Dobbs
Don Ottavio ....Gedda
Leporello ....Flagello
Masetto ....Marsh

February 17
LA FORZA DEL DESTINO (Verdi)
Same cast as February 1 except:
Don Alvaro ....Baum
Padre Guardiano ....Hines
Fra Melitone ....Pechner
Trabucco ....De Paolis

February 18
Benefit Free Milk Fund for
Babies, Inc.
AIDA (Verdi)
Same cast as November 9 except:
King ....Flagello
Amneris ....Simionato
Radames ....Bergonzi
Amonasro ....Guarrera
Ramfis ....Scott
Priestess ....Vanni

February 19
CAVALLERIA RUSTICANA
(Mascagni)
Same cast as October 31 except:
Conductor: Mitropoulos
Santuzza ....Curtis-Verna
Lola ....Amparan
Turiddu ....Tucker
Alfio ....Valentino

PAGLIACCI (Leoncavallo)
Same cast as October 31 except:
Conductor: Mitropoulos
Nedda ....Krall
Canio ....Baum
Tonio ....Merrill

February 20 (matinee)
DIE WALKUERE (Wagner)
Same cast as February 9

February 20
MACBETH (Verdi)
Same cast as January 2 except:
Macduff ....Morell
Warrior ....Marsh

February 22
MADAMA BUTTERFLY (Puccini)
Same cast as November 7 except:
B. F. Pinkerton ....Olvis
Suzuki ....Amparan
Goro ....De Paolis
Registrar ....Kessler

February 23
DER FLIEGENDE HOLLAENDER
(Wagner)
Same cast as January 13 except:
Daland ....Wildermann
Erik ....Da Costa
Mary ....Dunn
Steersman ....Franke

February 24
CAVALLERIA RUSTICANA
(Mascagni)
Same cast as October 31 except:
Conductor: Mitropoulos
Lola ....Vanni
Turiddu ....Barioni
Alfio ....Valentino

PAGLIACCI (Leoncavallo)
Same cast as October 31 except:
Conductor: Mitropoulos
Canio ....Bergonzi
Tonio ....Guarrera
Silvio ....Marsh

February 25
DON GIOVANNI (Mozart)
Same cast as January 16 except:
Don Giovanni ....London
Donna Elvira ....Amara
Zerlina ....Dobbs
Leporello ....Flagello

February 26
DIE WALKUERE (Wagner)
Same cast as February 9 except:
Fricka ....Rankin
Brünnhilde ....Harshaw

February 27 (matinee)
IL TROVATORE (Verdi)
Same cast as October 26 except:
Count Di Luna ......Bastianini

February 27
DER ROSENKAVALIER (R. Strauss)
Same cast as December 26 except:
Princess von Werdenberg .Steber
Octavian ....Miller
Faninal ....Rothmuller
Sophie ....Hurley
Valzacchi ....Kullman
Annina ....Roggero
Notary ....Pechner
Singer ....Baum
Blackamoor ....Hirschl

February 29
FIDELIO (Beethoven)
Same cast as January 28 except:
Don Fernando .....Wildermann
Rocco ....Ernster

March 1
Benefit Sponsored by the
Metropolitan Opera Guild for the
Production Fund
SIMON BOCCANEGRA (Verdi)
Conductor: Mitropoulos
Simon Boccanegra .....Warren
Amelia ....Curtis-Verna
Fiesco ....Tozzi
Gabriele Adorno ....Tucker
Paolo ....Flagello
Pietro ....Scott
Captain ....Nagy
Maid ....Vicos

March 2
DIE WALKUERE (Wagner)
Same cast as February 9 except:
Fricka ....Rankin
Brünnhilde ....Harshaw
Siegmund ....Liebl
Sieglinde ....Rysanek
Hunding ....Wildermann

March 3
AIDA (Verdi)
Same cast as November 9 except:
Amneris ....Simionato
Aida ....Stella
Radames ....Baum
Amonasro ....Lisitsian
Ramfis ....Moscona
Priestess ....Vanni

March 4 (matinee)
109th Metropolitan Opera
Guild Student Performance
DON GIOVANNI (Mozart)
Conductor: Adler
Don Giovanni ....Borg
Donna Anna ....Nelli
Donna Elvira ....Krall
Zerlina ....Allen
Don Ottavio ....Anthony
Commendatore ....Scott
Leporello ....Alvary
Masetto ....Marsh

March 4
LA FORZA DEL DESTINO (Verdi)
Same cast as February 1 except:
Leonora ....Tebaldi
Don Carlo ....Warren*
Padre Guardiano ....Hines
Fra Melitone ....Baccaloni
*The opera was terminated dur-
ing Act 2 due to the death of
Warren

March 5 (matinee)
DER FLIEGENDE HOLLAENDER
(Wagner)
Same cast as January 13

March 5
ANDREA CHENIER (Giordano)
Conductor: Cleva
Andrea Chénier ....Bergonzi
Maddalena ....Milanov
Countess di Coigny .....Lipton
Carlo Gérard ....Bastianini
Bersi ....Roggero
Fléville ....Cehanovsky
Abbé ....Carelli
Madelon ....Amparan
Mathieu ....Flagello
Spy ....De Paolis
Fouquier ....Scott
Dumas ....Hawkins
Roucher ....Valentino
Schmidt ....Marsh
Major domo ....Strang

March 7
DIE WALKUERE (Wagner)
Same cast as February 9 except:
Wotan ....Uhde
Fricka ....Rankin
Brünnhilde ....Moedl
Hunding ....Wildermann
Schwertleite ....Lansing

March 9
ANDREA CHENIER (Giordano)
Same cast as March 5 except:
Madelon ....Dunn

March 10
DER FLIEGENDE HOLLAENDER
(Wagner)
Same cast as January 13 except:
Daland ....Wildermann
Erik ....Da Costa
Mary ....Dunn

March 11
FIDELIO (Beethoven)
Same cast as January 28 except:
Don Fernando .....Wildermann
Don Pizarro ....Borg
Rocco ....Ernster

March 12 (matinee)
LA FORZA DEL DESTINO (Verdi)
Same cast as February 1 except:
Leonora ....Tebaldi
Don Carlo ....Sereni
Padre Guardiano ....Hines
Fra Melitone ....Baccaloni
Trabucco ....De Paolis

March 12
FAUST (Gounod)
Same cast as December 8 except:
Faust ....Morell
Marguerite ....Conner
Méphistophélès ....Hines
Siébel ....Vanni
Wagner ....Marsh

March 14
LA TRAVIATA (Verdi)
Same cast as November 4 except:
Conductor: Cleva
Violetta ....Albanese
Alfredo ....Fernandi
Germont ....Merrill
Flora ....Wall

March 15
SIMON BOCCANEGRA (Verdi)
Same cast as March 1 except:
Simon Boccanegra .....Guarrera
Amelia ....Tebaldi

March 16 (matinee)
110th Metropolitan Opera
Guild Student Performance
DON GIOVANNI (Mozart)
Same cast as March 4

March 16
FIDELIO (Beethoven)
Same cast as January 28 except:
Don Fernando ....Tozzi
Rocco ....Ernster
Jacquino ....Franke

March 17
DER ROSENKAVALIER (R. Strauss)
Same cast as December 26 except:
Princess von Werdenberg
Rysanek
Octavian ....Stevens
Faninal ....Rothmuller
Sophie ....Gueden
Valzacchi ....Kullman
Annina ....Lipton
Notary ....Pechner
Singer ....Da Costa
Blackamoor ....Hirschl

March 18
ANDREA CHENIER (Giordano)
Same cast as March 5 except:
Andrea Chénier ....Tucker
Maddalena ....Tebaldi

27

1959-60

March 19 (matinee)
TOSCA (Puccini)
Same cast as October 29 except:
Scarpia ....Cassel
Sacristan ....Pechner

March 19
DER FLIEGENDE HOLLAENDER
(Wagner)
Same cast as January 13

March 21
PARSIFAL (Wagner)
Conductor: Leinsdorf
Amfortas ....Uhde
Titurel ....Wildermann
Gurnemanz ....Hines
Parsifal ....Liebl
Klingsor ....Pechner
Kundry ....Moedl
Voice ....Amparan
Knights ....Stanz, Sgarro
Esquires ....Allen, Røggero,
Anthony, Nagy
Flower Maidens ..Hurley, Stratas,
Vanni, Krall, Wall, Dunn

March 22
TOSCA (Puccini)
Same cast as October 29 except:
Tosca ....Stella
Cavaradossi ....Bergonzi
Scarpia ....MacNeil
Sacristan ....Pechner

March 23 (matinee)
111th Metropolitan Opera
Guild Student Performance
DON GIOVANNI (Mozart)
Same cast as March 4 except:
Conductor: Schick
Donna Anna ......Curtis-Verna
Zerlina ....Stratas
Commendatore ....Moscona
Masetto ....Reitan

March 23
LA FORZA DEL DESTINO (Verdi)
Same cast as February 1 except:
Conductor: Adler
Leonora ....Tebaldi
Don Carlo ....Sereni
Don Alvaro ....Baum
Padre Guardiano ...Wildermann
Fra Melitone ....Pechner
Trabucco ....De Paolis

March 24 (matinee)
112th Metropolitan Opera
Guild Student Performance
DON GIOVANNI (Mozart)
Same cast as January 16 except:
Conductor: Rich
Don Giovanni ....Hines
Donna Anna ....Nelli
Donna Elvira ....Amara
Zerlina ....Hurley
Don Ottavio ....Carelli
Leporello ....Flagello

March 24
MADAMA BUTTERFLY (Puccini)
Same cast as November 7 except:
B. F. Pinkerton ....Fernandi
Imperial Commissioner ...Reitan
Registrar ....Kessler

March 25
SIMON BOCCANEGRA (Verdi)
Same cast as March 1 except:
Simon Boccanegra .....Guarrera
Amelia ....Milanov
Gabriele Adorno ......Bergonzi
Maid ....Yauger

March 26 (matinee)
ANDREA CHENIER (Giordano)
Same cast as March 5 except:
Andrea Chénier ....Tucker
Maddalena ....Tebaldi

March 26
LA TRAVIATA (Verdi)
Same cast as November 4 except:
Conductor: Cleva
Violetta ....Albanese
Alfredo ....Morell
Germont ....Cappuccilli
Gastone ....Anthony

March 28
DON GIOVANNI (Mozart)
Same cast as January 16 except:
Conductor: Rich
Don Giovanni ....Hines
Donna Elvira ....Amara
Don Ottavio ....Peerce
Leporello ....Flagello

March 29
AIDA (Verdi)
Same cast as November 9 except:
Aida ....Curtis-Verna
Radames ....Bergonzi
Amonasro ....Sereni
Ramfis ....Tozzi
Priestess ....Vanni

March 30
TOSCA (Puccini)
Same cast as October 29 except:
Tosca ....Tebaldi
Cavaradossi ....Morell
Scarpia ....Uhde
Sacristan ....Corena

March 31
ANDREA CHENIER (Giordano)
Same cast as March 5 except:
Andrea Chénier ....Tucker
Maddalena ....Stella
Mathieu ....Alvary
Roucher ....Harvuot

April 1 (matinee)
113th Metropolitan Opera
Guild Student Performance
DON GIOVANNI (Mozart)
Same cast as March 4 except:
Conductor: Schick
Donna Anna ......Curtis-Verna
Zerlina ....Stratas
Commendatore ....Moscona
Masetto ....Reitan

April 1
LA TRAVIATA (Verdi)
Same cast as November 4 except:
Conductor: Cleva
Violetta ....Moffo
Alfredo ....Peerce
Germont ....Merrill
Flora ....Wall

April 2 (matinee)
SIMON BOCCANEGRA (Verdi)
Same cast as March 1 except:
Simon Boccanegra ....Guarrera
Amelia ....Milanov
Gabriele Adorno ......Bergonzi
Maid ....Yauger

April 2
MADAMA BUTTERFLY (Puccini)
Same cast as November 7 except:
Conductor: Strasfogel
Cio-Cio-San ....Tebaldi
B. F. Pinkerton ....Fernandi
Suzuki ....Amparan
Imperial Commissioner ..Reitan
Registrar ....Kessler

April 4
ANDREA CHENIER (Giordano)
Same cast as March 5 except:
Andrea Chénier ....Tucker
Carlo Gérard ....Guarrera
Bersi ....Vanni
Mathieu ....Pechner
Spy ....Anthony
Roucher ....Harvuot

April 6
IL TROVATORE (Verdi)
Same cast as October 26 except:
Leonora ....Curtis-Verna
Count Di Luna ....Bastianini
Azucena ....Amparan
Inez ....Stratas
Gypsy ....Tomanelli

April 7 (matinee)
114th Metropolitan Opera
Guild Student Performance
DON GIOVANNI (Mozart)
Same cast as March 4 except:
Conductor: Taussig
Don Giovanni .....Wildermann
Don Ottavio ....Carelli
Commendatore ....Sgarro

28

April 7
SIMON BOCCANEGRA (Verdi)
Same cast as March 1 except:
Simon Boccanegra ...... Colzani
Amelia .... Tebaldi
Fiesco .... Hines

April 8
THE GYPSY BARON (J. Strauss)
Same cast as November 25 except:
Carnero .... Hawkins
Mirabella .... Votipka

April 9 (matinee)
PARSIFAL (Wagner)
Same cast as March 21 except:
Kundry .... Harshaw
Voice .... Dunn

April 9
TOSCA (Puccini)
Same cast as October 29 except:
Conductor: Schick
Tosca .... Albanese
Scarpia .... Uhde
Sacristan .... Alvary

April 10 (matinee)
MADAMA BUTTERFLY (Puccini)
Same cast as November 7 except:
Cio-Cio-San .... Tebaldi
Sharpless .... Sereni
Goro .... De Paolis
Registrar .... Kessler

April 11 (matinee)
115th Metropolitan Opera
Guild Student Performance
DON GIOVANNI (Mozart)
Same cast as March 4 except:
Conductor: Taussig
Don Giovanni ..... Wildermann
Don Ottavio .... Carelli
Commendatore .... Sgarro

April 11
SIMON BOCCANEGRA (Verdi)
Same cast as March 1 except:
Simon Boccanegra ...... Colzani
Amelia .... Milanov
Gabriele Adorno ...... Bergonzi
Maid .... Yauger

April 12
ANDREA CHENIER (Giordano)
Same cast as March 5 except:
Andrea Chénier .... Baum
Maddalena .... Curtis-Verna
Countess di Coigny ...... Dunn
Carlo Gérard .... Sereni
Bersi .... Vanni
Madelon .... Roggero
Mathieu .... Alvary
Spy .... Anthony
Roucher .... Reitan
Schmidt .... Sgarro

April 13
LA FORZA DEL DESTINO (Verdi)
Same cast as February 1 except:
Conductor: Adler
Leonora .... Tebaldi
Don Carlo .... Oppicelli
Don Alvaro .... Bergonzi
Fra Melitone .... Pechner
Trabucco .... De Paolis
Surgeon .... Cehanovsky

April 14
CARMEN (Bizet)
Same cast as October 31 except:
Carmen .... Amparan
Micaela .... Amara
Escamillo .... Guarrera
Zuniga .... Scott
Frasquita .... Lind
Mercédès .... Wall

April 15 (matinee)
PARSIFAL (Wagner)
Same cast as March 21 except:
Amfortas .... Borg
Titurel .... Moscona
Parsifal .... Kullman
Kundry .... Harshaw
Voice .... Dunn

April 16 (matinee)
MADAMA BUTTERFLY (Puccini)
Same cast as November 7 except:
Cio-Cio-San .... Kirsten
B. F. Pinkerton .... Fernandi
Sharpless .... Sereni
Imperial Commissioner ... Reitan
Registrar .... Kessler

April 16
DON GIOVANNI (Mozart)
Same cast as January 16 except:
Conductor: Leinsdorf
Donna Anna ...... Curtis-Verna
Don Ottavio .... Gedda

EXCERPTS FROM PRESS REVIEWS

NEW PRODUCTION OF Verdi's *Il Trovatore* and DEBUT OF GIULI-ETTA SIMIONATO, October 26, 1959

The prime impression of the Metropolitan Opera's new *Trovatore* is its freedom from vulgarity. It is so easy—and so customary—to strut, strike poses and roar out the infallibly popular tunes that an honest determination to treat Verdi's opera with respect comes as a pleasant surprise.

In this production there is no search for originality for its own sake, which ends by distorting or mocking the nature of the piece. The story, whatever its gaps and

involutions, takes place in medieval Aragon, and Motley's darkly colorful sets and costumes have authority and taste. ...

The staging, supervised by Herbert Graf, is neither fussy nor futile. It plays fair with Verdi, who was in earnest about this tale. ... Under Fausto Cleva's conducting the performance moves crisply and cleanly. His tempos, which can be metronomic, have elasticity without loss of vitality. The orchestra and chorus sound fresh, as well they might on opening night. And the cast is of a high caliber.

Giulietta Simionato is mentioned first, not only because she was the chief newcomer but also because Azucena of all the roles in the opera most fired Verdi's imagination. The Italian mezzo-soprano brings a rich, secure and cultivated voice to the Met. Her range is formidable; the high tones have accuracy and brilliance, and the low are firm and vibrant. She sings with stirring ardor and moves with intelligence. The Met has acquired a new artist of the first magnitude. —Howard Taubman, *New York Times*

NEW PRODUCTION of Mozart's *Le Nozze di Figaro*, and DEBUTS OF ELISABETH SOEDERSTROEM and KIM BORG, October 30, 1959

The season's first *Marriage of Figaro* at the Metropolitan Opera House last evening demonstrated what three gentlemen of taste can do when they combine their talents. These would be Oliver Messel, who has provided elegant settings and smart costumes; Cyril Ritchard, who has staged it with the verve of a Broadway musical; and Erich Leinsdorf, who was at his peak on the podium.

All eyes were focused on Messel's new décor last night. It was really something to see, for he is one of the most gifted designers of our era. And ears were attuned to the voices of Elisabeth Soederstroem and Kim Borg, making their debuts as Susanna and Count Almaviva at the Met.

Miss Soederstroem offered a pleasant and facile voice, and acted Susanna with winning coquetry. ... Borg displayed a good baritone and was properly pompous as the Count who forgets his dignity when he glimpses a pretty face and figure. They should be valuable assets to the roster.—Robert Coleman, *New York Daily Mirror*

DEBUT OF ANNA MOFFO as Violetta in *La Traviata,* November 14, 1959

[Miss Moffo] sang the role of Violetta, of course, and in at least one respect she lived up to advance billing: she is one of the most beautiful women ever to grace the stage of an opera house. As a singer it still is a case of "judgment reserved." Miss Moffo has quite a lovely voice, she is a sensitive artist and a graceful actress. So far, so good. But at this stage of her career her work still seems just a shade tentative.

Miss Moffo does everything skillfully, but she does not give the impression of having made the characterization her very own. She does not take over the stage as a major artist does, and her singing needs a little more personality. However, Miss Moffo is only twenty-five years old. She has come far in a short time. It could be that in a few years she will be one of the important sopranos.—Harold C. Schonberg, *New York Times*

NEW PRODUCTION of Johann Strauss' *The Gypsy Baron* and DEBUT OF WALTER SLEZAK, November 25, 1959

In the course of mounting *The Gypsy Baron* something somehow has gone terribly wrong at the Met. Nobody seems to have made up his mind what the work is all about, which is simply another way of indicating that the performance has neither an artistic point of view nor any stylistic consistency. As it stands, it is almost impossible to tell whether the company regards the *Baron* as funny, serious, real, make-believe, opera or operetta. This rip in concept is apparent even in Rolf Gérard's settings, which in the first and second acts are pure fairy tale and gingerbread, and in the third literal and breathtakingly photographic. . . .

Now, it is an indisputable fact that *The Gypsy Baron* is an old-fashioned number, which balks at any attempt to modernize it. Still, you cannot play it straight, and— apart from Szupán [Walter] Slezak—everybody seems to be doing just that. Cyril Ritchard, the director, appears to have duped the entire company into believing that they were dealing with an inviolate masterpiece, which would be deformed by any measure of lightness or jest. And Erich Leinsdorf, who has previously been revealed as a

Straussian of the utmost lilt and grace, contrives to conduct the work with a sobriety not the least becoming to the score. . . .

As for the singing itself, it is actually quite good, what with Regina Resnik bouncing lovely velvet tones from every wall, and Nicolai Gedda performing with more spunk and tonal vigor than I recall him possessing in the past. . . . Lisa Della Casa, however, is woefully miscast, as she is far too elegant of breeding to satisfy the demands of a hip-slinging gypsy, and, if I am not mistaken, she showed considerable discomfort attacking the upper tones of her scale. Mr. Slezak, though he is not likely to replace Leonard Warren, did more with his tunes than one would have thought possible.—Jay S. Harrison, *New York Herald Tribune*

DEBUT OF CHRISTA LUDWIG as Cherubino in *Le Nozze di Figaro,* December 10, 1959

Miss Ludwig sang and acted her role with good voice, style and enunciation of text. She may be a bit too effeminate in her movement and fuzzy in her general action, but she has identified herself with the inflections of the character. The audience liked her at once. She is undoubtedly an important addition to the company.—Miles Kastendieck, *New York Journal-American*

NEW PRODUCTION of Wagner's *Tristan und Isolde* and DEBUT OF BIRGIT NILSSON, December 18, 1959

The absorbing performance of *Tristan und Isolde* last night at the Metropolitan Opera proved that an operatic repertory without Wagner is a very incomplete one. But even when the management is willing to mount these great, difficult and expensive operas, they have difficulty in finding the heroic voices. . . .

Isolde is a stupendous role, calling for the most extraordinary vocal prowess and endurance. Now in the new Swedish soprano, Birgit Nilsson, the Met has an Isolde who can overwhelm not only everyone on the stage and in the auditorium but even the orchestra going at full tilt. Such a thing, ladies and gentlemen, has not been heard since Kirsten Flagstad.

Birgit Nilsson is the possessor of a magnificent voice—a clear, unobstructed, powerful soprano of ex-

traordinary brightness that can cut through the orchestral phalanx without ever being shrill, without giving the impression of forcing or even of any effort. And Miss Nilsson, to whom high B-flats and C's are just tones, perhaps a little higher than the ordinary run, but otherwise of no particular concern, can go down the scale all the way to an A. . . . Her musicianship is unquestionable, as are her serious artistic attitude and careful study of her role. The new Isolde is a true princess, not only in Ireland but in all the world of opera. . . .

Her bewitched paramour, Tristan, was sung by Karl Liebl, who is a gallant trouper but . . . not convincing in the role of a *Heldentenor*. . . . I do not think that there is a tenor now singing who can compete with Miss Nilsson on equal terms. Irene Dalis as Brangäne did some very fine singing, but she had occasional contretemps with sudden high notes. Walter Cassel (Kurvenal) and Jerome Hines (King Marke) were top-drawer. . . .

Karl Boehm is a conductor who accords equal solicitude to every phrase and every chord, and yet always has a firm concept of the whole. . . . How magnificently the Met's orchestra can play under such leadership!

As far as the rest of the new production is concerned, Teo Otto's sets are quite plainly opera décor, though they are far from plain décor. They have few of the arts and graces of good modern opera sets, but they provide a serviceable background. This, of course, considerably inhibited the stage director's work, but Herbert Graf, as usual, can extricate himself from such a dilemma with honor. He was especially successful with the difficult static scenes, which he composed into good tableaux.—Paul Henry Lang, *New York Herald Tribune*

REVIVAL of Wagner's *Der Fliegende Holländer,* January 13, 1960

When the *Fliegende Holländer* overture was last exciting patrons at the Metropolitan Opera under the direction of Fritz Reiner, the moments that followed the curtain rise seemed something of a letdown. In the current revival, for which Thomas Schippers is the conductor, this did not occur; the letdown occurred *before* the curtain was raised, as the prelude alternately stormed and stumbled, plodded and raced to its conclusion. . . .

Once the curtain was up, and George London appeared to sing his Bayreuth-bred Dutchman, the center of gravity shifted from pit to stage, with a settling effect all around. And Schippers' command of his responsibility was more secure, his expenditure of effort better mated to judgment. . . .

A particularly able, good-looking and strong-sounding cast had the central characterization of London as its axis. He towered over his first, second and third mates in artistic stature as he did in physical height, dispensing that indispensable "aura" without which a Dutchman is but a bearded man in dark clothes. . . . The other men were equally good and equally in the picture—Giorgio Tozzi as a Daland without the gruffness associated with Germanic bassos and a flicker of humor eminently appealing, Karl Liebl as an uncommonly persuasive Erik, and the young American William Olvis as a Steersman with a dramatic voice marked for bigger things.

Equally contributory to the total effect was the youthfully fervent Senta of Leonie Rysanek, who absorbed the eye with her romantically convincing appearance, whether or not she always charmed the ear with her singing.—Irving Kolodin, *Saturday Review*

DEBUT OF JON VICKERS as Canio in *Pagliacci*, January 17, 1960

A tenor who should be on the scene for some time to come made his Metropolitan debut with the first appearance of Jon Vickers. However, it is not likely that he will make his American career in such roles as Canio in *Pagliacci,* in which he introduced himself; he sings it with sure control, musical intelligence and dramatic persuasion, but with neither the vocal style nor the richness of sound favored in this part. —Irving Kolodin, *Saturday Review*

NEW PRODUCTION of Beethoven's *Fidelio*, January 28, 1960

Beethoven was merciless in his vocal demands, writing for voices as if they were instruments. *Fidelio* doesn't caress its performers, it whips them. Nonetheless, the principals in the Metropolitan Opera's new production not only survived last night, they thrived,

and one triumphed—Jon Vickers in the role of Leonore's maligned husband, Florestan.

Florestan's important singing is telescoped into one fiendish aria which he performs chained in a dungeon. . . . Despite the hurdles and hazards, Vickers sang with nobility of style and virility of tone. He managed to build his climaxes during the final *poco allegro* as if he had voice to spare. He also conveyed the despair of the situation with affecting emotion.

In the role of Leonore, disguised as Fidelio, the Norwegian soprano Aase Nordmo Loevberg sang easily and was able to support her male disguise believably despite the fact that, being feminine to the core, she is not ideally suited to the role. During her first-act aria . . . she didn't supply enough volume or intensity. In the second act, however, she elicited some brilliant notes and limbered up more in acting and singing.

In the role of the diabolical governor, Pizarro . . . Hermann Uhde proved a striking figure. His singing was uneven, but this, ironically, was in character, too. . . .

A combination of a superior supporting cast, a knowledgeable conductor, Karl Boehm, realistic sets and costumes by Horace Armistead and Herbert Graf's perceptive staging made this a competent *Fidelio* if not one of transcendent liberation.

[Boehm's] conception . . . was more gentle than incisive. In the buoyancy of his approach, this listener felt sometimes as if he were conducting Mozart. His tempos were often deliberate, which made it easier for the singers; but they missed something in a dynamic forcefulness which belongs to the composer who championed freedom in life as well as in music.— Harriett Johnson, *New York Post*

NEW PRODUCTION of Verdi's *Simon Boccanegra* and last complete performance by LEONARD WARREN, March 1, 1960

Because of the vagueness of its plot and the slightly too passive character of its hero, *Simon Boccanegra* has never ranked among the most popular of Verdi operas (a few performances ten years ago were all that we had heard here since the days of Lawrence Tibbett), but the revival of it at the Metropolitan on Tuesday night of last week proved again that it is well worth producing. . . .

The great Leonard Warren was

delivering his last complete performance. Three nights later, Mr. Warren died onstage in the middle of the second act of *La Forza del Destino,* leaving the art of opera immeasurably impoverished. . . . Mr. Warren sang the role of Simon with the nobility, the aristocratic sense of style and the profound dedication that characterized all his interpretations at the Metropolitan during the past two decades, in which he shone as one of the most memorable stars in its history and as the finest Verdi baritone of the era. The remainder of the production was, on the whole, well up to the lofty standard that he set. Richard Tucker sang the passionate tenor role of Gabriele Adorno superbly, and those admirable artists Giorgio Tozzi and Ezio Flagello outdid themselves as the conspirators Fiesco and Paolo. The staging was by Margaret Webster, a director who can be counted on to present operatic action with dignity, taste and sympathy; the new sets, by Frederick Fox, were both magnificent and agreeably unaffected in style; and the costumes, by Motley, fitted handsomely into the stage picture.

Dimitri Mitropoulos, at the helm in the orchestra pit, controlled the intricacies of the score with a firm and sensitive hand, turning out what was unquestionably his best piece of Verdi conducting to date.—Winthrop Sargeant, *The New Yorker*

DEBUT OF ANSELMO COLZANI as Simon Boccanegra, April 7, 1960

Mr. Colzani, after a short period of nervous flurry and adjustment to the new surroundings, proved himself a stalwart addition to the company. His big scene, as it is that of the opera, was that of the Council Chamber in the second act. There Mr. Colzani . . . rose splendidly to the demands of the music and the drama. Singing and acting combined to compelling purpose. This became a great impersonation.

Without being overresonant, Mr. Colzani's voice is strong and forceful, and he knows how to make every note, not to mention every word, count in the phrase. —Louis Biancolli, *New York World-Telegram and Sun*

1960-1961 SEASON

Male Artists
Alvary, Lorenzo
Anthony, Charles
Baccaloni, Salvatore
Backgren, Arthur
Balestrieri, Anthony
Barbusci, Nicola
Bardelli, Cesare
Baum, Kurt
Bergonzi, Carlo
Birlenbach, Erich
Borg, Kim
Carelli, Gabor
Cassel, Walter
Cehanovsky, George
Colzani, Anselmo
Cooke, Charles
Cooke, Thomas
Corelli, Franco
Corena, Fernando
Da Costa, Albert
Davidson, Lawrence
Del Ferro, Leonard
D'Elia, Frank
De Paola, Paul
De Paolis, Alessio
Fernandi, Eugenio
Flagello, Ezio
Folmer, Joseph
Formichini, Dino
Franke, Paul
Frydel, John
Gari, Giulio
Gedda, Nicolai
Ghazal, Edward
Giaiotti, Bonaldo
Guarrera, Frank
Harvuot, Clifford
Hawkins, Osie
Hemmerly, Walter
Herbert, Ralph
Hines, Jerome
Hopf, Hans
Kelley, Norman
Kessler, Kurt
Kuestner, Charles
Kullman, Charles
Liebl, Karl
London, George
MacNeil, Cornell
Marcella, Lou
Marsh, Calvin
Mayreder, Rudolf
Merrill, Robert
Miles, Roland
Morell, Barry
Moscona, Nicola
Nagy, Robert
Nikolov, Nikola
Olvis, William
Pechner, Gerhard
Peerce, Jan
Powell, Thomas
Prey, Hermann
Reitan, Roald
Ringland, Earl
Roberts, Hal
Rothmuller, Marko
Scott, Norman

Sereni, Mario
Sgarro, Louis
Siepi, Cesare
Strang, Lloyd
Sullivan, Brian
Testi, Lorenzo
Tomanelli, Carlo
Tozzi, Giorgio
Trehy, John
Tucker, Richard
Uhde, Hermann
Uppman, Theodor
Valentino, Frank
Vickers, Jon
Vinay, Ramon
Wächter, Eberhard
Wildermann, William

Female Artists
Albanese, Licia
Allen, Mildred
Amara, Lucine
Arroyo, Martina
Borkh, Inge
Brysac, Ada
Clark, Charleen
Coulter, Dorothy
Curtis-Verna, Mary
Cvejic, Biserka
Dalis, Irene
D'Angelo, Gianna
Davy, Gloria
De Florio, Evangeline
Della Casa, Lisa
De Los Angeles, Victoria
De Salvo, Dina
Di Franco, Loretta
Dobbs, Mattiwilda
Dunn, Mignon
Elias, Rosalind
Farrell, Eileen
Fercana, Mary
Greene, Ethel
Harshaw, Margaret
Hurley, Laurel
Jones, Lexi
Kailer, Lucille
Kirsten, Dorothy
Krall, Heidi
Kuchta, Gladys
Lewis, Brenda
Lind, Gloria
Lipton, Martha
Ludwig, Christa
MacKenzie, Mary
Madeira, Jean
Meyer, Kerstin
Milanov, Zinka
Miller, Mildred
Moffo, Anna
Munson, Pamela
Nelli, Herva
Nilsson, Birgit
Ordassy, Carlotta
Parsons, Meredith
Peters, Roberta
Pons, Lily
Price, Leontyne
Rankin, Nell
Reep, Nancy
Resnik, Regina

Rhodes, Jane
Roggero, Margaret
Rothenberger, Anneliese
Rysanek, Leonie
Santini, Nerina
Shawn, Dorothy
Simionato, Giulietta
Sims, Lilias
Soederstroem, Elisabeth
Steber, Eleanor
Stevens, Risë
Stratas, Teresa
Tebaldi, Renata
Thebom, Blanche
Tucci, Gabriella
Vanni, Helen
Vicos,. Athena
Votipka, Thelma
Wall, Joan
Yauger, Maria
Yeend, Frances

Ballet Soloists
Adams, Wally
Andrew, Thomas
Bausch, Pina
Bishop, Robert
Burdick, William
Crosson, Craig
Farrington, Hubert
Ferraro, Edilio
Horne, Kathryn
Jerell, Edith
Keane, Audrey
King, Nancy
Kroon, Carole
Marks, Bruce
Russell, Thomas
San Miguel, Lolita
Sayette, Howard
Sequoio, Ron

Conductors
Adler, Kurt
Boehm, Karl
Burger, Julius
Cleva, Fausto
Leinsdorf, Erich
Morel, Jean
Rich, Martin
Rosenstock, Joseph
Schick, George
Schippers, Thomas
Solti, Georg
Stokowski, Leopold
Strasfogel, Ignace
Taussig, Walter
Verchi, Nino

General Manager
Bing, Rudolf

October 24 (Opening Night)
NABUCCO (Verdi)
    Conductor: Schippers
Nabucco ....MacNeil
Abigaille ....Rysanek
Fenena ....Elias
Ismaele ....Fernandi
Zaccaria ....Siepi
High Priest of Baal .....Giaiotti
Abdallo ....Franke
Anna ....Ordassy

October 25
MANON LESCAUT (Puccini)
Conductor: Cleva
Manon .... Kirsten
Lescaut .... Sereni
Des Grieux .... Bergonzi
Geronte .... Flagello
Edmondo .... Gari
Ballet Master .... De Paolis
Innkeeper .... Davidson
Musician .... Wall
Sergeant .... Marsh
Lamplighter .... Nagy
Captain .... Sgarro
Madrigal singers .... Fercana,
Parsons, De Salvo, Jones

October 27
BORIS GODUNOV (Mussorgsky)
Conductor: Leinsdorf
Boris Godunov .... London
Fyodor .... Roggero
Xenia .... Allen
Nurse .... Dunn
Shuiski .... Kelley
Shchelkalov .... Marsh
Pimen .... Tozzi
Grigori .... Sullivan
Marina .... Thebom
Rangoni .... Borg
Varlaam .... Flagello
Missail .... Nagy
Innkeeper .... Lipton
Officer .... Hawkins
Simpleton .... Franke
Nikitich .... Sgarro
Boyar .... Carelli
Woman .... Votipka
Mityukh .... Powell
Khrushchov .... Balestrieri
Lavitski .... Trehy
Chernikovski .... Roberts

October 28
LA BOHEME (Puccini)
Conductor: Schippers
Rodolfo .... Tucker
Marcello .... Testi
Schaunard .... Reitan
Colline .... Siepi
Mimi .... Amara
Musetta .... Hurley
Benoit .... Pechner
Parpignol .... C. Cooke
Alcindoro .... Kelley
Sergeant .... Tomanelli
Customs Officer .... Ghazal

October 29 (matinee)
CARMEN (Bizet)
Conductor: Morel
Carmen .... Meyer
Don José .... Vickers
Micaela .... Amara
Escamillo .... Guarrera
Zuniga .... Scott
Morales .... Marsh
Frasquita .... Stratas
Mercédès .... Roggero
Dancaire .... Cehanovsky
Remendado .... Franke

October 29
MADAMA BUTTERFLY (Puccini)
Conductor: Morel
Cio-Cio-San .... Tucci
B. F. Pinkerton .... Bergonzi
Sharpless .... Harvuot
Suzuki .... Vanni
Kate Pinkerton .... Wall
Goro .... De Paolis
Yamadori .... Cehanovsky
Uncle-Priest .... Hawkins
Imperial Commissioner ... Reitan
Registrar .... Kessler

October 31
MANON LESCAUT (Puccini)
Same cast as October 25

November 1
NABUCCO (Verdi)
Same cast as October 24

November 2
BORIS GODUNOV (Mussorgsky)
Same cast as October 27

November 3
CARMEN (Bizet)
Same cast as October 29 except:
Mercédès .... Vanni

November 4
MADAMA BUTTERFLY (Puccini)
Same cast as October 29 except:
B. F. Pinkerton .... Olvis

November 5 (matinee)
LA BOHEME (Puccini)
Same cast as October 28 except:
Rodolfo .... Morell
Colline .... Wildermann

November 5
AIDA (Verdi)
Conductor: Verchi
King .... Sgarro
Amneris .... Simionato
Aida .... Rysanek
Radames .... Bergonzi
Amonasro .... Colzani
Ramfis .... Tozzi
Messenger .... Nagy
Priestess .... Dunn

November 6
Benefit Yeshiva University
Women's Organization
LE NOZZE DI FIGARO (Mozart)
Conductor: Leinsdorf
Almaviva .... Borg
Countess .... Della Casa
Susanna .... Soederstroem
Figaro .... Siepi
Cherubino .... Ludwig
Marcellina .... Dunn
Bartolo .... Flagello
Basilio .... Kelley
Don Curzio .... Carelli
Antonio .... Davidson
Barbarina .... Allen
Peasant Girls ..... Clark, Shawn

November 7
CARMEN (Bizet)
Same cast as October 29 except:
Don José .... Nikolov
Escamillo .... Testi

November 8
BORIS GODUNOV (Mussorgsky)
Same cast as October 27 except:
Xenia .... Stratas

November 9
AIDA (Verdi)
Same cast as November 5 except:
Aida .... Curtis-Verna
Ramfis .... Wildermann

November 10
LA BOHEME (Puccini)
Same cast as October 28 except:
Rodolfo .... Peerce
Marcello .... Sereni
Mimi .... Albanese
Benoit .... Davidson
Alcindoro .... De Paolis

November 11
NABUCCO (Verdi)
Same cast as October 24 except:
Zaccaria .... Tozzi

November 12 (matinee)
MADAMA BUTTERFLY (Puccini)
Same cast as October 29 except:
B. F. Pinkerton .... Olvis
Goro .... Franke

November 12
LE NOZZE DI FIGARO (Mozart)
Same cast as November 6

November 14
BORIS GODUNOV (Mussorgsky)
Same cast as October 27 except:
Boris Godunov .... Siepi
Fyodor .... Vanni
Xenia .... Stratas
Grigori .... Olvis
Marina .... Lewis
Varlaam .... Davidson
Missail .... Anthony
Boyar .... Nagy
Khrushchov .... Kessler

November 15
CARMEN (Bizet)
Same cast as October 29 except:
Carmen .... Rhodes
Don José .... Nikolov
Micaela .... Stratas
Escamillo .... Testi
Morales .... Harvuot
Frasquita .... Ordassy
Mercédès .... Vanni

November 16
LE NOZZE DI FIGARO (Mozart)
Same cast as November 6 except:
Countess .... Amara
Susanna .... Hurley
Cherubino .... Miller

33

November 17
MANON LESCAUT (Puccini)
Same cast as October 25 except:
Des Grieux .... Baum
Edmondo .... Anthony

November 18
ARABELLA (R. Strauss)
Conductor: Leinsdorf
Count Waldner .... Herbert
Adelaide .... Lipton
Arabella .... Della Casa
Zdenka .... Rothenberger
Mandryka .... London
Matteo .... Morell
Count Elemer .... Carelli
Count Dominik .... Reitan
Count Lamoral .... Scott
Fiakermilli .... Hurley
Fortune Teller .... Votipka
Welko .... Folmer
Djura .... Kuestner
Jankel .... Birlenbach
Waiter .... Mayreder

November 19 (matinee)
AIDA (Verdi)
Same cast as November 5 except:
Aida .... Curtis-Verna
Radames .... Fernandi
Ramfis .... Giaiotti

November 19
Benefit Mizrachi
Women's Organization
MADAMA BUTTERFLY (Puccini)
Same cast as October 29 except:
Cio-Cio-San .... Albanese
B. F. Pinkerton .... Morell
Sharpless .... Testi
Kate Pinkerton .... Allen
Imperial Commissioner ... Marsh

November 21
NABUCCO (Verdi)
Same cast as October 24 except:
Fenena .... Dunn
Ismaele .... Olvis

November 22
LA BOHEME (Puccini)
Same cast as October 28 except:
Rodolfo .... Bergonzi
Marcello .... Sereni
Colline .... Wildermann

November 23
MADAMA BUTTERFLY (Puccini)
Same cast as October 29 except:
Cio-Cio-San .... Kirsten
B. F. Pinkerton .... Morell
Sharpless .... Testi
Suzuki .... Elias
Imperial Commissioner ... Marsh

November 24
LE NOZZE DI FIGARO (Mozart)
Same cast as November 6 except:
Susanna .... Hurley
Barbarina .... Stratas

November 25
L'ELISIR D'AMORE (Donizetti)
Conductor: Cleva
Adina .... Soederstroem
Nemorino .... Formichini
Belcore .... Guarrera
Dulcamara .... Corena
Giannetta .... Allen

November 26 (matinee)
AIDA (Verdi)
Same cast as November 5 except:
Radames .... Fernandi
Ramfis .... Siepi
Priestess .... Ordassy

November 26
CARMEN (Bizet)
Same cast as October 29 except:
Don José .... Olvis
Micaela .... Krall
Escamillo .... Sereni
Frasquita .... Ordassy
Mercédès .... Vanni

November 28
ARABELLA (R. Strauss)
Same cast as November 18

November 30
CARMEN (Bizet)
Same cast as October 29 except:
Don José .... Del Ferro
Micaela .... Stratas
Morales .... Harvuot
Frasquita .... Ordassy
Mercédès .... Vanni

December 1
LA BOHEME (Puccini)
Same cast as October 28 except:
Rodolfo .... Morell
Colline .... Giaiotti
Parpignol .... Roberts

December 2
MANON LESCAUT (Puccini)
Same cast as October 25 except:
Geronte .... Baccaloni
Edmondo .... Anthony
Innkeeper .... Cehanovsky

December 3 (matinee)
NABUCCO (Verdi)
Same cast as October 24

December 3
BORIS GODUNOV (Mussorgsky)
Same cast as October 27 except:
Boris Godunov .... Hines
Fyodor .... Wall
Xenia .... Stratas
Shuiski .... Kullman
Marina .... Lewis
Varlaam .... Corena
Missail .... Anthony
Boyar .... Nagy
Khrushchov .... Kessler

December 5
LE NOZZE DI FIGARO (Mozart)
Same cast as November 6 except:
Susanna .... Peters
Figaro .... Tozzi
Cherubino .... Miller
Basilio .... De Paolis
Don Curzio .... Nagy
Antonio .... Alvary

December 6
ALCESTIS (Gluck)
Conductor: Leinsdorf
Admetus .... Gedda
Alcestis .... Farrell
High Priest .... Cassel
Apollo .... Olvis
Herald .... Marsh
Leaders .... Allen, Wall,
Anthony, Scott

December 7
NABUCCO (Verdi)
Same cast as October 24 except:
Nabucco .... Colzani
Zaccaria .... Hines

December 8
L'ELISIR D'AMORE (Donizetti)
Same cast as November 25

December 9
BORIS GODUNOV (Mussorgsky)
Same cast as October 27 except:
Boris Godunov .... Siepi
Fyodor .... Miller
Grigori .... Gedda
Marina .... Lewis
Varlaam .... Corena
Missail .... Anthony
Boyar .... Nagy
Khrushchov .... Kessler

December 10 (matinee)
MANON LESCAUT (Puccini)
Same cast as October 25 except:
Geronte .... Baccaloni
Edmondo .... Anthony
Innkeeper .... Cehanovsky

December 10
Benefit Hartman Homecrest
LA BOHEME (Puccini)
Same cast as October 28 except:
Colline .... Giaiotti
Mimi .... Della Casa
Parpignol .... Roberts

December 12
L'ELISIR D'AMORE (Donizetti)
Same cast as November 25

December 13
ARABELLA (R. Strauss)
Same cast as November 18 except:
Matteo .... Anthony

December 14
Benefit Employees' Welfare Fund

GALA PERFORMANCE

DON CARLO (Verdi)
(Act III, Scene 1)
Conductor: Adler
Philip II .... Siepi
Grand Inquisitor ... Wildermann
Elizabeth .... Curtis-Verna
Princess Eboli .... Dalis
Rodrigo .... Guarrera
Count Lerma .... Franke

MADAMA BUTTERFLY (Puccini)
(Act II)
Conductor: Morel
Cio-Cio-San .... Tebaldi
Sharpless .... Harvuot
Suzuki .... Elias
Goro .... De Paolis
Yamadori .... Cehanovsky

ARIAS
Ozean, du Ungeheuer (*Oberon*)
Farrell
No sleep, no rest (*Prince Igor*)
London
Conductor: Strasfogel
Quando le sere al placido (*Luisa
Miller*) .... Peerce
Caro nome (*Rigoletto*) .. Pons
Meine Lippen sie küssen so heiss
(*Giuditta*) .... Rysanek
Wanting you (*The New Moon*)
Soederstroem and Guarrera
Conductor: Rich
L'altra notte (*Mefistofele*)
Albanese
Vicino a te (*Andrea Chénier*)
Milanov and Tucker
Conductor: Cleva
Wherever I roam (*The Gypsy
Baron*) .... Gedda
Conductor: Strasfogel

December 15
MADAMA BUTTERFLY (Puccini)
Same cast as October 29 except:
Cio-Cio-San .... Albanese
Sharpless .... Testi
Suzuki .... Elias
Kate Pinkerton .... Allen
Imperial Commissioner ... Marsh

December 16
CARMEN (Bizet)
Same cast as October 29 except:
Carmen .... Thebom
Don José .... Baum
Micaela .... Hurley
Escamillo .... Merrill
Zuniga .... Sgarro
Morales .... Harvuot
Frasquita .... Ordassy
Mercédès .... Wall
Remendado .... Anthony

December 17 (matinee)
TANNHAUSER (Wagner)
Conductor: Solti
Hermann .... Hines
Tannhäuser .... Hopf
Wolfram .... Prey
Walther .... Nagy
Biterolf .... Rothmuller
Heinrich .... Franke
Reinmar .... Scott
Elisabeth .... Rysanek
Venus .... Dalis
Shepherd .... Allen
Pages .... Reep, Brysac,
Greene, Munson

December 17
ALCESTIS (Gluck)
Same cast as December 6

December 19
SIMON BOCCANEGRA (Verdi)
Conductor: Verchi
Simon Boccanegra ..... Guarrera
Amelia .... Tebaldi
Fiesco .... Tozzi
Gabriele Adorno .... Tucker
Paolo .... Flagello
Pietro .... Scott
Captain .... Nagy
Maid .... Yauger

December 21
LA BOHEME (Puccini)
Same cast as October 28 except:
Rodolfo .... Fernandi
Colline .... Moscona
Mimi .... Albanese
Benoit .... Baccaloni
Parpignol .... Roberts
Alcindoro .... Baccaloni
Sergeant .... Strang
Customs Officer .... Frydel

December 22
TANNHAUSER (Wagner)
Same cast as December 17

December 23
LE NOZZE DI FIGARO (Mozart)
Same cast as November 6 except:
Susanna .... Peters
Cherubino .... Miller
Basilio .... De Paolis
Don Curzio .... Nagy
Antonio .... Alvary
Second Peasant Girl ... De Salvo

December 24 (matinee)
L'ELISIR D'AMORE (Donizetti)
Same cast as November 25

December 24
LA BOHEME (Puccini)
Same cast as October 28 except:
Rodolfo .... Fernandi
Marcello .... Harvuot
Colline .... Moscona
Mimi .... Tebaldi
Parpignol .... Roberts
Sergeant .... Strang
Customs Officer .... Frydel

December 26
LA GIOCONDA (Ponchielli)
Conductor: Cleva
La Gioconda .... Farrell
Laura Adorno .... Rankin
Alvise Badoero .... Giaiotti
La Cieca .... Dunn
Enzo Grimaldo .... Tucker
Barnaba .... Merrill
Zuane .... Cehanovsky
Singers .... De Paola, Miles
Isepo .... De Paolis
Monk .... Sgarro
Steersman .... Barbusci

December 27
TANNHAUSER (Wagner)
Same cast as December 17 except:
Heinrich .... Anthony
Second Page .... Parsons

December 28
ARABELLA (R. Strauss)
Same cast as November 18 except:
Adelaide .... Dunn
Matteo .... Anthony
Elemer .... Nagy

December 29
MANON LESCAUT (Puccini)
Same cast as October 25 except:
Manon .... Tebaldi
Lescaut .... Testi
Des Grieux .... Tucker
Geronte .... Corena
Edmondo .... Anthony
Innkeeper .... Cehanovsky
Lamplighter .... Carelli

December 30
ALCESTIS (Gluck)
Same cast as December 6 except:
First Leader .... Stratas

December 31 (matinee)
RIGOLETTO (Verdi)
Conductor: Verchi
Duke .... Morell
Rigoletto .... MacNeil
Gilda .... Peters
Sparafucile .... Tozzi
Maddalena .... Dunn
Giovanna .... Votipka
Monterone .... Giaiotti
Marullo .... Harvuot
Borsa .... Carelli
Ceprano .... Cehanovsky
Countess .... Stratas
Page .... Wall
Guard .... De Paola

December 31
L'ELISIR D'AMORE (Donizetti)
Same cast as November 25

35

1960-61

January 2
MADAMA BUTTERFLY (Puccini)
Same cast as October 29 except:
Cio-Cio-San . . . . Tebaldi
B. F. Pinkerton . . . . Fernandi
Sharpless . . . . Uppman
Suzuki . . . . Roggero
Kate Pinkerton . . . . Allen
Goro . . . . Kelley

January 3
LE NOZZE DI FIGARO (Mozart)
Same cast as November 6 except:
Cherubino . . . . Vanni
Marcellina . . . . Resnik
Basilio . . . . De Paolis
Antonio . . . . Alvary

January 4
RIGOLETTO (Verdi)
Same cast as December 31 except:
Sparafucile . . . . Wildermann

January 5
ALCESTIS (Gluck)
Same cast as December 6 except:
First Leader . . . . Stratas

January 6
SIMON BOCCANEGRA (Verdi)
Same cast as December 19

January 7 (matinee)
BORIS GODUNOV (Mussorgsky)
Same cast as October 27 except:
Fyodor . . . . Vanni
Xenia . . . . Stratas
Nurse . . . . Roggero
Marina . . . . Dunn
Missail . . . . Anthony
Boyar . . . . Nagy

January 7
In Celebration of the Centenary
of the Unification of Italy
NABUCCO (Verdi)
Same cast as October 24 except:
Nabucco . . . . Colzani

January 9
LA BOHEME (Puccini)
Same cast as October 28 except:
Marcello . . . . Guarrera
Schaunard . . . . Harvuot
Mimi . . . . Tebaldi
Musetta . . . . Soederstroem
Benoit . . . . Corena
Parpignol . . . . Roberts
Alcindoro . . . . Alvary
Sergeant . . . . Strang
Customs Officer . . . . Frydel

January 11
ALCESTIS (Gluck)
Same cast as December 6 except:
Apollo . . . . Nagy
First Leader . . . . Stratas

January 12
SIMON BOCCANEGRA (Verdi)
Same cast as December 19 except:
Gabriele Adorno . . . . Olvis

January 13
L'ELISIR D'AMORE (Donizetti)
Same cast as November 25

January 14 (matinee)
DON GIOVANNI (Mozart)
Conductor: Leinsdorf
Don Giovanni . . . . Siepi
Donna Anna . . . . Steber
Donna Elvira . . . . Della Casa
Zerlina . . . . Hurley
Don Ottavio . . . . Gedda
Commendatore . . . . . Wildermann
Leporello . . . . Corena
Masetto . . . . Uppman

January 14
MANON LESCAUT (Puccini)
Same cast as October 25 except:
Manon . . . . Albanese
Lescaut . . . . Testi
Des Grieux . . . . Tucker
Geronte . . . . Baccaloni
Edmondo . . . . Anthony
Innkeeper . . . . Cehanovsky
Lamplighter . . . . Carelli

January 15
Benefit West Side
Institutional Synagogue
LA GIOCONDA (Ponchielli)
Same cast as December 26 except:
Enzo Grimaldo . . . . Baum

January 16
TANNHAUSER (Wagner)
Same cast as December 17 except:
Wolfram . . . . Cassel
Elisabeth . . . . . . De Los Angeles
Shepherd . . . . Stratas
First Page . . . . Di Franco

January 17
SIMON BOCCANEGRA (Verdi)
Same cast as December 19 except:
Simon Boccanegra . . . . . . Colzani
Amelia . . . . Milanov
Fiesco . . . . Siepi
Gabriele Adorno . . . . Olvis
Maid . . . . Vicos

January 18
MADAMA BUTTERFLY (Puccini)
Same cast as October 29 except:
Cio-Cio-San . . . . Tebaldi
B. F. Pinkerton . . . . Gedda
Sharpless . . . . Uppman
Suzuki . . . . Roggero
Imperial Commissioner . . . Marsh

January 19
RIGOLETTO (Verdi)
Same cast as December 31 except:
Conductor: Adler
Duke . . . . Formichini
Gilda . . . . Moffo
Sparafucile . . . . Wildermann

January 20
LA GIOCONDA (Ponchielli)
Same cast as December 26 except:
Laura Adorno . . . . Resnik
Alvise Badoero . . . . Siepi
Barnaba . . . . Colzani

January 21 (matinee)
ARABELLA (R. Strauss)
Same cast as November 18 except:
Adelaide . . . . Dunn
Elemer . . . . Nagy

January 21
AIDA (Verdi)
Same cast as November 5 except:
King . . . . Flagello
Amneris . . . . Rankin
Aida . . . . Amara
Radames . . . . Fernandi
Amonasro . . . . Merrill
Ramfis . . . . Wildermann
Priestess . . . . Ordassy

January 23
DON GIOVANNI (Mozart)
Same cast as January 14

January 24
RIGOLETTO (Verdi)
Same cast as December 31 except:
Duke . . . . Peerce
Rigoletto . . . . Colzani
Sparafucile . . . . Moscona

January 25
TANNHAUSER (Wagner)
Same cast as December 17 except:
Conductor: Strasfogel
Hermann . . . . Wildermann
Wolfram . . . . Wächter
Biterolf . . . . Harvuot
Elisabeth . . . . Nilsson
Venus . . . . Harshaw
Shepherd . . . . Stratas

January 26
Benefit Sponsored by the
Metropolitan Opera Guild for the
Production Fund
Conductor: Verchi
MARTHA (Flotow)
Lady Harriet . . . . De Los Angeles
Nancy . . . . Elias
Lionel . . . . Tucker
Plunkett . . . . Tozzi
Lord Tristram . . . . Alvary
Sheriff . . . . Pechner
Maids . . . . Allen, Stratas, Votipka
Lackeys . . . Hemmerly, Backgren,
Marcella
Farmer . . . . Frydel
Farmer's Wife . . . . Sims
Queen . . . . King

36

January 27
IL TROVATORE (Verdi)
Conductor: Cleva
Leonora .... Price
Manrico .... Corelli
Count Di Luna .... Merrill
Azucena .... Dalis
Inez .... Vanni
Ferrando .... Wildermann
Ruiz .... Anthony
Messenger .... Nagy
Gypsy .... Tomanelli

January 28 (matinee)
LE NOZZE DI FIGARO (Mozart)
Same cast as November 6 except:
Countess .... Amara
Susanna .... Peters
Cherubino .... Miller
Marcellina .... Resnik
Basilio .... Carelli
Don Curzio .... Nagy
Antonio .... Alvary

January 28
L'ELISIR D'AMORE (Donizetti)
Same cast as November 25 except:
Adina .... Moffo
Nemorino .... Gedda

January 30
ALCESTIS (Gluck)
Same cast as December 6 except:
Admetus .... Sullivan
High Priest .... Marsh
Apollo .... Nagy
Herald .... Sgarro
First Leader .... Stratas

January 31
TRISTAN UND ISOLDE (Wagner)
Conductor: Rosenstock
Tristan .... Vinay
Isolde .... Nilsson
King Marke .... Hines
Kurvenal .... Cassel
Brangäne .... Dalis
Melot .... Uhde
Steersman .... Sgarro
Shepherd .... Franke
Sailor's Voice .... Anthony

February 1
L'ELISIR D'AMORE (Donizetti)
Same cast as November 25 except:
Adina .... Peters
Belcore .... Sereni

February 2
DON GIOVANNI (Mozart)
Same cast as January 14 except:
Conductor: Rich
Commendatore .... Giaiotti
Leporello .... Flagello

February 3
TANNHAUSER (Wagner)
Same cast as December 17 except:
Conductor: Strasfogel
Hermann .... Wildermann
Wolfram .... Wächter
Biterolf .... Harvuot
Elisabeth .... Nilsson
Venus .... Dunn
Shepherd .... Stratas

February 4 (matinee)
IL TROVATORE (Verdi)
Same cast as January 27 except:
Count Di Luna .... Sereni
Inez .... Stratas

February 4
MARTHA (Flotow)
Same cast as January 26

February 5
MADAMA BUTTERFLY (Puccini)
Same cast as October 29 except:
Cio-Cio-San .... Tebaldi
B. F. Pinkerton .... Gedda
Sharpless .... Uppman
Suzuki .... Roggero
Kate Pinkerton .... Allen
Yamadori .... Marsh

February 6
TRISTAN UND ISOLDE (Wagner)
Same cast as January 31

February 8
IL TROVATORE (Verdi)
Same cast as January 27 except:
Azucena .... Madeira
Inez .... Stratas
Messenger .... Carelli

February 9
LA BOHEME (Puccini)
Same cast as October 28 except:
Conductor: Schick
Rodolfo .... Morell
Schaunard .... Harvuot
Colline .... Hines
Mimi .... Tebaldi
Musetta .... Krall
Parpignol .... Roberts
Sergeant .... Strang
Customs Officer .... Frydel

February 10
MARTHA (Flotow)
Same cast as January 26

February 11 (matinee)
ALCESTIS (Gluck)
Same cast as December 6 except:
Apollo .... Nagy

February 11
TANNHAUSER (Wagner)
Same cast as December 17 except:
Conductor: Strasfogel
Hermann .... Wildermann
Wolfram .... Wächter
Biterolf .... Harvuot
Elisabeth .... Nilsson
Venus .... Harshaw

February 13
ELEKTRA (R. Strauss)
Conductor: Rosenstock
Klytämnestra .... Madeira
Elektra .... Borkh
Chrysothemis .... Yeend
Aegisth .... Da Costa
Orest .... Cassel
Guardian of Orest .... Scott
Confidant .... Fercana
Trainbearer .... Vicos
Young Servant .... Anthony
Old Servant .... Ghazal
Overseer of Servants .... Votipka
Serving Women .... MacKenzie,
    Dunn, Roggero, Ordassy, Allen

February 14
LA BOHEME (Puccini)
Same cast as October 28 except:
Conductor: Schick
Rodolfo .... Morell
Marcello .... Sereni
Schaunard .... Harvuot
Colline .... Hines
Mimi .... Tebaldi
Parpignol .... Roberts
Alcindoro .... Alvary
Sergeant .... Strang
Customs Officer .... Frydel

February 15
MARTHA (Flotow)
Same cast as January 26 except:
First Lackey .... Powell

February 16
TRISTAN UND ISOLDE (Wagner)
Same cast as January 31 except:
Brangäne .... Dunn
Melot .... Marsh

February 17
RIGOLETTO (Verdi)
Same cast as December 31 except:
Duke .... Formichini
Rigoletto .... Merrill
Gilda .... Dobbs
Sparafucile .... Wildermann
Maddalena .... Roggero
Monterone .... Sgarro
Marullo .... Reitan

February 18 (matinee)
SIMON BOCCANEGRA (Verdi)
Same cast as December 19 except:
Maid .... Vicos

1960-61

February 18
IL TROVATORE (Verdi)
Same cast as January 27 except:
Leonora .... Amara
Count Di Luna .... Sereni
Azucena .... Rankin
Gypsy .... Ghazal

February 20
AIDA (Verdi)
Same cast as November 5 except:
King .... Flagello
Amneris .... Dalis
Aida .... Price
Radames .... Fernandi
Amonasro .... Merrill
Priestess .... Ordassy

February 21
MADAMA BUTTERFLY (Puccini)
Same cast as October 29 except:
Cio-Cio-San. .... Tebaldi
B. F. Pinkerton .... Gedda
Sharpless .... Uppman
Suzuki .... Roggero
Kate Pinkerton .... Allen
Goro .... Kelley

February 22
SIMON BOCCANEGRA (Verdi)
Same cast as December 19 except:
Simon Boccanegra ...... Colzani
Amelia .... Milanov
Fiesco .... Hines
Maid .... Vicos

February 23
IL TROVATORE (Verdi)
Same cast as January 27 except:
Leonora .... Amara
Manrico .... Baum
Inez .... Stratas
Ruiz .... Carelli
Gypsy .... Ghazal

February 24
Benefit Sponsored by the
Metropolitan Opera Guild for the
Production Fund
TURANDOT (Puccini)
Conductor: Stokowski
Turandot .... Nilsson
Emperor Altoum ..... De Paolis
Timur .... Giaiotti
Calaf .... Corelli
Liù .... Moffo
Ping .... Guarrera
Pang .... Nagy
Pong .... Anthony
Servants .Russell, Crosson, Bishop
Mandarin .... Marsh
Prince of Persia .... Ferraro
Executioners .... Sayette, Adams,
Burdick

February 25 (matinee)
MARTHA (Flotow)
Same cast as January 26 except:
Second Maid .... De Florio

February 25
LA GIOCONDA (Ponchielli)
Same cast as December 26 except:
Alvise Badoero .... Wildermann
Enzo Grimaldo .... Fernandi
Barnaba .... Colzani
Second Singer ...... Balestrieri

February 26
LA BOHEME (Puccini)
Same cast as October 28 except:
Conductor: Schick
Rodolfo .... Morell
Marcello .... Sereni
Colline .... Hines
Mimi .... Tebaldi
Parpignol .... Roberts
Alcindoro .... Alvary
Sergeant .... Strang
Customs Officer .... Frydel

February 27
RIGOLETTO (Verdi)
Same cast as December 31 except:
Duke .... Peerce
Rigoletto .... Merrill
Gilda .... Dobbs
Sparafucile .... Wildermann
Monterone .... Sgarro
Marullo .... Reitan
Borsa .... Nagy
Ceprano .... Marsh

March 1
TRISTAN UND ISOLDE (Wagner)
Same cast as January 31 except:
Tristan .... Liebl
Isolde .... Harshaw
Melot .... Marsh

March 2
LA GIOCONDA (Ponchielli)
Same cast as December 26 except:
La Gioconda .... Milanov
Laura Adorno .... Resnik
Alvise Badoero .... Tozzi
La Cieca .... MacKenzie
Enzo Grimaldo .... Morell
Second Singer ...... Balestrieri

March 3 (matinee)
116th Metropolitan Opera
Guild Student Performance
IL TROVATORE (Verdi)
Conductor: Rich
Leonora .... Amara
Manrico .... Gari
Count Di Luna .... Marsh
Azucena .... Elias
Inez .... Allen
Ferrando .... Scott
Ruiz .... Carelli
Messenger .... Marcella
Gypsy .... Ghazal

March 3
MADAMA BUTTERFLY (Puccini)
Same cast as October 29 except:
Cio-Cio-San .... Price
B. F. Pinkerton .... Olvis
Sharpless .... Testi

March 4 (matinee)
TURANDOT (Puccini)
Same cast as February 24

March 4
ELEKTRA (R. Strauss)
Same cast as February 13 except:
Klytämnestra .... Resnik
Chrysothemis .... Kuchta
Aegisth .... Liebl
Orest .... Uhde
Third Serving Woman .... Wall
Fifth Serving Woman .... Stratas

March 6
IL TROVATORE (Verdi)
Same cast as January 27 except:
Azucena .... Madeira
Gypsy .... Strang

March 7
ELEKTRA (R. Strauss)
Same cast as February 13 except:
Chrysothemis .... Kuchta
Aegisth .... Liebl
Fifth Serving Woman .... Stratas

March 8
LA GIOCONDA (Ponchielli)
Same cast as December 26 except:
La Gioconda .... Milanov
Alvise Badoero .... Tozzi
Enzo Grimaldo .... Morell
Barnaba .... Sereni
Second Singer ...... Balestrieri

March 9
TURANDOT (Puccini)
Same cast as February 24 except:
Liù .... Stratas

March 10
WOZZECK (Berg)
Conductor: Boehm
Wozzeck .... Uhde
Marie .... Steber
Margret .... Roggero
Captain .... Franke
Doctor .... Herbert
Drum Major .... Baum
Andres .... Anthony
Fool .... De Paolis
First Apprentice .... Flagello
Second Apprentice ...... Marsh
Soldier .... Ringland
Marie's Child .... T. Cooke
Townsman .... Kuestner

March 11 (matinee)
LA BOHEME (Puccini)
Same cast as October 28 except:
Conductor: Schick
Rodolfo .... Morell
Colline .... Wildermann
Mimi .... De Los Angeles
Musetta .... Krall
Benoit .... Corena
Parpignol .... Roberts
Sergeant .... Strang
Customs Officer .... Frydel

March 11
RIGOLETTO (Verdi)
Same cast as December 31 except:
Duke .... Formichini
Rigoletto .... Merrill
Gilda .... Santini
Sparafucile .... Wildermann
Maddalena .... Elias
Monterone .... Sgarro
Ceprano .... Marsh

March 13
TURANDOT (Puccini)
Same cast as February 24 except:
Liù .... Stratas

March 14
AIDA (Verdi)
Same cast as November 5 except:
Amneris .... Elias
Aida .... Price
Radames .... Olvis
Amonasro .... Bardelli
Ramfis .... Giaiotti
Priestess .... Ordassy

March 15
DON GIOVANNI (Mozart)
Same cast as January 14 except:
Conductor: Boehm
Don Giovanni .... London
Donna Elvira .... Amara
Don Ottavio .... Peerce
Commendatore .... Giaiotti
Leporello .... Flagello

March 16
DON CARLO (Verdi)
Conductor: Verchi
Philip II .... Tozzi
Don Carlo .... Fernandi
Rodrigo .... Merrill
Grand Inquisitor ... Wildermann
Elizabeth .... Curtis-Verna
Princess Eboli .... Dalis
Theobald .... Wall
Count Lerma .... Carelli
Friar .... Sgarro
Herald .... Nagy
Voice .... Arroyo
Countess Aremberg .... King

March 17
ELEKTRA (R. Strauss)
Same cast as February 13 except:
Chrysothemis .... Kuchta
Aegisth .... Vinay
Orest .... Uhde
Young Servant .... Nagy
Second Serving Woman ... Vanni
Fifth Serving Woman .... Stratas

March 18 (matinee)
TRISTAN UND ISOLDE (Wagner)
Same cast as January 31 except:
Tristan .... Liebl
Melot .... Marsh

March 18
Benefit Vassar Club
Scholarship Fund
IL TROVATORE (Verdi)
Same cast as January 27 except:
Azucena .... Dunn
Messenger .... Carelli
Gypsy .... Strang

March 20
WOZZECK (Berg)
Same cast as March 10

March 22
PARSIFAL (Wagner)
Conductor: Boehm
Amfortas .... Uhde
Titurel .... Wildermann
Gurnemanz .... Hines
Parsifal .... Vinay
Klingsor .... Herbert
Kundry .... Harshaw
Voice .... Dunn
Knights .... Carelli, Sgarro
Esquires .... Allen, Vanni,
                  Anthony, Nagy
Flower Maidens.. Hurley, Stratas,
      Vanni, Kailer, Wall, Roggero

March 23 (matinee)
117th Metropolitan Opera
Guild Student Performance
IL TROVATORE (Verdi)
Same cast as March 3 except:
Conductor: Taussig
Leonora .... Nelli
Count Di Luna .... Sereni
Azucena .... Dunn
Inez .... MacKenzie
Ferrando .... Sgarro
Messenger .... Ringland
Gypsy .... Strang

March 23
Benefit
Free Milk Fund for Babies
DON CARLO (Verdi)
Same cast as March 16 except:
Grand Inquisitor .... Uhde

March 24 (matinee)
118th Metropolitan Opera
Guild Student Performance
IL TROVATORE (Verdi)
Same cast as March 3 except:
Conductor: Burger
Leonora .... Nelli
Manrico .... Da Costa
Inez... .... Ordassy
Ruiz .... Nagy
Gypsy .... Strang

March 24
TURANDOT (Puccini)
Same cast as February 24 except:
Timur .... Wildermann
Liù .... Amara
Pong .... Carelli
Mandarin .... Cehanovsky
First Executioner .... Farrington

March 25 (matinee)
ELEKTRA (R. Strauss)
Same cast as February 13 except:
Chrysothemis .... Rysanek
Aegisth .... Vinay
Orest .... Uhde
Young Servant .... Nagy
Fifth Serving Woman .... Stratas

March 25
DON GIOVANNI (Mozart)
Same cast as January 14 except:
Conductor: Boehm
Don Giovanni .... London
Donna Anna .... Price
Donna Elvira ...... Curtis-Verna
Don Ottavio .... Anthony
Commendatore .... Giaiotti
Leporello .... Flagello

March 27
MARTHA (Flotow)
Same cast as January 26 except:
Plunkett .... Flagello
First Maid .... Reep
Queen .... Keane

March 28
DON CARLO (Verdi)
Same cast as March 16 except:
Philip II .... Hines
Rodrigo .... Guarrera
Grand Inquisitor .... Uhde
Elizabeth .... Rysanek
Countess Aremberg ...... Keane

March 29 (matinee)
119th Metropolitan Opera
Guild Student Performance
IL TROVATORE (Verdi)
Same cast as March 3 except:
Conductor: Burger
Leonora .... Davy
Manrico .... Da Costa
Inez .... Ordassy
Gypsy .... Strang

March 29
TURANDOT (Puccini)
Same cast as February 24 except:
Timur .... Wildermann
Calaf .... Gari*
Liù .... Price
Mandarin .... Cehanovsky
First Executioner .... Farrington
* Corelli fell ill after the first act

March 30 (matinee)
120th Metropolitan Opera
Guild Student Performance
IL TROVATORE (Verdi)
Same cast as March 3 except:
Conductor: Taussig
Leonora .... Nelli
Manrico .... Da Costa
Azucena .... Dunn
Inez .... Wall
Ferrando .... Sgarro
Messenger .... Ringland
Gypsy .... Strang

March 30
WOZZECK (Berg)
Same cast as March 10 except:
Doctor ....Alvary
Drum Major ....Da Costa

March 31 (matinee)
PARSIFAL (Wagner)
Same cast as March 22

April 1 (matinee)
LA GIOCONDA (Ponchielli)
Same cast as December 26 except:
Conductor: Schick
La Gioconda ....Milanov
Alvise Badoero ....Wildermann
Enzo Grimaldo ....Baum
Second Singer ....Balestrieri

April 1
NABUCCO (Verdi)
Same cast as October 24 except:
Ismaele ....Olvis
Zaccaria ....Tozzi
High Priest of Baal ....Scott

April 3
DON CARLO (Verdi)
Same cast as March 16 except:
Don Carlo ....Corelli
Rodrigo ....Sereni
Grand Inquisitor ....Uhde
Princess Eboli ....Rankin
Countess Aremberg ......Keane

April 4 (matinee)
IL TROVATORE (Verdi)
121st Metropolitan Opera
Guild Student Performance
Same cast as March 3 except:
Leonora ....Davy
Inez ....Wall

April 4
L'ELISIR D'AMORE (Donizetti)
Same cast as November 25 except:
Adina ....Hurley

April 5
RIGOLETTO (Verdi)
Same cast as December 31 except:
Duke ....Peerce
Rigoletto ....Merrill
Gilda ....D'Angelo
Sparafucile ....Wildermann
Monterone ....Sgarro
Ceprano ....Marsh

April 6
NABUCCO (Verdi)
Same cast as October 24 except:
Zaccaria ....Hines
High Priest of Baal ....Scott

April 7
PARSIFAL (Wagner)
Same cast as March 22 except:
Klingsor ....Pechner
Kundry ....Dalis

April 8 (matinee)
WOZZECK (Berg)
Same cast as March 10

April 8
TURANDOT (Puccini)
Same cast as February 24 except:
Liù ....Albanese
Mandarin ....Cehanovsky
First Executioner ....Farrington

April 10
LA BOHEME (Puccini)
Same cast as October 28 except:
Schippers fell ill after Act I
and was replaced by Schick.
Rodolfo ....Formichini
Marcello ....Valentino
Schaunard ....Cehanovsky
Colline ....Tozzi
Mimi ....De Los Angeles
Musetta ....Coulter
Benoit ....Corena
Parpignol ....D'Elia
Sergeant ....Strang
Customs Officer ....Frydel

April 11
TURANDOT (Puccini)
Same cast as February 24 except:
First Executioner ....Farrington

April 12
CARMEN (Bizet)
Same cast as October 29 except:
Carmen ....Stevens
Don José ....Olvis
Escamillo ....Merrill
Morales ....Harvuot
Frasquita ....Lind

April 13 (matinee)
IL TROVATORE (Verdi)
122nd Metropolitan Opera
Guild Student Performance
Same cast as March 3 except:
Leonora ....Nelli
Manrico ....Da Costa
Count Di Luna ....Guarrera
Azucena ....Dunn
Inez ....Wall
Ferrando ....Sgarro
Messenger ....Ringland

April 13
MARTHA (Flotow)
Same cast as January 26 except:
First Maid ....Reep
Queen ....Keane

April 14
AIDA (Verdi)
Same cast as November 5 except:
King ....Flagello

Amneris ....Cvejic
Aida ....Nilsson
Radames ....Baum
Ramfis ....Scott
Priestess ....Ordassy

April 15 (matinee)
DON CARLO (Verdi)
Same cast as March 16 except:
Philip II ....Hines
Don Carlo ....Corelli
Rodrigo ....Sereni
Grand Inquisitor ....Uhde
Countess Aremberg ......Keane

April 15
WOZZECK (Berg)
Same cast as March 10 except:
Marie ....Lewis
Drum Major ....Da Costa

EXCERPTS FROM PRESS REVIEWS

METROPOLITAN PREMIERE of Verdi's *Nabucco*, October 24, 1960

It was a new production of a very rare opera. Not only is [*Nabucco*] a newcomer to the Metropolitan but also in all likelihood it has not been seen in this city for a hundred years....

The music may be a little crude in spots, but it is full of ideas.... *Nabucco* gives the listener of today a chance to hear some remarkable vocal writing, many brilliant choruses, and a type of melodic intensity that no Italian composer except Verdi brought to his music.... Thus the revival proved fascinating. One wishes that the same could be said about the production.

The original four acts were compressed into three. This required some heavy cutting in the last two acts.... Not only that, but some scenes were transposed. ... More disturbing were the sets. This production can be considered low-budget *Nabucco* that is also low in imagination.

The singing last night was on a reasonably good level. The opera stands or falls on the role of Abigaille, and Leonie Rysanek made a brave attempt. The chances are that no living singer could handle the writing as Verdi composed it. Miss Rysanek simplified some of the coloratura and avoided all the trills. Nor does she have the low register to cope with the part. But she does have vocal intensity, a thrilling top and a good deal of command.

The other two important roles were that of Nabucco, sung by Cornell MacNeil, and Zaccaria, sung by Cesare Siepi. Mr. Mac-Neil sang and acted dependably. He never really took command of the stage, however, and one had hoped for a little more vocal weight. Mr. Siepi, in good voice, sang resonantly and acted with dignity. Eugenio Fernandi sang clearly and truly the little he had to do, and so did Miss Elias.

Thomas Schippers had things well controlled in the pit. . . . Like most efficient conductors, he inclines toward fast tempos, and here and there his soloists have trouble finding breathing spots. . . .

The choral parts are of the utmost importance in *Nabucco,* and the singers last night went about their work with fervor, clarity and precision.—Harold C. Schonberg, *New York Times*

DEBUT OF GABRIELLA TUCCI as Cio-Cio-San in *Madama Butterfly,* October 29, 1960

On the whole, [Miss Tucci's] performance as Cio-Cio-San was admirable and should find favor here if it holds up in the future. The soprano has an initial advantage of an attractive voice that seems solid in all registers. She is also very attractive and a persuasive actress.—Allen Hughes, *New York Times*

DEBUT OF ANNELIESE ROTHENBERGER as Zdenka in *Arabella,* November 18, 1960

Anneliese Rothenberger made her debut in the difficult role of Zdenka and achieved conspicuous success both as singer and actress. The role is hardly one to show her voice off to advantage, but the way she soared into the upper register immediately stamped her as a valuable acquisition to the company.—Miles Kastendieck, *New York Journal-American*

NEW PRODUCTION of Donizetti's *L'Elisir d'Amore* and DEBUT OF DINO FORMICHINI, November 25, 1960

By common agreement, operatic comedy is no laughing matter for producers. It succeeds only by a happy combination of good planning, high skills, and what Doolittle, Sr., called "a little bit of luck." Measured by the planning and high skills which resulted in such Metropolitan delights as *Fle-*

dermaus, Così Fan Tutte and *Perichole,* the current effort with Donizetti's *L'Elisir d'Amore* is on lower ground throughout. . . .

The happiest thought was the one that assigned Robert O'Hearn to the design problem. O'Hearn has provided a solution for the six situations required which is bright, airy, and above all highly functional. . . .

The cast, however, was not nearly so well matched to its problem . . . beginning with Fernando Corena's Dr. Dulcamara and continuing with Elisabeth Soederstroem's Adina. Corena performed up to the expectations of his hard-working comedy style, but with hardly the vocal substance for the doctor's "Udite, udite." Miss Soederstroem provided her usual kind of intelligent artistry, but Adina belongs to a special breed of operatic bird for which her vocal feathers are not...fine enough....

As replacement for the ailing [Cesare] Valletti, [Dino] Formichini performed courageously but with a quantity of sound that made Nemorino unhappily synonymous with *tenorino.* . . . Surprisingly sub-par, too, was the Belcore of Frank Guarrera, considering what he has done in some circumstances under other directors.

That, perhaps, puts the issue directly to Nathaniel Merrill, a member of the Metropolitan's technical staff, who had his first opportunity at staging a new production. . . . More often than not, the stage happenings were imposed on the situation rather than growing out of it, without any real regard for continuity, character, or, if the accusing word may be finally mentioned, style. Even so, it was in keeping with the musical direction of Fausto Cleva, which got over the ground without calling attention to the distinctive features of the terrain—Irving Kolodin, *Saturday Review*

NEW PRODUCTION of Gluck's *Alcestis* and DEBUT OF EILEEN FARRELL, December 6, 1960

Eileen Farrell's debut at the Metropolitan Opera House . . . was a long-awaited event, and brought forth several thunderous demonstrations of enthusiasm. . . . Miss Farrell possesses what is, as far as I am aware, the most powerful dramatic-soprano voice to be heard at the Met since Kirsten Flagstad, and it is also one of the

warmest, most expressive voices to come to light during this period.

The role of Alcestis is a terribly taxing one for any soprano's first appearance, since . . . it frequently requires the voice to make its own way, unsupported by lush orchestration, and demands from it the most scrupulous and refined sort of singing. There were one or two top notes in the role that sounded a little strained the other night, but aside from these imperfections, Miss Farrell sang with all the aplomb one had expected of her, ranging from beautiful pianissimos to rich and equally beautiful fortes, and showing [a] command of classical style. . . .

As a whole, the production was . . . somewhat unsatisfactory. . . . To my mind, neither the designer . . . Mr. Michael Manuel, nor the choreographer, Mr. Antony Tudor, succeeded in solving the problem suitably, perhaps because they both seemed over-anxious to counter the work's stark simplicity with arresting stagecraft. Mr. Manuel's scenery, the most notable feature of which was a quartet of mammoth sculptured figures . . . was neither Greek nor eighteenth-century in style. . . .

From the purely musical point of view, the evening was more satisfying. Nicolai Gedda sang the role of Admetus with lovely tone and style, and with immaculate English enunciation. The choruses were handled admirably; Walter Cassel did well enough by the role of the High Priest, though some of its lower notes were beyond his effective range . . . and if Erich Leinsdorf's conducting occasionally missed the dramatic intensity that was called for, it was at least smooth and expert.—Winthrop Sargeant, *The New Yorker*

NEW PRODUCTION of Flotow's *Martha,* January 26, 1961

There is nothing acutely objectionable in the revival of a work of such harmless nature, especially since very old hands will remember its erstwhile popularity, yet after hearing the performance one wonders why a great opera house should waste a magnificent cast on a flimsy period piece when masterpieces are neglected.

The staging presented difficulties, because what takes place between the set numbers is pretty thin stuff. Carl Ebert, the stage director, did very well, though perhaps a little more sophisticated treatment would have lessened the faint feeling of antique-shop felicity. Oliver Smith's sets are quite atmospheric, though he had to bring his own oxygen supply with him; the music supplied mighty little and the lyrics even less. . . .

All the singers were in top form. Miss de los Angeles' matchless art of mellifluous singing was in evidence all evening. . . . Rosalind Elias was pert and picturesque—the two ladies made a well-tuned pair. Mr. Tucker and Mr. Tozzi did not spare their magnificent voices, and Lorenzo Alvary completed the cast very satisfactorily. . . .

The fine production was well received, [though] the pitiful rhymes evoked laughter as well as embarrassment.—Paul Henry Lang, *New York Herald Tribune*

DEBUTS OF LEONTYNE PRICE and FRANCO CORELLI in *Il Trovatore*, January 27, 1961

Leontyne Price made an auspicious entry on the Metropolitan scene in a *Trovatore* that found her understandably tentative at the beginning, increasingly secure in the middle and finally triumphant in a treatment that was all finesse, glistening sound and warm artistry. There were qualities of musical distinction throughout, even when she was short of breath at the beginning, but the range and power of her voice, the poise and purpose of her action were positive factors all the way. A large contingent of well-wishers might have made her task more than normally difficult with their tumults of greeting, but she gave them, finally, an opportunity rightfully to roar. In dress and bearing Miss Price conducted herself as every inch the lady Leonora is supposed to be.

There was a good deal of roaring also for the new tenor, Franco Corelli. So good-looking a man need hardly be able to sing to make an appealing troubadour; thus the voluminous sound (of rather bland color) he pumped out early in the evening made an imposing effect. However, Verdi's requirements took the wind from his self-esteem if not from his tones in an "Ah sì, ben mio" that was crude and sobby and a "Di quella pira" that touched every base Italian instinct. He did some real singing later on, but what inclination will prevail in the future can only be a speculation.—Irving Kolodin, *Saturday Review*

DEBUT OF FRANCES YEEND as Chrysothemis in *Elektra*, February 13, 1961

A surprise was the Chrysothemis of Frances Yeend of City Center fame—a Metropolitan debut of significant voice and artistry, and one more proof that Rudolf Bing knows how to pick them and place them.—Louis Biancolli, *New York World-Telegram and Sun*

NEW PRODUCTION of Puccini's *Turandot* and DEBUT OF LEOPOLD STOKOWSKI, February 24, 1961

Making his Met debut in his late seventies, Leopold Stokowski, still crippled from his recent hip accident, last night conducted a powerful, magical performance of Puccini's final opera, *Turandot*. . . . Proceeding through the orchestra pit on crutches, Stokowski led the performance from the regular conductor's stool. He won a standing ovation at his first entrance and again at each reappearance.

The great interest in the production was due largely to the fact that it had not been presented at the Met in over thirty years. As if to make up for this loss, the Met mounted one of the most opulent and truly lovely productions the writer has ever seen. . . .

Birgit Nilsson made a splendid Turandot in eye-popping raiment. Her long, glorious and arduous aria "In questa reggia" was the thrilling core of the performance. Opposite her, the tall, handsome new tenor Franco Corelli, dressed to the nines in fancy fur hats and cloaks (two costume changes for him), pushed out his also-demanding music, culminating in the third-act "Nessun dorma," with fervor. Anna Moffo was a delightful Liù, Alessio De Paolis was excellent as the aging Emperor and the comedy trio of Ping, Pang and Pong were in the best of voices—those of Frank Guarrera, Robert Nagy and Charles Anthony.

Nathaniel Merrill, who supplanted the ailing Yoshio Aoyama as director, has done a remarkably fine job of staging the piece, especially in his handling of the all-important and huge chorus. The lavish yet entirely tasteful scenery and costumes are the work of Cecil Beaton.—Douglas Watt, *New York Daily News*

DEBUT OF GLADYS KUCHTA as Chrysothemis in *Elektra*, March 4, 1961

[Miss Kuchta] was not merely equal to the rigors of the role but brought a wealth of handsome singing and musical sensitivity to it. Chrysothemis is actually the opera's second biggest role, but the character functions dramatically as a pale contrast to her strong sister, Elektra, sung by Inge Borkh. It is not easy to bring her to life, but Miss Kuchta found a way. With a most beautiful vocal tone, she shaped expressive musical phrases that soared out above the orchestra with clarity, understanding and expressive feeling.—Eric Salzman, *New York Times*

DEBUT OF GIANNA D'ANGELO as Gilda in *Rigoletto*, April 5, 1961

A twenty-seven-year-old American soprano of whom the entire country can be proud made her Metropolitan Opera debut last night as Gilda in *Rigoletto*. Her name is Gianna d'Angelo . . . and even before she was finished with her first aria, "Caro nome," she had won an ovation. . . .

She has everything: beauty of face and figure, grace of movement, sensitivity of expression, a gorgeous voice and a professional sureness of touch born of a half-dozen years of experience in the leading houses of Europe.

With her first appearance in the second act, you get the impression of a girlish voice—fresh, unspoiled and perhaps even unsophisticated. But . . . she is a calculatingly adroit and polished singer far beyond her years, and you soon realize that she possesses formidable musicianship which has been trained to a high degree of perfection.—Ronald Eyer, *New York Herald Tribune*

DEBUT OF BISERKA CVEJIC as Amneris in *Aida*, April 14, 1961

Miss Cvejic so pleased her first Metropolitan audience that it demanded seven curtain calls at the end of the Judgment Scene. The Yugoslavian mezzo has a full, well-rounded, warm voice. It sounds best in the upper and lower register, suggesting a need for more support in the middle at dramatic moments. — Miles Kastendieck, *New York Journal-American*

1961-1962 SEASON

PERSONNEL
Male Artists
Alexander, John
Anthony, Charles
Baccaloni, Salvatore
Balestrieri, Anthony
Barbusci, Nicola
Bardelli, Cesare
Barioni, Daniele
Baum, Kurt
Bergonzi, Carlo
Borg, Kim
Borso, Umberto
Carelli, Gabor
Cassel, Walter
Cehanovsky, George
Chistiakov, Vladimir
Colzani, Anselmo
Cooke, Charles
Corelli, Franco
Corena, Fernando
Da Costa, Albert
Davidson, Lawrence
D'Elia, Frank
Dembaugh, William
De Paola, Paul
De Paolis, Alessio
Edelmann, Otto
Fernandi, Eugenio
Fischer, Alan
Flagello, Ezio
Formichini, Dino
Franke, Paul
Frick, Gottlob
Frydel, John
Gedda, Nicolai
Ghazal, Edward
Giaiotti, Bonaldo
Guarrera, Frank
Harvuot, Clifford
Hawkins, Osie
Hemmerly, Walter
Herbert, Ralph
Hines, Jerome
Hopf, Hans
Hundley, Richard
Kessler, Kurt
Kirschberg, Arnold
Konya, Sandor
Kuen, Paul
Kuestner, Charles
Liebl, Karl
London, George
MacNeil, Cornell
Mandile, Frank
Marcella, Lou
Marsh, Calvin
Mayreder, Rudolf
Meredith, Morley
Merrill, Robert
Mittelmann, Norman
Morell, Barry
Moscona, Nicola
Nagy, Robert
Olvis, William
Pechner, Gerhard
Peerce, Jan
Reitan, Roald
Ritchard, Cyril

Roberts, Hal
Scott, Norman
Sereni, Mario
Sgarro, Louis
Shirley, George
Siepi, Cesare
Sliker, Peter
Strang, Lloyd
Symonette, Randolph
Tagliavini, Ferruccio
Testi, Lorenzo
Tomanelli, Carlo
Tozzi, Giorgio
Trehy, John
Tucker, Richard
Uppman, Theodor
Velis, Andrea
Vichey, Luben
Vickers, Jon
Vinay, Ramon
Wiemann, Ernst
Wildermann, William
Zakariasen, William
Zampieri, Giuseppe

Female Artists
Albanese, Licia
Allen, Mildred
Amara, Lucine
Arroyo, Martina
Bjoner, Ingrid
Blair, Lynn
Chookasian, Lili
Coulter, Dorothy
Curtin, Phyllis
Curtis-Verna, Mary
Dalis, Irene
D'Angelo, Gianna
Della Casa, Lisa
De Salvo, Dina
Di Franco, Loretta
Dobbs, Mattiwilda
Dunn, Mignon
Elias, Rosalind
Farrell, Eileen
Fercana, Mary
Greene, Ethel
Harper, Elinor
Harshaw, Margaret
Hurley, Laurel
Jones, Lexi
Kirsten, Dorothy
Krall, Heidi
Kriese, Gladys
Kuchta, Gladys
Lammers, Gerda
Lansché, Ruth
Lewis, Brenda
Lind, Gloria
MacKenzie, Mary
Madeira, Jean
Meyer, Kerstin
Milanov, Zinka
Miller, Mildred
Moffo, Anna
Munson, Pamela
Nilsson, Birgit
Ordassy, Carlotta
Parada, Claudia

Parsons, Meredith
Peters, Roberta
Pracht, Mary Ellen
Price, Leontyne
Rankin, Nell
Raskin, Judith
Resnik, Regina
Rhodes, Jane
Roberti, Margherita
Roggero, Margaret
Rothenberger, **Anneliese**
Rysanek, Leonie
Shawn, Dorothy
Sims, Lilias
Stich-Randall, **Teresa**
Stratas, Teresa
Sutherland, Joan
Thebom, Blanche
Tucci, Gabriella
Välkki, Anita
Vanni, Helen
Vicos, Athena
Vishnevskaya, **Galina**
Votipka, Thelma
Wall, Joan
Yeend, Frances

Ballet Soloists
Ames, Suzanne
Andrew, Thomas
Blecker, Ingrid
Burdick, William
Chazin, Judith
Crosson, Craig
Farrington, Hubert
Ferraro, Edilio
Horne, Katharyn
Jones, Harry
Keane, Audrey
King, Nancy
Kroon, Carole
Mahler, Donald
Mitchell, Arthur
Russell, Thomas
San Miguel, Lolita
Sayette, Howard
Sequoio, Ron
Sibley, Louellen
Verdy, Violette
Wilder, Joan
Zelens, Richard

Conductors
Adler, Kurt
Behr, Jan
Cleva, Fausto
Leinsdorf, Erich
Morel, Jean
Rich, Martin
Rosenstock, Joseph
Santi, Nello
Schick, George
Stokowski, Leopold
Strasfogel, Ignace
Trucco, Victor
Varviso, Silvio
Verchi, Nino

General Manager
Bing, Rudolf

43

October 23 (Opening Night)
LA FANCIULLA DEL WEST
(Puccini)
Conductor: Cleva
Minnie ....Price
Dick Johnson ....Tucker
Jack Rance ....Colzani
Nick ....Franke
Ashby ....Scott
Sonora ....Harvuot
Trin ....Carelli
Sid ....Marsh
Handsome ....Cehanovsky
Harry ....Nagy
Joe ....Velis
Happy ....Reitan
Larkens ....Uppman
Billy Jackrabbit ....Pechner
Wowkle ....Roggero
Jake Wallace ....Flagello
José Castro ....Sgarro
Post Rider ....D'Elia

October 24
COSI FAN TUTTE (Mozart)
Conductor: Rosenstock
Fiordiligi ....Stich-Randall
Dorabella ....Elias
Despina ....Peters
Ferrando ....Shirley
Guglielmo ....Uppman
Don Alfonso ....Guarrera

October 26
LA BOHEME (Puccini)
Conductor: Verchi
Rodolfo ....Morell
Marcello ....Testi
Schaunard ....Reitan
Colline ....Giaiotti
Mimi ....Amara
Musetta ....Hurley
Benoit ....Corena
Parpignol ....Roberts
Alcindoro ....De Paolis
Sergeant ....Frydel
Customs Officer ....Ghazal

October 27
TOSCA (Puccini)
Conductor: Adler
Tosca ....Kirsten
Cavaradossi ....Tucker
Scarpia ....London
Angelotti ....Scott
Sacristan ....Corena
Spoletta ....Franke
Sciarrone ....Cehanovsky
Jailer ....Reitan
Shepherd ....Fischer

October 28 (matinee)
LA TRAVIATA (Verdi)
Conductor: Verchi
Violetta ....Moffo
Alfredo ....Peerce
Germont ....Merrill
Flora ....Wall
Gastone ....Carelli
Baron Douphol ....Marsh
Marquis d'Obigny ..Cehanovsky
Dr. Grenvil ....Sgarro

Annina ....Coulter
Giuseppe ....Marcella
Gardener ....Trehy

October 28
LOHENGRIN (Wagner)
Conductor: Rosenstock
King Henry ....Hines
Lohengrin ....Konya
Elsa ....Bjoner
Telramund ....Cassel
Ortrud ....Dalis
Herald ....Mittelmann
Nobles ....Kessler, Kirschberg,
Strang, Tomanelli

October 30
L'ELISIR D'AMORE (Donizetti)
Conductor: Cleva
Adina ....Peters
Nemorino ....Formichini
Belcore ....Sereni
Dulcamara ....Corena
Giannetta ....Coulter

October 31
LA FANCIULLA DEL WEST
(Puccini)
Same cast as October 23 except:
Minnie (Act III) ......Kirsten

November 1
LA BOHEME (Puccini)
Same cast as October 26 except:
Mimi ....Albanese
Musetta ....Krall

November 2
TOSCA (Puccini)
Same cast as October 27 except:
Tosca ....Curtis-Verna
Cavaradossi ....Barioni

November 3
MADAMA BUTTERFLY (Puccini)
Conductor: Cleva
Cio-Cio-San ....Kirsten
B. F. Pinkerton ....Olvis
Sharpless ....Harvuot
Suzuki ....Roggero
Kate Pinkerton ....Wall
Goro ....Velis
Yamadori ....Cehanovsky
Uncle-Priest ....Hawkins
Imperial Commissioner ...Marsh
Registrar ....Kessler

November 4 (matinee)
COSI FAN TUTTE (Mozart)
Same cast as October 24 except:
Fiordiligi ....Curtin

November 4
TURANDOT (Puccini)
Conductor: Stokowski
Turandot ....Nilsson
Emperor Altoum .... De Paolis
Timur ....Flagello
Calaf ....Tucker
Liù ....Amara
Ping ....Guarrera
Pang ....Nagy
Pong ....Carelli

Servants ....Russell,
Crosson, Jones
Mandarin ....Marsh
Prince of Persia ....Ferraro
Executioners ....Sayette,
Zelens, Burdick

November 6
AIDA (Verdi)
Conductor: Verchi
King ....Sgarro
Amneris ....Dunn
Aida ....Vishnevskaya
Radames ....Vickers
Amonasro ....Colzani
Ramfis ....Hines
Messenger ....Nagy
Priestess ....Ordassy

November 7
TURANDOT (Puccini)
Same cast as November 4

November 8
L'ELISIR D'AMORE (Donizetti)
Same cast as October 30

November 9
Benefit Bagby Music
Lovers' Foundation
LA BOHEME (Puccini)
Same cast as October 26 except:
Mimi ....Albanese
Musetta ....Krall

November 10
LA FANCIULLA DEL WEST
(Puccini)
Same cast as October 23 except:
Minnie ....Kirsten

November 11 (matinee)
LOHENGRIN (Wagner)
Same cast as October 28

November 11
Benefit Mizrachi
Women's Organization
LES CONTES D'HOFFMANN
(Offenbach)
Conductor: Morel
Hoffmann ....Gedda
Olympia ....Moffo
Giulietta ....Moffo
Antonia ....Moffo
Nicklausse ....Vanni
Lindorf ....London
Coppélius ....London
Dappertutto ....London
Dr. Miracle ....London
Spalanzani ....Franke
Schlemil ....Harvuot
Crespel ....Scott
Voice ....Dunn
Andrès ....De Paolis
Cochenille ....De Paolis
Pitichinaccio ....De Paolis
Frantz ....De Paolis
Luther ....Cehanovsky
Nathanael ....Nagy
Hermann ....Reitan
Stella ....Moffo

November 13
MADAMA BUTTERFLY (Puccini)
Same cast as November 3 except:
B. F. Pinkerton ....Shirley

November 14
LA TRAVIATA (Verdi)
Same cast as October 28 except:
Violetta ....Albanese

November 15
TOSCA (Puccini)
Same cast as October 27 except:
Cavaradossi ....Morell
Sacristan ....Flagello

November 16
AIDA (Verdi)
Same cast as November 6 except:
Amneris ....Dalis
Radames ....Baum
Ramfis ....Giaiotti

November 17
LOHENGRIN (Wagner)
Same cast as October 28 except:
King Henry ....Wiemann
Lohengrin ....Liebl
Telramund ....Symonette
Ortrud ....Rankin

November 18 (matinee)
LES CONTES D'HOFFMANN
(Offenbach)
Same cast as November 11 except:
Olympia ....Hurley
Giulietta ....Elias
Antonia ....Amara
Stella ....King

November 18
LA BOHEME (Puccini)
Same cast as October 26 except:
Rodolfo ....Barioni
Benoit ....Pechner
Alcindoro ....Velis

November 20
TOSCA (Puccini)
Same cast as October 27 except:
Tosca ....Milanov
Cavaradossi ....Zampieri
Sacristan ....Flagello

November 21
MADAMA BUTTERFLY (Puccini)
Same cast as November 3 except:
Cio-Cio-San ....Price

November 22
COSI FAN TUTTE (Mozart)
Same cast as October 24

November 23
LA FANCIULLA DEL WEST
(Puccini)
Same cast as October 23 except:
Minnie ....Kirsten
Dick Johnson ....Konya
Happy ....Hawkins
Larkens ....Reitan

November 24
LA TRAVIATA (Verdi)
Same cast as October 28 except:
Conductor: Strasfogel
Violetta ....Albanese
Alfredo ....Formichini
Annina ....Pracht
Gardener ....Chistiakov

November 25 (matinee)
AIDA (Verdi)
Same cast as November 6 except:
Conductor: Schick

November 25
LA PERICHOLE (Offenbach)
Conductor: Morel
Don Andres ....Ritchard
Don Pedro ....Hawkins
Panatellas ....Franke
Tarapote ....Scott
Perichole ....Moffo
Paquillo ....Uppman
Guadalena ....Coulter
Estrella ....Blair
Virginella ....Wall
Notaries ....Velis, Reitan
Old Prisoner ....De Paolis
Clown ....Andrew
Ballerina ....Ames
Jailer ....Mayreder
Ninetta ....Fercana
Frasquinella ....Sims
Brambilla ....Shawn
Manuelita ....Jones

November 26
Benefit Sponsored by the
Metropolitan Opera Guild for the
Production Fund
LUCIA DI LAMMERMOOR
(Donizetti)
Conductor: Varviso
Lucia ....Sutherland
Enrico Ashton ....Testi
Edgardo ....Tucker
Alisa ....Votipka
Raimondo ....Moscona
Arturo ....Anthony
Normanno ....Nagy

November 27
LES CONTES D'HOFFMANN
(Offenbach)
Same cast as November 11 except:
Olympia ....Hurley
Giulietta ....Elias
Antonia ....Amara
Stella ....King

November 28
TOSCA (Puccini)
Same cast as October 27 except:
Tosca ....Curtis-Verna
Cavaradossi ....Barioni
Scarpia ....Cassel

November 29
LOHENGRIN (Wagner)
Same cast as October 28 except:
Telramund ....Symonette
Ortrud ....Harshaw
Nobles ......Cooke, Dembaugh,
Sliker, Frydel

November 30
LA TRAVIATA (Verdi)
Same cast as October 28 except:
Conductor: Strasfogel
Alfredo ....Shirley
Annina ....Pracht

December 1
TURANDOT (Puccini)
Same cast as November 4 except:
Conductor: Adler
Liù ....Price
Pong ....Anthony

December 2 (matinee)
L'ELISIR D'AMORE (Donizetti)
Same cast as October 30 except:
Adina ....Hurley
Nemorino ....Gedda
Belcore ....Guarrera

December 2
Benefit Yeshiva University
Women's Organization
LUCIA DI LAMMERMOOR
(Donizetti)
Same cast as November 26 except:
Enrico Ashton ....Guarrera
Edgardo ....Peerce
Raimondo ....Giaiotti

December 4
LA FANCIULLA DEL WEST
(Puccini)
Same cast as October 23 except:
Dick Johnson ....Konya
Trin ....Marcella
Happy ....Hawkins
Larkens ....Reitan

December 5
MADAMA BUTTERFLY (Puccini)
Same cast as November 3 except:
Cio-Cio-San ......Vishnevskaya
Suzuki ....Vanni
Kate Pinkerton ......MacKenzie

December 6
LA PERICHOLE (Offenbach)
Same cast as November 25

December 7
LES CONTES D'HOFFMANN
(Offenbach)
Same cast as November 11 except:
Olympia ....Hurley
Giulietta ....Elias
Antonia ....Amara
Nathanael ....Velis
Stella ....King

1961-62

December 8
AIDA (Verdi)
Same cast as November 6 except:
Conductor: Schick
Amneris ....Elias
Radames ....Konya
Ramfis ....Tozzi
Messenger ....Franke

December 9 (matinee)
LUCIA DI LAMMERMOOR
(Donizetti)
Same cast as November 26 except:
Enrico Ashton ....Guarrera

December 9
GOETTERDAEMMERUNG (Wagner)
Conductor: Leinsdorf
Siegfried ....Hopf
Brünnhilde ....Nilsson
Gunther ....Mittelmann
Gutrune ....Bjoner
Alberich ....Herbert
Hagen ....Wiemann
Waltraute ....Dalis
Woglinde ....Arroyo
Wellgunde ....Elias
Flosshilde ....Dunn
Norns .....Dunn, Dalis, Arroyo
Vassals ....Kuestner, Trehy

December 11
LOHENGRIN (Wagner)
Same cast as October 28 except:
Ortrud ....Harshaw
Herald ....Marsh
Nobles .....Cooke, Dembaugh,
Sliker, Frydel

December 12
LA FORZA DEL DESTINO (Verdi)
Conductor: Schick
Marquis ....Sgarro
Leonora ....Farrell
Don Carlo ....Merrill
Don Alvaro ....Tucker
Padre Guardiano ....Hines
Fra Melitone ....Corena
Preziosilla ....Vanni
Curra ....Ordassy
Trabucco ....De Paolis
Surgeon ....Cehanovsky

December 13
AIDA (Verdi)
Same cast as November 6 except:
Conductor: Schick
King ....Flagello
Amneris ....Dalis
Aida ....Price
Radames ....Konya
Ramfis ....Tozzi

December 14
COSI FAN TUTTE (Mozart)
Same cast as October 24

December 15
LUCIA DI LAMMERMOOR
(Donizetti)
Same cast as November 26 except:
Edgardo ....Peerce
Raimondo ....Giaiotti
Normanno ....Carelli

December 16 (matinee)
Afternoon *Ring* cycle
DAS RHEINGOLD (Wagner)
Conductor: Leinsdorf
Wotan ....London
Donner ....Mittelmann
Froh ....Nagy
Loge ....Liebl
Alberich ....Herbert
Mime ....Kuen
Fasolt ....Hines
Fafner ....Wiemann
Fricka ....Dalis
Freia ....Krall
Erda ....Madeira
Woglinde ....Arroyo
Wellgunde ....Elias
Flosshilde ....Dunn

December 16
Benefit Hartman-Homecrest
L'ELISIR D'AMORE (Donizetti)
Same cast as October 30 except:
Belcore ....Guarrera
Dulcamara ....Flagello
Giannetta ....Allen

December 18
LA FORZA DEL DESTINO (Verdi)
Same cast as December 12 except:
Fra Melitone ....Pechner
Preziosilla ....Wall

December 19
COSI FAN TUTTE (Mozart)
Same cast as October 24 except:
Ferrando ....Alexander

December 20
MADAMA BUTTERFLY (Puccini)
Same cast as November 3 except:
Cio-Cio-San ....Price
B. F. Pinkerton ....Morell
Sharpless ....Marsh
Kate Pinkerton ......MacKenzie
Goro ....Franke
Imperial Commissioner ..Reitan

December 21
LUCIA DI LAMMERMOOR
(Donizetti)
Same cast as November 26 except:
Raimondo ....Giaiotti

December 22
LES CONTES D'HOFFMANN
(Offenbach)
Same cast as November 11 except:
Hoffmann ....Alexander
Olympia ....Hurley
Giulietta ....Dunn
Antonia ....Amara
Nicklausse ....Wall
Voice ....Kriese
Stella ....Keane

December 23 (matinee)
Afternoon *Ring* cycle
DIE WALKUERE (Wagner)
Conductor: Leinsdorf
Wotan ....Edelmann
Fricka ....Dalis
Brünnhilde ....Nilsson
Siegmund ....Vickers
Sieglinde ....Kuchta
Hunding ....Wiemann
Helmwige ....Krall
Gerhilde ....Ordassy
Ortlinde ....Arroyo
Rossweisse ....Roggero
Grimgerde ....MacKenzie
Waltraute ....Dunn
Siegrune ....Vanni
Schwertleite ....Kriese

December 23
AIDA (Verdi)
Same cast as November 6 except:
Conductor: Schick
Amneris ....Elias*
Aida ....Curtis-Verna
Radames ....Konya
Amonasro ....Symonette
Ramfis ....Tozzi
*Dalis sang in Act 4

December 25
LUCIA DI LAMMERMOOR
(Donizetti)
Same cast as November 26 except:
Lucia ....Moffo
Enrico Ashton ....Colzani
Alisa ....Ordassy
Raimondo ....Wildermann

December 26
LOHENGRIN (Wagner)
Same cast as October 28 except:
King Henry ....:.Wiemann
Elsa ....Kuchta
Ortrud ....Harshaw
Nobles .....Cooke, Dembaugh,
Sliker, Frydel

December 27
First evening *Ring* cycle
DAS RHEINGOLD (Wagner)
Same cast as December 16 except:
Froh ....Olvis
Fasolt ....Wiemann
Fafner ....Frick

December 28
L'ELISIR D'AMORE (Donizetti)
Same cast as October 30 except:
Belcore ....Testi
Giannetta ....Allen

December 29
First evening *Ring* cycle
DIE WALKUERE (Wagner)
Same cast as December 23 except:
Wotan ....Symonette
Hunding ....Frick
Schwertleite ....Madeira

46

December 30 (matinee)
LA FORZA DEL DESTINO (Verdi)
Same cast as December 12

December 30
LA FANCIULLA DEL WEST
(Puccini)
Same cast as October 23 except:
Minnie .... Kirsten
Dick Johnson .... Barioni
Jack Rance .... Guarrera
Happy .... Hawkins
Larkens .... Reitan

December 31
LA PERICHOLE (Offenbach)
Same cast as November 25 except:
Don Pedro .... Herbert
Ballerina .... King

January 1
COSI FAN TUTTE (Mozart)
Same cast as October 24 except:
Fiordiligi .... Amara
Despina .... Hurley
Ferrando .... Anthony

January 2
First evening Ring cycle
SIEGFRIED (Wagner)
Conductor: Leinsdorf
Wanderer .... London
Siegfried .... Hopf
Brünnhilde .... Nilsson
Erda .... Madeira
Mime .... Kuen
Alberich .... Herbert
Fafner .... Frick
Forest Bird .... Arroyo

January 3
LES CONTES D'HOFFMANN
(Offenbach)
Same cast as November 11 except:
Lindorf .... Meredith
Coppélius .... Meredith
Dappertutto .... Meredith
Dr. Miracle .... Meredith
Voice .... Roggero

January 4
RIGOLETTO (Verdi)
Conductor: Cleva
Duke .... Morell
Rigoletto .... Merrill
Gilda .... d'Angelo
Sparafucile .... Flagello
Maddalena .... Elias
Giovanna .... Votipka
Monterone .... Giaiotti
Marullo .... Harvuot
Borsa .... Carelli
Ceprano .... Marsh
Countess .... Wall
Page .... Blair
Guard .... De Paola

January 5
First evening Ring cycle
GOETTERDAEMMERUNG (Wagner)
Same cast as December 9 except:
Gunther .... Cassel
Gutrune .... Kuchta
Hagen .... Frick
Flosshilde .... Roggero
First Norn .... Madeira

January 6 (matinee)
LA FANCIULLA DEL WEST
(Puccini)
Same cast as October 23 except:
Minnie .... Kirsten

January 6
Benefit Vassar Club
Scholarship Fund
LA TRAVIATA (Verdi)
Same cast as October 28 except:
Conductor: Strasfogel
Alfredo .... Gedda
Germont .... Guarrera
Annina .... Blair
Giuseppe .... Zakariasen
Gardener .... Chistiakov

January 8
TURANDOT (Puccini)
Same cast as November 4 except:
Conductor: Adler
Timur .... Giaiotti
Calaf .... Konya
Pong .... Anthony

January 9
LES CONTES D'HOFFMANN
(Offenbach)
Same cast as November 11 except:
Olympia .... Hurley
Giulietta .... Elias
Antonia .... Amara
Voice .... Roggero
Andrès .... Kuen
Cochenille .... Kuen
Pitichinaccio .... Kuen
Frantz .... Kuen
Stella .... Keane

January 10
DIE WALKUERE (Wagner)
Same cast as December 23 except:
Fricka .... Dunn
Brünnhilde .... Harshaw
Hunding .... Frick
Schwertleite .... Greene
Note: Edelmann, who sang Wotan, fell ill after Act II; Symonette took over the role in Act III but found himself unable to continue. The curtain was lowered on Leinsdorf's orders, several pages of music cut, and Edelmann summoned back to finish the opera, beginning with Brünnhilde's words "War es so schmählich."

January 11
LE NOZZE DI FIGARO (Mozart)
Conductor: Leinsdorf
Almaviva .... Borg
Countess .... Della Casa
Susanna .... Rothenberger
Figaro .... Tozzi
Cherubino .... Miller
Marcellina .... Dunn
Bartolo .... Flagello
Basilio .... Velis
Don Curzio .... Carelli
Antonio .... Davidson
Barbarina .... Allen
Peasant Girls .. Di Franco, Shawn

January 12
COSI FAN TUTTE (Mozart)
Same cast as October 24 except:
Fiordiligi .... Amara
Despina .... Hurley
Ferrando .... Anthony

January 13 (matinee)
Afternoon Ring cycle
SIEGFRIED (Wagner)
Same cast as January 2

January 13
L'ELISIR D'AMORE (Donizetti)
Same cast as October 30 except:
Adina .... Moffo
Nemorino .... Tagliavini
Belcore .... Guarrera
Dulcamara .... Baccaloni
Giannetta .... Allen

January 14
Benefit West Side
Institutional Synagogue
LA FORZA DEL DESTINO (Verdi)
Same cast as December 12 except:
Leonora .... Curtis-Verna
Padre Guardiano .... Tozzi
Fra Melitone .... Baccaloni
Preziosilla .... Dunn

January 15
DAS RHEINGOLD (Wagner)
Same cast as December 16 except:
Wotan .... Hines
Fasolt .... Wiemann
Fafner .... Frick

January 16
LA PERICHOLE (Offenbach)
Same cast as November 25 except:
Perichole .... Hurley
Guadalena .... Allen
Ballerina .... King
Ninetta .... Parsons
Frasquinella .... Harper
Brambilla .... Munson
Manuelita .... Greene

January 17
LE NOZZE DI FIGARO (Mozart)
Same cast as January 11

January 18
MADAMA BUTTERFLY (Puccini)
Same cast as November 3 except:
Cio-Cio-San .... Albanese
Sharpless .... Uppman
Suzuki .... Elias
Kate Pinkerton ..... MacKenzie
Goro .... Franke

January 19
GOETTERDAEMMERUNG (Wagner)
Same cast as December 9 except:
Brünnhilde .... Harshaw
Gunther .... Cassel
Gutrune .... Kuchta
Hagen .... Frick
Alberich .... Pechner

January 20 (matinee)
LA BOHEME (Puccini)
Same cast as October 26 except:
Conductor: Rich
Benoit .... Pechner

January 20
LA FORZA DEL DESTINO (Verdi)
Same cast as December 12 except:
Don Carlo .... Colzani
Don Alvaro .... Peerce
Fra Melitone .... Baccaloni
Preziosilla .... Wall
Trabucco .... Velis

January 22
LA PERICHOLE (Offenbach)
Same cast as November 25 except:
Perichole .... Hurley
Guadalena .... Allen
Clown .... Zelens
Ballerina .... Wilder
Ninetta .... Parsons
Frasquinella .... Harper
Brambilla .... Munson
Manuelita .... Greene

January 23
DIE WALKUERE (Wagner)
Same cast as December 23 except:
Wotan .... Hines
Brünnhilde .... Välkki
Hunding .... Frick

January 24
RIGOLETTO (Verdi)
Same cast as January 4 except:
Rigoletto .... Colzani
Gilda .... Dobbs

January 25
UN BALLO IN MASCHERA (Verdi)
Conductor: Santi
Gustav III .... Bergonzi
Anckarström .... Merrill
Amelia .... Rysanek
Ulrica .... Madeira
Oscar .... Rothenberger
Christiano .... Marsh
Count de Horn .... Giaiotti
Count Warting .... Vichey
Chief Justice .... Velis
Servant .... Nagy

January 26
LA FORZA DEL DESTINO (Verdi)
Same cast as December 12 except:
Don Carlo .... Sereni
Don Alvaro .... Peerce
Preziosilla .... Wall
Trabucco .... Velis

January 27 (matinee)
Afternoon *Ring* cycle
GOETTERDAEMMERUNG (Wagner)
Same cast as December 9 except:
Gutrune .... Kuchta
Hagen .... Frick
First Norn .... Madeira

January 27
TOSCA (Puccini)
Same cast as October 27 except:
Tosca .... Roberti
Cavaradossi .... Corelli
Scarpia .... Colzani
Sacristan .... Baccaloni

January 29
SIEGFRIED (Wagner)
Same cast as January 2 except:
Brünnhilde .... Harshaw
Wanderer .... Symonette
Alberich .... Pechner

January 30
UN BALLO IN MASCHERA (Verdi)
Same cast as January 25

January 31
Benefit Sponsored by the
Metropolitan Opera Guild for the
Production Fund
TOSCA (Puccini)
Same cast as October 27 except:
Tosca .... Nilsson
Cavaradossi .... Corelli
Scarpia .... Colzani
Sacristan .... Baccaloni

February 1
GOETTERDAEMMERUNG (Wagner)
Same cast as December 9 except:
Siegfried .... Liebl
Brünnhilde .... Harshaw
Gutrune .... Krall
Hagen .... Frick
Alberich .... Pechner
Waltraute .... Madeira
Flosshilde .... Roggero
First Norn .... Madeira

February 2
SALOME (R. Strauss)
Conductor: Rosenstock
Herod .... Vinay
Herodias .... Thebom
Salome .... Rhodes
Jochanaan .... Cassel
Narraboth .... Olvis
Page .... Wall
First Nazarene .... Wiemann
Second Nazarene ...... Reitan
First Jew .... Anthony
Second Jew .... Nagy

Third Jew .... Carelli
Fourth Jew .... Velis
Fifth Jew .... Pechner
First Soldier .... Scott
Second Soldier .... Sgarro
Cappadocian .... Marsh
Slave .... Blair

February 3 (matinee)
MADAMA BUTTERFLY (Puccini)
Same cast as November 3 except:
Cio-Cio-San .... Tucci
B. F. Pinkerton ...... Bergonzi
Suzuki .... Vanni
Kate Pinkerton .... MacKenzie
Imperial Commissioner .. Reitan

February 3
LA BOHEME (Puccini)
Same cast as October 26 except:
Conductor: Rich
Rodolfo .... Formichini
Marcello .... Sereni
Colline .... Hines
Mimi .... Stratas
Benoit .... Pechner
Sergeant .... Strang
Customs Officer ...... Tomanelli

February 5
LE NOZZE DI FIGARO (Mozart)
Same cast as January 11 except:
Barbarina .... Stratas

February 6
TOSCA (Puccini)
Same cast as October 27 except:
Tosca .... Milanov
Cavaradossi .... Corelli
Scarpia .... Meredith
Sacristan .... Pechner

February 7
SALOME (R. Strauss)
Same cast as February 2

February 8
UN BALLO IN MASCHERA (Verdi)
Same cast as January 25

February 9
LA BOHEME (Puccini)
Same cast as October 26 except:
Conductor: Rich
Rodolfo .... Tagliavini
Musetta .... Lewis
Benoit .... Pechner
Sergeant .... Strang
Customs Officer ...... Tomanelli

February 10 (matinee)
LA PERICHOLE (Offenbach)
Same cast as November 25 except:
Perichole .... Hurley
Guadalena .... Allen
Ballerina .... King
Ninetta .... Parsons
Frasquinella .... Harper
Brambilla .... Munson
Manuelita .... Greene

February 10
LA TRAVIATA (Verdi)
Same cast as October 28 except:
Conductor: Strasfogel
Violetta ....Tucci
Alfredo ....Formichini
Germont ....Guarrera
Annina ....Pracht
Giuseppe ....Zakariasen
Gardener ....Chistiakov

February 12
UN BALLO IN MASCHERA (Verdi)
Same cast as January 25 except:
Ulrica ....Rankin

February 13 (matinee)
123rd Metropolitan Opera
Guild Student Performance
LA TRAVIATA (Verdi)
Same cast as October 28 except:
Conductor: Behr
Violetta ....Hurley
Alfredo ....Alexander
Germont ....Marsh
Flora ....Pracht
Gastone ....Nagy
Baron Douphol ....Reitan
Annina ....Blair

February 13
RIGOLETTO (Verdi)
Same cast as January 4 except:
Rigoletto ....Colzani
Gilda ....Dobbs
Monterone ....Sgarro

February 14
LA FORZA DEL DESTINO (Verdi)
Same cast as December 12 except:
Leonora ....Milanov
Don Alvaro ....Baum
Padre Guardiano ....Giaiotti
Fra Melitone ....Baccaloni

February 15
LA PERICHOLE (Offenbach)
Same cast as November 25 except:
Perichole ....Hurley
Clown ....Zelens
Ballerina ....Wilder
Ninetta ....Parsons
Frasquinella ....Harper
Brambilla ....Munson
Manuelita ....Greene

February 16
AIDA (Verdi)
Same cast as November 6 except:
Conductor: Schick
Amneris ....Dalis
Aida ....Rysanek
Radames ....Corelli
Ramfis ....Flagello

February 17 (matinee)
SALOME (R. Strauss)
Same cast as February 2 except:
Salome ....Lewis

February 17
LUCIA DI LAMMERMOOR
(Donizetti)
Same cast as November 26 except:
Conductor: Rich
Lucia ....Peters
Edgardo ....Bergonzi
Alisa ....Ordassy
Raimondo ....Scott

February 19
RIGOLETTO (Verdi)
Same cast as January 4 except:
Rigoletto ....MacNeil
Gilda ....Dobbs
Giovanna ....Ordassy
Monterone ....Sgarro
Borsa ....Franke
Countess ....Pracht

February 20
AIDA (Verdi)
Same cast as November 6 except:
Conductor: Schick
King ....Vichey
Amneris ....Rankin
Aida ....Roberti
Radames ....Baum
Amonasro ....Merrill
Ramfis ....Wildermann

February 21 (matinee)
124th Metropolitan Opera
Guild Student Performance
LA TRAVIATA (Verdi)
Same cast as October 28 except:
Conductor: Behr
Violetta ....Hurley
Alfredo ....Alexander
Germont ....Marsh
Flora ....Pracht
Gastone ....Nagy
Baron Douphol ....Harvuot
Annina ....Blair

February 21
LA TRAVIATA (Verdi)
Same cast as October 28 except:
Conductor: Strasfogel
Violetta ....Albanese
Alfredo ....Fernandi
Germont ....Guarrera
Annina ....Pracht
Giuseppe ....Zakariasen
Gardener ....Chistiakov

February 22
SALOME (R. Strauss)
Same cast as February 2 except:
Jochanaan ....Meredith
Narraboth ....Alexander
Page ....Roggero
First Nazarene .....Wildermann
Second Nazarene ....Strang

February 23
LE NOZZE DI FIGARO (Mozart)
Same cast as January 11 except:
Conductor: Strasfogel
Almaviva ....Cassel
Susanna ....Raskin
Basilio ....Carelli
Don Curzio ....Nagy
Barbarina ....Stratas
Peasant Girls..Lansché, De Salvo

February 24 (matinee)
TURANDOT (Puccini)
Same cast as November 4 except:
Conductor: Adler
Calaf ....Corelli
Liù ....Albanese
Pong ....Anthony
First Executioner ....Farrington

February 24
MACBETH (Verdi)
Conductor: Rosenstock
Macbeth ....Colzani
Lady Macbeth ....Rysanek
Banquo ....Tozzi
Macduff ....Bergonzi
Malcolm ....Shirley
Lady-in-Attendance .....Ordassy
Physician ....Pechner
Murderer ....Marsh
Warrior ....Sgarro
Bloody Child ....Blair
Crowned Child ....Allen
Manservant ....Tomanelli
King Duncan ....Hemmerly

February 26
LA BOHEME (Puccini)
Same cast as October 26 except:
Conductor: Rich
Rodolfo ....Tagliavini
Schaunard ....Harvuot
Mimi ....Stratas
Musetta ....Lewis
Benoit ....Pechner
Sergeant ....Strang
Customs Officer ......Tomanelli

February 27
UN BALLO IN MASCHERA (Verdi)
Same cast as January 25 except:
Conductor: Schick
Amelia ....Parada
Oscar ....Hurley
Servant ....Carelli

February 28
AIDA (Verdi)
Same cast as November 6 except:
Conductor: Schick
Amneris ....Dalis
Aida ....Tucci
Radames ....Corelli
Amonasro ....MacNeil
Ramfis ....Tozzi

49

1961-62

March 1
TURANDOT (Puccini)
Same cast as November 4 except:
Conductor: Adler
Timur ....Wildermann
Calaf ....Konya
Liù ....Stratas
Pong ....Anthony
First Executioner ....Farrington

March 2 (matinee)
125th Metropolitan Opera
Guild Student Performance
LA TRAVIATA (Verdi)
Same cast as October 28 except:
Conductor: Trucco
Violetta ....Yeend
Alfredo ....Shirley
Germont ....Marsh
Flora ....Pracht
Baron Douphol ....Reitan
Annina ....Blair
Giuseppe ....Zakariasen
Gardener ....Chistiakov

March 2
MACBETH (Verdi)
Same cast as February 24 except:
Banquo ....Giaiotti
Warrior ....Reitan

March 3 (matinee)
AIDA (Verdi)
Same cast as November 6 except:
Conductor: Schick
Amneris ....Dalis
Aida ....Tucci
Radames ....Corelli
Amonasro ....MacNeil
Ramfis ....Tozzi

March 3
ORFEO ED EURIDICE (Gluck)
Conductor: Morel
Orfeo ....Meyer
Euridice ....Amara
Amore ....Rothenberger

March 5
SALOME (R. Strauss)
Same cast as February 2 except:
Herodias ....Rankin
Jochanaan ....Meredith
First Nazarene ....Wildermann

March 6
LE NOZZE DI FIGARO (Mozart)
Same cast as January 11 except:
Conductor: Strasfogel
Susanna ....Hurley
Figaro ....Siepi
Cherubino ....Elias
Bartolo ....Pechner
Basilio ....De Paolis
Barbarina ....Stratas
Peasant Girls..Lansché, De Salvo

March 7
UN BALLO IN MASCHERA (Verdi)
Same cast as January 25 except:
Anckarström ....MacNeil
Amelia ....Parada

March 8
MACBETH (Verdi)
Same cast as February 24 except:
Banquo ....Giaiotti
Warrior ....Reitan

March 9 (matinee)
126th Metropolitan Opera
Guild Student Performance
LA TRAVIATA (Verdi)
Same cast as October 28 except:
Conductor: Behr
Violetta ....Yeend
Alfredo ....Anthony
Germont ....Marsh
Flora ....Pracht
Baron Douphol ....Harvuot
Annina ....Blair
Giuseppe ....Zakariasen
Gardener ....Chistiakov

March 9
LA GIOCONDA (Ponchielli)
Conductor: Cleva
La Gioconda ....Milanov
Laura Adorno ....Rankin
Alvise Badoero ....Tozzi
La Cieca ....Chookasian
Enzo Grimaldo ....Corelli
Barnaba ....Merrill
Zuane ....Cehanovsky
Singers ....De Paola, Balestrieri
Isepo ....De Paolis
Monk ....Sgarro
Steersman ....Barbusci

March 10 (matinee)
ORFEO ED EURIDICE (Gluck)
Same cast as March 3

March 10
RIGOLETTO (Verdi)
Same cast as January 4 except:
Conductor: Rich
Rigoletto ....MacNeil
Gilda ....Peters
Sparafucile ....Vichey
Maddalena ....Roggero
Giovanna ....Ordassy
Monterone ....Sgarro
Borsa ....Franke
Ceprano ....Cehanovsky
Countess ....Pracht

March 12
TURANDOT (Puccini)
Same cast as November 4 except:
Conductor: Adler
Turandot ....Curtis-Verna
Calaf ....Corelli
Liù ....Albanese
Ping ....Marsh
Pong ....Anthony
Mandarin ....Reitan
First Executioner ....Farrington

March 13 (matinee)
127th Metropolitan Opera
Guild Student Performance
LA TRAVIATA (Verdi)
Same cast as October 28 except:
Conductor: Trucco
Violetta ....Tucci
Alfredo ....Shirley
Germont ....Marsh
Flora ....Pracht
Gastone ....Velis
Baron Douphol ....Reitan
Annina ....Blair
Giuseppe ....Hundley
Gardener ....Barbusci

March 13
LA BOHEME (Puccini)
Same cast as October 26 except:
Conductor: Rich
Rodolfo ....Bergonzi
Marcello ....Sereni
Mimi ....Stratas
Benoit ....Pechner
Parpignol ....Mandile
Sergeant ....Strang
Customs Officer ......Tomanelli

March 14
MACBETH (Verdi)
Same cast as February 24 except:
Lady Macbeth ....Dalis
Warrior ....Reitan

March 15
TOSCA (Puccini)
Same cast as October 27 except:
Tosca ....Roberti
Cavaradossi ....Morell
Scarpia ....MacNeil
Sacristan ....Flagello
Spoletta ....Velis

March 16
ELEKTRA (R. Strauss)
Conductor: Rosenstock
Klytämnestra ....Madeira
Elektra ....Lammers
Chrysothemis ....Yeend
Aegisth ....Da Costa
Orest ....Cassel
Guardian of Orest ......Pechner
Confidant ....Fercana
Trainbearer ....Vicos
Young Servant ....Nagy
Old Servant ....Ghazal
Overseer of Servants ......Lind
Serving Women ....Kriese,
Vanni, Roggero, Ordassy, Stratas

March 17 (matinee)
UN BALLO IN MASCHERA (Verdi)
Same cast as January 25

March 17
LE NOZZE DI FIGARO (Mozart)
Same cast as January 11 except:
Conductor: Strasfogel
Susanna ....Hurley
Figaro ....Siepi
Cherubino ....Vanni
Basilio ....De Paolis
Peasant Girls..Lansché, De Salvo

March 19 (matinee)
128th Metropolitan Opera
Guild Student Performance
LA TRAVIATA (Verdi)
Same cast as October 28 except:
Conductor: Trucco
Violetta ....Hurley
Alfredo ....Anthony
Germont ....Reitan
Gastone ....Velis
Annina ....Blair
Giuseppe ....Hundley
Gardener ....Barbusci

March 19
LA FORZA DEL DESTINO (Verdi)
Same cast as December 12 except:
Leonora ....Amara
Don Alvaro ....Bergonzi
Padre Guardiano ....Giaiotti

March 20
AIDA (Verdi)
Same cast as November 6 except:
Conductor: Schick
King ....Vichey
Amneris ....Rankin
Aida ....Tucci
Radames ....Corelli
Amonasro ....Bardelli
Ramfis ....Tozzi

March 21
ORFEO ED EURIDICE (Gluck)
Same cast as March 3 except:
Euridice ....Tucci

March 22
TOSCA (Puccini)
Same cast as October 27 except:
Tosca ....Albanese
Cavaradossi ....Corelli
Scarpia ....Cassel
Sacristan ....Flagello

March 23
RIGOLETTO (Verdi)
Same cast as January 4 except:
Conductor: Rich
Duke ....Formichini
Rigoletto ....MacNeil
Gilda ....Hurley
Sparafucile ....Giaiotti
Maddalena ....Dunn
Giovanna ....Ordassy
Monterone ....Sgarro
Borsa ....Franke
Countess ....Pracht

March 24 (matinee)
MACBETH (Verdi)
Same cast as February 24 except:
Malcolm ....Olvis
Warrior ....Reitan

March 24
LA GIOCONDA (Ponchielli)
Same cast as March 9 except:
Second Singer ....Marcella

March 26
ELEKTRA (R. Strauss)
Same cast as March 16 except:
Fifth Serving Woman ....Allen

March 27
LA FORZA DEL DESTINO (Verdi)
Same cast as December 12 except:
Leonora ....Milanov
Don Carlo ....Sereni
Don Alvaro ....Bergonzi
Padre Guardiano ....Tozzi
Preziosilla ....Wall
Trabucco ....Velis

March 28
TURANDOT (Puccini)
Same cast as November 4 except:
Conductor: Adler
Turandot ....Curtis-Verna
Timur ....Wildermann
Calaf ....Corelli
Liù ....Albanese
Ping ....Marsh
Pong ....Anthony
Mandarin ....Reitan

March 29
ORFEO ED EURIDICE (Gluck)
Same cast as March 3 except:
Euridice ....Tucci
Amore ....Allen

March 30 (matinee)
129th Metropolitan Opera
Guild Student Performance
LA TRAVIATA (Verdi)
Same cast as October 28 except:
Conductor: Behr
Violetta ....Coulter
Alfredo ....Carelli
Germont ....Reitan
Flora ....Pracht
Annina ....Blair
Giuseppe ....Hundley
Gardener ....Barbusci

March 30
L'ELISIR D'AMORE (Donizetti)
Same cast as October 30 except:
Adina ....Hurley
Nemorino ....Tagliavini
Belcore ....Testi
Giannetta ....Allen

March 31 (matinee)
LA GIOCONDA (Ponchielli)
Same cast as March 9 except:
La Gioconda ....Farrell
La Cieca ....Dunn
Singers ....Trehy, Marcella
Steersman ....Sliker

March 31
LA TRAVIATA (Verdi)
Same cast as October 28 except:
Conductor: Strasfogel
Violetta ....Tucci
Alfredo ....Morell
Germont ....Sereni
Annina ....Pracht
Giuseppe ....Zakariasen
Gardener ....Chistiakov

April 1
TOSCA (Puccini)
Same cast as October 27 except:
Tosca ....Price
Scarpia ....MacNeil
Sciarrone ....Marsh

April 2
MACBETH (Verdi)
Same cast as February 24 except:
Lady Macbeth ....Dalis
Malcolm ....Anthony
Warrior ....Reitan

April 3
ELEKTRA (R. Strauss)
Same cast as March 16 except:
Klytämnestra ....Resnik
Aegisth ....Liebl
Orest ....Meredith

April 4
LUCIA DI LAMMERMOOR
(Donizetti)
Same cast as November 26 except:
Conductor: Rich
Lucia ....Moffo
Edgardo ....Morell
Alisa ....Ordassy
Raimondo ....Scott

April 5
LA GIOCONDA (Ponchielli)
Same cast as March 9 except:
La Gioconda ....Farrell
Laura Adorno ....Elias
Alvise Badoero ....Hines
La Cieca ....Roggero
Enzo Grimaldo ....Tucker
Barnaba ....Sereni
Singers ....Trehy, Marcella
Steersman ....Sliker

April 6
UN BALLO IN MASCHERA (Verdi)
Same cast as January 25 except:
Conductor: Schick
Amelia ....Curtis-Verna
Ulrica ....Rankin
Oscar ....Hurley
Chief Justice ....Nagy
Servant ....Carelli

April 7 (matinee)
TOSCA (Puccini)
Same cast as October 27 except:
Tosca ....Price
Cavaradossi ....Corelli
Scarpia ....MacNeil
Sacristan ....Flagello

April 7
COSÌ FAN TUTTE (Mozart)
Same cast as October 24

April 16
LA GIOCONDA (Ponchielli)
Same cast as March 9 except:
La Gioconda ....Farrell
Laura Adorno ....Elias
Alvise Badoero ....Hines
Enzo Grimaldo ....Borso
Singers ....Trehy, Marcella
Steersman ....Sliker

April 17
LUCIA DI LAMMERMOOR
(Donizetti)
Same cast as November 26 except:
Conductor: Rich
Lucia ....d'Angelo
Edgardo ....Bergonzi
Alisa ....Ordassy
Raimondo ....Scott
Arturo ....Carelli

April 18
LA FANCIULLA DEL WEST
(Puccini)
Same cast as October 23 except:
Minnie ....Kirsten
Dick Johnson ....Konya
Jack Rance ....Cassel
Happy ....Hawkins
Larkens ....Reitan

April 19
ELEKTRA (R. Strauss)
Same cast as March 16 except:
Klytämnestra ....Resnik
Aegisth ....Liebl

April 20
ORFEO ED EURIDICE (Gluck)
Same cast as March 3 except:
Euridice ....Tucci
Amore ....Hurley

April 21 (matinee)
LA TRAVIATA (Verdi)
Same cast as October 28 except:
Alfredo ....Morell
Germont ....Sereni
Annina ....Pracht
Giuseppe ....Zakariasen
Gardener ....Chistiakov

April 21
MADAMA BUTTERFLY (Puccini)
Same cast as November 3 except:
B. F. Pinkerton ....Bergonzi
Sharpless ....Uppman
Suzuki ....Vanni
Kate Pinkerton ....Pracht
Imperial Commissioner ...Reitan
Registrar ....Kuestner

EXCERPTS FROM PRESS REVIEWS

REVIVAL OF Puccini's *La Fanciulla del West*, October 23, 1961

Puccini's *La Fanciulla del West* ... had not been in the vicinity of the Metropolitan since the 1931-32 season. For this occasion the production was borrowed from the Lyric Opera of Chicago, which had successfully revived the work a short time ago.

Last night's performance was brilliant. The Chicago sets, completely realistic, set the mood. Henry Butler, in his debut at the Metropolitan, staged the performance with skill, handling the crowd scenes deftly, making the best of the awkward situations in the libretto....

The three principals were splendid. Indeed, the entire cast was.... Leontyne Price acted well and sang beautifully, up to the soaring C's that dot the part. Richard Tucker ... sounded clear, even clarion, and he gave a convincing impersonation. The best acting of the evening, however, came from Anselmo Colzani as Jack Rance, the Sheriff. Aside from one or two typically Italianate gestures, he went through his part with all the aplomb of a heavy in a cowboy film. And vocally he did all that could have been desired.

Mr. Cleva not only worked well with his singers—that he always does—but he also brought a good deal of force and personality to his conducting. In this kind of repertory he is first-class. One could go so far as to say that he is one of the most underestimated conductors on the Metropolitan staff.—Harold C. Schonberg, *New York Times*

DEBUTS OF TERESA STICH-RANDALL and GEORGE SHIRLEY in *Così Fan Tutte*, October 24, 1961

Teresa Stich-Randall ... is a singer of extraordinary musicianship. The way she phrases, makes elisions, bends a little cadenza or negotiates a complicated bit of coloratura is just wonderful to hear. She has a fine voice that can soar, but it is a trifle cool and on rare occasion flutelike. The Met acquired in the Connecticut girl a remarkable artist.

Ferrando was sung by . . . George Shirley, who on short notice substituted for Charles Anthony. Mr. Shirley has a nicely rounded, warm tenor, not big but remarkably suave for someone so young. He acted well and gave the impression of a very promising artist.—Paul Henry Lang, *New York Herald Tribune*

DEBUTS OF INGRID BJONER, SÁNDOR KÓNYA and NORMAN MITTELMANN in *Lohengrin*, October 28, 1961

The most impressive of the three [debuts] was made by Ingrid Bjoner, a tall, slender and blonde Norwegian soprano who made a stunning Elsa. She has a warm, large, expertly produced voice. Her top tones were spread a bit in the first act, but the fuzziness disappeared thereafter as she sang with increasing beauty and brilliance.

There was a new Lohengrin as well, in the person of Sándor Kónya, a Hungarian tenor with an appealing stage presence and a lyric voice that he used mostly to fine effect. Only the occasional catches in his voice, mannered little sobs, marred his performance for me, and then only slightly.

The third debut singer was Norman Mittelmann, a Canadian baritone heard as the Herald, a part he sang and acted in an accomplished manner.—Douglas Watt, *New York Daily News*

DEBUT OF PHYLLIS CURTIN as Fiordiligi in *Così Fan Tutte*, November 4, 1961

Long a favorite at the City Center, Phyllis Curtin, the West Virginia-born soprano, showed every sign of becoming one at the Metropolitan Saturday afternoon. In her debut as Fiordiligi in Mozart's *Così Fan Tutte*, she proved once more that in voice and acting she is an artistic adornment to any company smart enough to negotiate for her services. Mistress of many styles, from the most classic to the most modern, she was the true Mozartean on Saturday, exquisite with word and note.—Louis Biancolli, *New York World Telegram and Sun*

DEBUT OF GALINA VISHNEVSKA-YA as Aida, November 6, 1961

Mme. Vishnevskaya, schooled in Russia and a member of the Bolshoi Opera Theater troupe, is on the short side but has the frame to support a big voice. It's fairly powerful, wide-ranged and facile, but the top notes and tone expansions are rather shrill. It's at its best when Mme. Vishnevskaya uses it with deliberate control, particularly in softer passages.

It is a voice that can be heard over an orchestra. The lower register is notably good in an era where chest tones are too often absent, or almost so. But for us it lacks color, the color that makes a great favorite.—Robert Coleman, *New York Daily Mirror*

DOROTHY KIRSTEN as Minnie in *La Fanciulla del West,* November 10, 1961

[Miss Kirsten's first Metropolitan Minnie] was well-routined, vocally and dramatically. Her voice warmed up as the evening went along, and it rang out effectively in the second act, with all its high-lying phrases, as it had not in the first act. But throughout there were many tender passages that she sang with loving care and a caressing tone.

The soprano's good looks worked against a convincing dramatic portrayal. With her slim figure, handsome features, beautifully marcelled blond hair and natty costume, she seemed like a fugitive from a dude ranch in an opera that is supposed to take place around 1850. . . . With respect to movement alone, Miss Kirsten acted intelligently and threw herself feverishly into the famous poker game with Jack Rance, winning an enthusiastic reception from the audience after the curtain fell.—Raymond Ericson, *New York Times*

DEBUTS OF RANDOLPH SYMO-NETTE and ERNST WIEMANN in *Lohengrin,* November 17, 1961

Mr. Symonette is a huge man, with a voice of similar size. It is not a particularly subtle voice, nor one of great beauty. But it is an impressive instrument nonetheless. He sang with accuracy and power, and invested his singing with intense villainy. His stage movements were something less than graceful, but since much of what

Telramund has to do consists in standing still, looking blackly and sounding evil, Mr. Symonette more than filled the bill.

Herr Wiemann made of King Henry a gentle, rather paternal figure. His voice is rich and it is filled with the accents of compassion. It sounded rather small in the vastness of the Metropolitan Opera House, however, and when it was forced it tended to wobble. —Alan Rich, *New York Times*

DEBUTS OF JOAN SUTHERLAND and SILVIO VARVISO in *Lucia di Lammermoor,* November 26, 1961

Joan Sutherland came, sang and conquered the Metropolitan Opera House in her awaited debut as Lucia. This mode of putting it means there was never much doubt of her ability to deliver Donizetti's music with distinction. But how it would sound in a theater that has devoured many another famous voice was something else. This, however, was quickly determined after her entrance aria in the Fountain Scene; broad, fluent, perfectly in pitch, fastidious in style, a treat to the ear and an incitement to the enthusiasm of the audience that filled every salable spot.

Thereafter it was a matter of sitting back to enjoy a superlative demonstration of vocalism. . . . This is a voice consistent in timbre through two octaves (E-flat to E-flat in this part) with scarcely a break—full, ringing and clear at the top, solid in the middle, viola-mellow at the bottom.

When it comes to character portrayal, however, Miss Sutherland has work to do. Prior to the Mad Scene she projected Lucia as a maid all sad of mien, cast over with a sense of tragedy to come, with a mid-century (nineteenth) slant of the body to compose her tall figure in an angular attitude of "suffering." For the Mad Scene she wore her auburn hair at shoulder length and a faraway look that searched out the cleverly contrived actions to fill the musical gaps with pantomime and movement. One especially apt incident accompanied an echo effect in the music, in which she turned her back to the audience, apparently listening (to herself). But all the artifice did not generate compulsion, develop conviction or magnetize the observer into involvement with anything but vocal virtuosity. . . .

Her entrance was accompanied . . . by the young Swiss-Italian [conductor] Silvio Varviso. There was nothing in the least old-fashioned about his treatment of the score except a virtuous attention to detail, a well-discriminated distribution of emphasis between stage and pit.—Irving Kolodin, *Saturday Review*

DEBUT OF JOHN ALEXANDER as Ferrando in *Così Fan Tutte,* December 19, 1961

Musically and dramatically, his performance showed the thorough ensemble spirit which marks the Metropolitan's current presentation of this perennially ingratiating operatic comedy. His voice combined good volume with prevailing musicianship and dynamic discretion, and apart from an occasionally spread upper note, his tones were firm and fluent and expressively evocative. His impersonation was also convincing from the visual point of view, both in humorous scenes and in his reaction to the news of his fiancée's temporary perfidy.—Francis D. Perkins, *New York Herald Tribune*

DEBUT OF GOTTLOB FRICK as Fafner in *Das Rheingold,* December 27, 1961

Mr. Frick . . . managed to display a strong voice of attractive quality that rang out with brilliance in the bass-baritone range. He may be a valuable asset to the company in more rewarding roles.—Ronald Eyer, *New York Herald Tribune*

PAUL KUEN as Mime in *Siegfried,* January 2, 1962

His brief appearance in *Rheingold* [debut as Mime, December 16, 1961] suggested that he has a voice of just the right timbre and flexibility for Mime, but his *Siegfried* characterization has to be seen to be fully appreciated. He is wholly at home in the suitable hovel provided for him in the Simonson setting, whether taunting Siegfried, rebuffing the Wanderer or busily brewing a meal for himself as visual counterpoint to the forging of Nothung. This is a virtuoso effort that proceeds from a real affection for the character and a range of dramatic resources wide enough to convey servile flattery (when the hero he has raised has killed the dragon) or abject terror (when he realizes he has overreached himself). — Irving Kolodin, *Saturday Review*

DEBUT OF MORLEY MEREDITH, as Lindorf, Coppélius, Dappertutto and Dr. Miracle in *Les Contes d'Hoffmann*, January 3, 1962

To portray the four sides of Hoffmann's evil genius calls for accomplishment in acting as well as in singing. [Meredith] met both demands successfully. As the performance progressed, he revealed stronger characterization and a high level of vocal attainment. His voice has quality and power, flexible enough to meet the various aspects of his assignment. . . . More sharpness in action, particularly in the final role, would increase the effectiveness of his acting.—Miles Kastendieck, *New York Journal-American*

DEBUT OF ANITA VÄLKKI as Brünnhilde in *Die Walküre*, January 23, 1962

[Miss Välkki] had a big, open tone that was full but true. There was plenty of projection and firm, heroic phrasing. It was a straight-forward Brünnhilde, solid and a little unyielding in character, but certainly impressive. In fact, as the performance went on, her singing grew stronger and more sensitive; the third act was a triumph. Miss Välkki showed the voice, range and the power of a first-class Wagnerian soprano. With a deeper sense of line and phrase, she will easily rank with the best of that rare species.—Eric Salzman, *New York Times*

NEW PRODUCTION of Verdi's *Un Ballo in Maschera* and DEBUT OF NELLO SANTI, January 25, 1962

On Thursday night the Metropolitan revived Verdi's *Un Ballo in Maschera*, once more in its original Swedish setting. . . . The new sets and costumes, by Ita Maximowna, were elaborate and expensive—very handsome 'in the last act, and, I am afraid, rather self-conscious and arty in the earlier ones. (Ulrica does her fortune-telling . . . beside what looked like an expressionist sculptor's conception of the pier at Atlantic City, suggesting a rather conspicuous . . . locale for such secret goings-on).

The artistic contributions that to me made the evening memorable were, in order of merit, Robert Merrill's magnificent and stylistically authentic singing as Renato; Carlo Bergonzi's somewhat light but very pleasing and elegant interpretation of Riccardo; the conducting of Nello Santi, a new Italian maestro, who is extremely efficient and whose musical ideas are at least very vigorous; Leonie Rysanek's forceful, distinctly erratic but now and then quite agreeable Amelia; and Jean Madeira's valiant struggles with the role of Ulrica, a fairly thankless one, demanding a great range and an enormous amount of stentorian tone and never, in my experience, letting its interpreter sound at her best. Anneliese Rothenberger was visually delectable but vocally just adequate as the page, Oscar.—Winthrop Sargeant, *The New Yorker*

DEBUT OF MARGHERITA ROBERTI as Floria Tosca, January 27, 1962

The young, Iowa-born [soprano] is a very handsome girl who has a dossier of fine performances behind her (primarily abroad) and who has sung this role before.

But it seemed to this reviewer that to finally sing "Vissi d'arte" at the glittering Met must have been an enormous strain on the lady's emotions. The fact is that Miss Roberti has a nice, big voice, not without luster, but one that, despite the nerves, lacks that singular quality of beauty that sets one singer's voice apart from all the rest. One detected splendid training, excellent diction and a genuine musical understanding. As for Floria Tosca, she is a woman of great depth and her emotions multi-faceted. Miss Roberti's portrayal, at least last Saturday, seemed alarmingly one-dimensional. — John Gruen, *New York Herald Tribune*

DEBUT OF JUDITH RASKIN as Susanna in *Le Nozze di Figaro*, February 23, 1962

Miss Raskin has proved to be an enchanting Susanna in performances with the New York City Opera, and her characterization has lost none of its delightful qualities in the move downtown. The soprano's fine-spun voice carried easily in the larger house, and she seemed so at ease in the Metro-

politan production as to be enjoying the evening.

Just the natural way she affectionately pushed Cherubino away when he buzzed around her indicated her complete identification with the part. Pretty as a picture, never forcing her musical phrases nor overplaying the comedy, enunciating the Italian like a veteran, Miss Raskin was as appealing a Susanna as the Metropolitan could wish for.—Raymond Ericson, *New York Times*

DEBUT OF LILI CHOOKASIAN as La Cieca in *La Gioconda*, March 9, 1962

The splendor of American contralto Lili Chookasian's voice as the blind old La Cieca was in direct contrast to the moth-eaten red canopy which was suspended above her in Act I of Ponchielli's *La Gioconda*. . . . Miss Chookasian, of Armenian descent and a pupil of Rosa Ponselle, was making her Met debut. She disclosed a rich quality, freely produced and equalized from top to bottom. Her voice was consistently beautiful, and in interpretation she made an affecting figure. She is a welcome addition to a roster more abundantly stocked with mezzos than altos.—Harriett Johnson, *New York Post*

DEBUT OF GERDA LAMMERS as Elektra, March 16, 1962

Gerda Lammers, who made her debut in the title role, is a fine artist with a very good voice, though it is not quite large enough for this fearful role. At times she gave the impression that she is holding back, or perhaps she is not used to such an immense theater as the Met. . . .

The voice is a clear soprano, basically more lyric than dramatic, and she turned some exquisite phrases. . . . At times the voice sailed beautifully above the roaring orchestra, at others it was somewhat swamped. Nor is her temperament exactly a dramatic temperament; in the great recognition scene her gestures were awkward, and the climactic scene lacked the scorching intensity it requires. But on the whole, Miss Lammers did well, and she should do even better if she can cast off her reserve.—Paul Henry Lang, *New York Herald Tribune*

NICOLAI GEDDA as Faust

LEONIE RYSANEK as Abigaille in *Nabucco*

GIULIETTA SIMIONATO as Azucena in
Il Trovatore

BARRY MORELL as Lt. B. F. Pinkerton in
Madama Butterfly

CORNELL MACNEIL as Nabucco

ANNA MOFFO as Manon

55

BIRGIT NILSSON as Isolde

JON VICKERS as Florestan in *Fidelio*

ANSELMO COLZANI as Sir John Falstaff

GABRIELLA TUCCI as Alice Ford in *Falstaff*

EILEEN FARRELL as Alcestis

EZIO FLAGELLO as the Maharajah in
The Last Savage

LEONTYNE PRICE as Leonora in *Il Trovatore*

FRANCO CORELLI as Calaf in *Turandot*

SÁNDOR KÓNYA as Walther von Stolzing in
Die Meistersinger

JOAN SUTHERLAND as Lucia di Lammermoor

JUDITH RASKIN as Anne in *Falstaff*

JAMES MCCRACKEN as Otello

57

RÉGINE CRESPIN as the Marschallin in
Der Rosenkavalier

JESS THOMAS as Lohengrin

GERAINT EVANS as Leporello in *Don Giovanni*

ELISABETH SCHWARZKOPF as Donna Elvira in
Don Giovanni

MIRELLA FRENI as Adina in *L'Elisir d'Amore*

NICOLAI GHIAUROV as Méphistophélès in *Faust*

1962-1963 SEASON

PERSONNEL
Male Artists
Aldridge, Erbert
Alexander, John
Alperstein, Max
Alvary, Lorenzo
Anthony, Charles
Bardelli, Cesare
Barioni, Daniele
Bergonzi, Carlo
Borso, Umberto
Carelli, Gabor
Caruso, Mariano
Cassel, Walter
Cehanovsky, George
Chistiakov, Vladimir
Colzani, Anselmo
Corelli, Franco
Corena, Fernando
D'Elia, Frank
Dembaugh, William
De Paola, Paul
De Paolis, Alessio
Dickie, Murray
Doench, Karl
Edelmann, Otto
Flagello, Ezio
Fliether, Herbert
Folmer, Joseph
Formichini, Dino
Franke, Paul
Gedda, Nicolai
Ghazal, Edward
Giaiotti, Bonaldo
Gilford, Jack
Guarrera, Frank
Harvuot, Clifford
Hawkins, Osie
Herbert, Ralph
Hines, Jerome
Konya, Sandor
Kuestner, Charles
Labo, Flaviano
Liebl, Karl
London, George
MacNeil, Cornell
Macurdy, John
Marcella, Lou
Marsh, Calvin
Mayreder, Rudolf
McCracken, James
Meredith, Morley
Merrill, Robert
Mittelmann, Norman
Morell, Barry
Nagy, Robert
Olvis, William
Patterson, Robert
Pechner, Gerhard
Peerce, Jan
Reitan, Roald
Roberts, Hal
Ruzdak, Vladimir
Schoeffler, Paul
Scott, Norman
Sereni, Mario
Sergi, Arturo

Sgarro, Louis
Shirley, George
Siepi, Cesare
Sliker, Peter
Stanz, William
Strang, Lloyd
Testi, Lorenzo
Thomas, Jess
Tomanelli, Carlo
Tozzi, Giorgio
Trehy, John
Tucker, Richard
Uppman, Theodor
Velis, Andrea
Vichey, Luben
Vickers, Jon
Walker, William
Wiemann, Ernst
Wiener, Otto
Wildermann, William
Zakariasen, William

Female Artists
Albanese, Licia
Amara, Lucine
Bjoner, Ingrid
Blair, Lynn
Brewer, Nadyne
Calabrese, Ada
Chookasian, Lili
Crespin, Régine
Curtis-Verna, Mary
Cvejic, Biserka
Dalis, Irene
D'Angelo, Gianna
Della Casa, Lisa
De Salvo, Dina
Di Franco, Loretta
Dobbs, Mattiwilda
Dunn, Mignon
Elias, Rosalind
Farrell, Eileen
Fercana, Mary
Gorr, Rita
Harper, Elinor
Hurley, Laurel
Jones, Lexi
Kabaivanska, Raina
Kirsten, Dorothy
Kriese, Gladys
Kuchta, Gladys
Madeira, Jean
Martin, Janis
Meyer, Kerstin
Milanov, Zinka
Miller, Mildred
Moffo, Anna
Munson, Pamela
Nilsson, Birgit
Ordassy, Carlotta
Parada, Claudia
Peters, Roberta
Pracht, Mary Ellen
Price, Leontyne
Rankin, Nell
Raskin, Judith
Resnik, Regina

Roggero, Margaret
Rothenberger, Anneliese
Rysanek, Leonie
Scovotti, Jeanette
Shawn, Dorothy
Simionato, Giulietta
Sims, Lilias
Soederstroem, Elisabeth
Steber, Eleanor
Stich-Randall, Teresa
Stratas, Teresa
Sutherland, Joan
Tebaldi, Renata
Thebom, Blanche
Töpper, Hertha
Tucci, Gabriella
Vanni, Helen
Votipka, Thelma

Ballet Soloists
Ames, Suzanne
Andrew, Thomas
Burdick, William
Chazin, Judith
Crosson, Craig
Eddington, Lawrence
Enckell, Thomas
Farrington, Hubert
Ferraro, Edilio
Heyes, Patricia
Hillyer, Jane
Horne, Katharyn
Jerell, Edith
Jones, Harry
Kapilow, Gloria
Keane, Audrey
King, Nancy
Kroon, Carole
Mahler, Donald
Martin, Carolyn
Meister, Hans
San Miguel, Lolita
Sayette, Howard
Sequoio, Ron
Warren, Marsha
Wilder, Joan
Wilder, Kenlin
Youskevitch, Igor

Conductors
Adler, Kurt
Ansermet, Ernest
Boehm, Karl
Cleva, Fausto
Maazel, Lorin
Rich, Martin
Rosenstock, Joseph
Santi, Nello
Schick, George
Schippers, Thomas
Solti, Georg
Strasfogel, Ignace
Varviso, Silvio

General Manager
Bing, Rudolf

59

1962-63

October 15 (Opening Night)
ANDREA CHENIER (Giordano)
Conductor: Cleva
Andrea Chénier	Corelli
Maddalena	Farrell
Countess di Coigny	Dunn
Carlo Gérard	Merrill
Bersi	Elias
Fléville	Cehanovsky
Abbé	Carelli
Madelon	Madeira
Mathieu	Alvary
Spy	Velis
Fouquier	Scott
Dumas	Hawkins
Roucher	Marsh
Schmidt	Reitan
Major domo	Strang

October 16
MADAMA BUTTERFLY (Puccini)
Conductor: Varviso
Cio-Cio-San	Kirsten
B. F. Pinkerton	Morell
Sharpless	Sereni
Suzuki	Roggero
Kate Pinkerton	Pracht
Goro	De Paolis
Yamadori	Cehanovsky
Uncle-Priest	Hawkins
Imperial Commissioner	Walker
Registrar	Alperstein
Cio-Cio-San's Child	Kapilow

October 17
AIDA (Verdi)
Conductor: Santi
King	Sgarro
Amneris	Gorr
Aida	Price
Radames	Bergonzi
Amonasro	Colzani
Ramfis	Giaiotti
Messenger	Nagy
Priestess	Vanni

October 18
DIE MEISTERSINGER (Wagner)
Conductor: Rosenstock
Hans Sachs	Wiener
Pogner	Flagello
Eva	Bjoner
Magdalene	Vanni
Walther	Konya
Beckmesser	Doench
Kothner	Mittelmann
Vogelgesang	Franke
Nachtigall	Marsh
Zorn	Velis
Eisslinger	Nagy
Moser	Carelli
Ortel	Reitan
Schwarz	Scott
Foltz	Sgarro
David	Dickie
Night Watchman	Harvuot

October 19
ANDREA CHENIER (Giordano)
Same cast as October 15

October 20
AIDA (Verdi)
Same cast as October 17

October 22
MADAMA BUTTERFLY (Puccini)
Same cast as October 16

October 23
DIE MEISTERSINGER (Wagner)
Same cast as October 18

October 24
FLEDERMAUS (J. Strauss)
Conductor: Varviso
Eisenstein	Uppman
Rosalinda	Soederstroem
Adele	Rothenberger
Ida	King
Alfred	Formichini
Orlofsky	Madeira
Dr. Falke	Guarrera
Frank	Reitan
Dr. Blind	Velis
Frosch	Gilford

October 25
ANDREA CHENIER (Giordano)
Same cast as October 15

October 26
AIDA (Verdi)
Same cast as October 17 except:
Amneris	Dalis
Radames	Borso

October 27 (matinee)
MADAMA BUTTERFLY (Puccini)
Same cast as October 16 except:
Sharpless	Harvuot
Cio-Cio-San's Child	K. Wilder

October 27
CAVALLERIA RUSTICANA (Mascagni)
Conductor: Cleva
Santuzza	Gorr
Lola	Elias
Turiddu	Morell
Alfio	Testi
Lucia	Chookasian

PAGLIACCI (Leoncavallo)
Conductor: Cleva
Nedda	Kabaivanska
Canio	Bergonzi
Tonio	Sereni
Beppe	Shirley
Silvio	Mittelmann
Villagers	Dembaugh, Tomanelli

October 29
AIDA (Verdi)
Same cast as October 17 except:
Aida	Amara
Priestess	Pracht

October 30
ANDREA CHENIER (Giordano)
Same cast as October 15 except:
Andrea Chénier	Borso
Carlo Gérard	Sereni

October 31
MADAMA BUTTERFLY (Puccini)
Same cast as October 16 except:
Sharpless	Harvuot

November 1
DON GIOVANNI (Mozart)
Conductor: Maazel
Don Giovanni	Siepi
Donna Anna	Steber
Donna Elvira	Tucci
Zerlina	Peters
Don Ottavio	Gedda
Commendatore	Wiemann
Leporello	Flagello
Masetto	Uppman

November 2
CAVALLERIA RUSTICANA (Mascagni)
Same cast as October 27
PAGLIACCI (Leoncavallo)
Same cast as October 27

November 3 (matinee)
DIE MEISTERSINGER (Wagner)
Same cast as October 18 except:
Pogner	Wiemann

November 3
FLEDERMAUS (J. Strauss)
Same cast as October 24 except:
Rosalinda	Kirsten

November 5
CAVALLERIA RUSTICANA (Mascagni)
Same cast as October 27 except:
Santuzza	Farrell

PAGLIACCI (Leoncavallo)
Same cast as October 27 except:
Canio	Borso
Tonio	Colzani

November 6
MADAMA BUTTERFLY (Puccini)
Same cast as October 16 except:
Cio-Cio-San	Amara
B. F. Pinkerton	Olvis
Suzuki	Dunn

November 7
DIE MEISTERSINGER (Wagner)
Same cast as October 18 except:
Pogner	Wiemann

November 8
DON GIOVANNI (Mozart)
Same cast as November 1

November 9
FLEDERMAUS (J. Strauss)
Same cast as October 24

November 10 (matinee)
ERNANI (Verdi)
Conductor: Schippers
Carlo ....MacNeil
Silva ....Hines
Elvira ....Price
Ernani ....Corelli
Don Riccardo ....Nagy
Jago ....Reitan
Giovanna ....Roggero

November 10
ANDREA CHENIER (Giordano)
Same cast as October 15 except:
Andrea Chénier ....Barioni
Maddalena ....Tucci
Carlo Gérard ....Sereni
Bersi ....Roggero
Madelon ....Chookasian
Schmidt ....Walker

November 12
DON GIOVANNI (Mozart)
Same cast as November 1

November 13
CAVALLERIA RUSTICANA
(Mascagni)
Same cast as October 27 except:
Santuzza ....Simionato
Lola ....Roggero
Turiddu .... Olvis
Alfio ....Cassel
PAGLIACCI (Leoncavallo)
Same cast as October 27 except:
Beppe ....Anthony

November 14
ERNANI (Verdi)
Same cast as November 10

November 15
FLEDERMAUS (J. Strauss)
Same cast as October 24 except:
Eisenstein ....Alexander
Adele ....Scovotti
Frank ....Harvuot

November 16
MADAMA BUTTERFLY (Puccini)
Same cast as October 16 except:
Cio-Cio-San ....Amara
B. F. Pinkerton ....Shirley
Sharpless ....Harvuot
Suzuki ....Dunn
Cio-Cio-San's Child ..K. Wilder

November 17 (matinee)
ANDREA CHENIER (Giordano)
Same cast as October 15 except:
Maddalena ....Milanov
Carlo Gérard ....Colzani
Bersi ....Roggero
Madelon ....Chookasian
Schmidt ....Walker

November 17
Benefit Mizrachi
Women's Organization
DON GIOVANNI (Mozart)
Same cast as November 1 except:
Don Giovanni ....London
Donna Anna ....Price

November 19
DER ROSENKAVALIER (R. Strauss)
Conductor: Maazel
Princess von Werdenberg.Crespin
Baron Ochs ....Edelmann
Octavian ....Töpper
Faninal ....Doench
Sophie ....Rothenberger
Marianne ....Votipka
Valzacchi ....Franke
Annina ....Elias
Police Commissioner ......Scott
Major domo of Princess ..Nagy
Major domo of Faninal ...Velis
Notary ....Pechner
Innkeeper ....Anthony
Singer ....Barioni
Orphans ....Calabrese, L. Jones,
Shawn
Milliner ....Fercana
Hairdresser ....H. Jones
Leopold ....Aldridge
Animal Vendor ....D'Elia
Blackamoor ....Warren
Lackeys ....Folmer, Trehy,
Marcella, Ghazal

November 20
AIDA (Verdi)
Same cast as October 17 except:
Amneris ....Simionato
Aida ....Amara
Radames ....Corelli
Amonasro ....Ruzdak
Ramfis ....Tozzi

November 21
ANDREA CHENIER (Giordano)
Same cast as October 15 except:
Andrea Chénier ......Bergonzi
Carlo Gérard ....Colzani
Bersi ....Roggero
Madelon ....Chookasian
Schmidt ....Walker

November 22
ERNANI (Verdi)
Same cast as November 10 except:
Giovanna ....Ordassy

November 23
DON GIOVANNI (Mozart)
Same cast as November 1 except:
Don Giovanni ....London
Zerlina ....Hurley

November 24 (matinee)
AIDA (Verdi)
Same cast as October 17 except:
Aida ....Curtis-Verna
Radames ....Labo
Amonasro ....Ruzdak
Ramfis ....Tozzi
Priestess ....Pracht

November 24
DER ROSENKAVALIER (R. Strauss)
Same cast as November 19 except:
Faninal ....Herbert
Singer ....Konya

November 25
IL BARBIERE DI SIVIGLIA (Rossini)
Conductor: Schippers
Almaviva ....Formichini
Dr. Bartolo ....Corena
Rosina ....Simionato
Figaro ....Merrill
Don Basilio ....Siepi
Berta ....Vanni
Fiorello ....Cehanovsky
Sergeant ....De Paolis
Ambrogio ....Mayreder

November 26
ERNANI (Verdi)
Same cast as November 10 except:
Silva ....Tozzi
Ernani ....Bergonzi
Giovanna ....Ordassy

November 27
DER ROSENKAVALIER (R. Strauss)
Same cast as November 19 except:
Faninal ....Herbert
Marianne ....Ordassy

November 28
IL BARBIERE DI SIVIGLIA (Rossini)
Same cast as November 25

November 29
DIE MEISTERSINGER (Wagner)
Same cast as October 18 except:
Hans Sachs ....-..Edelmann
David ....Anthony

November 30
PELLEAS ET MELISANDE (Debussy)
Conductor: Ansermet
Mélisande ....Moffo
Arkel ....Hines
Pelléas ....Uppman
Golaud ....London
Geneviève ....Thebom
Yniold ....Stratas
Physician ....Harvuot
Shepherd ....Walker

December 1 (matinee)
AIDA (Verdi)
Same cast as October 17 except:
Amneris ....Simionato
Aida ....Tucci
Radames ....Konya
Amonasro ....Merrill
Ramfis ....Siepi
Priestess ....Pracht

December 1
ERNANI (Verdi)
Same cast as November 10 except:
Silva ....Tozzi
Ernani ....Bergonzi
Giovanna ....Ordassy

61

1962-63

December 3
FLEDERMAUS (J. Strauss)
Same cast as October 24 except:
Eisenstein ....Alexander
Rosalinda ....Kirsten
Adele ....Peters
Ida ....Ames
Dr. Falke ....Meredith
Frank ....Harvuot

December 4
ANDREA CHENIER (Giordano)
Same cast as October 15 except:
Andrea Chénier ......Bergonzi
Countess di Coigny ....Roggero
Carlo Gérard ....Sereni
Madelon ....Chookasian
Mathieu ....Corena
Spy ....De Paolis
Schmidt ....Walker

December 5
DON GIOVANNI (Mozart)
Same cast as November 1 except:
Donna Anna ....Price
Donna Elvira ......Della Casa
Zerlina ....Hurley
Don Ottavio ....Anthony
Commendatore ....Wildermann
Leporello ....Corena
Masetto ....Marsh

December 6
PELLEAS ET MELISANDE (Debussy)
Same cast as November 30

December 7
DER ROSENKAVALIER (R. Strauss)
Same cast as November 19 except:
Faninal ....Herbert
Sophie ....Soederstroem
Marianne ....Ordassy
Singer ....Konya

December 8 (matinee)
CAVALLERIA RUSTICANA
(Mascagni)
Same cast as October 27 except:
Santuzza ....Dalis
Alfio ....Cassel
PAGLIACCI (Leoncavallo)
Same cast as October 27

December 8
Benefit Yeshiva University
Women's Organization
UN BALLO IN MASCHERA (Verdi)
Conductor: Santi
Gustav III ....Tucker
Anckarström ....Merrill
Amelia ....Rysanek
Ulrica ....Chookasian
Oscar ....Dobbs
Cristiano ....Marsh
Count de Horn ....Giaiotti
Count Warting ....Macurdy
Chief Justice ....Velis
Servant ....Nagy

December 10
PELLEAS ET MELISANDE (Debussy)
Same cast as November 30 except:
Pelléas ....Gedda

December 11
DIE MEISTERSINGER (Wagner)
Same cast as October 18 except:
Hans Sachs ....'.....Schoeffler
Walther ....Thomas
David ....Anthony

December 12
CAVALLERIA RUSTICANA
(Mascagni)
Same cast as October 27 except:
Santuzza ....Farrell
Lola ....Vanni
Turiddu ....Peerce
Alfio ....Cassel
PAGLIACCI (Leoncavallo)
Same cast as October 27 except:
Tonio ....Guarrera
Silvio ....Marsh

December 13
UN BALLO IN MASCHERA (Verdi)
Same cast as December 8 except:
Amelia ....Crespin
Cristiano ....Reitan

December 14
DER ROSENKAVALIER (R. Strauss)
Same cast as November 19 except:
Conductor: Strasfogel
Princess von Werdenberg
Della Casa
Faninal ....Herbert
Sophie ....Soederstroem
Marianne ....Ordassy
Singer ....Konya
Orphans ....Di Franco, Brewer,
De Salvo
Milliner ....Sims

December 15 (matinee)
AIDA (Verdi)
Same cast as October 17 except:
King ....Macurdy
Aida ....Amara
Amonasro ....Sereni
Ramfis ....Siepi

December 15
MADAMA BUTTERFLY (Puccini)
Same cast as October 16 except:
Conductor: Schick
Cio-Cio-San ....Price
B. F. Pinkerton ......Alexander
Sharpless ....Harvuot
Cio-Cio-San's Child ..K. Wilder

December 17
ANDREA CHENIER (Giordano)
Same cast as October 15 except:
Andrea Chénier ....Tucker
Maddalena ....Milanov
Countess di Coigny ....Roggero
Madelon ....Chookasian
Mathieu ....Corena

Spy ....Caruso
Schmidt ....Walker

December 18
FLEDERMAUS (J. Strauss)
Same cast as October 24 except:
Conductor: Rich
Eisenstein ....Alexander
Adele ....Hurley
Ida ....J. Wilder
Dr. Falke ....Meredith

December 19
LA TRAVIATA (Verdi)
Conductor: Santi
Violetta ....Moffo
Alfredo ....Morell
Germont ....Sereni
Flora ....Martin
Gastone ....Carelli
Baron Douphol ....Reitan
Marquis d'Obigny ..Cehanovsky
Dr. Grenvil ....Macurdy
Annina ....Blair
Giuseppe ....Kuestner
Gardener ....Sliker

December 20
DON GIOVANNI (Mozart)
Same cast as November 1 except:
Conductor: Schick
Donna Anna ....Price
Donna Elvira ......Della Casa
Zerlina ....Stratas
Commendatore ....Wildermann
Leporello ....Corena
Masetto ....Marsh

December 21
IL BARBIERE DI SIVIGLIA (Rossini)
Same cast as November 25 except:
Almaviva ....Shirley
Rosina ....Peters
Berta ....Roggero

December 22 (matinee)
DER ROSENKAVALIER (R. Strauss)
Same cast as November 19 except:
Faninal ....Herbert
Singer ....Konya
Orphans ....Di Franco, Brewer,
De Salvo
Milliner ....Sims

December 22
PELLEAS ET MELISANDE (Debussy)
Same cast as November 30 except:
Arkel ....Tozzi
Pelléas ....Gedda

December 24
CAVALLERIA RUSTICANA
(Mascagni)
Same cast as October 27 except:
Santuzza ....Farrell
Turiddu ....Tucker
PAGLIACCI (Leoncavallo)
Same cast as October 27 except:
Nedda ....Amara
Canio ....Borso
Silvio ....Marsh

December 25
DON GIOVANNI (Mozart)
Same cast as November 1 except:
Don Giovanni ....London
Donna Elvira ....Della Casa
Don Ottavio ....Peerce
Commendatore ....Wildermann
Leporello ....Corena
Masetto ....Reitan

December 26
AIDA (Verdi)
Same cast as October 17 except:
King ....Macurdy
Amneris ....Dalis
Radames ....Konya
Amonasro ....Mittelmann
Ramfis ....Tozzi
Priestess ....Martin

December 27
MADAMA BUTTERFLY (Puccini)
Same cast as October 16 except:
Suzuki ....Dunn
Goro ....Caruso
Uncle-Priest ....Macurdy
Cio-Cio-San's Child ..K. Wilder

December 28
DIE MEISTERSINGER (Wagner)
Same cast as October 18 except:
Hans Sachs ....Edelmann
Pogner ....Tozzi
Eva ....Amara
Walther ....Liebl
David ....Anthony

December 29 (matinee)
PELLEAS ET MELISANDE (Debussy)
Pelléas ....Gedda

December 29
ARIADNE AUF NAXOS (R. Strauss)
Conductor: Boehm
Major domo ....Meredith
Music Master ....Cassel
Composer ....Meyer
Bacchus ....Thomas
Officer ....Nagy
Dancing Master ....Franke
Wigmaker ....Reitan
Lackey ....Pechner
Zerbinetta ....d'Angelo
Ariadne ....Rysanek
Harlekin ....Uppman
Scaramuccio ....Velis
Truffaldin ....Flagello
Brighella ....Anthony
Najade ....Hurley
Dryade ....Kriese
Echo ....Scovotti

December 31
FLEDERMAUS (J. Strauss)
Same cast as October 24 except:
Eisenstein ....Alexander
Adele ....Peters
Ida ....Ames
Frank ....Harvuot

January 1
LA TRAVIATA (Verdi)
Same cast as December 19 except:
Germont ....Merrill
Flora ....Pracht

January 2
DER ROSENKAVALIER (R. Strauss)
Same cast as November 19 except:
Faninal ....Herbert
Marianne ....Ordassy
Singer ....Konya
Orphans ....Di Franco, Brewer,
                       De Salvo
Milliner ....Sims
Leopold ....Zakariasen

January 3
ARIADNE AUF NAXOS (R. Strauss)
Same cast as December 29

January 4
AIDA (Verdi)
Same cast as October 17 except:
Radames ....Thomas
Amonasro ....Sereni
Ramfis ....Hines
Priestess ....Martin

January 5 (matinee)
DIE MEISTERSINGER (Wagner)
Same cast as October 18 except:
Hans Sachs ....Edelmann
Eva ....Della Casa
David ....Anthony

January 5
IL BARBIERE DI SIVIGLIA (Rossini)
Same cast as November 25 except:
Almaviva ....Shirley
Rosina ....Peters
Figaro ....Guarrera
Berta ....Roggero
Fiorello ....Walker

January 7
DER ROSENKAVALIER (R. Strauss)
Same cast as November 19 except:
Baron Ochs ....Alvary
Faninal ....Herbert
Marianne ....Ordassy
Valzacchi ....De Paolis
Annina ....Dunn
Major domo of Faninal ..Carelli
Singer ....Morell
First Orphan ....Di Franco
Third Orphan ....De Salvo
Milliner ....Sims
Leopold ....Zakariasen

January 8
ERNANI (Verdi)
Same cast as November 10 except:
Carlo ....Sereni
Silva ....Tozzi
Giovanna ....Ordassy

January 9
UN BALLO IN MASCHERA (Verdi)
Same cast as December 8 except:
Amelia ....Nilsson
Cristiano ....Reitan
Count de Horn ....Wildermann
Chief Justice ....Franke

January 10
IL BARBIERE DI SIVIGLIA (Rossini)
Same cast as November 25 except:
Rosina ....Peters
Figaro ....Guarrera
Berta ....Roggero
Fiorello ....Walker

January 11
DER FLIEGENDE HOLLAENDER
                       (Wagner)
Conductor: Boehm
Daland ....Tozzi
Senta ....Rysanek
Erik ....Konya
Mary ....Chookasian
Steersman ....Shirley
Dutchman ....London

January 12 (matinee)
UN BALLO IN MASCHERA (Verdi)
Same cast as December 8 except:
Amelia ....Nilsson
Ulrica ....Madeira
Cristiano ....Reitan

January 12
LA TRAVIATA (Verdi)
Same cast as December 19 except:
Alfredo ....Alexander
Flora ....Pracht
Gastone ....Velis
Baron Douphol ....Marsh
Dr. Grenvil ....Sgarro

January 13
Benefit West Side
Institutional Synagogue
MADAMA BUTTERFLY (Puccini)
Same cast as October 16 except:
Cio-Cio-San ....Price
B. P. Pinkerton ....Konya
Sharpless ....Testi
Suzuki ....Dunn
Kate Pinkerton ....Martin
Cio-Cio-San's Child ..K. Wilder

January 14
DIE MEISTERSINGER (Wagner)
Same cast as October 18 except:
Hans Sachs ....Schoeffler
Pogner ....Wiemann
Eva ....Della Casa
Walther ....Thomas
Beckmesser ....Herbert
Kothner ....Patterson
David ....Anthony

January 15
UN BALLO IN MASCHERA (Verdi)
Same cast as December 8 except:
Renato ....Sereni
Amelia ....Nilsson
Cristiano ....Reitan
Count Warting ....Vichey

January 16
ARIADNE AUF NAXOS (R. Strauss)
Same cast as December 29 except:
Bacchus ....Konya
Zerbinetta ....Peters

January 17
DER ROSENKAVALIER (R. Strauss)
Same cast as November 19 except:
Princess von Werdenberg
                        Della Casa
Octavian ....Elias
Faninal ....Herbert
Marianne ....Ordassy
Valzacchi ....De Paolis
Annina ....Dunn
Singer ....Shirley
Orphans ....Di Franco, Munson,
                        De Salvo
Milliner ....Sims
Leopold ....Zakariasen

January 18
AIDA (Verdi)
Same cast as October 17 except:
King ....Macurdy
Amneris ....Rankin
Aida ....Nilsson
Radames ....Thomas
Amonasro ....Guarrera
Priestess ....Martin

January 19 (matinee)
DON GIOVANNI (Mozart)
Same cast as November 1 except:
Donna Anna ....Price
Donna Elvira ....Amara
Zerlina ....Hurley
Don Ottavio ....Peerce
Leporello ....Corena

January 19
DER FLIEGENDE HOLLAENDER
                        (Wagner)
Same cast as January 11 except:
Senta ....Crespin

January 21
Benefit Sponsored by the
Metropolitan Opera Guild for
the Production Fund
ADRIANA LECOUVREUR (Cilèa)
Conductor: Varviso
Adriana ....Tebaldi
Princess ....Dalis
Jouvenot ....Hurley
Dangeville ....Vanni
Maurizio ....Corelli
Abbé ....Franke
Michonnet ....Colzani
Prince de Bouillon ..Wildermann
Quinault ....Scott

Poisson ....Velis
La Duclos ....Keane
Major domo ....Trehy

January 22
ARIADNE AUF NAXOS (R. Strauss)
Same cast as December 29 except:
Music Master ....Schoeffler
Zerbinetta ....Peters
Ariadne ....Della Casa
Najade ....Pracht

January 23
DER FLIEGENDE HOLLAENDER
                        (Wagner)
Same cast as January 11 except:
Daland ....Wildermann
Erik ....Liebl

January 24
ERNANI (Verdi)
Same cast as November 10 except:
Carlo ....Sereni
Silva ....Tozzi
Giovanna ....Ordassy

January 25
ANDREA CHENIER (Giordano)
Same cast as October 15 except:
Conductor: Schick
Andrea Chénier ....Tucker
Maddalena ....Parada
Carlo Gérard ....Colzani
Bersi ....Roggero
Spy ....De Paolis
Dumas ....Sgarro
Roucher ....Reitan
Schmidt ....Walker

January 26 (matinee)
FIDELIO (Beethoven)
Conductor: Boehm
Don Fernando ....Flagello
Don Pizarro ....Meredith
Florestan ....Vickers
Leonore ....Nilsson
Rocco ....Wiemann
Marzelline ....Raskin
Jacquino ....Anthony
First Prisoner ....Shirley
Second Prisoner ....Marsh

January 26
DIE MEISTERSINGER (Wagner)
Same cast as October 18 except:
Hans Sachs ....Schoeffler
Pogner ....Tozzi
Eva ....Della Casa
Walther ....Thomas
Beckmesser ....Herbert
Kothner ....Patterson
David ....Anthony

January 28
ADRIANA LECOUVREUR (Cilèa)
Same cast as January 21

January 29
ARIADNE AUF NAXOS (R. Strauss)
Same cast as December 29 except:
Dancing Master ....Velis
Ariadne ....Della Casa
Scaramuccio ....Folmer
                (Prologue only)
Najade ....Pracht

January 30
TURANDOT (Puccini)
Conductor: Adler
Turandot ....Nilsson
Emperor Altoum ......De Paolis
Timur ....Giaiotti
Calaf ....Tucker
Liù ....Amara
Ping ....Guarrera
Pang ....Nagy
Pong ....Anthony
Servants ....Eddington,
                Crosson, H. Jones
Mandarin ....Marsh
Prince of Persia ....Ferraro
Executioners ....Sayette,
                Sequoio, Burdick

January 31
CAVALLERIA RUSTICANA
                        (Mascagni)
Same cast as October 27 except:
Conductor: Adler
Santuzza ....Curtis-Verna
Lola ....Miller
Alfio ....Meredith
PAGLIACCI (Leoncavallo)
Same cast as October 27 except:
Conductor: Adler
Nedda ....Stratas
Canio ....Vickers
Tonio ....Colzani
Silvio ....Marsh

February 1
ADRIANA LECOUVREUR (Cilèa)
Same cast as January 21 except:
Princess ....Cvejic
Prince de Bouillon ......Alvary

February 2 (matinee)
ARIADNE AUF NAXOS (R. Strauss)
Same cast as December 29 except:
Zerbinetta ....Peters

February 2
Benefit Vassar Club
Scholarship Fund
TURANDOT (Puccini)
Same cast as January 30 except:
Emperor Altoum ....Velis

February 4
LA TRAVIATA (Verdi)
Same cast as December 19 except:
Conductor: Adler
Violetta ....Albanese
Alfredo ....Alexander
Germont ....Ruzdak

February 5
ADRIANA LECOUVREUR (Cilèa)
Same cast as January 21 except:
Princess .... Cvejic

February 6
DER FLIEGENDE HOLLAENDER
(Wagner)
Same cast as January 11 except:
Senta .... Kuchta

February 7
FIDELIO (Beethoven)
Same cast as January 26 except:
Florestan .... Thomas
Leonore .... Rysanek

February 8
TRISTAN UND ISOLDE (Wagner)
Conductor: Solti
Tristan .... Liebl
Isolde .... Nilsson
King Marke .... Hines
Kurvenal .... Cassel
Brangäne .... Dalis
Melot .... Marsh
Steersman .... Sgarro
Shepherd .... Franke
Sailor's Voice .... Shirley

February 9 (matinee)
ADRIANA LECOUVREUR (Cilèa)
Same cast as January 21 except:
Princess .... Cvejic

February 9
DON GIOVANNI (Mozart)
Same cast as November 1 except:
Conductor: Rich
Don Giovanni .... London
Donna Anna ..... Stich-Randall
Donna Elvira .... Della Casa
Zerlina .... Hurley

February 11
TRISTAN UND ISOLDE (Wagner)
Same cast as February 8

February 12
DER FLIEGENDE HOLLAENDER
(Wagner)
Same cast as January 11 except:
Daland .... Wiemann

February 13
ADRIANA LECOUVREUR (Cilèa)
Same cast as January 21 except:
Princess .... Dunn

February 14
AIDA (Verdi)
Same cast as October 17 except:
Conductor: Schick
Amneris .... Cvejic
Aida .... Nilsson
Radames .... Labo
Amonasro .... Ruzdak
Ramfis .... Flagello
Priestess .... Pracht

February 15
FIDELIO (Beethoven)
Same cast as January 26 except:
Don Fernando .... Patterson
Don Pizarro .... Fliether
Leonore .... Kuchta

February 16 (matinee)
DER FLIEGENDE HOLLAENDER
(Wagner)
Same cast as January 11

February 16
UN BALLO IN MASCHERA (Verdi)
Same cast as December 8 except:
Conductor: Schick
Amelia .... Kuchta
Ulrica .... Cvejic
Oscar .... Hurley
Cristiano .... Reitan
Count de Horn .... Wildermann

February 17
TURANDOT (Puccini)
Same cast as January 30 except:
Calaf .... Corelli
Liù .... Albanese

February 18
DER FLIEGENDE HOLLAENDER
(Wagner)
Same cast as January 11 except:
Daland .... Wiemann

February 19
LA TRAVIATA (Verdi)
Same cast as December 19 except:
Conductor: Adler
Germont .... Ruzdak
Dr. Grenvil .... Sgarro

February 20
FIDELIO (Beethoven)
Same cast as January 26 except:
Don Fernando .... Patterson
Don Pizarro .... Fliether
Leonore .... Kuchta
Rocco .... Wildermann
Jacquino .... Franke

February 21
Benefit Sponsored by the
Metropolitan Opera Guild for the
Employees Welfare Fund and
the Guild's Education Program
LA SONNAMBULA (Bellini)
Conductor: Varviso
Amina .... Sutherland
Elvino .... Gedda
Rodolfo .... Tozzi
Lisa .... Scovotti
Teresa .... Chookasian
Alessio .... Macurdy
Notary .... Velis

February 22
TURANDOT (Puccini)
Same cast as January 30 except:
Turandot .... Curtis-Verna
Timur .... Flagello
Liù .... Albanese

February 23 (matinee)
TRISTAN UND ISOLDE (Wagner)
Same cast as February 8

February 23
ADRIANA LECOUVREUR (Cilèa)
Same cast as January 21 except:
Adriana .... Albanese
Princess .... Cvejic
Maurizio .... Morell
Major domo .... Tomanelli

February 25
UN BALLO IN MASCHERA (Verdi)
Same cast as December 8 except:
Conductor: Schick
Anckarström .... Ruzdak
Ulrica .... Dunn
Oscar .... Scovotti
Cristiano .... Reitan

February 26
TURANDOT (Puccini)
Same cast as January 30 except:
Timur .... Flagello
Calaf .... Labo
First Executioner .... Farrington

February 27
LA SONNAMBULA (Bellini)
Same cast as February 21

February 28
LA TRAVIATA (Verdi)
Same cast as December 19 except:
Conductor: Cleva
Violetta .... Albanese
Alfredo .... Labo
Germont .... Ruzdak
Dr. Grenvil .... Sgarro

March 1
FIDELIO (Beethoven)
Same cast as January 26 except:
Don Fernando .... Patterson
Don Pizarro .... Cassel

March 2 (matinee)
ANDREA CHENIER (Giordano)
Same cast as October 15 except:
Andrea Chénier .... Tucker
Maddalena .... Milanov
Carlo Gérard .... Colzani
Bersi .... Vanni
Madelon .... Chookasian
Spy .... De Paolis
Dumas .... Sgarro
Schmidt .... Walker

March 2
ARIADNE AUF NAXOS (R. Strauss)
Same cast as December 29 except:
Composer .... Miller
Bacchus .... Konya
Zerbinetta .... Peters
Ariadne .... Della Casa
Najade .... Pracht

March 4
LA SONNAMBULA (Bellini)
Same cast as February 21

65

1962-63

March 5
TURANDOT (Puccini)
Same cast as January 30 except:
Turandot .... Kuchta
Timur .... Wildermann
Calaf .... Labo
Liù .... Albanese
Ping .... Marsh
Mandarin .... Reitan

March 6
FIDELIO (Beethoven)
Same cast as January 26 except:
Don Fernando .... Patterson
Don Pizarro .... Cassel
Marzelline .... Hurley

March 7
LA SONNAMBULA (Bellini)
Same cast as February 21

March 8
ARIADNE AUF NAXOS (R. Strauss)
Same cast as December 29 except:
Composer .... Miller
Bacchus .... Konya
Officer .... Carelli
Zerbinetta .... Dobbs
Najade .... Pracht

March 9 (matinee)
IL BARBIERE DI SIVIGLIA (Rossini)
Same cast as November 25 except:
Conductor: Strasfogel
Almaviva .... Shirley
Rosina .... d'Angelo
Figaro .... Guarrera
Don Basilio .... Tozzi
Berta .... Roggero
Fiorello .... Walker

March 9
TRISTAN UND ISOLDE (Wagner)
Same cast as February 8 except:
Conductor: Rosenstock
Brangäne .... Dunn
Sailor's Voice .... Anthony

March 10
Benefit Sponsored by the
Metropolitan Opera Guild for the
Production Fund
OTELLO (Verdi)
Conductor: Solti
Otello .... McCracken
Desdemona .... Tucci
Iago .... Merrill
Emilia .... Dunn
Cassio .... Franke
Roderigo .... Velis
Lodovico .... Giaiotti
Montano .... Harvuot
Herald .... Reitan

March 11
FIDELIO (Beethoven)
Same cast as January 26 except:
Don Fernando .... Patterson
Don Pizarro .... Fliether
Leonore .... Kuchta

March 12
TURANDOT (Puccini)
Same cast as January 30 except:
Timur .... Wildermann
Calaf .... Konya
Liù .... Albanese
Ping .... Marsh
Pang .... Marcella
    (Acts II and III)
Mandarin .... Reitan
First Executioner .... Farrington

March 13
OTELLO (Verdi)
Same cast as March 10

March 14
LA SONNAMBULA (Bellini)
Same cast as February 21 except:
Elvino .... Formichini
Rodolfo .... Hines

March 15
UN BALLO IN MASCHERA (Verdi)
Same cast as December 8 except:
Conductor: Schick
Gustav III .... Labo
Anckarström .... Sereni
Amelia .... Nilsson
Ulrica .... Resnik
Oscar .... Scovotti
Cristiano .... Reitan
Count de Horn .... Wildermann
Servant .... Carelli

March 16 (matinee)
LA TRAVIATA (Verdi)
Same cast as December 19 except:
Conductor: Cleva
Violetta .... Tucci
Germont .... Merrill
Flora .... Pracht
Dr. Grenvil .... Sgarro

March 16
BORIS GODUNOV (Mussorgsky)
Conductor: Solti
Boris Godunov .... London
Fyodor .... Vanni
Xenia .... Blair
Nurse .... Chookasian
Shuiski .... Franke
Shchelkalov .... Walker
Pimen .... Flagello
Grigori .... Gedda
Marina .... Elias
Rangoni .... Cassel
Varlaam .... Corena
Missail .... Velis
Innkeeper .... Dunn
Officer .... Macurdy
Simpleton .... Shirley
Nikitich .... Sgarro
Boyar .... Carelli
Woman .... Harper
Mityukh .... Chistiakov
Khrushchov .... Stanz
Lavitski .... De Paola
Chernikovski .... Roberts

March 18
OTELLO (Verdi)
Same cast as March 10 except:
Roderigo .... Nagy

March 19 (matinee)
130th Metropolitan Opera Guild
Student Performance
IL BARBIERE DI SIVIGLIA (Rossini)
Same cast as November 25 except:
Conductor: Strasfogel
Almaviva .... Shirley
Dr. Bartolo .... Pechner
Rosina .... Miller
Figaro .... Sereni
Don Basilio ...... Wildermann
Berta .... Martin
Fiorello .... Walker
Ambrogio .... Sliker

March 19
LA SONNAMBULA (Bellini)
Same cast as February 21 except:
Elvino .... Formichini

March 20
BORIS GODUNOV (Mussorgsky)
Same cast as March 16 except:
Varlaam .... Alvary
Innkeeper .... Martin
Boyar .... Nagy
Chernikovski .... Zakariasen

March 21
TRISTAN UND ISOLDE (Wagner)
Same cast as February 8 except:
Sailor's Voice .... Anthony

March 22 (matinee)
131st Metropolitan Opera Guild
Student Performance
IL BARBIERE DI SIVIGLIA (Rossini)
Same cast as November 25 except:
Conductor: Strasfogel
Almaviva .... Shirley
Dr. Bartolo .... Pechner
Rosina .... Miller
Figaro .... Sereni
Don Basilio ...... Wildermann
Berta .... Martin
Ambrogio .... Sliker

March 22
LA TRAVIATA (Verdi)
Same cast as December 19 except:
Conductor: Cleva
Violetta .... Albanese
Germont .... Colzani
Flora .... Pracht

March 23 (matinee)
OTELLO (Verdi)
Same cast as March 10 except:
Emilia .... Martin
Roderigo .... Anthony

March 23
LA SONNAMBULA (Bellini)
Same cast as February 21 except:
Rodolfo .... Flagello

March 25
BORIS GODUNOV (Mussorgsky)
Same cast as March 16 except:
Boris Godunov .... Hines
Fyodor .... Roggero
Xenia .... Scovotti
Shchelkalov .... Harvuot
Pimen .... Tozzi
Grigori .... Sergi
Innkeeper .... Martin
Simpleton .... Anthony
Boyar .... Marcella
Mityukh .... Tomanelli

March 26 (matinee)
132nd Metropolitan Opera Guild
Student Performance
IL BARBIERE DI SIVIGLIA (Rossini)
Same cast as November 25 except:
Conductor: Rich
Dr. Bartolo .... Flagello
Rosina .... Vanni
Figaro .... Marsh
Don Basilio .... Macurdy
Berta .... Martin
Fiorello .... Reitan
Ambrogio .... Sliker

March 26
IL BARBIERE DI SIVIGLIA (Rossini)
Same cast as November 25 except:
Conductor: Strasfogel
Almaviva .... Shirley
Rosina .... d'Angelo
Figaro .... Sereni
Don Basilio .... Giaiotti
Berta .... Roggero
Fiorello .... Reitan

March 27
UN BALLO IN MASCHERA (Verdi)
Same cast as December 8 except:
Conductor: Schick
Gustav III .... Labo
Amelia .... Tucci
Ulrica .... Cvejic
Oscar .... Hurley
Cristiano .... Reitan
Count de Horn .... Wildermann
Count Warting .... Alvary
Servant .... Carelli

March 28 (matinee)
133rd Metropolitan Opera Guild
Student Performance
IL BARBIERE DI SIVIGLIA (Rossini)
Same cast as November 25 except:
Conductor: Rich
Almaviva ..... Anthony (Act I)
              Carelli (Acts II & III)
Rosina .... Vanni
Figaro .... Marsh
Don Basilio .... Macurdy
Berta .... Martin
Fiorello .... Walker
Ambrogio .... Sliker

March 28
ADRIANA LECOUVREUR (Cilèa)
Same cast as January 21 except:
Adriana .... Albanese
Maurizio .... Morell
Jouvenot .... Blair
Prince de Bouillon ..... Alvary
Major domo .... Tomanelli

March 29
BORIS GODUNOV (Mussorgsky)
Same cast as March 16 except:
Boris Godunov .... Tozzi
Fyodor .... Roggero
Xenia .... Scovotti
Shchelkalov .... Marsh
Pimen .... Hines
Grigori .... Olvis
Innkeeper .... Martin
Boyar .... Marcella
Lavitski .... Ghazal
Chernikovski .... Zakariasen

March 30 (matinee)
LA SONNAMBULA (Bellini)
Same cast as February 21 except:
Rodolfo .... Flagello

March 30
OTELLO (Verdi)
Same cast as March 10 except:
Emilia .... Martin
Roderigo .... Anthony
Lodovico .... Macurdy

April 1 (matinee)
134th Metropolitan Opera Guild
Student Performance
IL BARBIERE DI SIVIGLIA (Rossini)
Same cast as November 25 except:
Conductor: Rich
Rosina .... Scovotti
Figaro .... Marsh
Don Basilio .... Scott
Berta .... Martin
Fiorello .... Walker
Ambrogio .... Sliker

April 1
CAVALLERIA RUSTICANA
                    (Mascagni)
Same cast as October 27 except:
Santuzza .... Dalis
Lola .... Roggero
Turiddu .... Labo
Alfio .... Bardelli
PAGLIACCI (Leoncavallo)
Same cast as October 27 except:
Nedda .... Hurley
Canio .... McCracken
Silvio .... Reitan

April 2
LA SONNAMBULA (Bellini)
Same cast as February 21 except:
Rodolfo .... Hines

April 3
ADRIANA LECOUVREUR (Cilèa)
Same cast as January 21 except:
Adriana .... Albanese
Jouvenot .... Blair
Princess .... Cvejic
Maurizio .... Morell
Major domo .... Tomanelli

April 4
OTELLO (Verdi)
Same cast as March 10 except:
Desdemona .... Milanov
Emilia .... Martin
Roderigo .... Nagy
Lodovico .... Macurdy
Herald .... Walker

April 5 (matinee)
135th Metropolitan Opera Guild
Student Performance
IL BARBIERE DI SIVIGLIA (Rossini)
Same cast as November 25 except:
Conductor: Strasfogel
Almaviva .... Carelli
Rosina .... Scovotti
Figaro .... Reitan
Don Basilio .... Sgarro
Berta .... Kriese
Fiorello .... Walker
Sergeant .... Velis

April 5
MADAMA BUTTERFLY (Puccini)
Same cast as October 16 except:
Cio-Cio-San .... Albanese
B. F. Pinkerton .... Shirley
Sharpless .... Harvuot
Yamadori .... Reitan
Registrar .... D'Elia
Cio-Cio-San's Child .. K. Wilder

April 6 (matinee)
BORIS GODUNOV (Mussorgsky)
Same cast as March 16 except:
Boris Godunov .... Hines
Shchelkalov .... Marsh
Pimen .... Tozzi
Varlaam .... Alvary
Innkeeper .... Martin
Boyar .... Nagy
Lavitski .... Ghazal
Chernikovski .... Zakariasen

April 6
LA TRAVIATA (Verdi)
Same cast as December 19 except:
Conductor: Cleva
Violetta .... Tucci
Alfredo .... Labo
Marquis d'Obigny .... Sgarro
Annina .... Pracht

April 8 (matinee)
136th Metropolitan Opera Guild
Student Performance
IL BARBIERE DI SIVIGLIA (Rossini)
Same cast as November 25 except:
Conductor: Strasfogel
Almaviva . . . . Carelli
Dr. Bartolo . . . . Flagello
Rosina . . . . Hurley
Figaro . . . . Reitan
Don Basilio . . . . Sgarro
Berta . . . . Kriese
Fiorello . . . . Walker
Sergeant . . . . Velis

April 8
IL BARBIERE DI SIVIGLIA (Rossini)
Same cast as November 25 except:
Conductor: Rich
Rosina . . . . d'Angelo
Don Basilio . . . . Tozzi
Berta . . . . Roggero
Fiorello . . . . Walker

April 9
OTELLO (Verdi)
Same cast as March 10 except:
Desdemona . . . . Milanov
Iago . . . . Colzani
Emilia . . . . Martin
Roderigo . . . . Nagy
Lodovico . . . . Macurdy

April 10
LA TRAVIATA (Verdi)
Same cast as December 19 except:
Conductor: Cleva
Violetta . . . . Tucci
Marquis d'Obigny . . . . Sgarro
Annina . . . . Pracht

April 11
BORIS GODUNOV (Mussorgsky)
Same cast as March 16 except:
Boris Godunov . . . . Tozzi
Shchelkalov . . . . Marsh
Pimen . . . . Hines
Grigori . . . . Sergi
Marina . . . . Dunn
Innkeeper . . . . Martin
Boyar . . . . Nagy

April 12
LA SONNAMBULA (Bellini)
Same cast as February 21 except:
Rodolfo . . . . Flagello

April 13 (matinee)
FLEDERMAUS (J. Strauss)
Same cast as October 24 except:
Eisenstein . . . . Alexander
Rosalinda . . . . Kirsten
Adele . . . . Scovotti
Ida . . . . Ames
Frank . . . . Harvuot

April 13
ADRIANA LECOUVREUR (Cilèa)
Same cast as January 21 except:
Adriana . . . . Curtis-Verna
Jouvenot . . . . Blair
Major domo . . . . Tomanelli

EXCERPTS FROM PRESS REVIEWS

DEBUT OF RITA GORR as Amneris
in *Aida,* October 17, 1962

Miss Gorr is one of a relatively small clan of singers who are as much at home in Wagner as in Verdi. The voice is big enough, and certainly penetrating enough, to cope with the rigors of German opera. But it also has the flexibility and subtlety of inflection to join sinuously with the slave girl in the second-act duet in *Aida.*

While she is billed as a mezzo, her voice has a definite contralto hue and, to these ears, is best in its lower ranges. The top, while big and impressive, tends to become brassy. But you know there is a singer in the house. Her vast reserves of power can be felt, and she commands great dignity and aristocracy of style.—Ronald Eyer, *New York Herald Tribune*

NEW PRODUCTION of Wagner's *Die Meistersinger* and DEBUTS OF OTTO WIENER and MURRAY DICKIE, October 18, 1962

Everything was new about Wagner's *Die Meistersinger* last night at the Metropolitan Opera.

Most of the singers were new, and two of them—Otto Wiener as Hans Sachs and Murray Dickie as David—made their debuts on this occasion. Even certain elements of the score sounded new [for] Joseph Rosenstock, who conducted, opened many . . . cuts.

Robert O'Hearn designed the sets and costumes. The sets are among the most ambitious in Metropolitan history. Here the opera house has eschewed symbolism and presented a completely naturalistic *Meistersinger,* with St. Katherine's Church looking as though it is rooted in stone and marble, and with the streets of Nuremberg in the second act as solid as, well, the streets of Nuremberg. So confident was the Metropolitan in the strength of its scenery that it even had Mr. Dickie shinnying down the side of

Sachs' house to get at Beckmesser.

The third act opens with the interior of Sachs' house, for all the world a realization of a Dürer engraving. And the finale is played against a backdrop showing the city in the distance as the various guilds disport themselves on the Pegnitz meadows. The Metropolitan Opera has not in years had so stunning a production, and it is the kind of atmospheric production that *Die Meistersinger* needs.

As the new sets, so the performance—idiomatic, handsomely sung, full of style and tradition. Mr. Wiener was a most absorbing Sachs, young and virile-looking, the poet-philosopher and also man of action that Wagner intended.

His foil, Beckmesser, was sung by Karl Doench. Mr. Doench's characterization has previously been admired. His Beckmesser fully equals that of any singer who has attempted the role this last generation. It is completely rounded and subtle, with every detail worked out, and with plenty of voice to support the details.

Sándor Kónya sang Walther for the first time at the Metropolitan. In such a fine cast of specialists, his acting was a little primitive. But purely as a vocalist he sang the brightest Walther heard in many a year. . . .

Ingrid Bjoner, lovely in looks, was the Eva. She too was a fine stylist, and not even the slight wobble that afflicts her voice when she lets it out detracted from the finish of her conception. Mr. Dickie, a light-voiced tenor, as the role of David demands, gave a traditional performance: traditionally sung, with the usual exertion in the high notes, and traditionally acted, with swinging of arms . . . to suggest the adolescent.

Ezio Flagello sang Pogner for the first time, giving us a characterization that had warmth and style. And so on down the line. Helen Vanni was an admirable Magdalene, Norman Mittelmann an amusing . . . touching Kothner.

A special vote of thanks should go to Mr. Rosenstock, whose conducting had vitality and a good infusion of poetry. He is the kind of dependable musician who never is spasmodic, who is secure in the tradition of German opera and whose taste is impeccable. Thanks to him and the unusually fine body of singing musicians . . . New York has a *Meistersinger* that is the equal of that of any opera house in the world.—Harold C. Schonberg, *New York Times*

DEBUT OF RAINA KABAIVANSKA as Nedda in *Pagliacci*, October 27, 1962

[Miss Kabaivanska's] Nedda was exciting, partly for its unusual persuasiveness and partly as an augury for the kind of artist she should become. She is slim, dark and very pretty, so that in her scene as Colombina she looked doll-like. Yet her Nedda was a sensual, vital creature, who in the end became vulnerably pathetic. Miss Kabaivanska's lyric voice was sizable and clear, if a little cool, and her singing, with a few exceptions, was highly musical.—Raymond Ericson, *New York Times*

DEBUT OF LORIN MAAZEL, conducting *Don Giovanni*, November 1, 1962

Mr. Maazel had a tough assignment. Gifted young man that he is, he has much to offer. He showed more promise than achievement on this occasion, though he obviously knew the score and the style. He has yet to attain the orchestral refinement to match his sense of style and to impart dramatic inflection to his interpretation of the score.

His youthful bounce and crisp procedure had merit. Being a little too anxious, however, he stepped up the pace injudiciously at times and phrased too rigidly at others. —Miles Kastendieck, *New York Journal-American*

DEBUT OF JEANETTE SCOVOTTI as Adele in *Fledermaus*, November 15, 1962

A petite, neatly turned out young lady, Miss Scovotti kicked up her heels, showed a pretty leg and let loose with some fireworks that made you feel she was a real comer. Her voice is fresh, works best in high coloratura passages, but can also shift with ease to other registers. What is more, the tone has clarity and sweetness, and she can spin a phrase with delectable purity.—John Gruen, *New York Herald Tribune*

DEBUTS OF RÉGINE CRESPIN and HERTHA TÖPPER in *Der Rosenkavalier*, November 19, 1962

First things first. In Miss Crespin, the Metropolitan and *Der Rosenkavalier* have a singer worthy of the great tradition of the house and opera. . . . A rather

large and handsome woman, she proved a brilliant actress who handled herself with . . . finesse.

Her voice is extremely large, but as she sings the sound is never extended. . . . Lack of vibrato makes the voice tend a little toward coolness, but that does not mean there is no color in it. Miss Crespin . . . employed all kinds of delicate shading. The most unusual thing about the voice, though, was its absolute security. . . . She never had to slide into a note or grope for it, and was in complete command. And when she did let out, the voice soared over the orchestra and all over the house—big, confident, beautiful.

Miss Töpper proved a reliable singer, one well versed in the tradition of the opera. Her costuming was a bit against her. She has the figure of Octavian. Then why a second-act costume that emphasized her femininity? . . . But she is a strong singer, and a good musician besides, who worked well with the orchestra and her colleagues onstage. — Harold C. Schonberg, *New York Times*

DEBUT OF ERNEST ANSERMET, conducting *Pelléas et Mélisande*, November 30, 1962

The performance the other night owed most of its distinction to the conducting of Ernest Ansermet, a maestro who understands all the opera's subtleties but whose understanding never leads to forgetfulness of the grand line, as frequently happens with other conductors. His was an unusually vertebrate *Pelléas*, constructed with complete intellectual control from start to finish, and building to what in this work may be regarded as some pretty smashing climaxes. — Winthrop Sargeant, *The New Yorker*

DEBUT OF JESS THOMAS as Walther von Stolzing in *Die Meistersinger*, December 11, 1962

Everything about his bearing, poise and good routine sustained the reports that had preceded him from Germany. He also has a voice of size and quality, with an uncommonly flaring top for a performer of German roles. The timbre is a little harder, dryer than might be preferred, but it may be that his schooling in three R's of vocalism — ring, resonance and richness—will show itself in high degree next time.—Irving Kolodin, *Saturday Review*

METROPOLITAN PREMIERE of Richard Strauss' *Ariadne auf Naxos*, December 29, 1962

Offhand, one might think it was about time that this classic of operatic satire received a hearing at our foremost opera house. . . . The fact remains, however, that the Met is not the ideal place to hear it in. *Ariadne*'s intimate scale is such that the opera gets lost in so vast an auditorium, its chamber-music-size orchestra does not shine with quite the brilliance it has in smaller surroundings, and a good deal of its light-hearted comedy fails to come over the footlights.

Nevertheless, the production, with a tricky set by Oliver Messel and with the slapstick very much broadened by Carl Ebert, who directed it, was well worth attending, mainly because full stage presentations of *Ariadne* are seldom encountered hereabouts.

The opera within an opera, which is by far the finest part of the spectacle, was sung the other night in the original German, while the prelude was done in English, in a commendable translation by John Gutman. A host of characters—among them Morley Meredith as the Major-domo, Walter Cassel as the Music Master and Paul Franke as the Dancing Master —managed to project Mr. Gutman's text admirably, but regrettably not a syllable of the role that should dominate the episode—that of the Composer, here sung by Kerstin Meyer—was intelligible.

[In] the opera proper, things improved greatly. Leonie Rysanek made a presentable Ariadne, her voice being a little hollow here and there in the lower and middle registers but sufficiently loud and expressive at the top to fill the auditorium. Her three attendant nymphs—Laurel Hurley, Gladys Kriese and Jeanette Scovotti—sang their Rhinemaidenish roles beautifully. Gianna d'Angelo . . . sang Zerbinetta almost to perfection. . . . As her four male companions, Theodor Uppman, Andrea Velis, Ezio Flagello and Charles Anthony were amusing enough. Then there was the Bacchus of Jess Thomas. . . . He is a handsome young man and acts acceptably, by operatic standards. But the closing episode of *Ariadne* calls for a tenor who can trumpet in such a way as to introduce an aura of grandeur that lasts right up to the final curtain, and this is something that Mr. Thomas had neither the power nor the assured style to do.

Mr. Boehm is a conductor with good and less good points. He is, as far as I have been able to make out from repeated hearings, a soulful but not an overwhelmingly brilliant maestro. *Ariadne*, unfortunately, requires overwhelming brilliance—the sort of brilliance that makes horns and oboes seem to jump out of the pit and join the singers.—Winthrop Sargeant, *The New Yorker*

NEW PRODUCTION of Cilèa's *Adriana Lecouvreur*, January 21, 1963

Occasionally people forget an opera justifiably. If it received only two performances fifty years ago, the neglect might be considered well-founded. The revival of Cilèa's *Adriana Lecouvreur* at the Metropolitan on Monday night qualifies it as the kind of period piece that may not be worth all the attention given it in spite of the flutter of interest surrounding it.

Renata Tebaldi is of course chiefly responsible for its revival. Why the title role should appeal so much to her becomes a good question in the light of the present presentation. She has to share honors with at least three other singers. Though the story identifies the heroine with "the most celebrated actress of her day," the music is hardly memorable enough to make such a reference significant. . . .

Mme. Tebaldi is a thinner prima donna and at the moment quite a restrained one vocally. She resorts to a great deal of pianissimo singing, some of which is wholly ineffectual. Her studied gestures detract noticeably from her portrayal. Perhaps she considers the role type casting for her, but her first performance conveyed no such idea.

Franco Corelli has the requisite brilliance if not the suavity to hold his own beside Tebaldi, and . . . he has certainly gained artistic stature since last season. Irene Dalis as the Princess and Anselmo Colzani as Michonnet gave the most impassioned accounts of their roles, with Mr. Colzani supplying the only real characterization of the evening. . . . Silvio Varviso conducted acceptably. Nathaniel Merrill probably had some good ideas for the staging but encountered such independent ones among the principal singers as to be thwarted in his attempt to pull the story together.—Miles Kastendieck, *Christian Science Monitor*

NEW PRODUCTION of Bellini's *La Sonnambula*, February 21, 1963

When *La Sonnambula* was last given here, it was in a lightly embroidered version stitched by Lily Pons in her best petit point. By comparison, this is a Gobelin tapestry . . . that Miss Sutherland is offering, a tribute first to her artistry as a musician and second to a singer of bewitching facility. The order of importance is decreed by the taste and good sense with which the printed text is embellished by the optional ornaments traditional in the realization of such music. These are a collation, from traditional and other sources, by her husband-coach Richard Bonynge. This recovery of a lost art is not the least of the singular services Miss Sutherland presents in her Amina. Among the others, the demonstration that glossy ease and vocal virtuosity are not incompatible with the strength to run this exacting course ranks high.

Miss Sutherland's big frame and broad features are not the materials of pictorial illusion in this part, but she has worked hard to suggest lightness in action, as she has made it her serious concern to suggest "peril" in her walk across the bridge. . . . Her associates ranged from the distinguished effort of the always reliable Giorgio Tozzi as Rodolfo through the brave if sometimes labored one of Nicolai Gedda as Elvino. Whereas the former was settled comfortably into a range in which he could exploit his best skills, the latter was working act after act at a cruelly high part which only artistry and [power at the price of quality] brought within his compass. . . .

There is much more in praise of [the Swiss landscape] in Bellini's score than in Rolf Gérard's scenic design. The latter are among the most budget-conscious the Met has given us in some time, with prettified costumes more suitable for a revived *Song of Norway*. . . . Its lack of distinction is paralleled by the fussy posturing of Henry Butler's stage direction (simplicity would have been much preferable). I can understand the need to provide some enlivening ballet action during the choruses, but why such courtly, nonpastoral conceptions as Mattlyn Gavers'? All this, and Silvio Varviso, too, cannot dim the luster shed by Sutherland or lessen the conviction that what she is doing will be remembered in history.—Irving Kolodin, *Saturday Review*

NEW PRODUCTION of Verdi's *Otello*, March 10, 1963

In singing the title role in Verdi's *Otello* last night for the first time at the Metropolitan Opera, thirty-five-year-old, Indiana-born James McCracken has accomplished what is generally considered impossible. He left the Met in 1957 as its chief onstage tenor messenger and spear carrier and has returned in triumph in the title role of one of the greatest operas ever written.

True dramatic tenors these days are as rare as the ivory-billed woodpecker, and McCracken's debut marks him as probably, everything considered, the leading protagonist of the role in the world today. Herbert Graf gave the tenor his first chance at Otello in 1960 at the Zurich Opera, where he was general director. Since then he has sung the role more than fifty times, and now this looks like only the beginning. Graf himself was back at the Met last night, as director of the new production.

Georg Solti conducted with excitement and vitality the fast, dramatic portions, such as the opening storm scene. Where subtlety and poetry were required [however], as in the love duet of the first act, Solti manifested noticeable lack of color and heart.

Gabriella Tucci . . . has a voice that is essentially too lyric for [Desdemona], and she started out looking and acting more like a wispy Mélisande than the wife of the volcanic Moor. But her death scene in Act IV proved deeply touching, while she sang the "Ave Maria" with beauty, climaxed by a pianissimo high A-flat. Robert Merrill, a luscious-voiced Iago, . . . didn't begin to communicate the core of his twisted, poisonous depravity. Paul Franke was an excellent Cassio.

Eugene Berman's costumes were fussy and not always functional. Berman has designed an assortment of colorful costumes and startling headgear . . . which certainly indicate that fifteenth-century Cyprus under the Venetian and Turkish influence had independent thinkers, at least in dress. Among the evening's highlights was the powerful, decisive singing of Verdi's magnificent choruses.—Harriett Johnson, *New York Post*

1963-1964 SEASON

PERSONNEL

Male Artists

Aldridge, Erbert
Alexander, John
Alva, Luigi
Alvary, Lorenzo
Anthony, Charles
Bardelli, Cesare
Bergonzi, Carlo
Campora, Giuseppe
Carelli, Gabor
Caruso, Mariano
Cassel, Walter
Cehanovsky, George
Chistiakov, Vladimir
Christopher, Russell
Colzani, Anselmo
Cooke, Charles
Corelli, Franco
Corena, Fernando
Davidson, Lawrence
D'Elia, Frank
Dembaugh, William
De Paola, Paul
De Paolis, Alessio
Diakov, Anton
Diaz, Justino
Dickie, Murray
Doench, Karl
Dooley, William
Edelmann, Otto
Ernster, Dezso
Evans, Geraint
Ferrin, Agostino
Filip, Emil
Fischer, Stuart
Flagello, Ezio
Folmer, Joseph
Formichini, Dino
Franke, Paul
Frydel, John
Gedda, Nicolai
Ghazal, Edward
Ghitti, Franco
Giaiotti, Bonaldo
Gilford, Jack
Gobbi, Tito
Gorin, Igor
Graham, Arthur
Gramm, Donald
Guarrera, Frank
Harvuot, Clifford
Hemmerly, Walter
Herlea, Nicolae
Hines, Jerome
Hopf, Hans
Kirschberg, Arnold
Konya, Sandor
Kuestner, Charles
Labo, Flaviano
Liebl, Karl
London, George
MacNeil, Cornell
Macurdy, John
Marcella, Lou
Marsh, Calvin
McCracken, James
McLuckey, William

Meredith, Morley
Merrill, Robert
Mittelmann, Norman
Morell, Barry
Nagy, Robert
Patterson, Robert
Pechner, Gerhard
Peerce, Jan
Roberts, Hal
Ruzdak, Vladimir
Schoeffler, Paul
Scott, Norman
Sereni, Mario
Sergi, Arturo
Sgarro, Louis
Shirley, George
Siepi, Cesare
Simoneau, Leopold
Sliker, Peter
Smith, Kenneth
Stanz, William
Strang, Lloyd
Thomas, Jess
Tomanelli, Carlo
Tozzi, Giorgio
Trehy, John
Tucker, Richard
Uhde, Hermann
Uppman, Theodor
Velis, Andrea
Verreau, Richard
Walker, William
Ward, David
Wiemann, Ernst
Wildermann, William
Zakariasen, William

Female Artists

Amara, Lucine
Baldwin, Marcia
Bjoner, Ingrid
Blair, Lynn
Chookasian, Lili
Clements, Joy
Costa, Mary
Crespin, Régine
Curtis-Verna, Mary
Cvejic, Biserka
Dalis, Irene
D'Angelo, Gianna
Della Casa, Lisa
Dobbs, Mattiwilda
Dunn, Mignon
Elias, Rosalind
Farrell, Eileen
Fenn, Jean
Gorr, Rita
Gray, Maria
Grillo, Joann
Harshaw, Margaret
Hurley, Laurel
Jones, Junetta
Kabaivanska, Raina
Kirsten, Dorothy
Kriese, Gladys
Kuchta, Gladys
Love, Shirley
Madeira, Jean

Malagrida, Luisa
Martin, Janis
Meneguzzer, Jolanda
Milanov, Zinka
Miller, Mildred
Moffo, Anna
Nilsson, Birgit
Ordassy, Carlotta
Panni, Nicoletta
Pavek, Janet
Peters, Roberta
Pracht, Mary Ellen
Price, Leontyne
Rankin, Nell
Raskin, Judith
Resnik, Regina
Rothenberger, Anneliese
Rysanek, Leonie
Scovotti, Jeanette
Shawn, Dorothy
Soederstroem, Elisabeth
Stich-Randall, Teresa
Stratas, Teresa
Sutherland, Joan
Tebaldi, Renata
Thebom, Blanche
Thomaz, Neyde
Tucci, Gabriella
Vicos, Athena
Yeend, Frances

Ballet Soloists

Ames, Suzanne
Brayley, Sally
Collins, Eugene
Crosson, Craig
Ehrenberg, Miriam
Heyes, Patricia
Horne, Katharyn
Jerell, Edith
Jorgenson, Rhodie
Kroon, Carole
Mahler, Donald
Marritt, Naomi
Martin, Carolyn
Meister, Hans
Mihalic, Melanija
Oliver, Jess
Pourfarrokh, Ali
Sayette, Howard
Tol Padu, Khemfoia
Warren, Marsha

Conductors

Adler, Kurt
Allers, Franz
Behr, Jan
Bernstein, Leonard
Cleva, Fausto
Rich, Martin
Rosenstock, Joseph
Santi, Nello
Schick, George
Schippers, Thomas
Solti, Georg
Strasfogel, Ignace
Varviso, Silvio

General Manager

Bing, Rudolf

71

1963-64

October 14 (Opening Night)
AIDA (Verdi)
Conductor: Solti
King ....Macurdy
Amneris ....Dalis
Aida ....Nilsson
Radames ....Bergonzi
Amonasro ....Sereni
Ramfis ....Tozzi
Messenger ....Nagy
Priestess ....Pracht

October 15
DIE MEISTERSINGER (Wagner)
Conductor: Rosenstock
Hans Sachs ....Schoeffler
Pogner ....Flagello
Eva ....Della Casa
Magdalene ....Thebom
Walther ....Konya
Beckmesser ....Doench
Kothner ....Mittelmann
Vogelgesang ....Franke
Nachtigall ....Marsh
Zorn ....Velis
Eisslinger ....Nagy
Moser ....Carelli
Ortel ....Patterson
Schwarz ....Scott
Foltz ....Sgarro
David ....Dickie
Night Watchman ......Harvuot

October 16
LA BOHEME (Puccini)
Conductor: Cleva
Rodolfo ....Shirley
Marcello ....Marsh
Schaunard ....Harvuot
Colline ....Diakov
Mimi ....Kabaivanska
Musetta ....Gray
Benoit ....Corena
Parpignol ....Filip
Alcindoro ....Alvary
Sergeant ....Strang
Customs Officer ....Ghazal

October 17
MANON (Massenet)
Conductor: Schippers
Manon ....Moffo
Lescaut ....Guarrera
Des Grieux ....Gedda
Count des Grieux ....Tozzi
Poussette ....Scovotti
Javotte ....Baldwin
Rosette ....Grillo
Guillot ....De Paolis
Brétigny ....Walker
Innkeeper ....Patterson
Guards ....Kuestner, Tomanelli
Servant ....Vicos
Sergeant ....Stanz

October 18
DON GIOVANNI (Mozart)
Conductor: Rosenstock
Don Giovanni ....Siepi
Donna Anna ......Stich-Randall
Donna Elvira ....Amara

Zerlina ....Thomaz
Don Ottavio ....Simoneau
Commendatore ....Wiemann
Leporello ....Corena
Masetto ....Uppman

October 19
AIDA (Verdi)
Same cast as October 14

October 21
LA BOHEME (Puccini)
Same cast as October 16 except:
Benoit ....Pechner

October 22
AIDA (Verdi)
Same cast as October 14

October 23
RIGOLETTO (Verdi)
Conductor: Cleva
Duke ....Morell
Rigoletto ....MacNeil
Gilda ....d'Angelo
Sparafucile ....Giaiotti
Maddalena ....Elias
Giovanna ....Ordassy
Monterone ....Diaz
Marullo ....Marsh
Borsa ....Graham
Ceprano ....Patterson
Countess ....Clements
Page ....Blair
Guard ....Sliker

October 24
DIE MEISTERSINGER (Wagner)
Same cast as October 15 except:
Hans Sachs ....Edelmann

October 25
MANON (Massenet)
Same cast as October 17 except:
Des Grieux ....Shirley

October 26 (matinee)
LA BOHEME (Puccini)
Same cast as October 16 except:
Rodolfo ....Bergonzi
Benoit ....Pechner

October 26
DON GIOVANNI (Mozart)
Same cast as October 18

October 28
DIE MEISTERSINGER (Wagner)
Same cast as October 15 except:
Hans Sachs ....Edelmann
Night Watchman ....Diaz

October 29
RIGOLETTO (Verdi)
Same cast as October 23

October 30
MANON (Massenet)
Same cast as October 17 except:
Lescaut ....Ruzdak
Des Grieux ....Shirley

October 31
DON CARLO (Verdi)
Conductor: Solti
Philip II ....Hines
Don Carlo ....Tucker
Rodrigo ....Merrill
Grand Inquisitor .....Schoeffler
Elizabeth ....Kabaivanska
Princess Eboli ....Gorr
Theobald ....Baldwin
Count Lerma ....Carelli
Friar ....Diaz
Herald ....Nagy
Voice ....Jones
Countess Aremberg .....Brayley

November 1
AIDA (Verdi)
Same cast as October 14 except:
Aida ....Curtis-Verna
Amonasro ....Guarrera

November 2 (matinee)
DON GIOVANNI (Mozart)
Same cast as October 18

November 2
Benefit Mizrachi
Women's Organization
RIGOLETTO (Verdi)
Same cast as October 23 except:
Duke ....Peerce

November 4
AIDA (Verdi)
Same cast as October 14 except:
Amonasro ....Guarrera

November 5
RIGOLETTO (Verdi)
Same cast as October 23 except:
Conductor: Strasfogel
Duke ....Tucker
Maddalena ....Dunn

November 6
FAUST (Gounod)
Conductor: Cleva
Faust ....Campora
Marguerite ....Moffo
Méphistophélès ....Siepi
Valentin ....Sereni
Siébel ....Elias
Marthe ....Chookasian
Wagner ....Sgarro

November 7
DIE MEISTERSINGER (Wagner)
Same cast as October 15 except:
Hans Sachs ....Edelmann
Pogner ....Tozzi
Walther ....Liebl

November 8
DON CARLO (Verdi)
Same cast as October 31

November 9 (matinee)
LA BOHEME (Puccini)
Same cast as October 16 except:
Rodolfo ....Alexander
Schaunard ....Walker
Colline ....Giaiotti

Mimi ....Panni
Musetta ....Pavek
Benoit ....Davidson
Alcindoro ....Velis

November 9
MANON (Massenet)
Same cast as October 17 except:
Lescaut ....Ruzdak
Des Grieux ....Shirley
Count des Grieux ....Alvary

November 10
AIDA (Verdi)
Same cast as October 14 except:
Amonasro ....MacNeil
Ramfis ....Hines

November 11
FAUST (Gounod)
Same cast as November 6 except:
Faust ....Morell

November 12
DON GIOVANNI (Mozart)
Same cast as October 18 except:
Don Giovanni ....Tozzi
Donna Elvira ....Della Casa
Zerlina ....Scovotti
Commendatore ....Giaiotti
Leporello ....Flagello

November 13
DON CARLO (Verdi)
Same cast as October 31

November 14
GOETTERDAEMMERUNG (Wagner)
Conductor: Rosenstock
Siegfried ....Hopf
Brünnhilde ....Nilsson
Gunther ....Mittelmann
Gutrune ....Curtis-Verna
Alberich ....Pechner
Hagen ....Wiemann
Waltraute ....Dalis
Woglinde ....Pracht
Wellgunde ....Elias
Flosshilde ....Kriese
Norns ......Chookasian, Dunn,
                    Curtis-Verna
Vassals ......Dembaugh, Trehy

November 15
LA BOHEME (Puccini)
Same cast as October 16 except:
Rodolfo ....Bergonzi
Marcello ....Ruzdak
Schaunard ....Walker
Colline ....Giaiotti
Mimi ....Panni
Musetta ....Pavek
Benoit ....Davidson

November 16 (matinee)
RIGOLETTO (Verdi)
Same cast as October 23 except:
Conductor: Strasfogel
Sparafucile ....Flagello
Maddalena ....Dunn

November 16
Benefit Yeshiva University
Women's Organization
FAUST (Gounod)
Same cast as November 6 except:
Faust ....Peerce
Siébel ....Baldwin

November 18
DON GIOVANNI (Mozart)
Same cast as October 18 except:
Don Giovanni ....Hines
Donna Anna ....Kuchta
Donna Elvira ....Della Casa
Zerlina ....Scovotti
Don Ottavio ....Dickie
Commendatore ....Macurdy
Masetto ....Marsh

November 19
AIDA (Verdi)
Same cast as October 14 except:
Amneris ....Gorr
Ramfis ....Siepi

November 20
Benefit Sponsored by the
Metropolitan Opera Guild
for the
Metropolitan Opera Association
GALA PERFORMANCE
Celebrating the 50th Anniversary
of Giovanni Martinelli's
debut at the Metropolitan
Overture (La Forza del Destino)
Prologue (Pagliacci)
    MacNeil
Ah fors'è lui (La Traviata)
    d'Angelo
Nessun dorma (Turandot)
    Morell
Tacea la notte (Il Trovatore)
    Amara
Infelice (Ernani)
    Flagello
Suicidio (La Gioconda)
    Kabaivanska
Che gelida manina (La Bohème)
    Alexander
                Conductor: Cleva
Prelude (Carmen)
                Conductor: Rosenstock
Nemico della patria
    Merrill   (Andrea Chénier)
Un bel di vedremo
    Moffo   (Madama Butterfly)
Il lacerato spirito
    Tozzi   (Simon Boccanegra)
Amour, viens aider
    Gorr   (Samson et Dalila)
Salce, Salce; Ave Maria (Otello)
    Milanov
Piff! Paff! (Les Huguenots)
    Siepi
                Conductor: Schick

AIDA (Verdi) (Act II, Scene 2)
Same cast as October 14 except:
Conductor: Adler
Aida ....Curtis-Verna
Ramfis ....Giaiotti
[Editor's note: during a cere-
mony prior to the scene from
Aida, a group of Martinelli's col-
leagues—Mmes. Albanese, Bran-
zell, Bampton, Case, Miller, Mor-
gana, C. Ponselle, Sayao and Eva
Turner and Messrs. Bamboschek,
Brownlee, Chalmers, Chamlee,
Jagel and Sved—gathered onstage
to honor the tenor.]

November 21
RIGOLETTO (Verdi)
Same cast as October 23 except:
Gilda ....Scovotti
Maddalena ....Grillo

November 23 (matinee)
DIE MEISTERSINGER (Wagner)
Same cast as October 15 except:
Pogner ....Tozzi
Night Watchman ....Diaz

November 23
LA BOHEME (Puccini)
Same cast as October 16 except:
Rodolfo ....Tucker
Colline ....Siepi
Musetta ....Meneguzzer
Benoit ....Davidson

November 26
AIDA (Verdi)
Same cast as October 14 except:
Amneris ....Gorr
Ramfis ....Giaiotti

November 27
DON GIOVANNI (Mozart)
Same cast as October 18 except:
Don Giovanni ....Tozzi
Donna Elvira ....Della Casa
Don Ottavio ....Shirley
Commendatore ....Macurdy
Leporello ....Flagello
Masetto ....Marsh

November 28
FAUST (Gounod)
Same cast as November 6 except:
Faust ....Verreau
Marguerite ....Panni
Méphistophélès ....Hines
Valentin ....Ruzdak
Siébel ....Baldwin
Marthe ....Kriese

November 29
GOETTERDAEMMERUNG (Wagner)
Same cast as November 14 except:
Siegfried ....Liebl
Brünnhilde ....Kuchta
Alberich ....Davidson
Waltraute ....Gorr

73

November 30 (matinee)
FLEDERMAUS (J. Strauss)
Conductor: Allers

Eisenstein ....Franke
Rosalinda ....Kirsten
Adele ....Rothenberger
Ida ....Ames
Alfred ....Formichini
Orlofsky ....Madeira
Dr. Falke ....Guarrera
Frank ....Walker
Dr. Blind ....Carelli
Frosch ....Gilford

November 30
THE MAGIC FLUTE (Mozart)
Conductor: Varviso

Sarastro ....Siepi
Tamino ....Gedda
High Priest ....Cassel
Priest ....Carelli
Queen of the Night ....d'Angelo
Pamina ....Moffo
Ladies .....Pracht, Love, Kriese
Papageno ....Uppman
Papagena ....Scovotti
Monostatos ....Velis
Genii ....Jones, Baldwin, Grillo
Guards ....Nagy, Diaz
Slaves..D'Elia, Kuestner, Roberts

December 2
DON CARLO (Verdi)
Same cast as October 31 except:
Philip II ....Siepi
Don Carlo ....Labo
Princess Eboli ....Dalis
Herald ....Graham

December 3
LA BOHEME (Puccini)
Same cast as October 16 except:
Rodolfo ....Bergonzi
Marcello ....Ruzdak
Mimi ....Kirsten
Musetta ....Rothenberger
Benoit ....Pechner

December 4
GOETTERDAEMMERUNG (Wagner)
Same cast as November 14 except:
Gunther ....Cassel
Gutrune ....Yeend
Alberich ....Davidson
Hagen ....Ernster
Waltraute ....Gorr
First Norn ....Kriese
Third Norn ....Ordassy

December 5
LA SONNAMBULA (Bellini)
Conductor: Varviso

Amina ....Sutherland
Elvino ....Alexander
Rodolfo ....Tozzi
Lisa ....Scovotti
Teresa ....Martin
Alessio ....Macurdy
Notary ....Graham

December 6
DIE MEISTERSINGER (Wagner)
Same cast as October 15 except:
Pogner ....Wiemann
Magdalene ....Kriese
Eisslinger ....Roberts

December 7 (matinee)
AIDA (Verdi)
Same cast as October 14 except:
Amneris ....Gorr
Aida ....Price
Ramfis ....Siepi
Priestess ....Martin

December 7
FLEDERMAUS (J. Strauss)
Same cast as November 30 except:
Alfred ....Carelli
Dr. Blind ....Velis

December 9
THE MAGIC FLUTE (Mozart)
Same cast as November 30 except:
Sarastro ....Hines

December 10
LA SONNAMBULA (Bellini)
Same cast as December 5

December 11
IL TROVATORE (Verdi)
Conductor: Schippers

Leonora ....Price
Manrico ....Tucker
Count Di Luna ....Merrill
Azucena ....Dalis
Inez ....Martin
Ferrando ....Diakov
Ruiz ....Nagy
Gypsy ....Ghazal
Messenger ....Roberts

December 12
FLEDERMAUS (J. Strauss)
Same cast as November 30 except:
Rosalinda ....Fenn
Dr. Falke ....Meredith
Dr. Blind ....Velis

December 13
RIGOLETTO (Verdi)
Same cast as October 23 except:
Rigoletto ....Merrill
Gilda ....Meneguzzer
Sparafucile ....Flagello
Maddalena ....Grillo
Monterone ....Macurdy

December 14 (matinee)
GOETTERDAEMMERUNG (Wagner)
Same cast as November 14 except:
Waltraute ....Dunn

December 14
Benefit Sponsored by the
Metropolitan Opera Guild for the
Production Fund
LA TRAVIATA (Verdi)
Conductor: Schick

Violetta ....Sutherland
Alfredo ....Konya
Germont ....Sereni

Flora ....Martin
Gastone ....Carelli
Baron Douphol ....Walker
Marquis d'Obigny ..Christopher
Dr. Grenvil ....Diaz
Annina ....Blair
Giuseppe ....Marcella
Gardener ....De Paola

December 16
THE MAGIC FLUTE (Mozart)
Same cast as November 30 except:
High Priest ....Smith
Third Slave ....Frydel

December 17
DON CARLO (Verdi)
Same cast as October 31 except:
Conductor: Adler

Philip II ....Siepi
Don Carlo ....Labo
Grand Inquisitor ....Ernster
Elizabeth ....Curtis-Verna
Friar ....Macurdy

December 18
DIE MEISTERSINGER (Wagner)
Same cast as October 15 except:
Hans Sachs ....Edelmann
Pogner ....Wiemann
Eva ....Bjoner
Walther ....Liebl

December 19
IL TROVATORE (Verdi)
Same cast as December 11 except:
Count Di Luna ....Sereni
Gypsy ....Tomanelli

December 20
DON GIOVANNI (Mozart)
Same cast as October 18 except:
Donna Anna ....Bjoner
Zerlina ....Scovotti
Don Ottavio ....Peerce
Commendatore ....Diaz

December 21 (matinee)
MANON (Massenet)
Same cast as October 17 except:
Innkeeper ....Davidson

December 21
FAUST (Gounod)
Same cast as November 6 except:
Faust ....Morell
Marguerite ....Panni
Méphistophélès ....Hines
Valentin ....Mittelmann
Siébel ....Miller

December 23
LA SONNAMBULA (Bellini)
Same cast as December 5 except:
Rodolfo ....Macurdy
Teresa ....Chookasian
Alessio ....Sgarro

December 24
THE MAGIC FLUTE (Mozart)
Same cast as November 30 except:
Conductor: Strasfogel
Tamino ....Shirley
High Priest ....Meredith
Papageno ....Walker
Papagena ....Blair
Second Guard ....Sgarro

December 25
ARIADNE AUF NAXOS (R. Strauss)
Conductor: Varviso
Major domo ....Meredith
Music Master ....Cassel
Composer ....Stratas
Bacchus ....Konya
Officer ....Nagy
Dancing Master ....Franke
Wigmaker ....Christopher
Lackey ....Pechner
Zerbinetta ....Peters
Ariadne ....Kuchta
Harlekin ....Uppman
Scaramuccio ....Velis
Truffaldin ....Alvary
Brighella ....Anthony
Najade ....Pracht
Dryade ....Kriese
Echo ....Clements

December 26
IL TROVATORE (Verdi)
Same cast as December 11 except:
Leonora ....Malagrida
Azucena ....Gorr
Gypsy ....Tomanelli

December 27
LA SONNAMBULA (Bellini)
Same cast as December 5 except:
Amina ....d'Angelo
Lisa ....Clements
Teresa ....Chookasian

December 28 (matinee)
DON GIOVANNI (Mozart)
Same cast as October 18 except:
Donna Anna ....Kuchta
Zerlina ....Scovotti
Don Ottavio ....Peerce
Commendatore ....Giaiotti

December 28
LA TRAVIATA (Verdi)
Same cast as December 14

December 30
AIDA (Verdi)
Same cast as October 14 except:
Conductor: Adler
King ....Diaz
Amneris ....Gorr
Aida ....Price
Radames ....Labo
Amonasro ....London
Ramfis ....Giaiotti

December 31
FLEDERMAUS (J. Strauss)
Same cast as November 30 except:
Eisenstein ....Alexander
Alfred ....Carelli
Dr. Falke ....Meredith
Dr. Blind ....Velis

January 1
ARIADNE AUF NAXOS (R. Strauss)
Same cast as December 25

January 2
LA TRAVIATA (Verdi)
Same cast as December 14 except:
Alfredo ....Labo

January 3
THE MAGIC FLUTE (Mozart)
Same cast as November 30 except:
Sarastro ....Ward
Tamino ....Alexander
High Priest ....Meredith
Pamina ....Price
Papageno ....Walker
Papagena ....Blair
Monostatos ....Franke
First Genie ....Clements

January 4 (matinee)
FAUST (Gounod)
Same cast as November 6 except:
Faust ....Morell
Valentin ....Ruzdak
Siébel ....Martin
Marthe ....Kriese

January 4
RIGOLETTO (Verdi)
Same cast as October 23 except:
Conductor: Strasfogel
Duke ....Tucker
Rigoletto ....Merrill
Maddalena ....Dunn
Monterone ....Harvuot
Page ....Jones

January 5
Benefit West Side
Institutional Synagogue
GALA PERFORMANCE
LA TRAVIATA (Verdi) (Act I)
Same cast as December 14
Mad Scene; Fra poco a me
(Lucia di Lammermoor)
Sutherland, Tucker, Diakov
LA SONNAMBULA (Bellini)
(Act III)
Same cast as December 5 except:
Elvino ....Gedda
Teresa ....Chookasian

January 6
LA TRAVIATA (Verdi)
Same cast as December 14 except:
Violetta ....Costa
Alfredo ....Labo
Flora ....Baldwin
Marquis d'Obigny ...Cehanovsky

January 7
LA BOHEME (Puccini)
Same cast as October 16 except:
Conductor: Schick
Marcello ....Uppman
Colline ....Siepi
Mimi ....Amara
Musetta ....Meneguzzer
Benoit ....Pechner
Alcindoro ....Velis

January 8
LA SONNAMBULA (Bellini)
Same cast as December 5 except:
Conductor (Act III): Rich
Rodolfo ....Giaiotti
Lisa ....Clements

January 9
FAUST (Gounod)
Same cast as November 6 except:
Conductor: Strasfogel
Faust ....Morell
Marguerite ....Kirsten
Valentin ....Mittelmann
Siébel ....Miller
Marthe ....Kriese
Wagner ....Patterson

January 10
ARIADNE AUF NAXOS (R. Strauss)
Same cast as December 25 except:
Ariadne ....Amara
Truffaldin ....Gramm
Brighella ....Carelli

January 11 (matinee)
LA TRAVIATA (Verdi)
Same cast as December 14 except:
Alfredo ....Gedda
Flora ....Baldwin
Marquis d'Obigny ...Cehanovsky

January 11
DON CARLO (Verdi)
Same cast as October 31 except:
Conductor: Adler
Philip II ....Tozzi
Grand Inquisitor ....Ward
Elizabeth ....Curtis-Verna
Princess Eboli ....Cvejic
Friar ....Macurdy
Voice ....Clements

January 13
AIDA (Verdi)
Same cast as October 14 except:
Conductor: Adler
King ....Diaz
Amneris ....Cvejic
Aida ....Price
Radames ....Konya
Amonasro ....Ruzdak
Ramfis ....Macurdy

January 14
LA SONNAMBULA (Bellini)
Same cast as December 5 except:
Conductor: Rich
Amina ....d'Angelo
Elvino ....Gedda
Rodolfo ....Giaiotti

January 15
FLEDERMAUS (J. Strauss)
Same cast as November 30 except:
Conductor: Behr
Rosalinda ....Fenn
Eisenstein ....Uppman
Adele ....Hurley
Ida ....Kroon
Alfred ....Carelli
Frank ....Harvuot
Dr. Blind ....Velis

January 16
THE MAGIC FLUTE (Mozart)
Same cast as November 30 except:
Conductor: Strasfogel
Sarastro ....Ward
Tamino ....Alexander
Pamina ....Price
Papagena ....Blair
Monostatos ....Franke

January 17
LA TRAVIATA (Verdi)
Same cast as December 14 except:
Alfredo ....Labo
Flora ....Baldwin
Marquis d'Obigny ..Cehanovsky

January 18 (matinee)
IL TROVATORE (Verdi)
Same cast as December 11 except:
Ferrando ....Macurdy
Gypsy ....Tomanelli

January 18
ARIADNE AUF NAXOS (R. Strauss)
Same cast as December 25 except:
Conductor: Rich
Composer ....Miller
Zerbinetta ....Scovotti
Ariadne ....Amara
Truffaldin ....Gramm
Brighella ....Carelli

January 20
FLEDERMAUS (J. Strauss)
Same cast as November 30 except:
Conductor: Behr
Rosalinda ....Fenn
Eisenstein ....Uppman
Adele ....Hurley
Ida ....Kroon
Alfred ....Carelli
Dr. Blind ....Velis

January 21
LA TRAVIATA (Verdi)
Same cast as December 14 except:
Alfredo ....Tucker
Germont ....Ruzdak
Flora ....Baldwin
Marquis d'Obigny ...Cehanovsky

January 22
AIDA (Verdi)
Same cast as October 14 except:
Conductor: Adler
King ....Diaz
Amneris ....Cvejic
Aida ....Price
Radames ....Labo
Amonasro ....Guarrera
Ramfis ....Giaiotti

January 23
THE LAST SAVAGE (Menotti)
Conductor: Schippers
Maharajah ....Flagello
Maharanee ....Chookasian
Kodanda ....Gedda
Scattergood ....Meredith
Kitty ....Peters
Abdul ....London
Sardula ....Stratas
Learned Men .....Franke, Velis
Philosopher ....Harvuot
Composer ....Walker
Doctor ....Pechner
Protestant Pastor ....Marsh
Catholic Priest ......Patterson
Rabbi ....Aldridge
Orthodox Priest .....Dembaugh
Scientist ....Graham
Painter ....Marcella
Poet ....Carelli
Tailors .....Franke, Velis, Scott
Businesswoman ....Ordassy
Singer ....Martin
Woman ....Shawn
Major domo ....McLuckey

January 24
LA TRAVIATA (Verdi)
Same cast as December 14 except:
Alfredo ....Morell
Flora ....Baldwin
Dr. Grenvil ....Harvuot

January 25 (matinee)
THE MAGIC FLUTE (Mozart)
Same cast as November 30 except:
Tamino ....Shirley
Queen of the Night .....Peters
Pamina ....Amara
Papagena ....Blair
Monostatos ....Franke

January 25
IL TROVATORE (Verdi)
Same cast as December 11 except:
Leonora ....Malagrida
Manrico ....Labo
Azucena ....Cvejic
Ferrando ....Macurdy
Gypsy ....Tomanelli

January 26
AIDA (Verdi)
Same cast as October 14 except:
Conductor: Adler
King ....Diaz
Aida ....Price
Radames ....Labo
Amonasro ....Colzani

January 27
ARIADNE AUF NAXOS (R. Strauss)
Same cast as December 25 except:
Zerbinetta ....d'Angelo
Ariadne ....Bjoner
Bacchus ....Thomas
Truffaldin ....Gramm
Brighella ....Carelli

January 28
THE LAST SAVAGE (Menotti)
Same cast as January 23

January 29
AIDA (Verdi)
Same cast as October 14 except:
Conductor: Adler
King ....Diaz
Aida ....Amara
Radames ....Labo
Amonasro ....Colzani
Ramfis ....Hines
Messenger ....Franke

January 30
LA BOHEME (Puccini)
Same cast as October 16 except:
Rodolfo ....Morell
Marcello ....Uppman
Schaunard ....Walker
Colline ....Giaiotti
Mimi ....Amara
Musetta ....Hurley
Benoit ....Pechner
Alcindoro ....Velis

January 31
FAUST (Gounod)
Same cast as November 6 except:
Faust ....Gedda
Marguerite ....Kirsten
Méphistophélès ....London
Valentin ....Ruzdak
Wagner ....Patterson

February 1 (matinee)
LOHENGRIN (Wagner)
Conductor: Rosenstock
King Henry ....Wiemann
Lohengrin ....Konya
Elsa ....Crespin
Telramund ....Cassel
Ortrud ....Rankin
Herald ....Marsh
Nobles ......Stanz, Kirschberg,
            Trehy, Chistiakov

February 1
Benefit Bagby Music
Lovers' Foundation, Inc.
IL TROVATORE (Verdi)
Same cast as December 11 except:
Manrico ....Corelli
Count Di Luna ....Sereni
Azucena ....Cvejic
Inez ....Baldwin
Ferrando ....Macurdy

February 3
RIGOLETTO (Verdi)
Same cast as October 23 except:
Duke ....Alexander
Rigoletto ....Merrill
Gilda ....Dobbs
Maddalena ....Grillo

February 4
IL TROVATORE (Verdi)
Same cast as December 11 except:
Manrico ....McCracken
Count Di Luna ....Sereni
Azucena ....Dunn
Inez ....Baldwin
Ferrando ....Macurdy

February 5
LOHENGRIN (Wagner)
Same cast as February 1

February 6
LA SONNAMBULA (Bellini)
Same cast as December 5 except:
Conductor: Rich
Amina ....Peters
Elvino ....Gedda
Teresa ....Kriese
Alessio ....Sgarro

February 7
AIDA (Verdi)
Same cast as October 14 except:
Conductor: Adler
King ....Diaz
Amneris ....Rankin
Aida ....Amara
Radames ....Corelli
Ramfis ....Hines

February 8 (matinee)
THE LAST SAVAGE (Menotti)
Same cast as January 23

February 8
Benefit Vassar Club
Scholarship Fund
OTELLO (Verdi)
Conductor: Santi
Otello ....McCracken
Desdemona ....Rysanek
Iago ....Merrill
Emilia ....Martin
Cassio ....Alexander
Roderigo ....Nagy
Lodovico ....Wildermann
Montano ....Harvuot
Herald ....Patterson

February 10
LA TRAVIATA (Verdi)
Same cast as December 14 except:
Violetta ....Costa
Alfredo ....Alexander
Germont ....Gorin
Flora ....Baldwin
Marquis d'Obigny ...Cehanovsky
Dr. Grenvil ....Sgarro

February 11
LOHENGRIN (Wagner)
Same cast as February 1 except:
Telramund (Act I) ....Uhde
Ortrud ....Harshaw

February 12
OTELLO (Verdi)
Same cast as February 8 except:
Cassio ....Franke

February 13
AIDA (Verdi)
Same cast as October 14 except:
Conductor: Adler
King . ...Sgarro
Amneris ....Rankin
Aida ....Amara
Radames ....Corelli
Ramfis ....Macurdy

February 14
THE LAST SAVAGE (Menotti)
Same cast as January 23 except:
Maharajah ....Gramm
Abdul ....Cassel

February 15 (matinee)
OTELLO (Verdi)
Same cast as February 8 except:
Iago ....Colzani

February 15
EUGENE ONEGIN (Tchaikovsky)
Conductor: Schippers
Larina ....Kriese
Tatyana ....Price
Olga ....Elias
Onegin ....Dooley
Lenski ....Thomas
Prince Gremin ....Tozzi
Filippyevna ....Chookasian
Captain ....Sgarro
Zaretski ....Cehanovsky
Triquet ....Velis

February 17
LOHENGRIN (Wagner)
Same cast as February 1 except:
King Henry ....Hines
Lohengrin ....Sergi
Ortrud ....Dalis
Herald ....Dooley

February 18
OTELLO (Verdi)
Same cast as February 8 except:
Desdemona ....Milanov
Cassio ....Franke

February 19
EUGENE ONEGIN (Tchaikovsky)
Same cast as February 15

February 20
ARIADNE AUF NAXOS (R. Strauss)
Same cast as December 25 except:
Conductor: Rich
Composer ....Soederstroem
Zerbinetta ....d'Angelo
Ariadne ....Rysanek
Truffaldin ....Gramm
Brighella ....Carelli

February 21
IL TROVATORE (Verdi)
Same cast as December 11 except:
Leonora ....Tucci
Manrico ....Corelli
Count Di Luna ....Marsh
Azucena ....Rankin
Inez ....Baldwin
Ferrando ....Wildermann
Gypsy ....Tomanelli

February 22 (matinee)
RIGOLETTO (Verdi)
Same cast as October 23 except:
Duke ....Tucker
Rigoletto ....Merrill
Gilda ....Peters
Maddalena ....Dunn
Monterone ....Macurdy
Page ....Jones

February 22
THE LAST SAVAGE (Menotti)
Same cast as January 23 except:
Maharajah ....Gramm
Kitty ....Hurley

February 24
IL TROVATORE (Verdi)
Same cast as December 11 except:
Manrico ....Corelli
Count Di Luna ....Marsh
Inez ....Baldwin
Ferrando ....Wildermann
Gypsy ....Tomanelli

February 25
OTELLO (Verdi)
Same cast as February 8 except:
Otello ....Sergi
Desdemona ....Milanov
Emilia ....Dunn
Cassio ....Franke
Roderigo ....Carelli
Lodovico ....Macurdy
Herald ....Christopher

February 26
THE LAST SAVAGE (Menotti)
Same cast as January 23 except:
Maharajah ....Gramm
Kodanda ....Alexander

February 27
LOHENGRIN (Wagner)
Same cast as February 1 except:
King Henry ....Hines
Lohengrin ....Liebl
Ortrud ....Dalis
Herald ....Dooley
Nobles ......Cooke, Zakariasen,
Sliker, Frydel

February 28
OTELLO (Verdi)
Same cast as February 8 except:
Emilia ....Dunn
Cassio ....Franke
Roderigo ....Carelli
Lodovico ....Macurdy
Herald ....Christopher

February 29 (matinee)
EUGENE ONEGIN (Tchaikovsky)
Same cast as February 15

February 29
LA BOHEME (Puccini)
Same cast as October 16 except:
Rodolfo ....Corelli
Marcello ....Guarrera
Schaunard ....Walker
Colline ....Giaiotti
Mimi ....Tucci
Musetta ....Soederstroem
Alcindoro ....De Paolis

March 2
THE LAST SAVAGE (Menotti)
Same cast as January 23 except:
Maharajah ....Gramm
Kodanda ....Alexander

March 3
ARIADNE AUF NAXOS (R. Strauss)
Same cast as December 25 except:
Conductor: Rich
Composer ....Soederstroem
Bacchus ....Thomas
Officer ....Graham
Zerbinetta ....d'Angelo
Ariadne ....Rysanek
Scaramuccio ....Nagy
Truffaldin ....Gramm
Brighella ....Carelli

March 4
LOHENGRIN (Wagner)
Same cast as February 1 except:
King Henry ....Hines
Herald ....Walker
Nobles ......Cooke, Zakariasen,
Sliker, Frydel

March 5
EUGENE ONEGIN (Tchaikovsky)
Same cast as February 15 except:
Olga ....Grillo
Lenski ....Morell
Zaretski ....Walker
Triquet ....De Paolis

March 6
Benefit Sponsored by the
Metropolitan Opera Guild for the
Production Fund
FALSTAFF (Verdi)
Conductor: Bernstein
Sir John Falstaff ....Colzani
Ford ....Sereni
Fenton ....Alva
Dr. Caius ....Franke
Bardolph ....Velis
Pistol ....Scott
Mistress Ford ....Tucci
Anne ....Raskin
Dame Quickly ....Resnik
Mistress Page ....Elias

March 7 (matinee)
DON CARLO (Verdi)
Same cast as October 31 except:
Conductor: Adler
Philip II ....Tozzi
Don Carlo ....Corelli
Rodrigo ....Herlea
Grand Inquisitor ....Uhde
Elizabeth ....Rysanek
Princess Eboli ....Dalis

March 7
LA SONNAMBULA (Bellini)
Same cast as December 5 except:
Conductor: Rich
Amina ....Peters
Elvino ....Shirley
Rodolfo ....Giaiotti
Lisa ....Clements
Teresa ....Kriese
Alessio ....Sgarro

March 9
OTELLO (Verdi)
Same cast as February 8 except:
Desdemona ....Milanov
Iago ....Colzani

Emilia ....Dunn
Cassio ....Franke
Roderigo ....Carelli
Herald ....Christopher

March 10
LOHENGRIN (Wagner)
Same cast as February 1 except:
King Henry ....Hines
Lohengrin ....Thomas
Elsa ....Rysanek
Telramund ....Uhde
Ortrud ....Harshaw
Herald ....Walker
Nobles ......Cooke, Zakariasen,
Sliker, Frydel

March 11
CAVALLERIA RUSTICANA
(Mascagni)
Conductor: Santi
Santuzza ....Farrell
Lola ....Grillo
Turiddu ....Sergi
Alfio ....Bardelli
Lucia ....Ordassy
PAGLIACCI (Leoncavallo)
Conductor: Santi
Nedda ....Amara
Canio ....Corelli
Tonio ....Herlea
Beppe ....Ghitti
Silvio ....Marsh
Villagers ......Folmer, Strang

March 12
FALSTAFF (Verdi)
Same cast as March 6 except:
Sir John Falstaff ....Corena

March 13
EUGENE ONEGIN (Tchaikovsky)
Same cast as February 15 except:
Conductor: Strasfogel
Olga ....Grillo
Onegin ....Meredith
Lenski ....Morell
Zaretski ....Walker

March 14 (matinee)
LA BOHEME (Puccini)
Same cast as October 16 except:
Rodolfo ....Konya
Marcello ....Guarrera
Colline ....Hines
Mimi ....Tebaldi
Musetta ....Hurley

March 14
LOHENGRIN (Wagner)
Same cast as February 1 except:
Lohengrin ....Thomas
Elsa ....Rysanek
Telramund ....Uhde
Herald ....Walker
Nobles ......Cooke, Zakariasen,
Sliker, Frydel

March 16
FALSTAFF (Verdi)
Same cast as March 6 except:
Sir John Falstaff ....Corena
Dr. Caius ....Caruso

March 17
FAUST (Gounod)
Same cast as November 6 except:
Faust ....Alexander
Marguerite ....Amara
Méphistophélès ....Hines
Valentin ....Guarrera
Siébel ....Martin
Marthe ....Kriese
Wagner ....Patterson

March 18
OTELLO (Verdi)
Same cast as February 8 except:
Otello ....Sergi
Desdemona ....Milanov
Iago ....Colzani
Emilia ....Dunn
Cassio ....Franke
Lodovico ....Macurdy
Herald ....Christopher

March 19
MACBETH (Verdi)
Conductor: Santi
Macbeth ....MacNeil
Lady Macbeth ....Nilsson
Banquo ....Hines
Macduff ....Shirley
Malcolm ....Ghitti
Lady-in-Attendance .....Ordassy
Physician ....Pechner
Murderer ....Christopher
Warrior ....Walker
Bloody Child ....Blair
Crowned Child ....Clements
Manservant ....Ghazal
King Duncan ....Hemmerly

March 20
CAVALLERIA RUSTICANA
(Mascagni)
Same cast as March 11 except:
Turiddu ....Morell
Alfio ....Meredith
Lucia ....Chookasian
PAGLIACCI (Leoncavallo)
Same cast as March 11

March 21 (matinee)
FALSTAFF (Verdi)
Same cast as March 6 except:
Dr. Caius ....Caruso

March 21
OTELLO (Verdi)
Same cast as February 8 except:
Desdemona ....Milanov
Cassio ....Franke
Lodovico ....Ferrin
Herald ....Christopher

March 22
TOSCA (Puccini)
Conductor: Cleva
Tosca ....Tebaldi
Cavaradossi ....Corelli
Scarpia ....Gobbi
Angelotti ....Diaz
Sacristan ....Corena
Spoletta ....Caruso
Sciarrone ....Walker
Jailer ....Christopher
Shepherd ....Fischer

March 23
MACBETH (Verdi)
Same cast as March 19

March 24
EUGENE ONEGIN (Tchaikovsky)
Same cast as February 15 except:
Tatyana ....Amara
Olga ....Grillo
Onegin ....Meredith
Prince Gremin ....Macurdy

March 25
FALSTAFF (Verdi)
Same cast as March 6 except:
Sir John Falstaff ....Evans
Dr. Caius ....Caruso

March 26 (matinee)
137th Metropolitan Opera Guild
Student Performance
LA BOHEME (Puccini)
Same cast as October 16 except:
Conductor: Behr
Rodolfo ....Ghitti
Marcello ....Walker
Schaunard ....Patterson
Colline ....Diaz
Mimi ....Pracht
Musetta ....Clements
Benoit ....Pechner
Parpignol ....D'Elia
Alcindoro ....Caruso

March 26
TOSCA (Puccini)
Same cast as March 22 except:
Cavaradossi ....Morell

March 27
PARSIFAL (Wagner)
(Act III, Scene 1)
Conductor: Solti
Parsifal ....Thomas
Gurnemanz ....Hines
Kundry ....Baldwin
MESSA DA REQUIEM (Verdi)
Conductor: Solti
Soloists ....Price, Elias,
Bergonzi, Siepi

March 28 (matinee)
PARSIFAL (Wagner)
(Act III, Scene 1)
Same cast as March 27
MESSA DA REQUIEM (Verdi)
Same soloists as March 27

March 28
CAVALLERIA RUSTICANA
(Mascagni)
Same cast as March 11 except:
Santuzza ....Dalis
Lola ....Dunn
Turiddu ....Corelli
Lucia ....Chookasian
PAGLIACCI (Leoncavallo)
Same cast as March 11 except:
Canio ....McCracken
Silvio ....Walker

March 30 (matinee)
138th Metropolitan Opera Guild
Student Performance
LA BOHEME (Puccini)
Same cast as October 16 except:
Conductor: Behr
Rodolfo ....Ghitti
Marcello ....Walker
Colline ....Diaz
Mimi ....Pracht
Musetta ....Clements
Benoit ....Pechner
Parpignol ....D'Elia
Alcindoro ....Caruso

March 30
TOSCA (Puccini)
Same cast as March 22 except:
Angelotti ....Scott

March 31
EUGENE ONEGIN (Tchaikovsky)
Same cast as February 15 except:
Tatyana ....Amara
Onegin ....Guarrera
Prince Gremin ....Diaz

April 1
MACBETH (Verdi)
Same cast as March 19 except:
Lady Macbeth ....Dalis
Banquo ....Giaiotti
Macduff ....Morell

April 2 (matinee)
139th Metropolitan Opera Guild
Student Performance
LA BOHEME (Puccini)
Same cast as October 16 except:
Conductor: Adler
Rodolfo ....Ghitti
Marcello ....Harvuot
Schaunard ....Christopher
Colline ....Macurdy
Mimi ....Pracht
Musetta ....Clements
Benoit ....Pechner
Parpignol ....D'Elia
Alcindoro ....Caruso
Customs Officer ....Trehy

April 2
CAVALLERIA RUSTICANA
(Mascagni)
Same cast as March 11 except:
Santuzza ....Curtis-Verna
Lola ....Martin
Turiddu ....Corelli
Lucia ....Chookasian
PAGLIACCI (Leoncavallo)
Same cast as March 11 except:
Canio ....McCracken
Tonio ....Merrill
Beppe ....Shirley
Silvio ....Walker

April 3
FALSTAFF (Verdi)
Same cast as March 6 except:
Sir John Falstaff ....Corena
Dr. Caius ....Caruso

April 4 (matinee)
MACBETH (Verdi)
Same cast as March 19 except:
Lady Macbeth ....Dalis
Banquo ....Giaiotti
Macduff ....Morell

April 4
OTELLO (Verdi)
Same cast as February 8 except:
Desdemona ....Tebaldi
Iago ....Colzani
Lodovico ....Ferrin
Herald ....Christopher

April 6
EUGENE ONEGIN (Tchaikovsky)
Same cast as February 15 except:
Onegin ....Guarrera
Prince Gremin ....Giaiotti

April 7
FALSTAFF (Verdi)
Same cast as March 6 except:
Sir John Falstaff ....Evans
Dr. Caius ....Caruso

April 8 (matinee)
140th Metropolitan Opera Guild
Student Performance
LA BOHEME (Puccini)
Same cast as October 16 except:
Conductor: Adler
Rodolfo ....Ghitti
Marcello ....Walker
Schaunard ....Christopher
Colline ....Diaz
Mimi ....Pracht
Musetta ....Clements
Benoit ....Pechner
Parpignol ....D'Elia
Alcindoro ....Caruso
Customs Officer ....Trehy

April 8
TOSCA (Puccini)
Same cast as March 22 except:
Tosca ....Curtis-Verna
Scarpia ....MacNeil
Angelotti ....Scott
Spoletta ....Franke
Sciarrone ....Marsh
Jailer ....Patterson

April 9
OTELLO (Verdi)
Same cast as February 8 except:
Desdemona ....Tebaldi
Iago ....Colzani
Lodovico ....Ferrin

April 10
LA BOHEME (Puccini)
Same cast as October 16 except:
Rodolfo ....Morell
Marcello ....Guarrera
Schaunard ....Walker
Colline ....Macurdy
Mimi ....Tucci
Musetta ....Fenn
Alcindoro ....Caruso

79

April 11 (matinee)
CAVALLERIA RUSTICANA
(Mascagni)
Same cast as March 11 except:
Lola ....Miller
Turiddu ....Tucker
Lucia ....Chookasian
PAGLIACCI (Leoncavallo)
Same cast as March 11 except:
Tonio ....Colzani

April 11
MACBETH (Verdi)
Same cast as March 19 except:
Lady Macbeth ....Dalis
Banquo ....Giaiotti
Macduff ....Sergi

WORLD'S FAIR SEASON
April 27
FALSTAFF (Verdi)
Same cast as March 6 except:
Dr. Caius ....Caruso

April 28
MACBETH (Verdi)
Same cast as March 19 except:
Banquo ....Tozzi
Macduff ....Bergonzi
Bloody Child ....Pracht

April 29 (matinee)
141st Metropolitan Opera Guild
Student Performance
LA BOHEME (Puccini)
Same cast as October 16 except:
Conductor: Adler
Rodolfo ....Alexander
Marcello ....Harvuot
Schaunard ....Walker
Colline ....Diaz
Mimi ....Fenn
Musetta ....Clements
Benoit ....Pechner
Parpignol ....D'Elia
Alcindoro ....Velis
Customs Officer ....Trehy

April 29
DON GIOVANNI (Mozart)
Same cast as October 18 except:
Donna Anna ....Price
Donna Elvira ....Della Casa
Zerlina ....Peters
Don Ottavio ....Gedda
Commendatore ....Macurdy

April 30 (matinee)
142nd Metropolitan Opera Guild
Student Performance
LA BOHEME (Puccini)
Same cast as October 16 except:
Conductor: Adler
Marcello ....Walker
Schaunard ....Christopher
Colline ....Diaz
Mimi ....Hurley
Musetta ....Clements
Benoit ....Pechner
Parpignol ....D'Elia
Alcindoro ....Velis
Customs Officer ....Trehy

April 30
OTELLO (Verdi)
Same cast as February 8 except:
Desdemona ....Tebaldi
Emilia ....Dunn
Lodovico ....Macurdy
Herald ....Marsh

May 1
AIDA (Verdi)
Same cast as October 14 except:
Conductor: Varviso
King ....Diaz
Radames ....Corelli
Amonasro ....MacNeil
Ramfis ....Flagello

May 2 (matinee)
IL TROVATORE (Verdi)
Same cast as December 11 except:
Leonora ....Tucci
Count Di Luna ....Sereni
Azucena ....Gorr
Ferrando ....Macurdy

May 2
MANON (Massenet)
Same cast as October 17 except:
Guillot ....Caruso

May 3
LA SONNAMBULA (Bellini)
Same cast as December 5 except:
Rodolfo ....Hines
Teresa ....Chookasian
Alessio ....Sgarro

May 4
FALSTAFF (Verdi)
Same cast as March 6 except:
Sir John Falstaff ....:.Corena
Dr. Caius ....Caruso

May 5 (matinee)
143rd Metropolitan Opera Guild
Student Performance
LA BOHEME (Puccini)
Same cast as October 16 except:
Conductor: Adler
Rodolfo ....Alexander
Marcello ....Harvuot
Schaunard ....Christopher
Colline ....Macurdy
Mimi ....Hurley
Musetta ....Clements
Benoit ....Pechner
Parpignol ....D'Elia
Alcindoro ....Velis

May 5
CAVALLERIA RUSTICANA
(Mascagni)
Same cast as March 11 except:
Lola ....Dunn
Turiddu ....Tucker
Lucia ....Chookasian
PAGLIACCI (Leoncavallo)
Same cast as March 11 except:
Tonio ....Colzani

May 6
AIDA (Verdi)
Same cast as October 14 except:
Conductor: Varviso
King ....Diaz
Amneris ....Gorr
Radames ....Thomas
Amonasro ....MacNeil
Ramfis ....Hines

May 7
AIDA (Verdi)
Same cast as October 14 except:
Conductor: Varviso
Aida ....Price
Amonasro ....MacNeil
Ramfis ....Flagello

May 8
IL TROVATORE (Verdi)
Same cast as December 11 except:
Leonora ....Tucci
Manrico ....Corelli
Azucena ....Resnik
Ferrando ....Wildermann
Gypsy ....Tomanelli

May 9 (matinee)
OTELLO (Verdi)
Same cast as February 8 except:
Desdemona ....Tebaldi
Iago ....Colzani
Emilia ....Dunn
Lodovico ....Diaz
Herald ....Marsh

May 9
LA SONNAMBULA (Bellini)
Same cast as December 5 except:
Elvino ....Gedda
Teresa ....Kriese
Alessio ....Sgarro

May 10 (matinee)
DON GIOVANNI (Mozart)
Same cast as October 18 except:
Donna Anna ....Price
Donna Elvira ....Della Casa
Zerlina ....Peters
Don Ottavio ....Alva
Commendatore ....Diaz
Leporello ....Flagello

EXCERPTS FROM PRESS REVIEWS

NEW PRODUCTION of Verdi's
Aida, October 14, 1963

The Met has a new production
of *Aida* on its hands, and it's a
dandy. The evening was full of
stars, and some were of the first
magnitude, but they were all out-
shone by Robert O'Hearn, the
young man who designed this new
production, and Nathaniel Merrill,

0

the director who filled it full of action.

By the time the singing begins we are face to face with a magnificent expansion of yellows and crimson that seems to extend from Broadway right up to the banks of the Nile. Later on there is an equally sumptuous temple. . . . For the Triumphal Scene the stage once again extends back to infinity, the colors turn to browns, orange and gold. . . . The Nile Scene . . . looks for once like the bank of a river, and its moon looks like a moon. Mr. O'Hearn has operated from the basis of the music. His sets look the way *Aida* sounds, and that makes his achievement all the more impressive. Mr. Merrill knows what he is doing, too; his groupings make strong dramatic sense, and they avoid beautifully the fearful symmetry that many directors settle for these days.

There was much to hear, too, and most of it was superb. Georg Solti conducted a taut, alert performance that brought out lines in the orchestra that are usually submerged in mud, and [he] balanced beautifully the sounds in the pit with the sounds onstage. Birgit Nilsson was in her very best form . . . and cut through the ensemble with searing accuracy. . . . Carlo Bergonzi, whose voice is not in itself an absorbing instrument, was nevertheless able to demonstrate in his singing the way to make a Verdian line touch the heart. . . . Irene Dalis, the Amneris, and Mario Sereni, the Amonasro, were up to their usual dependable level, but no further.—Alan Rich, *New York Herald Tribune*

NEW PRODUCTION of Massenet's *Manon*, October 17, 1963

The Metropolitan last night came up with a new production of Massenet's *Manon* and perhaps demonstrated why Mr. Bing approaches French opera with caution. The Metropolitan could and did provide the external trappings —costumes, scenery, direction. But when it came to the important element—singing in the French style —there was a dull thud, accompanied by faint ectoplasmic shrieks of protest from Mary Garden and Maggie Teyte.

Aside from a shabby second-act set, the production was colorful and evocative. Renoir-like pastel shadings predominated, and the Cours la Reine scene, with colored balloons and trees, was especially successful. That scene, too, was

helped by Alicia Markova's stylish choreography.

The direction, too, was for the most part excellent. Günther Rennert's staging was direct and clear, except for those few moments when he carried on with transparent scrims. . . . In the second act, the maid serving dinner goes out the door with a tray. At the end of the act, the whole set becomes transparent . . . and the door through which the maid disappeared is seen facing the street.

Manon . . . needs above all two things: elegance of style and sensuousness of voice. Neither was much in evidence last night. Nicolai Gedda could not seem to unblock himself. When he used a forte attack . . . he sounded strained; when he sang pianissimo . . . there was none of the caressing sound so necessary to ["Le Rêve"]. Much the same could be said of Anna Moffo in the title role. She was as lovely-looking a Manon as the Metropolitan stage has ever contained. But she had little success floating a line or shading a phrase. . . .

The most stylish singing came in those few moments Giorgio Tozzi, as the Count des Grieux, was onstage. Here, at least, was the sonorous sound and smooth vocalism lacking everywhere else.

Thomas Schippers, who conducted, displayed little stylistic empathy in his noisy approach to the score. And the orchestra distinguished itself by some alarmingly out-of-tune playing.—Harold C. Schonberg, *New York Times*

DEBUTS OF LÉOPOLD SIMONEAU and NEYDE THOMAZ in *Don Giovanni*, October 18, 1963

It is indeed a great pleasure to welcome the Canadian tenor Léopold Simoneau to the company. . . . As Don Ottavio, he brought the vocal finesse and stylistic elegance so necessary to the role. Furthermore, he merged the tenor's two famous arias with the performance more skillfully than most tenors have. . . .

Making her debut as Zerlina, Neyde Thomaz of Brazil found herself in excellent company, including Cesare Siepi as the Don, who found Zerlina more than usually attractive on this occasion. She succumbed, at first revealing a somewhat small but fresh, sweet voice.—Miles Kastendieck, *New York Journal-American*

DEBUT OF DAVID WARD as Sarastro in *The Magic Flute*, January 3, 1964

When he had adjusted himself to his surroundings, [David] Ward demonstrated not merely a sonorous voice, with a secure cushion on the low F required for "O Isis and Osiris," but also the authority and musicianship to make the sounds meaningful. As an exhilarating plus, he spoke the English text as well as he sang the notes, which is to say better than anyone else in the cast.—Irving Kolodin, *Saturday Review*

DEBUT OF MARY COSTA as Violetta in *La Traviata*, January 6, 1964

A dazzling blonde named Mary Costa, a Knoxville, Tennessee, girl who sold cars on a non-singing television commercial only short years ago, last night made it all the way to the Metropolitan Opera.

It was a pleasure to gaze upon the vivacious Miss Costa, wearing her own stunning white ball gown in the first-act party scene, and it turned out to be a pleasure to listen to her, too. She has an ample and velvety soprano that she employed with considerable skill once she got past an initial nervousness that left her voice dry. . . .

She negotiated the darting "Sempre libera" that brings Act I to a close sufficiently well to win several curtain calls from the sold-out house.—Douglas Watt, *New York Daily News*

DEBUT OF DONALD GRAMM as Truffaldin in *Ariadne auf Naxos*, January 10, 1964

The Truffaldin was Donald Gramm, who was making his debut with the company. The part is hardly big enough to warrant a very sophisticated judgment on how Mr. Gramm will fare in the house, but there was enough to suggest that the [bass-baritone], familiar figure on the American musical scene, brings to the company a vocal quality and character style as well as a good musical and stage presence.—Eric Salzman, *New York Times*

AMERICAN PREMIERE of Menotti's *The Last Savage*, January 23, 1964

After a none-too-successful premiere in October 1963, at the

Paris Opéra Comique, *The Last Savage* arrived on the current occasion in a revised version and hilarious translation from Menotti's original Italian. As always, he has written his own libretto; and, as often, functioned as his own stage director. Thomas Schippers conducted . . . with élan, and with both the instinctive and craftsman's understanding that the transparent orchestra must be underplayed during the solo singing. . . .

During the opera's three acts we roam from India in all its splendor to Chicago, to the Indian jungle. . . . Along the way, Menotti spoofs and exposes . . . habits, people, ideas, concepts—from the cocktail party to the avant-garde painter and the "electro-dodecaphonic" composer. . . . Menotti's score spouts concerted pieces, which include trio, quartet, quintet, sextet and final septet, with . . . the skill apparent since his first opera, *Amelia Goes to the Ball.*

Of sheer musical invention and inspiration there is, however, little. . . . His current triumph is as a librettist, not a composer. . . . His curtailment of Act I, and other revisions, have benefited the score. Also, Beni Montresor's sets and costumes, new for this production, are lavishly stunning.

The cast is perfect. Besides [George] London . . . Roberta Peters as Kitty, Lili Chookasian as the Maharani and Teresa Stratas as Sardula were wonderful. Morley Meredith as Scattergood, Nicolai Gedda as Kodanda and Ezio Flagello as the Maharaja hadn't quite the scope Menotti gave his women but were magically equal to all their challenges. . . .—Harriett Johnson, *New York Post*

DEBUT OF WILLIAM DOOLEY as Eugene Onegin, February 15, 1964

Mr. Dooley is a thirty-one-year-old Californian who has sung some workshop performances in this country and a number of leads in major European houses; his pattern is, therefore, a classic one among American singers.

He gave an excellent performance in a difficult role. . . . Mr. Dooley's voice seemed a little dry at times, but it came through strong and clear. One missed, perhaps, a touch of the burning passion of the role. . . . But one heard singing and saw acting that was full of intelligence.—Alan Rich, *New York Herald Tribune*

NEW PRODUCTION of Verdi's *Falstaff* and DEBUTS OF LUIGI ALVA and LEONARD BERNSTEIN, March 6, 1964

In this sixth *Falstaff* that [Franco] Zeffirelli has staged and designed in various parts of the world, the light as well as the shade are so brilliantly depicted in the action that even the unknowing should be captivated by its recreation of a bygone era. . . . From its beginning in the musty but solid interior of the Garter Inn, through the sunlit garden with its flowering shrubbery and the elegant "lived-in" living room of Ford's house to the strikingly evocative conclusion in the moonlit forest, it is a triumph of artistic mind over the highly material obstacle of flat floors, no machinery and inadequate ways of getting things on and off between scenes. . . .

Into this self-created visual world, the still youthful Italian has cajoled into being a dramatic action that is animated but not stagy, full of lifelike touches—such as the burlap sack Falstaff plucks off the Garter wall in Scene 1 of Act III to wrap around him after his immersion in the Thames—that are ingenious without being obtrusive.

As [Leonard] Bernstein is five *Falstaff* productions behind Zeffirelli, his direction does not yet command the same assurance of touch. But there is no conceivable doubt that musical theater is his predestined milieu, that he gives more to it and it takes more from him than even his concert conducting. He plunged into the performance with a kind of bull-in-a-china-shop recklessness, tending to pull up and slow down when something fragile impends. But by the strength of his impulse, as well as the fertility of his mind, he achieved a sense of exhilaration in the pleasures of this marvelous score that is enormously infectious.

So much for the B to Z within the parentheses of Bernstein and Zeffirelli. Currently lacking is the A of a really distinguished Falstaff. Anselmo Colzani works hard, plays well, sings perhaps too much, doesn't characterize as successfully as the text and words permit. There is little but joy in the musical ensemble otherwise (that little is the Ford of Mario Sereni, a rather stock Italian model rather than the English type wanted). Gabriella Tucci sings a delightful Alice and looks the *sirena* de-

scribed in the text. Rosalind Elias is almost demure as Meg, and Regina Resnik reaches her career's peak with a Dame Quickly that is not merely chucklesome but lovable. Judith Raskin was a sweet-sounding Nannetta and a delight to watch, a worthy companion to the assured Fenton of the accomplished Luigi Alva in his debut.
—Irving Kolodin, *Saturday Review*

DEBUT OF NICOLAE HERLEA as Rodrigo in *Don Carlo,* March 7, 1964

Of primary interest was the debut of Nicolae Herlea, a young Rumanian baritone . . . who appeared as Rodrigo. It was a role he had just had a success in at La Scala, Milan, so it was no surprise that he performed with complete assurance. He sensibly kept his movements to a minimum, since he did not seem wholly familiar with the stage direction here.

What was important was the easy brilliance of his voice and the fine legato he could summon for "Per me giunto." If he was sometimes at odds with the conductor, Kurt Adler, on musical matters, so were many of the singers, and it will be interesting to see what Mr. Herlea can do in a more fully prepared production. — Raymond Ericson, *New York Times*

DEBUT OF GERAINT EVANS as Falstaff, March 25, 1964

Mr. Evans has a magnificent voice—a voice that can roar with drunken anger or soar with courtly elegance, according to the requirements of the moment. His Italian is beautifully enunciated, and every word can be clearly heard throughout the large auditorium. Moreover, he has created a character far above the usual slapstick one. His Falstaff is often understaged, and is no less funny for that. His stage business never seems to fall into clichés; every pantomimic motion he makes has not only a definite significance but a fresh significance, reflecting the inner psychology of the Fat Knight. . . . In short, Mr. Evans is a great actor in the British tradition as well as a great singer in the Italian one.—Winthrop Sargeant, *The New Yorker*

1964-1965 SEASON

PERSONNEL

Male Artists
Aldridge, Erbert
Alexander, John
Alva, Luigi
Alvary, Lorenzo
Anthony, Charles
Bacquier, Gabriel
Bardelli, Cesare
Bastianini, Ettore
Baum, Kurt
Bergonzi, Carlo
Campora, Giuseppe
Carelli, Gabor
Caruso, Mariano
Cassel, Walter
Cehanovsky, George
Christopher, Russell
Colzani, Anselmo
Corelli, Franco
Corena, Fernando
Davidson, Lawrence
D'Elia, Frank
Dembaugh, William
De Paola, Paul
Diaz, Justino
Dickie, Murray
Di Stefano, Giuseppe
Doench, Karl
Dooley, William
Edelmann, Otto
Esparza, Elfego
Evans, Geraint
Ferrin, Agostino
Filip, Emil
Finkelstein, Gary
Fischer, Stuart
Flagello, Ezio
Folmer, Joseph
Forero, Luis
Franke, Paul
Gedda, Nicolai
Ghazal, Edward
Giaiotti, Bonaldo
Giffin, Norman
Gobbi, Tito
Goodloe, Robert
Graham, Arthur
Gramm, Donald
Guarrera, Frank
Harvuot, Clifford
Hawkins, Osie
Hecht, Joshua
Herlea, Nicolae
Hines, Jerome
Konya, Sandor
Kuestner, Charles
Labo, Flaviano
Langdon, Michael
Liebl, Karl
London, George
MacNeil, Cornell
Macurdy, John
Marcella, Lou
Marsh, Calvin
McCracken, James
McLuckey, William
Meredith, Morley
Merrill, Robert
Mittelmann, Norman
Morell, Barry
Nagy, Robert
Paskalis, Kostas

Patterson, Robert
Pechner, Gerhard
Peerce, Jan
Prevedi, Bruno
Prey, Hermann
Roberts, Hal
Rothmuller, Marko
Schoeffler, Paul
Scott, Norman
Sereni, Mario
Sergi, Arturo
Sgarro, Louis
Shirley, George
Siepi, Cesare
Sliker, Peter
Souzay, Gérard
Stanz, William
Strang, Lloyd
Thomas, Jess
Tomanelli, Carlo
Tozzi, Giorgio
Trehy, John
Tucker, Richard
Uzunov, Dimiter
Velis, Andrea
Verreau, Richard
Vickers, Jon
Walker, William
Ward, David
Wiemann, Ernst
Zakariasen, William

Female Artists
Albanese, Licia
Amara, Lucine
Arroyo, Martina
Baldwin, Marcia
Berlin, Patricia
Bjoner, Ingrid
Blair, Lynn
Bower, Beverly
Brewer, Nadyne
Calabrese, Ada
Callas, Maria
Casei, Nedda
Cernei, Elena
Chookasian, Lili
Clements, Joy
Costa, Mary
Crespin, Régine
Curtis-Verna, Mary
Cvejic, Biserka
Dalis, Irene
D'Angelo, Gianna
Della Casa, Lisa
De Salvo, Dina
Di Franco, Loretta
Dunn, Mignon
Elias, Rosalind
Fenn, Jean
Fercana, Mary
Gorr, Rita
Grillo, Joann
Hurley, Laurel
Jones, Alexandra
Jones, Junetta
Kabaivanska, Raina
Kirsten, Dorothy
Kouba, Maria
Kriese, Gladys
Kuchta, Gladys
Lewis, Brenda
Martin, Janis

Milanov, Zinka
Miller, Mildred
Moffo, Anna
Munson, Pamela
Nilsson, Birgit
Ordassy, Carlotta
Owen, Lynn
Peters, Roberta
Pilarczyk, Helga
Pracht, Mary Ellen
Price, Leontyne
Rankin, Nell
Raskin, Judith
Resnik, Regina
Rothenberger, Anneliese
Rysanek, Leonie
Schwarzkopf, Elisabeth
Scovotti, Jeanette
Shawn, Dorothy
Sims, Lilias
Stratas, Teresa
Sutherland, Joan
Tebaldi, Renata
Thebom, Blanche
Tucci, Gabriella
Välkki, Anita
Vanni, Helen
Vicos, Athena

Ballet Soloists
Allen, Ivan
Brayley, Sally
Burdick, William
Crosson, Craig
Eddington, Lawrence
Ehrenberg, Miriam
Enckell, Thomas
Heyes, Patricia
Horne, Katharyn
Jerell, Edith
Jones, Harry
Jorgenson, Rhodie
Lyall, Christopher
MacLarnon, Fern
Mahler, Donald
Maloney, William
Marritt, Naomi
Martin, Carolyn
Meister, Hans
Mickens, Jan
Paaz, Nira
Sayette, Howard
Warren, Marsha
Zelens, Richard

Conductors
Adler, Kurt
Behr, Jan
Boehm, Karl
Cleva, Fausto
La Marchina, Robert
Prêtre, Georges
Rich, Martin
Rosenstock, Joseph
Santi, Nello
Schick, George
Schippers, Thomas
Steinberg, William
Strasfogel, Ignace
Varviso, Silvio

General Manager
Bing, Rudolf

83

1964-65

October 12 (Opening Night)
LUCIA DI LAMMERMOOR
(Donizetti)
Conductor: Varviso
Lucia .... Sutherland
Enrico Ashton .... Merrill
Edgardo .... Konya
Alisa .... Ordassy
Raimondo .... Giaiotti
Arturo .... Anthony
Normanno .... Nagy

October 13
DER ROSENKAVALIER (R. Strauss)
Conductor: Schippers
Princess von
Werdenberg .... Schwarzkopf
Baron Ochs .... Edelmann
Octavian .... Della Casa
Faninal .... Mittelmann
Sophie .... Rothenberger
Marianne .... Owen
Valzacchi .... Velis
Annina .... Dunn
Police Commissioner .... Scott
Major domo of Princess .... Carelli
Major domo of Faninal .... Graham
Notary .... Pechner
Innkeeper .... Anthony
Singer .... Konya
Orphans .... Fercana, A. Jones,
Shawn
Milliner .... Di Franco
Hairdresser .... H. Jones
Leopold .... Aldridge
Animal Vendor .... D'Elia
Blackamoor .... Warren
Lackeys .... Folmer, Trehy,
Marcella, Ghazal

October 14
RIGOLETTO (Verdi)
Conductor: Santi
Duke .... Bergonzi
Rigoletto .... Herlea
Gilda .... Peters
Sparafucile .... Diaz
Maddalena .... Casei
Giovanna .... Ordassy
Monterone .... Macurdy
Marullo .... Marsh
Borsa .... Carelli
Ceprano .... Patterson
Countess .... Blair
Page .... J. Jones
Guard .... Sliker

October 15
MADAMA BUTTERFLY (Puccini)
Conductor: Schick
Cio-Cio-San .... Tucci
B. F. Pinkerton .... Shirley
Sharpless .... Sereni
Suzuki .... Miller
Kate Pinkerton .... Baldwin
Goro .... Franke
Yamadori .... Cehanovsky
Uncle-Priest .... Hawkins
Commissioner .... Christopher
Registrar .... Roberts

October 16
LUCIA DI LAMMERMOOR
(Donizetti)
Same cast as October 12

October 17
SAMSON ET DALILA (Saint-Saëns)
Conductor: Prêtre
Dalila .... Gorr
Samson .... Thomas
High Priest .... Bacquier
Abimelech .... Diaz
Old Hebrew .... Macurdy
Philistine Messenger .... Nagy
Philistines .... Carelli, Goodloe

October 19
RIGOLETTO (Verdi)
Same cast as October 14 except:
Duke .... Alexander

October 20
MADAMA BUTTERFLY (Puccini)
Same cast as October 15

October 21
DIE MEISTERSINGER (Wagner)
Conductor: Rosenstock
Hans Sachs .... Edelmann
Pogner .... Flagello
Eva .... Bjoner
Magdalene .... Kriese
Walther .... Konya
Beckmesser .... Doench
Kothner .... Mittelmann
Vogelgesang .... Franke
Nachtigall .... Marsh
Zorn .... Velis
Eisslinger .... Nagy
Moser .... Carelli
Ortel .... Patterson
Schwarz .... Scott
Foltz .... Sgarro
David .... Dickie
Night Watchman .... Harvuot

October 22
SAMSON ET DALILA (Saint-Saëns)
Same cast as October 17

October 23
TOSCA (Puccini)
Conductor: Santi
Tosca .... Rysanek
Cavaradossi .... Labo
Scarpia .... Merrill
Angelotti .... Diaz
Sacristan .... Corena
Spoletta .... Caruso
Sciarrone .... Christopher
Jailer .... Patterson
Shepherd .... Fischer

October 24 (matinee)
LUCIA DI LAMMERMOOR
(Donizetti)
Same cast as October 12 except:
Enrico Ashton .... Sereni

October 24
DER ROSENKAVALIER (R. Strauss)
Same cast as October 13 except:
Singer .... Morell

October 26
RIGOLETTO (Verdi)
Same cast as October 14

October 27
LUCIA DI LAMMERMOOR
(Donizetti)
Same cast as October 12

October 28
SAMSON ET DALILA (Saint-Saëns)
Same cast as October 17

DER ROSENKAVALIER (R. Strauss)
Same cast as October 13 except:
Singer .... Morell

October 30
TOSCA (Puccini)
Same cast as October 23

October 31 (matinee)
FALSTAFF (Verdi)
Conductor: Rosenstock
Sir John Falstaff .... Colzani
Ford .... Sereni
Fenton .... Alva
Dr. Caius .... Caruso
Bardolph .... Velis
Pistol .... Scott
Mistress Ford .... Tucci
Anne .... Raskin
Dame Quickly .... Resnik
Mistress Page .... Miller

October 31
MADAMA BUTTERFLY (Puccini)
Same cast as October 15 except:
Cio-Cio-San .... Kirsten
B. F. Pinkerton .... Alexander
Sharpless .... Marsh
Suzuki .... Casei

November 2
DER ROSENKAVALIER (R. Strauss)
Same cast as October 13 except:
Baron Ochs .... Langdon
Leopold .... Zakariasen

November 3
SAMSON ET DALILA (Saint-Saëns)
Same cast as October 17 except:
High Priest .... Mittelmann

November 4
TOSCA (Puccini)
Same cast as October 23 except:
Scarpia .... Bacquier

November 5
LUCIA DI LAMMERMOOR
(Donizetti)
Same cast as October 12 except:
Lucia .... d'Angelo
Edgardo .... Sergi

November 6
DIE MEISTERSINGER (Wagner)
Same cast as October 21

November 7 (matinee)
RIGOLETTO (Verdi)
Same cast as October 14 except:
Duke ....Morell
Sparafucile ....Giaiotti
Borsa ....Graham

November 7
Benefit Mizrachi
Women's Organization
OTELLO (Verdi)
Conductor· Schippers
Otello ....Uzunov
Desdemona ....Kabaivanska
Iago ....MacNeil
Emilia ....Grillo
Cassio ....Alexander
Roderigo ....Anthony
Lodovico ....Ferrin
Montano ....Harvuot
Herald ....Goodloe

November 9
SAMSON ET DALILA (Saint-Saëns)
Same cast as October 17

November 10
TOSCA (Puccini)
Same cast as October 23 except:
Scarpia ....Bacquier
Sacristan ....Esparza

November 11
FALSTAFF (Verdi)
Same cast as October 31 except:
Sir John Falstaff ....Evans

November 12
DER ROSENKAVALIER (R. Strauss)
Same cast as October 13 except:
Singer ....Morell
Orphans ....Calabrese, Munson,
                                    De Salvo
Milliner ....Sims
Animal Vendor ....Filip
Lackeys ....Dembaugh, Strang,
                                Roberts, Forero

November 13
LES SYLPHIDES (Chopin)
Conductor: Varviso
Soloists: Horne, Martin, Heyes,
    Meister
DON PASQUALE (Donizetti)
Conductor: Varviso
Don Pasquale ....Corena
Ernesto ....Alva
Norina ....d'Angelo
Dr. Malatesta ....Guarrera
Notary ....Velis

November 14 (matinee)
DIE MEISTERSINGER (Wagner)
Same cast as October 21 except:
Hans Sachs ....Schoeffler

November 14
LUCIA DI LAMMERMOOR
                            (Donizetti)
Same cast as October 12 except:
Enrico Ashton ....Herlea
Edgardo ....Labo

November 16
MADAMA BUTTERFLY (Puccini)
Same cast as October 15 except:
B. F. Pinkerton ....Alexander
Sharpless ....Marsh
Suzuki ....Casei
Kate Pinkerton ....Clements
Goro ....Caruso
Uncle-Priest ....Scott
Registrar ....Stanz

November 17
DER ROSENKAVALIER (R. Strauss)
Same cast as October 13 except:
Singer ....Alexander
Orphans ....Calabrese, Munson,
                                    De Salvo
Milliner ....Sims
Animal Vendor ....Filip
Lackeys #2, 3, 4 ....Strang,
                            Roberts, Forero

November 18
MANON (Massenet)
Conductor: Schippers
Manon ....Fenn
Lescaut ....Bacquier
Des Grieux ....Verreau
Count des Grieux ....Macurdy
Poussette ....Clements
Javotte ....Baldwin
Rosette ....Grillo
Guillot ....Franke
Brétigny ....Walker
Innkeeper ....Patterson
Guards ....Kuestner, Tomanelli
Servant ....Vicos
Sergeant ....Stanz

November 19
TOSCA (Puccini)
Same cast as October 23 except:
Tosca ....Kirsten
Cavaradossi ....Konya
Scarpia ....Colzani
Sacristan ....Esparza

November 20
LUCIA DI LAMMERMOOR
                            (Donizetti)
Same cast as October 12 except:
Edgardo ....Labo

November 21 (matinee)
OTELLO (Verdi)
Same cast as November 7 except:
Desdemona ....Milanov

November 21
LES SYLPHIDES (Chopin)
Same soloists as November 13
DON PASQUALE (Donizetti)
Same cast as November 13

November 23
FALSTAFF (Verdi)
Same cast as October 31 except:
Ford ....Guarrera
Mistress Ford ....Kabaivanska

November 24
DIE MEISTERSINGER (Wagner)
Same cast as October 21 except:
Hans Sachs ....Schoeffler
Eva ....Fenn
Walther ....Thomas

November 25
LES SYLPHIDES (Chopin)
Soloists: Jerell, Martin, Brayley,
    Meister
DON PASQUALE (Donizetti)
Same cast as November 13

November 26
LA FORZA DEL DESTINO (Verdi)
Conductor: Santi
Marquis ....Sgarro
Leonora ....Tucci
Don Carlo ....Herlea
Don Alvaro ....Bergonzi
Padre Guardiano ....Siepi
Fra Melitone ....Corena
Preziosilla ....Grillo
Curra ....Ordassy
Trabucco ....Velis
Surgeon ....Goodloe

November 27
RIGOLETTO (Verdi)
Same cast as October 14 except:
Duke ....Peerce
Rigoletto ....Merrill
Sparafucile ....Giaiotti
Borsa ....Graham
Guard ....De Paola

November 28 (matinee)
MANON (Massenet)
Same cast as November 18

November 28
OTELLO (Verdi)
Same cast as November 7

November 29
GALA PERFORMANCE
Benefit Welfare and Pension
Funds
DER ROSENKAVALIER (R. Strauss)
(Act 1)
Same cast as October 13 except:
Annina ....Kriese
Singer ....Morell
Orphans ....Calabrese,
                            Munson, De Salvo

85

Milliner ....Sims
Animal Vendor ....Filip
Lackeys ....Dembaugh, Strang,
Roberts, Forero
LA BOHEME (Puccini) (Act 1)
Conductor: Schick
Rodolfo ....Bergonzi
Marcello ....Marsh
Schaunard ....Harvuot
Colline ....Siepi
Mimi ....Tebaldi
Benoit ....Corena
LA TRAVIATA (Verdi) (Act 1)
Conductor: Schick
Violetta ....Sutherland
Alfredo ....Alexander
Flora ....Baldwin
Gastone ....Carelli
Baron Douphol ....Walker
Marquis d'Obigny .....Cehanovsky
Dr. Grenvil ....Sgarro

November 30
LES SYLPHIDES (Chopin)
Soloists: Horne, Martin,
Brayley, Lyall
DON PASQUALE (Donizetti)
Same cast as November 13 except:
Norina ....Peters

December 1
SAMSON ET DALILA (Saint-Saëns)
Same cast as October 17

December 2
LE NOZZE DI FIGARO (Mozart)
Conductor: Rosenstock
Almaviva ....Prey
Countess ....Della Casa
Susanna ....Raskin
Figaro ....Siepi
Cherubino ....Stratas
Marcellina ....Kriese
Bartolo ....Esparza
Basilio ....Caruso
Don Curzio ....Carelli
Antonio ....Alvary
Barbarina ....Clements
Peasant Girls .. Di Franco, Shawn

December 3
FALSTAFF (Verdi)
Same cast as October 31 except:
Sir John Falstaff ....Flagello
Ford ....Guarrera
Mistress Ford ....Kabaivanska
Anne ....Scovotti

December 4
OTELLO (Verdi)
Same cast as November 7 except:
Otello ....McCracken
Desdemona ....Milanov
Cassio ....Franke

December 5 (matinee)
LUCIA DI LAMMERMOOR
(Donizetti)
Same cast as October 12 except:
Enrico Ashton ....Herlea

December 5
DIE MEISTERSINGER (Wagner)
Same cast as October 21 except:
Pogner ....Macurdy
Walther ....Sergi
Kothner ....Walker

December 7
MANON (Massenet)
Same cast as November 18 except:
Des Grieux ....Gedda
Poussette ....Blair

December 8
DER ROSENKAVALIER (R. Strauss)
Same cast as October 13 except:
Faninal ....Rothmuller
Sophie ....Raskin
Annina ....Kriese
Singer ....Alexander
Lackeys #1, 2, 4 ....Dembaugh,
Strang, Forero

December 9
SIMON BOCCANEGRA (Verdi)
Conductor: Cleva
Simon Boccanegra ....Colzani
Amelia ....Tebaldi
Fiesco ....Tozzi
Gabriele Adorno ....Shirley
Paolo ....Walker
Pietro ....Scott
Captain ....Nagy
Maid ....Brewer

December 10
LE NOZZE DI FIGARO (Mozart)
Same cast as December 2 except:
Cherubino ....Elias

December 11
DIE MEISTERSINGER (Wagner)
Same cast as October 21 except:
Hans Sachs ....Schoeffler
Pogner ....Macurdy
Magdalene ....Thebom
Walther ....Thomas
Kothner ....Walker

December 12 (matinee)
RIGOLETTO (Verdi)
Same cast as October 14 except:
Rigoletto ....MacNeil
Gilda ....d'Angelo
Guard ....De Paola

December 12
Benefit Yeshiva University
Women's Organization
TOSCA (Puccini)
Same cast as October 23 except:
Tosca ....Tebaldi
Cavaradossi ....Morell
Angelotti ....Scott
Jailer ....Goodloe

December 14
LUCIA DI LAMMERMOOR
(Donizetti)
Same cast as October 12 except:
Enrico Ashton ....Colzani
Edgardo ....Alexander

December 15
LE NOZZE DI FIGARO (Mozart)
Same cast as December 2 except:
Almaviva ....Bacquier
Figaro ....Tozzi
Barbarina ....Blair

December 16
LA FORZA DEL DESTINO (Verdi)
Same cast as November 26 except:
Leonora ....Kabaivanska

December 17
SAMSON ET DALILA (Saint-Saëns)
Same cast as October 17 except:
Dalila ....Dalis
Old Hebrew ....Giaiotti

December 18
LES CONTES d'HOFFMANN
(Offenbach)
Conductor: Varviso
Hoffmann ....Gedda
Olympia ....Scovotti
Giulietta ....Cvejic
Antonia ....Amara
Nicklausse ....Martin
Lindorf ....Dooley
Coppélius ....Dooley
Dappertutto ....Dooley
Dr. Miracle ....Dooley
Spalanzani ....Franke
Schlemil ....Harvuot
Crespel ....Macurdy
Voice ....Kriese
Andrès ....Velis
Cochenille ....Velis
Pitichinaccio ....Velis
Frantz ....Velis
Luther ....Sgarro
Nathanael ....Graham
Hermann ....Christopher
Stella ....Brayley

December 19 (matinee)
DER ROSENKAVALIER (R. Strauss)
Same cast as October 13 except:
Faninal ....Doench
Sophie ....Raskin
Annina ....Kriese
Singer ....Shirley
Lackeys ....Dembaugh, Strang,
Roberts, Forero

December 19
SIMON BOCCANEGRA (Verdi)
Same cast as December 9 except:
Paolo ....Diaz

December 21
LA FORZA DEL DESTINO (Verdi)
Same cast as November 26 except:
Leonora ....Kabaivanska
Padre Guardiano ....Giaiotti

December 22
MANON (Massenet)
Same cast as November 18 except:
Manon ....Costa
Des Grieux ....Gedda
Count des Grieux ....Tozzi

December 23
OTELLO (Verdi)
Same cast as November 7 except:
Conductor: Adler
Desdemona ....Tebaldi
Iago ....Merrill
Emilia ....Martin
Cassio ....Franke
Herald ....Christopher

December 24
LUCIA DI LAMMERMOOR
(Donizetti)
Same cast as October 12 except:
Enrico Ashton ....Colzani
Edgardo ....Alexander

December 25
DER ROSENKAVALIER (R. Strauss)
Same cast as October 13 except:
Princess
von Werdenberg .....Della Casa
Octavian ....Elias
Faninal ....Rothmuller
Sophie ....Raskin
Annina ....Kriese
Notary ....Davidson
Singer ....Shirley
Orphans ....Calabrese, Munson,
De Salvo
Milliner ....Sims
Animal Vendor ....Filip

December 26 (matinee)
SAMSON ET DALILA (Saint-Saëns)
Same cast as October 17 except:
Dalila ....Dalis

December 26
FALSTAFF (Verdi)
Same cast as October 31 except:
Sir John Falstaff ....Flagello
Ford ....Guarrera
Mistress Ford ....Curtis-Verna
Anne ....Scovotti
Mistress Page ....Baldwin

December 28
LES CONTES d'HOFFMANN
(Offenbach)
Same cast as December 18 except:
Olympia ....Hurley

December 29
OTELLO (Verdi)
Same cast as November 7 except:
Conductor: Adler
Desdemona ....Tebaldi
Iago ....Merrill
Emilia ....Martin
Cassio ....Franke
Herald ....Christopher

December 30
DER ROSENKAVALIER (R. Strauss)
Same cast as October 13 except:
Conductor: Strasfogel
Princess
von Werdenberg .....Della Casa
Baron Ochs ....Esparza
Octavian ....Elias
Faninal ....Rothmuller
Sophie ....Raskin
Annina ....Kriese
Police Commissioner .....Hawkins
Notary ....Davidson
Innkeeper ....Carelli
Singer ....Shirley
Orphans ....Calabrese, Munson,
De Salvo
Milliner ....Sims
Animal Vendor ....Filip

December 31
THE LAST SAVAGE (Menotti)
Conductor: La Marchina
Maharajah ....Gramm
Maharanee ....Chookasian
Kodanda ....Alexander
Scattergood ....Meredith
Kitty ....Peters
Abdul ....London
Sardula ....Stratas
Learned Men ....Franke, Velis
Philosopher ....Harvuot
Composer ....Walker
Doctor ....Pechner
Protestant Pastor ....Marsh
Catholic Priest ....Sgarro
Rabbi ....Aldridge
Orthodox Priest ....Dembaugh
Scientist ....Nagy
Painter ....Marcella
Poet ....Carelli
Tailors ....Franke, Velis, Scott
Businesswoman ....Ordassy
Singer ....Martin
Woman ....Shawn
Major domo ....McLuckey

January 1
MANON (Massenet)
Same cast as November 18 except:
Conductor: Rich
Manon ....Costa
Lescaut ....Guarrera
Des Grieux ....Gedda

January 2 (matinee)
LE NOZZE DI FIGARO (Mozart)
Same cast as December 2 except:
Figaro ....Tozzi
Barbarina ....Blair

January 2
AIDA (Verdi)
Conductor: Steinberg
King ....Diaz
Amneris ....Dalis
Aida ....Price

Radames ....Tucker
Amonasro ....Sereni
Ramfis ....Flagello
Messenger ....Franke
Priestess ....Pracht

January 4
LUCIA DI LAMMERMOOR
(Donizetti)
Same cast as October 12 except:
Lucia ....Moffo
Enrico Ashton ....Colzani
Edgardo ....Bergonzi
Normanno ....Graham

January 5
FALSTAFF (Verdi)
Same cast as October 31 except:
Sir John Falstaff ....Corena
Mistress Ford ....Curtis-Verna
Dame Quickly ....Chookasian

January 6
SIMON BOCCANEGRA (Verdi)
Same cast as December 9 except:
Gabriele Adorno ....Campora
Paolo ....Diaz

January 7
THE LAST SAVAGE (Menotti)
Same cast as December 31 except:
Protestant Pastor ......Christopher

January 8
AIDA (Verdi)
Same cast as January 2 except:
Amneris ....Cvejic
Messenger ....Nagy

January 9 (matinee)
LES SYLPHIDES (Chopin)
Soloists, Horne, Marritt, Heyes,
Meister
DON PASQUALE (Donizetti)
Same cast as November 13 except:
Norina ....Peters

January 9
LES CONTES d'HOFFMANN
(Offenbach)
Same cast as December 18 except:
Hoffmann ....Alexander
Olympia ....Hurley

January 11
MADAMA BUTTERFLY (Puccini)
Same cast as October 15 except:
B. F. Pinkerton ....Konya
Sharpless ....Harvuot
Suzuki ....Grillo
Kate Pinkerton ....Clements
Goro ....Velis
Uncle-Priest ....Scott
Registrar ....Stanz

1964-65

January 12
Tosca (Puccini)
Same cast as October 23 except:
Tosca ....Tebaldi
Cavaradossi ....Tucker
Scarpia ....Colzani
Spoletta ....Franke

January 13
Turandot (Puccini)
Conductor: Cleva
Turandot ....Nilsson
Emperor Altoum ....Caruso
Timur ....Giaiotti
Calaf ....Thomas
Liù ....Amara
Ping ....Guarrera
Pang ....Nagy
Pong ....Anthony
Servants ...... Eddington, Crosson,
H. Jones
Mandarin ....Goodloe
Prince of Persia ....Lyall
Executioners .... Sayette, Zelens,
Burdick

January 14
Les Sylphides (Chopin)
Soloists: Horne, Marritt,
Brayley, Meister
Don Pasquale (Donizetti)
Same cast as November 13 except:
Don Pasquale ....Esparza
Norina ....Moffo

January 15
The Last Savage (Menotti)
Same cast as December 31 except:
Abdul ....Cassel
Sardula ....Clements
Protestant Pastor ...... Christopher

January 16 (matinee)
Turandot (Puccini)
Same cast as January 13

January 16
Le Nozze Di Figaro (Mozart)
Same cast as December 2 except:
Almaviva ....Dooley
Countess ....Bjoner
Figaro ....Evans
Barbarina ....J. Jones

January 17
Benefit West Side
Institutional Synagogue
Aida (Verdi)
Same cast as January 2 except:
King ....Sgarro
Amonasro ....Merrill
Messenger ....Nagy

January 18
Tosca (Puccini)
Same cast as October 23 except:
Tosca ....Tebaldi
Scarpia ....Colzani
Angelotti ....Scott
Sacristan ....Esparza
Spoletta ....Velis

January 19
Der Fliegende Hollaender
(Wagner)
Conductor: Boehm
Daland ....Tozzi
Senta ....Rysanek
Erik ....Konya
Mary ....Kriese
Steersman ....Shirley
Dutchman ....London

January 20
Madama Butterfly (Puccini)
Same cast as October 15 except:
Sharpless ....Harvuot
Suzuki ....Grillo
Kate Pinkerton ....Clements
Uncle-Priest ....Scott
Registrar ....Stanz

January 21
Le Nozze Di Figaro (Mozart)
Same cast as December 2 except:
Almaviva ....Souzay
Countess ....Bjoner
Figaro ....Evans
Barbarina ....J. Jones

January 22
Turandot (Puccini)
Same cast as January 13 except:
Liù ....Stratas
Second Executioner ....Mahler

January 23 (matinee)
Falstaff (Verdi)
Same cast as October 31 except:
Sir John Falstaff ....Evans
Fenton ....Shirley

January 23
Lucia di Lammermoor
(Donizetti)
Same cast as October 12 except:
Lucia ....d'Angelo
Edgardo ....Morell

January 25
Der Fliegende Hollaender
(Wagner)
Same cast as January 19 except:
Steersman ....Anthony

January 26
Falstaff (Verdi)
Same cast as October 31 except:
Sir John Falstaff ....Evans
Fenton ....Shirley
Dame Quickly ....Chookasian

January 27
Les Contes d'Hoffmann
(Offenbach)
Same cast as December 18 except:
Hoffmann ....Di Stefano
Olympia ....Hurley
Giulietta ....Rankin
Antonia ....Stratas
Lindorf ....Meredith
Coppélius ....Meredith
Dappertutto ....Meredith
Dr. Miracle ....Meredith

January 28
Turandot (Puccini)
Same cast as January 13 except:
Turandot .... Curtis-Verna
Ping ....Marsh
Ping's Servant ....Allen
Second Executioner ....Meister

January 29
La Forza del Destino (Verdi)
Same cast as November 26 except:
Don Carlo ....Bastianini
Don Alvaro ....Corelli
Padre Guardiano ....Tozzi
Fra Melitone ....Esparza

January 30 (matinee)
Simon Boccanegra (Verdi)
Same cast as December 9 except:
Fiesco ....Hines
Paolo ....Diaz

January 30
Cosi Fan Tutte (Mozart)
Conductor: Rosenstock
Fiordiligi ....Price
Dorabella ....Elias
Despina ....Peters
Ferrando ....Tucker
Guglielmo ....Uppman
Don Alfonso ....Gramm

February 1
Turandot (Puccini)
Same cast as January 13 except:
Turandot .... Curtis-Verna
Calaf ....Corelli
Liù ....Albanese
Ping ....Marsh
Ping's Servant ....Allen
Second Executioner ....Mahler

February 2
Aida (Verdi)
Same cast as January 2 except:
King ....Sgarro
Amneris ....Rankin
Aida ....Tucci
Radames ....Labo
Amonasro ....Colzani
Ramfis ....Hines
Messenger ....Nagy

February 3
Benefit Sponsored by the
Metropolitan Opera Guild
for the
Production Fund
Don Juan (R. Strauss)
Salome (R. Strauss)
Conductor: Boehm
Herod ....Liebl
Herodias ....Dalis
Salome ....Nilsson
Jochanaan ....Dooley
Narraboth ....Alexander
Page ....Baldwin
First Nazarene ....Wiemann
Second Nazarene ....Marsh
First Jew ....Anthony
Second Jew ....Nagy

Third Jew ....Carelli
Fourth Jew ....Velis
Fifth Jew ....Pechner
First Soldier ....Diaz
Second Soldier ....Sgarro
Cappadocian ....Walker
Slave ....Graham

February 4
COSI FAN TUTTE (Mozart)
Same cast as January 30 except:
Don Alfonso ....Guarrera

February 5
DER FLIEGENDE HOLLAENDER
(Wagner)
Same cast as January 19 except:
Daland ....Wiemann
Dutchman ....Ward

February 6 (matinee)
LA FORZA DEL DESTINO (Verdi)
Same cast as November 26 except:
Don Carlo ....Bastianini
Don Alvaro ....Corelli
Padre Guardiano ....Tozzi
Fra Melitone ....Esparza

February 6
AIDA (Verdi)
Same cast as January 2 except:
King ....Sgarro
Amneris ....Rankin
Aida ....Arroyo
Radames ....Labo
Ramfis ....Hines
Messenger ....Nagy

February 8
COSI FAN TUTTE (Mozart)
Same cast as January 30 except:
Don Alfonso ....Guarrera

February 9
DON JUAN (R. Strauss)
SALOME (R. Strauss)
Same cast as February 3 except:
Jochanaan ....Cassel

February 10
LUCIA DI LAMMERMOOR
(Donizetti)
Same cast as October 12 except:
Lucia ....Peters
Enrico Ashton ....Bastianini
Edgardo ....Labo
Raimondo ....Diaz
Normanno ....Graham

February 11
LES CONTES d'HOFFMANN
(Offenbach)
Same cast as December 18 except:
Hoffmann ....Alexander
Giulietta ....Rankin
Antonia ....Fenn
Nicklausse ....Baldwin
Lindorf ....Meredith
Coppélius ....Meredith
Dappertutto ....Meredith
Dr. Miracle ....Meredith
Nathanael ....Dembaugh

February 12
DON JUAN (R. Strauss)
SALOME (R. Strauss)
Same cast as February 3 except:
Salome ....Kouba
Jochanaan ....Cassel
Second Jew ....Zakariasen

February 13 (matinee)
DER FLIEGENDE HOLLAENDER
(Wagner)
Same cast as January 19 except:
Dutchman ....Ward

February 13
Benefit Vassar Club
Scholarship Fund
TOSCA (Puccini)
Same cast as October 23 except:
Conductor: Cleva
Tosca ....Tucci
Cavaradossi ....Tucker
Scarpia ....Bastianini
Angelotti ....Scott
Sacristan ....Esparza
Sciarrone ....Marsh
Jailer ....Goodloe

February 14
TURANDOT (Puccini)
Same cast as January 13 except:
Calaf ....Corelli
Liù ....Albanese
Pang ....Franke
Second Executioner ....Mahler

February 15
DON JUAN (R. Strauss)
SALOME (R. Strauss)
Same cast as February 3 except:
Salome ....Kouba
Jochanaan ....Cassel
Narraboth ....Shirley
Second Jew ....Zakariasen

February 16
LUCIA DI LAMMERMOOR
(Donizetti)
Same cast as October 12 except:
Lucia ....Peters
Enrico Ashton ....Bastianini
Edgardo ....Labo
Normanno ....Graham

February 17
LA FORZA DEL DESTINO (Verdi)
Same cast as November 26 except:
Conductor: Rich
Don Carlo ....Paskalis
Don Alvaro ....Corelli
Fra Melitone ....Esparza

February 18
LES CONTES d'HOFFMANN
(Offenbach)
Same cast as December 18 except:
Hoffmann ....Alexander
Antonia ....Fenn
Nicklausse ....Baldwin
Lindorf ....Meredith

Coppélius ....Meredith
Dappertutto ....Meredith
Dr. Miracle ....Meredith
Spalanzani ....Velis
Cochenille ....Anthony
Nathanael ....Dembaugh

February 19
WOZZECK (Berg)
Conductor: Boehm
Wozzeck ....Dooley
Marie ....Pilarczyk
Margret ....Martin
Captain ....Carelli
Doctor ....Gramm
Drum Major ....Baum
Andres ....Anthony
Fool ....Velis
First Apprentice ....Diaz
Second Apprentice ....Goodloe
Soldier ....Zakariasen
Marie's Child ....Finkelstein
Townsman ....Giffin

February 20 (matinee)
COSI FAN TUTTE (Mozart)
Same cast as January 30 except:
Don Alfonso ....Guarrera

February 20
DER FLIEGENDE HOLLAENDER
(Wagner)
Same cast as January 19 except:
Senta ....Välkki
Dutchman ....Ward

February 22
DIE WALKUERE (Wagner)
Conductor: Steinberg
Wotan ....London
Fricka ....Dalis
Brünnhilde ....Nilsson
Siegmund ....Vickers
Sieglinde ....Rysanek
Hunding ....Ward
Helmwige ....Owen
Gerhilde ....Ordassy
Ortlinde ....Bower
Rossweisse ....Martin
Grimgerde ....Grillo
Waltraute ....Dunn
Siegrune ....Vanni
Schwertleite ....Kriese

February 23
SIMON BOCCANEGRA (Verdi)
Same cast as December 9 except:
Simon Boccanegra ....MacNeil
Amelia ....Milanov
Fiesco ....Siepi
Gabriele Adorno ....Tucker

February 24
WOZZECK (Berg)
Same cast as February 19 except:
Marie ....Lewis
Captain ....Franke
Second Apprentice ....Marsh

February 25
DER FLIEGENDE HOLLAENDER
(Wagner)
Same cast as January 19 except:
Senta ....Välkki
Erik ....Liebl
Dutchman ....Cassel

February 26
COSI FAN TUTTE (Mozart)
Same cast as January 30 except:
Dorabella ....Vanni

Ferbuary 27 (matinee)
LES CONTES d'HOFFMANN
(Offenbach)
Same cast as December 18 except:
Hoffmann ....Alexander

February 27
DON JUAN (R. Strauss)
SALOME (R. Strauss)
Same cast as February 3 except:
Jochanaan ....Cassel
Narraboth ....Shirley
First Nazarene ....Ward

March 1
DER FLIEGENDE HOLLAENDER
(Wagner)
Same cast as January 19 except:
Daland ....Wiemann
Senta ....Kouba
Erik ....Vickers
Dutchman ....Cassel

March 2
WOZZECK (Berg)
Same cast as February 19 except:
Captain ....Franke

March 3
TOSCA (Puccini)
Same cast as October 23 except:
Conductor: Cleva
Tosca ....Kirsten
Cavaradossi ....Tucker
Scarpia ....Bastianini
Angelotti ....Scott
Sacristan ....Davidson
Spoletta ....Velis
Jailer ....Goodloe

March 4
DON JUAN (R. Strauss)
SALOME (R. Strauss)
Same cast as February 3 except:
Salome ....Kouba
Jochanaan ....Cassel
Narraboth ....Shirley
First Nazarene ....Ward

March 5
ERNANI (Verdi)
Conductor: Schippers
Carlo ....MacNeil
Silva ....Hines
Elvira ....Price
Ernani ....Sergi

Don Riccardo ....Anthony
Jago ....Christopher
Giovanna ....Ordassy

March 6 (matinee)
DIE WALKUERE (Wagner)
Same cast as February 22

March 6
TOSCA (Puccini)
Same cast as October 23 except:
Conductor: Cleva
Tosca ....Kirsten
Cavaradossi ....Prevedi
Scarpia ....Bastianini
Angelotti ....Scott
Sacristan ....Davidson
Spoletta ....Franke
Jailer ....Goodloe

March 8
COSI FAN TUTTE (Mozart)
Same cast as January 30 except:
Fiordiligi ....Amara
Dorabella ....Vanni
Despina ....Hurley
Don Alfonso ....Meredith

March 9
DIE WALKUERE (Wagner)
Same cast as February 22

March 10
WOZZECK (Berg)
Same cast as February 19 except:
Captain ....Franke
Doctor ....Alvary
Drum Major ....Nagy

March 11
ERNANI (Verdi)
Same cast as March 5 except:
Ernani ....Corelli

March 12
DER FLIEGENDE HOLLAENDER
(Wagner)
Same cast as January 19 except:
Daland ....Wiemann
Erik ....Liebl

March 13 (matinee)
DON JUAN (R. Strauss)
SALOME (R. Strauss)
Same cast as February 3 except:
Jochanaan ....Cassel
Narraboth ....Shirley

March 13
VANESSA (Barber)
Conductor: Steinberg
Vanessa ....Costa
Erika ....Elias
Baroness ....Thebom
Anatol ....Alexander
Doctor ....Tozzi
Major domo ....Christopher
Footman ....Graham

March 15
ERNANI (Verdi)
Same cast as March 5 except:
Silva ....Siepi
Ernani ....Corelli

March 16
DON JUAN (R. Strauss)
SALOME (R. Strauss)
Same cast as February 3 except:
Narraboth ....Shirley
Cappadocian ....Christopher

March 17 (matinee)
144th Metropolitan Opera Guild
Student Performance
DER FLIEGENDE HOLLAENDER
(Wagner)
Conductor: Adler
Daland ....Macurdy
Senta ....Kouba
Erik ....Nagy
Mary ....Grillo
Steersman ....Anthony
Dutchman ....Cassel

March 17
SAMSON ET DALILA (Saint-Saëns)
Same cast as October 17 except:
Conductor: Cleva
Dalila ....Cernei
Samson ....Vickers
High Priest ....Walker
Old Hebrew ....Giaiotti

March 18 (matinee)
145th Metropolitan Opera Guild
Student Performance
DER FLIEGENDE HOLLAENDER
(Wagner)
Same cast as March 17 except:
Daland ....Wiemann
Senta ....Välkki
Erik ....Liebl
Mary ....Kriese
Dutchman ....Hecht

March 18
VANESSA (Barber)
Same cast as March 13

March 19
Benefit Sponsored by the
Metropolitan Opera Guild
for the
Production Fund
TOSCA (Puccini)
Same cast as October 23 except:
Conductor: Cleva
Tosca ....Callas
Cavaradossi ....Corelli
Scarpia ....Gobbi
Angelotti ....Harvuot
Sacristan ....Davidson
Spoletta ....Velis
Jailer ....Goodloe

March 20 (matinee)
AIDA (Verdi)
Same cast as January 2 except:
King ....Sgarro
Amneris ....Cernei
Aida ....Nilsson
Amonasro ....MacNeil
Ramfis ....Tozzi
Messenger ....Nagy

March 20
LA FORZA DEL DESTINO (Verdi)
Same cast as November 26 except:
Conductor: Rich
Leonora ....Amara
Don Carlo ....Sereni
Don Alvaro ....Prevedi
Fra Melitone ....Pechner

March 22 (matinee)
146th Metropolitan Opera Guild
Student Performance
DER FLIEGENDE HOLLAENDER
(Wagner)
Same cast as March 17 except:
Daland ....Scott
Senta ....Kuchta

March 22
VANESSA (Barber)
Same cast as March 13

March 23
ERNANI (Verdi)
Same cast as March 5 except:
Carlo ....Sereni
Silva ....Siepi
Ernani ....Corelli

March 24
DIE WALKUERE (Wagner)
Same cast as February 22 except:
Wotan ....Hines
Fricka ....Dunn
Brünnhilde ....Välkki
Sieglinde ....Crespin
Hunding ....Wiemann
Waltraute ....Berlin

March 25
TOSCA (Puccini)
Same cast as October 23 except:
Conductor: Cleva
Tosca ....Callas
Cavaradossi ....Tucker
Scarpia ....Gobbi
Angelotti ....Harvuot
Sacristan ....Davidson
Spoletta ....Velis
Jailer ....Goodloe

March 26
SAMSON ET DALILA (Saint-Saëns)
Same cast as October 17 except:
Conductor: Cleva
Dalila ....Dunn
Samson ....Vickers
High Priest ....Walker

March 27 (matinee)
MADAMA BUTTERFLY (Puccini)
Same cast as October 15 except:
Cio-Cio-San ....Kirsten
B. F. Pinkerton ....Morell
Sharpless ....Uppman
Suzuki ....Baldwin
Kate Pinkerton ....Clements
Uncle-Priest ....Scott
Registrar ....Stanz

March 27
TURANDOT (Puccini)
Same cast as January 13 except:
Turandot ....Kuchta
Calaf ....Konya
Liù ....Albanese
Ping ....Marsh
Prince of Persia ....Enckell
Second Executioner ....Mahler

March 28
AIDA (Verdi)
Same cast as January 2 except:
King ....Scott
Amneris ....Elias
Aida ....Nilsson
Radames ....Corelli
Ramfis ....Seipi
Messenger ....Nagy
Priestess ....Martin

March 29
SIMON BOCCANEGRA (Verdi)
Same cast as December 9 except:
Simon Boccanegra ....MacNeil
Amelia ....Milanov
Fiesco ....Hines
Gabriele Adorno ....Tucker

March 30 (matinee)
147th Metropolitan Opera Guild
Student Performance
DER FLIEGENDE HOLLAENDER
(Wagner)
Same cast as March 17 except:
Senta ....Bower
Erik ....Sergi
Mary ....Kriese

March 30
MADAMA BUTTERFLY (Puccini)
Same cast as October 15 except:
Cio-Cio-San ....Kirsten
B. F. Pinkerton ....Konya
Sharpless ....Uppman
Suzuki ....Baldwin
Kate Pinkerton ....Clements
Goro ....Velis
Registrar ....Stanz

March 31 (matinee)
148th Metropolitan Opera Guild
Student Performance
DER FLIEGENDE HOLLAENDER
(Wagner)
Same cast as March 17 except:
Daland ....Scott
Senta ....Owen

Erik ....Liebl
Mary ....Kriese
Dutchman ....Hecht

March 31
GALA PERFORMANCE
LA BOHEME (Puccini) (Act 1)
Conductor: Schick
Rodolfo ....Corelli
Marcello ....Marsh
Schaunard ....Harvuot
Colline ....Siepi
Mimi ....Tebaldi
Benoit ....Pechner
LA TRAVIATA (Verdi) (Act 2)
Conductor: Schick
Violetta ....Costa
Alfredo ....Morell
Germont ....MacNeil
Annina ....Di Franco
Giuseppe ....Marcella
Gardener ....De Paola
TURANDOT (Puccini) (Act 3)
Same cast as January 13 except:
Conductor: Adler
Turandot ....Välkki
Calaf ....Corelli
Liù ....Albanese
Ping ....Marsh
Second Executioner ....Mahler

April 1
AIDA (Verdi)
Same cast as January 2 except:
King ....Scott
Amneris ....Dunn
Aida ....Arroyo
Radames ....Prevedi
Amonasro ....Guarrera
Ramfis ....Hines
Messenger ....Nagy
Priestess ....Martin

April 2
DIE WALKUERE (Wagner)
Same cast as February 22 except:
Wotan ....Hines
Fricka ....Dunn
Sieglinde ....Kuchta
Hunding ....Wiemann
Waltraute ....Berlin
Schwertleite ....Munson

April 3 (matinee)
VANESSA (Barber)
Same cast as March 13

April 3
TOSCA (Puccini)
Same cast as October 23 except:
Conductor: Cleva
Tosca ....Crespin
Cavaradossi ....Corelli
Scarpia ....London
Angelotti ....Scott
Sacristan ....Pechner
Spoletta ....Franke
Sciarrone ....Marsh
Jailer ....Goodloe

April 5
AIDA (Verdi)
Same cast as January 2 except:
King .... Scott
Amneris .... Cernei
Aida .... Kuchta
Radames .... Konya
Ramfis .... Diaz
Messenger .... Nagy
Priestess .... Martin

April 6 (matinee)
149th Metropolitan Opera Guild
Student Performance
DER FLIEGENDE HOLLAENDER
(Wagner)
Same cast as March 17 except:
Senta .... Bower
Erik .... Sergi
Mary .... Kriese

April 6
TOSCA (Puccini)
Same cast as October 23 except:
Conductor: Cleva
Tosca .... Crespin
Cavaradossi .... Morell
Scarpia .... MacNeil
Angelotti .... Scott
Sacristan .... Pechner
Spoletta .... Franke
Sciarrone .... Marsh
Jailer .... Goodloe

April 7
TURANDOT (Puccini)
Same cast as January 13 except:
Turandot .... Välkki
Calaf .... Konya
Liù .... Moffo
Ping .... Marsh
Second Executioner .... Mahler

April 8
AIDA (Verdi)
Same cast as January 2 except:
King .... Scott
Amneris .... Cernei
Aida .... Arroyo
Radames .... Sergi
Amonasro .... Bardelli
Ramfis .... Diaz
Messenger .... Nagy
Priestess .... Martin

April 9
SIMON BOCCANEGRA (Verdi)
Same cast as December 9 except:
Simon Boccanegra .... MacNeil
Amelia .... Milanov
Gabriele Adorno .... Morell

April 10 (matinee)
ERNANI (Verdi)
Same cast as March 5 except:
Carlo .... Sereni
Silva .... Siepi
Ernani .... Corelli

April 10
DIE WALKUERE (Wagner)
Same cast as February 22 except:
Wotan .... Hines
Fricka .... Kriese
Brünnhilde .... Välkki
Sieglinde .... Crespin
Hunding .... Wiemann
Waltraute .... Berlin
Schwertleite .... Munson

April 11
BALLET EVENING
LES SYLPHIDES (Chopin)
Conductor: Behr
Soloists: Horne, Martin,
Brayley, Meister
THE MIRACULOUS MANDARIN
(Bartók)
Conductor: La Marchina
Woman .... MacLarnon
Mandarin .... Meister
Boys ..... Enckell, Sayette, Maloney
Old Man .... Jones
Adolescent .... Eddington
LE PAS DE QUATRE (Pugni)
Conductor: Behr
Marie Taglioni .... Heyes
Lucille Grahn .... Paaz
Carlotta Grisi .... Ehrenberg
Fanny Cerrito .... Marritt
BLUEBIRD "PAS DE DEUX"
(The Sleeping Beauty)
(Tchaikovsky)
Conductor: Behr
Soloists: Horne, Allen
BACCHANALE (Samson et Dalila)
(Saint-Saëns)
Conductor: Cleva
Soloists: Jerell, Mickens, Mahler

April 12
TURANDOT (Puccini)
Same cast as January 13 except:
Turandot .... Kuchta
Calaf .... Konya
Liù .... Moffo
Pang .... Franke
Prince of Persia .... Enckell
Second Executioner .... Mahler

April 13 (matinee)
150th Metropolitan Opera Guild
Student Performance
DER FLIEGENDE HOLLAENDER
(Wagner)
Same cast as March 17 except:
Conductor: Rosenstock
Daland .... Wiemann
Senta .... Välkki
Erik .... Vickers
Mary .... Kriese

April 13
VANESSA (Barber)
Same cast as March 13

April 14
AIDA (Verdi)
Same cast as January 2 except:
King .... Sgarro
Amneris .... Cernei
Aida .... Amara
Radames .... Konya
Amonasro .... Merrill
Ramfis .... Hines
Messenger .... Nagy
Priestess .... Martin

April 15
OTELLO (Verdi)
Same cast as November 7 except:
Desdemona .... Milanov
Cassio .... Franke
Lodovico .... Diaz
Montano .... Marsh
Herald .... Christopher

April 16
SAMSON ET DALILA (Saint-Saëns)
Same cast as October 17 except:
Conductor: Cleva
Dalila .... Cernei
Samson .... Vickers
High Priest .... Mittelmann
Philistine Messenger .... Caruso

April 17 (matinee)
TOSCA (Puccini)
Same cast as October 23 except:
Conductor: Cleva
Tosca .... Crespin
Cavaradossi .... Konya
Angelotti .... Scott
Sacristan .... Flagello
Spoletta .... Franke
Jailer .... Goodloe

April 17
RIGOLETTO (Verdi)
Same cast as October 14 except:
Conductor: Behr
Duke .... Morell
Rigoletto .... MacNeil
Sparafucile .... Giaiotti
Maddalena .... Dunn
Monterone .... Diaz
Marullo .... Harvuot
Borsa .... Graham
Ceprano .... Sgarro
Countess .... Clements
Page .... Di Franco

EXCERPTS FROM PRESS REVIEWS

NEW PRODUCTION of Donizetti's
Lucia di Lammermoor, October
12, 1964
The Metropolitan Opera has
needed a replacement for its old
production of *Lucia di Lammer-*

moor for as long as most of us have been going to opera. It got one, and unveiled it last night at the gala opening of its eightieth season at the Opera House. It's an improvement, all right . . . but it is a long way from the *Lucia* some of us have dreamed about. . . .

[Attilio] Colonnello has designed a series of murky, ponderous settings; the buildings reflect a spot of college-campus Gothic, and the exteriors are rank with underbrush and pre-Raphaelite clutter. [Stage director Margherita] Wallmann has translated this all into action that seldom moves but spends most of its time striking poses.

All this might have been acceptable at some time in the past, but it is not today. The main reason that it isn't is that we have in our generation two great singers, Maria Callas and Joan Sutherland, who have restored this repertory to its rightful respectability. . . . Having in Miss Sutherland a woman who is not only a specialized Donizetti stylist but also a stupendously endowed singer by any standard, one would have thought that the Metropolitan might have gone all the way with her, shining up the looks of *Lucia* as well as the sound. . . .

Just one of the traditional cuts has been restored . . . a short trio for Lucia, Enrico and Raimondo midway in the Mad Scene. That leaves about fifty-two more cuts to be closed before we can have the score as the composer wrote it.—Alan Rich, *New York Herald Tribune*

DEBUT OF ELISABETH SCHWARZKOPF as the Marschallin in *Der Rosenkavalier*, October 13, 1964

Miss Schwarzkopf was making her belated appearance on the Metropolitan's stage in the same part that served for her American operatic debut nine years ago, in San Francisco. . . . Since the first act is more or less the Marschallin's, the audience knew what to make of [her] performance by the time the act was over. The soprano conquered her listeners, and the roar that filled the house when she took her bows must be the kind that the most vain prima donna could ask for.

When she has sung in *Rosenkavalier* elsewhere, Miss Schwarzkopf's interpretation has inspired some controversy. Last night her performance was never less than admirable, and often it was deeply

moving. With her blond radiance, she looked beautiful and behaved with the aristocratic manner expected of the Marschallin. She was constantly projecting the most minute dramatic details suggested by the text in terms of vocal phrasing and coloration and of facial and bodily expression.

If these never seemed artificial, there were times when the emotions swept by so quickly and easily [that] one was a little uneasy in their presence. But she was able to do one thing superbly and uncannily: after looking so youthfully happy in her early love scenes with Octavian, she seemed to age physically as she began to think about the passing years and about losing her lover. . . .

Vocally, Miss Schwarzkopf is no longer the fresh, pure-voiced artist she used to be. The voice has grown larger. At times it is more shrill; at times it has its old blandishments, and she can still manage lovely high pianissimos. —Raymond Ericson, *New York Times*

NEW PRODUCTION of Saint-Saëns' *Samson et Dalila* and DEBUTS OF GEORGES PRÊTRE and GABRIEL BACQUIER, October 17, 1964

High hopes for the future of the French repertory at the Metropolitan were prompted by the debut of the estimable Georges Prêtre as conductor of the new production of *Samson et Dalila*, the first hearing of Saint-Saëns' cultivated score here in seven years. What this fortyish Frenchman has suggested at his concert performances in New York was affirmed in the more demanding conditions of the theater—that he is a conductor with not only the mind and the heart but also the ear to restore the glow to a repertory tarnished by disuse, not to say abuse. It was comforting to hear the high spots of the score so well projected, [and] it was an absolute delight to experience the duet "Près de moi" of Act II shaped with such certainty, flow and sensitivity.

In this duet as well as elsewhere, most of what was Prêtreworthy on the stage came from Rita Gorr, who poured out a stream of well-modulated sound as Dalila, and from Gabriel Bacquier, who made himself welcome as the High Priest. Gorr has never sounded so good nor acted so effectively in prior roles (mostly Italian) as she did in this French one. Visually as well as aurally,

she commands the voluptuous means to make Dalila a figure of some grandeur. . . . Such singing, when combined with the leadership of Prêtre, subdues complaints that *Samson* is static or nontheatrical.

A little more of the same from Jess Thomas would have muted them altogether. He has both the range and the physique for a convincing Samson, but his background in the German theater has perhaps left him uneasy as yet in French. It is not a voice of much sensuous appeal but, then, neither is Bacquier's, which nevertheless served that performer effectively. for he, thanks to Parisian training, knew exactly what he was doing at all times. Thanks are due also to John Macurdy for his sonorous Old Hebrew.

Nathaniel Merrill and Robert O'Hearn have applied to this new production the stage sense that has commended their previous work at the Metropolitan, plus a warm range of colors to suit the Near Eastern locale. . . . Had Zachary Solov's choreography matched this standard it would have greatly enhanced the opportunities provided by Saint-Saëns' skillful score, but his temple dance was limpid, his Bacchanale trite. . . . However, while Prêtre and Gorr are performing their leading roles, this is better French opera than the Met has offered in a decade.—Irving Kolodin, *Saturday Review*

METROPOLITAN PREMIÈRE of Fokine's *Les Sylphides*, November 13, 1964

The Metropolitan Opera got around to producing its first independent ballet classic in several decades last evening with the presentation of Michel Fokine's one-act *Les Sylphides*, a necessary staple in the repertories of most major ballet companies.

The new staging, with scenery and costumes by Rolf Gérard, was arranged by the Met's opera ballet director, Dame Alicia Markova, a foremost interpreter of the leading role in *Les Sylphides* before her retirement from the stage two years ago.

Under Dame Alicia's guidance, the Metropolitan Opera ballet dances the measures Fokine created to music of Chopin very neatly, very prettily and somewhat blandly. True, the ballet seeks to capture the mood of reverie, but there are opportunities for the subtle disclosure of individuality among the principals. This was not really touched upon last evening. A quiet level of dynamics was observed by all, the three principal ladies and the single gentleman.

The corps of sixteen girls accomplished the Fokine patterns easily and tidily and, with a few individual exceptions, captured the lyrical Fokine style which Dame Alicia required of them.

The Met's new venture into ballet production, then, was a quiet one, not at all startling, but a welcome beginning none the less. The audience received *Les Sylphides* graciously but reserved its most enthusiastic applause for Dame Alicia in her solo bow on the great stage.—Walter Terry, *New York Herald Tribune*

DEBUT OF WILLIAM STEINBERG, conducting *Aida*, January 2, 1965

Steinberg proved a welcome addition to the company's thin conductorial ranks. Although he failed to reveal anything really novel or individual in the score, he elicited superior playing from the orchestra, maintained excellent balance between stage and pit, restored law and order to what is often a laissez-faire opera and kept things moving at a lively clip. At times (the end of the Nile Scene duet, for instance) the pace was more frantic than spirited, but more often (the Triumphal Scene ensemble, for instance) it provided an exciting impulse of its own. —Martin Bernheimer, *New York Post*

NEW PRODUCTION of Richard Strauss' *Salome,* February 3, 1965

If nothing else, the sets for the new production of Richard Strauss' *Salome* are a study in decadence. The dominant feature is a necrophilic moon, rotting away in different colors, slowly setting, turning the skies around it awful venomous shades. . . .

The other sets matched. A netlike mesh dominated the entire back part of the stage, and the building from which Herod and his entourage emerged was full of the sick-dappled pimples and quality of an Albright painting. There probably was some symbolism in the netting; Jochanaan was clad in a net, and that too was the motif of Herod's costume. The sets and costumes were designed by Rudolf Heinrich, the staging was Günther Rennert's. . . .

[It has] been a long time be-

tween great Salomes. In recent years, Ljuba Welitsch for two seasons (1948 to 1950) set the standard. Strauss, of course, asked the impossible—an Isolde voice in the body of an adolescent. . . . But Miss Nilsson has recorded *Salome,* and her brilliant vocalism there whetted the appetite. Could she overcome handicaps of figure and age to represent, with any degree of conviction, the teen-age, perverted Salome?

The answer is, not really. What standard gesture could do, what basically an old-fashioned and operatic acting method could do, was dramatically not enough. At least Miss Nilsson was wise enough not to make a big thing of the dance. She did not even attempt to disrobe, as have most sopranos in immediate memory. But her characterization, depending as it did on stock gesture, on an open mouth and extended fingers, on writhings and gaspings, was a long way from the ideal Salome.

So let's forget it and discuss the singing. And there Miss Nilsson erased all previous memories. The great, accurate, flawless voice soared through the house. . . .

Karl Liebl, as Herod, turned in a thoroughly competent but not very subtle characterization. . . . Nor was the Herodias, Irene Dalis, a very commanding figure, though she too went competently through the role. Some strong singing was contributed by William Dooley, an austere Jochanaan, and by John Alexander as Narraboth. Mr. Boehm's conducting was knowledgeable and accurate; and with Miss Nilsson he could let the orchestra out as much as he desired.—Harold C. Schonberg, *New York Times*

DEBUT OF BRUNO PREVEDI as Cavaradossi in *Tosca,* March 6, 1965

The New York debut of Bruno Prevedi on Saturday night as Cavaradossi in *Tosca* may not have been one of the most sensational in Metropolitan Opera history, but it introduced a tenor who has the potential for a long and prosperous career here by virtue of musicality, good looks and sensitivity to dramatic situations, which is not often met among this high-register, unpredictable breed. . . . The rich, dark quality of his voice augurs well for development in the lyric and dramatic repertory.— Louis Snyder, *New York Herald Tribune*

MARIA CALLAS as Tosca, March 19, 1965

Here we have a woman who, like her or not, is the most important person singing in opera today. Her greatness, as she demonstrated beyond any doubt last night, is a fierce and all-pervasive power to realize every dramatic nuance of a character, and to recreate that realization through the overwhelming use of her body and voice. For this generation at least, Maria Callas is the supreme embodiment of the drama inherent in the romantic Mediterranean operatic language, which in turn is a language of broad and impassioned drama. . . .

The performance she gave last night had in it the white heat of creation. It was a performance that left unrealized no aspect of the human being at the center of this drama. It was also a stunning revelation of the power of the human voice to serve as a dramatic vehicle. Miss Callas sang gorgeously, just in case I haven't made that clear up to now. . . .

But one cannot, with this kind of total performance, concentrate on any single element without regarding the entire achievement. That is Callas' way. What she did with her voice in the first act was an extension of the totally delightful, girlish conception she has devised. What she did with it in the second act was even more remarkable, because it stripped this piece of old-fashioned broad melodrama down to human proportions. Her "Vissi d'arte," soft and floating, became what it is supposed to be: a prayer from a frightened, confused, trapped human being. The whole act, in fact, was a stunning study in humanity. Callas never once betrayed the woman in Tosca to the unsubtle and cheap tigress that the unsubtle have wrongly found there. Her murder of Scarpia was brilliant, because it was not the act of a murderess. It was a study in fear, in the instinct of self-preservation, that swept aside all memories of what others have here accomplished. The third act was no less magnificent, although there were one or two notes here and there that did escape from control. For once, however, this act seemed culmination rather than anticlimax. Her work here was, in a sense, the synthesis of simplicity and triumph, and the final accents of horror were intoned with no sense of grotesquerie.—Alan Rich, *New York Herald Tribune*

1965-1966 SEASON

PERSONNEL

Male Artists
Alexander, John
Alva, Luigi
Alvary, Lorenzo
Anthony, Charles
Bacquier, Gabriel
Bardelli, Cesare
Bardini, Gaetano
Bastianini, Ettore
Baum, Kurt*
Bergonzi, Carlo
Birlenbach, Erich
Boucher, Gene
Carelli, Gabor
Caruso, Mariano
Cassel, Walter
Cehanovsky, George
Chistiakov, Vladimir
Christopher, Russell
Colzani, Anselmo
Corelli, Franco
Corena, Fernando
Davidson, Lawrence
D'Elia, Frank
De Paola, Paul
Diaz, Justino
Dooley, William
Dunlap, John Robert
Edelmann, Otto
Esparza, Elfego
Evans, Geraint
Filip, Emil
Fischer, Stuart
Flagello, Ezio
Folmer, Joseph
Forero, Luis
Franke, Paul
Gedda, Nicolai
Ghazal, Edward
Ghiaurov, Nicolai
Ghiuselev, Nicola
Giaiotti, Bonaldo
Gobbi, Tito
Goodloe, Robert
Gramm, Donald
Guarrera, Frank
Harvuot, Clifford
Herlea, Nicolae
Hines, Jerome
King, James
Konya, Sandor
Kraus, Alfredo
Kuestner, Charles
Labo, Flaviano
Liebl, Karl
London, George
MacNeil, Cornell
Macurdy, John
Marcella, Lou

Marck, Dan
Marsh, Calvin
McCracken, James
Meredith, Morley
Merrill, Robert
Michalski, Raymond
Milnes, Sherrill
Morell, Barry
Nagy, Robert
Nuotio, Pekka
Peerce, Jan
Piso, Ion
Prevedi, Bruno
Raimondi, Gianni
Reardon, John
Ritchard, Cyril
Roberts, Hal
Schmorr, Robert
Scott, Norman
Sereni, Mario
Sergi, Arturo
Sgarro, Louis
Shirley, George
Siepi, Cesare
Sliker, Peter
Stanz, William
Stewart, Thomas
Strang, Lloyd
Thomas, Jess
Tomanelli, Carlo
Tozzi, Giorgio
Trehy, John
Tucker, Richard
Uppman, Theodor
Velis, Andrea
Vichey, Luben
Vickers, Jon
Vinay, Ramon
Walker, William
Ward, David
Wiemann, Ernst
Zakariasen, William

Female Artists
Albanese, Licia
Amara, Lucine
Arroyo, Martina
Baldwin, Marcia
Bjoner, Ingrid
Bower, Beverly
Bumbry, Grace
Caballé, Montserrat
Casei, Nedda
Cernei, Elena
Chookasian, Lili
Clements, Joy
Costa, Mary
Crespin, Régine
Curtis-Verna, Mary
Cvejic, Biserka
Dalis, Irene

D'Angelo, Gianna
Della Casa, Lisa
De Salvo, Dina
Di Franco, Loretta
Dunn, Mignon
Dvorakova, Ludmila
Elias, Rosalind
Eure, Ella
Farrell, Eileen
Fenn, Jean
Fercana, Mary
Freni, Mirella
Gorr, Rita
Grillo, Joann
Grist, Reri
Jones, Alexandra
Kabaivanska, Raina
Kailer, Lucille
Kalil, Margaret
Kirsten, Dorothy
Kouba, Maria
Krall, Heidi
Kriese, Gladys
Lansché, Ruth
Lorengar, Pilar
Love, Shirley
Madeira, Jean
McIlhenny, Helen
Milanov, Zinka
Miller, Mildred
Moffo, Anna
Munson, Pamela
Nilsson, Birgit
Ordassy, Carlotta
Owen, Lynn
Peters, Roberta
Pospinov, Ruza
Pracht, Mary Ellen
Price, Leontyne
Rankin, Nell
Raskin, Judith
Resnik, Regina
Rigal, Delia*
Roberto, Francesca
Rothenberger, Anneliese
Rysanek, Leonie
Schwarzkopf, Elisabeth
Scotto, Renata
Scovotti, Jeanette
Shawn, Dorothy
Sims, Lilias
Steber, Eleanor
Stich-Randall, Teresa
Stratas, Teresa
Sukis, Lilian
Tebaldi, Renata
Thebom, Blanche
Tucci, Gabriella
Välkki, Anita
Votipka, Thelma*
Weathers, Felicia

Ballet Soloists
Allen, Ivan
Aragno, Anna
Aschieri, Susana
Brayley, Sally
Burdick, William
Davis, Robert
Eddington, Lawrence
Emanuel, Nicolyn
Friedman, Martin
Gregory, Josef
Grinvald, Sylvia
Heyes, Patricia
Jerell, Edith
Jones, Harry
Jorgenson, Rhodie
Knitzer, Pauline
Levy, Diana
MacLarnon, Fern
Mahler, Donald
Maloney, William
Marritt, Naomi
Martin, Carolyn
Meister, Hans
Mickens, Jan
Milnes, David
Morse, Janet
O'Connell, Sharon
Paaz, Nira
Santiago, Anthony
Sayette, Howard
Westergard, Lance
Wilson, Lee
Yezer, Franklin

Conductors
Adler, Kurt
Allers, Franz
Behr, Jan
Boehm, Karl
Cleva, Fausto
Gardelli, Lamberto
Leinsdorf, Erich*
Lombard, Alain
Mehta, Zubin
Molinari-Pradelli,
    Francesco
Prêtre, Georges
Rich, Martin
Rosenstock, Joseph
Rudolf, Max*
Schick, George
Schippers, Thomas
Stokowski, Leopold*
Strasfogel, Ignace
Varviso, Silvio

General Manager
Bing, Rudolf

*Guest artist at Gala Farewell

95

September 27 (Opening Night)
FAUST (Gounod)
    Conductor: Prêtre
Faust .... Gedda
Marguerite .... Tucci
Méphistophélès .... Siepi
Valentin .... Merrill
Siébel .... Baldwin
Marthe .... Kriese
Wagner .... Christopher

September 28
QUEEN OF SPADES (Tchaikovsky)
    Conductor: Schippers
Countess .... Resnik
Lisa .... Stratas
Pauline (Daphnis) .... Elias
Gherman .... Vickers
Count Tomsky .... Reardon
Prince Yeletsky .... Walker
Chekalinsky .... Franke
Surin .... Alvary
Chaplitsky .... Carelli
Narumov .... Sgarro
Master of Ceremonies ... Boucher
Chloë .... Pracht
Masha .... Ordassy

September 29
LA BOHEME (Puccini)
    Conductor: Cleva
Rodolfo .... Raimondi
Marcello .... Marsh
Schaunard .... Harvuot
Colline .... Macurdy
Mimi .... Freni
Musetta .... Krall
Benoit .... Alvary
Parpignol .... Filip
Alcindoro .... Velis
Sergeant .... Ghazal
Customs Officer .... Trehy

September 30
LUCIA DI LAMMERMOOR
    (Donizetti)
    Conductor: Varviso
Lucia .... Moffo
Enrico Ashton .... Sereni
Edgardo .... Piso
Alisa .... Ordassy
Raimondo .... Giaiotti
Arturo .... Marek
Normanno .... Velis

October 1
ARABELLA (R. Strauss)
    Conductor: Prêtre
Count Waldner .... Gramm
Adelaide .... Thebom
Arabella .... Della Casa
Zdenka .... Rothenberger
Mandryka .... Cassel
Matteo .... Morell
Count Elemer .... Anthony
Count Dominik .... Goodloe
Count Lamoral .... Scott
Fiakermilli .... Kailer
Fortune Teller .... Owen
Welko .... Folmer
Djura .... Kuestner
Jankel .... Sliker
Waiter .... Birlenbach

October 2
FAUST (Gounod)
Same cast as September 27

October 4
QUEEN OF SPADES (Tchaikovsky)
Same cast as September 28

October 5
LA BOHEME (Puccini)
Same cast as September 29 except:
Mimi .... Albanese

October 6
FAUST (Gounod)
Same cast as September 27

October 7
DON CARLO (Verdi)
    Conductor: Schippers
Philip II .... Hines
Don Carlo .... Prevedi
Rodrigo .... Bastianini
Grand Inquisitor .... Diaz
Elizabeth .... Kabaivanska
Princess Eboli .... Bumbry
Theobald .... Pracht
Count Lerma .... Carelli
Friar .... Sgarro
Herald .... Nagy
Voice .... Kalil
Countess Aremberg ..... Brayley

October 8
LA BOHEME (Puccini)
Same cast as September 29

October 9 (matinee)
LUCIA DI LAMMERMOOR
    (Donizetti)
Same cast as September 30

October 9
ARABELLA (R. Strauss)
Same cast as October 1

October 11
LA BOHEME (Puccini)
Same cast as September 29 except:
    Conductor: Schick

October 12
FAUST (Gounod)
Same cast as September 27

October 13
MADAMA BUTTERFLY (Puccini)
    Conductor: Schick
Cio-Cio-San .... Scotto
B. F. Pinkerton ...... Alexander
Sharpless .... Dunlap
Suzuki .... Grillo
Kate Pinkerton .... Love
Goro .... Schmorr
Yamadori .... Christopher
Uncle-Priest .... Scott
Commissioner .... Boucher
Registrar .... Stanz

October 14
ARABELLA (R. Strauss)
Same cast as October 1 except:
Mandryka .... Reardon
Fiakermilli .... Scovotti

October 15
DON CARLO (Verdi)
Same cast as October 7

October 16 (matinee)
QUEEN OF SPADES (Tchaikovsky)
Same cast as September 28

October 16
LUCIA DI LAMMERMOOR
    (Donizetti)
Same cast as September 30 except:
Lucia .... d'Angelo
Edgardo .... Raimondi

October 18
MADAMA BUTTERFLY (Puccini)
Same cast as October 13

October 19
ARABELLA (R. Strauss)
Same cast as October 1 except:
Mandryka .... Reardon
Fiakermilli .... Scovotti

October 20
IL TROVATORE (Verdi)
    Conductor: Prêtre
Leonora .... Tucci
Manrico .... Labo
Count Di Luna .... Merrill
Azucena .... Dalis
Inez .... Love
Ferrando .... Macurdy
Ruiz .... Anthony
Gypsy .... Forero
Messenger .... Roberts

October 21
QUEEN OF SPADES (Tchaikovsky)
Same cast as September 28 except:
Lisa .... Weathers
Chloë .... Di Franco

October 22
LUCIA DI LAMMERMOOR
    (Donizetti)
Same cast as September 30 except:
Enrico Ashton .... Bastianini
Edgardo .... Morell

October 23 (matinee)
FAUST (Gounod)
Same cast as September 27

October 23
LA BOHEME (Puccini)
Same cast as September 29 except:
    Conductor: Schick
Marcello .... Sereni
Colline .... Hines
Mimi .... Tucci
Musetta .... Bower

October 25
MANON LESCAUT (Puccini)
Conductor: Adler
Manon . . . . Kabaivanska
Lescaut . . . . Walker
Des Grieux . . . . Alexander
Geronte . . . . Esparza
Edmondo . . . . Anthony
Ballet Master . . . . Velis
Innkeeper . . . . Cehanovsky
Musician . . . . Baldwin
Sergeant . . . . Goodloe
Lamplighter . . . . Marek
Captain . . . . Boucher
Madrigal Singers . . . . Fercana,
Lansché, De Salvo, Munson

October 26
IL TROVATORE (Verdi)
Same cast as October 20

October 27
LUCIA DI LAMMERMOOR
(Donizetti)
Same cast as September 30 except:
Conductor: Rich
Enrico Ashton . . . . . . Bastianini
Edgardo . . . . Alexander
Normanno . . . . Schmorr

October 28
LA BOHEME (Puccini)
Same cast as September 29 except:
Conductor: Schick
Marcello . . . . Sereni
Mimi . . . . Stratas
Musetta . . . . Bower

October 29
FALSTAFF (Verdi)
Conductor: Rosenstock
Sir John Falstaff . . . . Evans
Ford . . . . Guarrera
Fenton . . . . Shirley
Dr. Caius . . . . Franke
Bardolph . . . . Velis
Pistol . . . . Scott
Mistress Ford . . . . Costa
Anne . . . . Raskin
Dame Quickly . . . . Resnik
Mistress Page . . . . Miller

October 30 (matinee)
MADAMA BUTTERFLY (Puccini)
Same cast as October 13 except:
Cio-Cio-San . . . . Albanese
B. F. Pinkerton . . . . . . Raimondi

October 30
DON CARLO (Verdi)
Same cast as October 7 except:
Philip II . . . . Siepi
Elizabeth . . . . Arroyo
Princess Eboli . . . . Cvejic

November 1
FAUST (Gounod)
Same cast as September 27 except:
Valentin . . . . Sereni

November 2
LUCIA DI LAMMERMOOR
(Donizetti)
Same cast as September 30 except:
Conductor: Rich
Enrico Ashton . . . . Colzani
Edgardo . . . . Raimondi
Normanno . . . . Schmorr

November 3
MANON LESCAUT (Puccini)
Same cast as October 25 except:
Des Grieux . . . . Tucker
Innkeeper . . . . Christopher

November 4
DON CARLO (Verdi)
Same cast as October 7 except:
Philip II . . . . Siepi
Elizabeth . . . . Curtis-Verna
Princess Eboli . . . . Cvejic
Friar . . . . Scott

November 5
FALSTAFF (Verdi)
Same cast as October 29

November 6 (matinee)
LA BOHEME (Puccini)
Same cast as September 29 except:
Conductor: Schick
Marcello . . . . Sereni
Colline . . . . Diaz
Benoit . . . . Esparza
Alcindoro . . . . Alvary

November 6
Benefit Yeshiva University
Women's Organization
IL TROVATORE (Verdi)
Same cast as October 20 except:
Manrico . . . . Tucker
Ferrando . . . . Sgarro

November 8
FAUST (Gounod)
Same cast as September 27 except:
Faust . . . . Morell
Marguerite . . . . Fenn
Méphistophélès . . . . . . Ghiaurov

November 10
DON CARLO (Verdi)
Same cast as October 7 except:
Philip II . . . . Giaiotti
Grand Inquisitor . . . . Ward
Elizabeth . . . . Arroyo
Princess Eboli . . . . Cvejic

November 11
LA BOHEME (Puccini)
Same cast as September 29 except:
Conductor: Schick
Marcello . . . . Guarrera
Colline . . . . Diaz
Mimi . . . . Stratas
Musetta . . . . Bower
Benoit . . . . Esparza
Alcindoro . . . . Alvary

November 12
L'ELISIR D'AMORE (Donizetti)
Conductor: Schippers
Adina . . . . Freni
Nemorino . . . . Gedda
Belcore . . . . Sereni
Dulcamara . . . . Corena
Giannetta . . . . Clements

November 13 (matinee)
MANON LESCAUT (Puccini)
Same cast as October 25 except:
Des Grieux . . . . Tucker
Innkeeper . . . . Christopher

November 13
MADAMA BUTTERFLY (Puccini)
Same cast as October 13 except:
B. F. Pinkerton . . . . . . Raimondi

November 15
IL TROVATORE (Verdi)
Same cast as October 20 except:
Manrico . . . . Prevedi
Count Di Luna . . . . Colzani
Azucena . . . . Cvejic
Inez . . . . Owen

November 16
DON CARLO (Verdi)
Same cast as October 7 except:
Philip II . . . . Ghiaurov
Don Carlo . . . . Tucker
Rodrigo . . . . Merrill
Grand Inquisitor . . . . Ward
Princess Eboli . . . . Dalis
Friar . . . . Vichey

November 17
L'ELISIR D'AMORE (Donizetti)
Same cast as November 12

November 18
MANON LESCAUT (Puccini)
Same cast as October 25 except:
Manon . . . . Albanese
Lescaut . . . . Guarrera
Innkeeper . . . . Christopher

November 19
FAUST (Gounod)
Same cast as September 27 except:
Méphistophélès . . . . . . Ghiaurov
Valentin . . . . Walker

November 20 (matinee)
MADAMA BUTTERFLY (Puccini)
Same cast as October 13 except:
Cio-Cio-San . . . . Arroyo
B. F. Pinkerton . . . . . . Raimondi
Kate Pinkerton . . . . Owen
Yamadori . . . . Boucher
Commissioner . . . . Goodloe

November 20
QUEEN OF SPADES (Tchaikovsky)
Same cast as September 28 except:
Count Tomsky . . . . Cassel
Chloë . . . . Di Franco

97

1965-66

November 22
DON CARLO (Verdi)
Same cast as October 7 except:
Philip II ....Ghiaurov
Rodrigo ....Merrill
Grand Inquisitor ....Ward
Elizabeth ....Curtis-Verna
Princess Eboli ....Dalis
Count Lerma ....Marcella

November 23
ARABELLA (R. Strauss)
Same cast as October 1 except:
Mandryka ....Dooley

November 24
QUEEN OF SPADES (Tchaikovsky)
Same cast as September 28 except:
Lisa ....Weathers
Pauline (Daphnis) ......Grillo
Count Tomsky ....Cassel
Chloë ....Di Franco

November 25
IL TROVATORE (Verdi)
Same cast as October 20 except:
Manrico ....Prevedi
Azucena ....Gorr
Inez ....Owen
Ferrando ....Giaiotti

November 26
MADAMA BUTTERFLY (Puccini)
Same cast as October 13 except:
Conductor: Cleva
Cio-Cio-San ....Albanese
B. F. Pinkerton ....Morell

November 27 (matinee)
L'ELISIR D'AMORE (Donizetti)
Same cast as November 12

November 27
FAUST (Gounod)
Same cast as September 27 except:
Faust ....Alexander
Marguerite ....Fenn
Méphistophélès ......Ghiaurov
Valentin ....Walker

November 29
DON CARLO (Verdi)
Same cast as October 7 except:
Philip II ....Flagello
Rodrigo ....Merrill
Grand Inquisitor ....Dooley
Count Lerma ....Marcella
Friar ....Vichey

November 30
L'ELISIR D'AMORE (Donizetti)
Same cast as November 12

December 1
LA FANCIULLA DEL WEST
(Puccini)
Conductor: Cleva
Minnie ....Kirsten
Dick Johnson ....Corelli

Jack Rance ....Colzani
Nick ....Franke
Ashby ....Scott
Sonora ....Harvuot
Trin ....Carelli
Sid ....Goodloe
Handsome ....Cehanovsky
Harry ....Nagy
Joe ....Velis
Happy ....Christopher
Larkens ....Boucher
Billy Jackrabbit ....Ghazal
Wowkle ....Love
Jake Wallace ....Flagello
José Castro ....Sgarro
Post Rider ....D'Elia

December 2
FAUST (Gounod)
Same cast as September 27 except:
Faust ....Alexander
Marguerite ....Costa
Méphistophélès ....Diaz
Valentin ....Sereni

December 3
QUEEN OF SPADES (Tchaikovsky)
Same cast as September 28 except:
Conductor: Rich
Countess ....Thebom
Count Tomsky ....Cassel
Chloë ....Di Franco

December 4 (matinee)
IL TROVATORE (Verdi)
Same cast as October 20 except:
Manrico ....Prevedi
Azucena ....Cvejic
Ferrando ....Giaiotti

December 4
Benefit Mizrachi
Women's Organization
LA BOHEME (Puccini)
Same cast as September 29 except:
Conductor: Schick
Rodolfo ....Corelli
Marcello ....Guarrera
Colline ....Giaiotti
Mimi ....Tebaldi
Musetta ....Rothenberger
Benoit ....Corena
Alcindoro ....Alvary

December 6
SAMSON ET DALILA (Saint-Saëns)
Conductor: Prêtre
Dalila ....Gorr
Samson ....McCracken
High Priest ....Bacquier
Abimelech ....Diaz
Old Hebrew ....Giaiotti
Philistine Messenger ......Nagy
Philistines ....Schmorr, Goodloe

December 7
LA FANCIULLA DEL WEST
(Puccini)
Same cast as December 1

December 8
ARABELLA (R. Strauss)
Same cast as October 1 except:
Mandryka ....Dooley
Fiakermilli ....Scovotti

December 9
FAUST (Gounod)
Same cast as September 27 except:
Faust ....Alexander
Marguerite ....Fenn
Méphistophélès ....Diaz

December 10
LA BOHEME (Puccini)
Same cast as September 29 except:
Conductor: Schick
Rodolfo ....Konya
Marcello ....Guarrera
Colline ....Giaiotti
Mimi ....Tebaldi
Musetta ....Rothenberger
Benoit ....Corena
Alcindoro ....Alvary

December 11 (matinee)
DON CARLO (Verdi)
Same cast as October 7 except:
Elizabeth ....Arroyo
Princess Eboli ....Cvejic

December 11
L'ELISIR D'AMORE (Donizetti)
Same cast as November 12

December 13
LUCIA DI LAMMERMOOR
(Donizetti)
Same cast as September 30 except:
Conductor: Rich
Lucia ....Scotto
Enrico Ashton ....Colzani
Edgardo ....Konya
Normanno ....Schmorr

December 14
LA BOHEME (Puccini)
Same cast as September 29 except:
Rodolfo ....Corelli
Marcello ....Guarrera
Colline ....Hines
Mimi ....Tebaldi
Musetta ....Rothenberger
Benoit ....Corena
Alcindoro ....Alvary

December 15
SAMSON ET DALILA (Saint-Saëns)
Same cast as December 6

December 16
L'ELISIR D'AMORE (Donizetti)
Same cast as November 12 except:
Adina ....Scovotti

98

December 17
LA FANCIULLA DEL WEST
(Puccini)
Same cast as December 1 except:
Conductor: Behr
Jake Wallace . . . . Giaiotti

December 18 (matinee)
ARABELLA (R. Strauss)
Same cast as October 1 except:
Mandryka . . . . Dooley
Fiakermilli . . . . Scovotti

December 18
Benefit Bagby Music
Lovers Foundation
LA PERICHOLE (Offenbach)
Conductor: Allers
Don Andres . . . . Ritchard
Don Pedro . . . . Gramm
Panatellas . . . . Franke
Tarapote . . . . Alvary
Perichole . . . . Stratas
Paquillo . . . . Uppman
Guadalena . . . . Clements
Estrella . . . . Pracht
Virginella . . . . Baldwin
Notaries . . . . . . Schmorr, Boucher
Old Prisoner . . . . Velis
Clown . . . . Mickens
Ballerina . . . . Aragno
Jailer . . . . Chistiakov

December 19
IL TROVATORE (Verdi)
Same cast as October 20 except:
Manrico . . . . McCracken
Count Di Luna . . . . Colzani
Ferrando . . . . Sgarro

December 20
SAMSON ET DALILA (Saint-Saëns)
Same cast as December 6 except:
Dalila . . . . Cvejic
Samson . . . . Vickers
High Priest . . . . Walker
Abimelech . . . . Sgarro

December 21
TOSCA (Puccini)
Conductor: Schick
Tosca . . . . Tebaldi
Cavaradossi . . . . Konya
Scarpia . . . . Bacquier
Angelotti . . . . Harvuot
Sacristan . . . . Corena
Spoletta . . . . Velis
Sciarrone . . . . Christopher
Jailer . . . . Boucher
Shepherd . . . . Fischer

December 22
FAUST (Gounod)
Same cast as September 27 except:
Faust . . . . Alexander
Marguerite . . . . Caballé
Méphistophélès . . . . Diaz
Valentin . . . . Milnes

December 23
LA FANCIULLA DEL WEST
(Puccini)
Same cast as December 1 except:
Jake Wallace . . . . Giaiotti

December 24
L'ELISIR D'AMORE (Donizetti)
Same cast as November 12 except:
Adina . . . . Scotto
Nemorino . . . . Shirley
Belcore . . . . Guarrera

December 25 (matinee)
LA PERICHOLE (Offenbach)
Same cast as December 18

December 25
IL TROVATORE (Verdi)
Same cast as October 20 except:
Conductor: Schippers
Leonora . . . . Arroyo
Manrico . . . . McCracken
Ruiz . . . . Marek

December 27
TOSCA (Puccini)
Same cast as December 21

December 28
QUEEN OF SPADES (Tchaikovsky)
Same cast as September 28 except:
Countess . . . . Thebom
Pauline (Daphnis) . . . . . . Grillo
Gherman . . . . McCracken
Count Tomsky . . . . Meredith
Prince Yeletsky . . . . Milnes
Chloë . . . . Di Franco

December 29
AIDA (Verdi)
Conductor: Mehta
King . . . . Michalski
Amneris . . . . Gorr
Aida . . . . Tucci
Radames . . . . Corelli
Amonasro . . . . Colzani
Ramfis . . . . Ghiuselev
Messenger . . . . Nagy
Priestess . . . . Pracht

December 30
LA BOHEME (Puccini)
Same cast as September 29 except:
Conductor (Acts 2, 3, 4): Schick
Rodolfo . . . . Konya
Marcello . . . . Sereni
Schaunard . . . . Goodloe
Colline . . . . Hines
Mimi . . . . Tebaldi

December 31
LA PERICHOLE (Offenbach)
Same cast as December 18

January 1 (matinee)
SAMSON ET DALILA (Saint-Saëns)
Same cast as December 6 except:
Conductor: Adler
Dalila . . . . Dalis
Old Hebrew . . . . Macurdy

January 1
MADAMA BUTTERFLY (Puccini)
Same cast as October 13

January 3
AIDA (Verdi)
Same cast as December 29 except:
Priestess . . . . Baldwin

January 4
SAMSON ET DALILA (Saint-Saëns)
Same cast as December 6 except:
Conductor: Adler
Dalila . . . . Dalis
Samson . . . . Thomas
Old Hebrew . . . . Macurdy

January 5
MADAMA BUTTERFLY (Puccini)
Same cast as October 13 except:
Cio-Cio-San . . . . Roberto
B. F. Pinkerton . . . . Shirley
Sharpless . . . . Sereni

January 6
QUEEN OF SPADES (Tchaikovsky)
Same cast as September 28 except:
Countess . . . . Madeira
Lisa . . . . Weathers
Pauline (Daphnis) . . . . . . Grillo
Gherman . . . . McCracken
Count Tomsky . . . . Meredith
Prince Yeletsky . . . . Milnes
Chloë . . . . Di Franco

January 7
TOSCA (Puccini)
Same cast as December 21 except:
Sacristan . . . . Alvary

January 8 (matinee)
LA FANCIULLA DEL WEST
(Puccini)
Same cast as December 1 except:
Conductor: Behr
Billy Jackrabbit . . . . . . Michalski
Jake Wallace . . . . Macurdy

January 8
FIDELIO (Beethoven)
Conductor: Boehm
Don Fernando . . . . Milnes
Don Pizarro . . . . Evans
Florestan . . . . King
Leonore . . . . Nilsson
Rocco . . . . Edelmann
Marzelline . . . . Pracht
Jacquino . . . . Anthony
First Prisoner . . . . Shirley
Second Prisoner . . . . Christopher

January 9
Benefit West Side
Institutional Synagogue
LUCIA DI LAMMERMOOR
(Donizetti)
Same cast as September 30 except:
Conductor: Rich
Lucia . . . . Scotto
Edgardo . . . . Konya
Raimondo . . . . Diaz
Normanno . . . . Nagy

January 10
AIDA (Verdi)
Same cast as December 29 except:
Amneris .... Rankin
Radames .... Thomas

January 11
LA BOHEME (Puccini)
Same cast as September 29 except:
Conductor: Schick
Rodolfo .... Corelli
Marcello .... Uppman
Schaunard .... Goodloe
Colline .... Ghiuselev
Mimi .... Tebaldi
Benoit .... Michalski
Sergeant .... Forero

January 12
FIDELIO (Beethoven)
Same cast as January 8 except:
Leonore .... Dvorakova

January 13
MADAMA BUTTERFLY (Puccini)
Same cast as October 13 except:
B. F. Pinkerton .... Morell
Sharpless .... Sereni
Kate Pinkerton .... Owen

January 14
SALOME (R. Strauss)
Conductor: Boehm
Herod .... Liebl
Herodias .... Dalis
Salome .... Nilsson
Jochanaan .... Dooley
Narraboth .... Shirley
Page .... Casei
First Nazarene .... Macurdy
Second Nazarene ...... Goodloe
First Jew .... Anthony
Second Jew .... Nagy
Third Jew .... Carelli
Fourth Jew .... Velis
Fifth Jew .... Davidson
First Soldier .... Michalski
Second Soldier .... Sgarro
Cappodocian .... Christopher
Slave .... Marek

January 15 (matinee)
QUEEN OF SPADES (Tchaikovsky)
Same cast as September 28 except:
Countess .... Madeira
Gherman .... McCracken
Count Tomsky .... Cassel
Chloë .... Di Franco

January 15
LA BOHEME (Puccini)
Same cast as September 29 except:
Conductor: Schick
Rodolfo .... Konya
Marcello .... Uppman
Schaunard .... Goodloe
Colline .... Ghiuselev
Mimi .... Tebaldi
Benoit .... Michalski

January 17
LA FANCIULLA DEL WEST
(Puccini)
Same cast as December 1 except:
Conductor: Behr
Minnie .... Steber
Dick Johnson (Acts 2 & 3) Bardini
Jake Wallace .... Macurdy

January 18
LA PERICHOLE (Offenbach)
Same cast as December 18 except:
Conductor: Strasfogel

January 19
SALOME (R. Strauss)
Same cast as January 14

January 20
MANON LESCAUT (Puccini)
Same cast as October 25 except:
Manon .... Albanese
Lescaut .... Sereni
Des Grieux .... Tucker
Geronte .... Gramm
Innkeeper .... Christopher
Madrigal Singers .... Sims,
    McIlhenny, Eure, A. Jones

January 21
SAMSON ET DALILA (Saint-Saëns)
Same cast as December 6 except:
Conductor: Adler
Dalila .... Dunn
Samson .... Thomas
Old Hebrew .... Macurdy

January 22 (matinee)
FIDELIO (Beethoven)
Same cast as January 8

January 22
AIDA (Verdi)
Same cast as December 29 except:
Amneris .... Dalis
Aida .... Arroyo
Amonasro .... Milnes
Ramfis .... Macurdy

January 24
LA BOHEME (Puccini)
Same cast as September 29 except:
Conductor: Schick
Rodolfo .... Tucker
Marcello .... Sereni
Schaunard .... Goodloe
Colline .... Ghiuselev
Mimi .... Amara
Benoit .... Michalski

January 25
TOSCA (Puccini)
Same cast as December 21 except:
Tosca .... Nilsson
Cavaradossi .... Corelli
Scarpia .... Colzani
Angelotti .... Scott
Sacristan .... Alvary

January 26
AIDA (Verdi)
Same cast as December 29 except:
Amneris .... Rankin
Aida .... Arroyo
Radames .... Thomas
Amonasro .... Merrill
Ramfis .... Macurdy

January 27
FIDELIO (Beethoven)
Same cast as January 8 except:
Don Fernando .... Flagello
Don Pizarro .... Dooley
Leonore .... Dvorakova

January 28
SALOME (R. Strauss)
Same cast as January 14 except:
Jochanaan .... Cassel

January 29 (matinee)
DON GIOVANNI (Mozart)
Conductor: Rosenstock
Don Giovanni .... Siepi
Donna Anna ..... Stich-Randall
Donna Elvira ...... Schwarzkopf
Zerlina .... Elias
Don Ottavio .... Peerce
Commendatore .... Ghiuselev
Leporello .... Evans
Masetto .... Uppman

January 29
MANON LESCAUT (Puccini)
Same cast as October 25 except:
Manon .... Kirsten
Lescaut .... Sereni
Des Grieux .... Tucker
Geronte .... Gramm
Innkeeper .... Christopher
Madrigal Singers .... Sims,
    McIlhenny, Eure, A. Jones

January 30
Benefit Sponsored by the
Metropolitan Opera Guild
for the
Production Fund
ANDREA CHENIER (Giordano)
Conductor: Gardelli
Andrea Chénier .... Corelli
Maddalena .... Tebaldi
Countess di Coigny ...... Kriese
Carlo Gérard .... Colzani
Bersi .... Casei
Fléville .... Boucher
Abbé .... Carelli
Madelon .... Dunn
Mathieu .... Michalski
Spy .... Velis
Fouquier .... Scott
Dumas .... Christopher
Roucher .... Walker
Schmidt .... Sgarro
Major domo .... Strang

January 31
FIDELIO (Beethoven)
Same cast as January 8 except:
Don Pizarro .... Dooley

February 1
DON GIOVANNI (Mozart)
Same cast as January 29 except:
Donna Elvira . . . . Amara

February 2
LA PERICHOLE (Offenbach)
Same cast as December 18 except:
Ballerina . . . . Wilson

February 3
TOSCA (Puccini)
Same cast as December 21 except:
Tosca . . . . Kirsten
Cavaradossi . . . . Tucker
Scarpia . . . . Cassel
Angelotti . . . . Scott
Sacristan . . . . Alvary

February 4
DON GIOVANNI (Mozart)
Same cast as January 29 except:
Donna Elvira . . . . Amara

February 5 (matinee)
ANDREA CHENIER (Giordano)
Same cast as January 30

February 5
SALOME (R. Strauss)
Same cast as January 14 except:
Herodias . . . . Rankin
Jochanaan . . . . Cassel

February 7
UN BALLO IN MASCHERA (Verdi)
Conductor: Molinari-Pradelli
Gustav III . . . . Bergonzi
Anckarström . . . . Merrill
Amelia . . . . Price
Ulrica . . . . Dunn
Oscar . . . . Peters
Cristiano . . . . Goodloe
Count de Horn . . . . Macurdy
Count Warting . . . . Sgarro
Chief Justice . . . . Velis
Servant . . . . Schmorr

February 8 (matinee)
151st Metropolitan Opera Guild
Student Performance
LA FANCIULLA DEL WEST
(Puccini)
Conductor: Behr
Minnie . . . . Owen
Dick Johnson . . . . Bardini
Jack Rance . . . . Milnes
Nick . . . . Anthony
Ashby . . . . Scott
Sonora . . . . Boucher
Trin . . . . Marcella
Sid . . . . De Paola
Handsome . . . . Sliker
Harry . . . . Zakariasen
Joe . . . . Marek
Happy . . . . Strang
Larkens . . . . Dunlap
Billy Jackrabbit . . . . . Tomanelli
Wowkle . . . . Shawn
Jack Wallace . . . . Sgarro
José Castro . . . . Michalski
Post Rider . . . . D'Elia

February 8
SALOME (R. Strauss)
Same cast as January 14 except:
Herodias . . . . Rankin
Salome . . . . Kouba
Narraboth . . . . Alexander

February 9
FIDELIO (Beethoven)
Same cast as January 8 except:
Don Pizarro . . . . Cassel
Florestan . . . . Thomas
Leonore . . . . Dvorakova
Marzelline . . . . Clements

February 10
ANDREA CHENIER (Giordano)
Same cast as January 30 except:
Andrea Chénier . . . . Bergonzi
Madelon . . . . Madeira
Mathieu . . . . Esparza

February 11
DON GIOVANNI (Mozart)
Same cast as January 29 except:
Donna Elvira . . . . Lorengar

February 12 (matinee)
AIDA (Verdi)
Same cast as December 29 except:
Amneris . . . . Dalis
Aida . . . . Price
Radames . . . . Tucker
Amonasro . . . . Merrill

February 12
TOSCA (Puccini)
Same cast as December 21 except:
Tosca . . . . Kirsten
Cavaradossi . . . . Morell
Scarpia . . . . Cassel
Angelotti . . . . Scott
Sacristan . . . . Esparza
Spoletta . . . . Schmorr

February 14
DON GIOVANNI (Mozart)
Same cast as January 29 except:
Donna Elvira . . . . Lorengar

February 15
ANDREA CHENIER (Giordano)
Same cast as January 30 except:
Andrea Chénier . . . . Bergonzi
Carlo Gérard . . . . Milnes
Madelon . . . . Madeira
Mathieu . . . . Esparza

February 16
RIGOLETTO (Verdi)
Conductor: Molinari-Pradelli
Duke . . . . Kraus
Rigoletto . . . . MacNeil
Gilda . . . . Peters
Sparafucile . . . . Macurdy
Maddalena . . . . Pospinov
Giovanna . . . . Ordassy
Monterone . . . . Michalski
Marullo . . . . Goodloe
Borsa . . . . Carelli
Ceprano . . . . Boucher
Countess . . . . Di Franco
Page . . . . Shawn
Guard . . . . De Paola

February 17
FALSTAFF (Verdi)
Same cast as October 29 except:
Fenton . . . . Alva
Dr. Caius . . . . Caruso
Mistress Ford . . . . Lorengar
Dame Quickly . . . . . . Chookasian

February 18
AIDA (Verdi)
Same cast as December 29 except:
Amneris . . . . Rankin
Aida . . . . Arroyo
Radames . . . . Tucker
Amonasro . . . . MacNeil

February 19 (matinee)
LUCIA DI LAMMERMOOR
(Donizetti)
Same cast as September 30 except:
Lucia . . . . Peters
Enrico Ashton . . . . Guarrera
Edgardo . . . . Konya
Raimondo . . . . Diaz
Normanno . . . . Nagy

February 19
UN BALLO IN MASCHERA (Verdi)
Same cast as February 7 except:
Oscar . . . . Scovotti

February 21
DON GIOVANNI (Mozart)
Same cast as January 29 except:
Donna Anna . . . . Bjoner
Donna Elvira . . . . Lorengar
Commendatore . . . . Diaz
Leporello . . . . Esparza

February 22
RIGOLETTO (Verdi)
Same cast as February 16 except:
Monterone . . . . Diaz

February 23
FALSTAFF (Verdi)
Same cast as October 29 except:
Fenton . . . . Alva
Dr. Caius . . . . Caruso
Mistress Ford . . . . Lorengar
Dame Quickly . . . . . . Chookasian

February 24 (matinee)
152nd Metropolitan Opera Guild
Student Performance
LA FANCIULLA DEL WEST
(Puccini)
Same cast as February 8

February 24
LA FANCIULLA DEL WEST
(Puccini)
Same cast as December 1 except:
Conductor: Behr
Dick Johnson . . . . Tucker
Jack Rance . . . . Guarrera
Jake Wallace . . . . Macurdy

February 25
IL BARBIERE DI SIVIGLIA
(Rossini)
Conductor: Varviso
Almaviva . . . . Shirley
Dr. Bartolo . . . . Corena
Rosina . . . . Grist
Figaro . . . . Herlea
Don Basilio . . . . Tozzi
Berta . . . . Kriese
Fiorello . . . . Boucher
Sergeant . . . . Velis
Ambrogio . . . . Sliker

February 26 (matinee)
UN BALLO IN MASCHERA (Verdi)
Same cast as February 7

February 26
TOSCA (Puccini)
Same cast as December 21 except:
Cavaradossi . . . . Alexander
Scarpia . . . . Gobbi
Angelotti . . . . Scott
Spoletta . . . . Schmorr

February 28 (matinee)
153rd Metropolitan Opera Guild
Student Performance
LA FANCIULLA DEL WEST
(Puccini)
Same cast as February 8 except:
Dick Johnson . . . . Nagy
Jack Rance . . . . Bardelli
Nick . . . . Franke

February 28
IL TROVATORE (Verdi)
Same cast as October 20 except:
Conductor: Schick
Leonora . . . . Arroyo
Manrico . . . . Tucker
Count Di Luna . . . . MacNeil
Azucena . . . . Rankin
Ferrando . . . . Sgarro

March 1
UN BALLO IN MASCHERA (Verdi)
Same cast as February 7

March 2
IL BARBIERE DI SIVIGLIA
(Rossini)
Same cast as February 25

March 3
RIGOLETTO (Verdi)
Same cast as February 16 except:
Gilda . . . . Scovotti
Monterone . . . . Diaz
Page . . . . A. Jones

March 4
MANON LESCAUT (Puccini)
Same cast as October 25 except:
Des Grieux . . . . Tucker
Captain . . . . Christopher
Madrigal Singers . . . . Sims,
McIlhenney, Eure, A. Jones

March 5 (matinee)
L'ELISIR D'AMORE (Donizetti)
Same cast as November 12 except:
Adina . . . . Peters
Nemorino . . . . Bergonzi
Belcore . . . . Guarrera
Giannetta . . . . Di Franco

March 5
FALSTAFF (Verdi)
Same cast as October 29 except:
Sir John Falstaff . . . . Gobbi
Fenton . . . . Alva
Dr. Caius . . . . Caruso
Mistress Ford . . . . Lorengar
Dame Quickly . . . . . . Chookasian

March 7
ANDREA CHENIER (Giordano)
Same cast as January 30 except:
Conductor: Molinari-Pradelli
Andrea Chénier . . . . Bergonzi
Maddalena . . . . Milanov
Carlo Gérard . . . . Merrill
Mathieu . . . . Esparza

March 8
DON GIOVANNI (Mozart)
Same cast as January 29 except:
Donna Anna . . . . Bjoner
Donna Elvira . . . . Lorengar
Zerlina . . . . Scovotti
Don Ottavio . . . . Kraus
Commendatore . . . . Diaz
Leporello . . . . Flagello

March 9
FALSTAFF (Verdi)
Same cast as October 29 except:
Sir John Falstaff . . . . Gobbi
Ford . . . . Stewart
Fenton . . . . Alva
Dr. Caius . . . . Caruso
Mistress Ford . . . . Lorengar
Dame Quickly . . . . . . Chookasian

March 10
PARSIFAL (Wagner)
Conductor: Prêtre
Amfortas . . . . London
Titurel . . . . Diaz
Gurnemanz . . . . Hines
Parsifal . . . . Konya
Klingsor . . . . Meredith
Kundry . . . . Crespin
Voice . . . . Pospinov
Knights . . . . Nagy, Goodloe
Esquires . . . . Pracht, Love,
Anthony, Marek
Flower Maidens . . Krall, Clements,
Sukis, Di Franco,
Baldwin, Casei

March 11
RIGOLETTO (Verdi)
Same cast as February 16 except:
Sparafucile . . . . Diaz
Maddalena . . . . Casei
Page . . . . A. Jones

March 12 (matinee)
MANON LESCAUT (Puccini)
Same cast as October 25 except:
Des Grieux . . . . Tucker
Innkeeper . . . . Christopher

March 12
Benefit Vassar Club
Scholarship Fund
IL BARBIERE DI SIVIGLIA
(Rossini)
Same cast as February 25 except:
Almaviva . . . . Alva
Don Basilio . . . . Siepi

March 13
AIDA (Verdi)
Same cast as December 29 except:
Amneris . . . . Cernei
Aida . . . . Price
Amonasro . . . . Milnes
Ramfis . . . . Hines

March 14
ANDREA CHENIER (Giordano)
Same cast as January 30 except:
Conductor: Molinari-Pradelli
Andrea Chénier . . . . Bergonzi
Maddalena . . . . Farrell
Carlo Gérard . . . . Merrill
Bersi . . . . Baldwin
Mathieu . . . . Esparza

March 15
FALSTAFF (Verdi)
Same cast as October 29 except:
Sir John Falstaff . . . . Gobbi
Fenton . . . . Alva
Dr. Caius . . . . Caruso
Mistress Ford . . . . . . Kabaivanska
Dame Quickly . . . . . . Chookasian
Mistress Page . . . . Baldwin

March 16
PARSIFAL (Wagner)
Same cast as March 10 except:
Amfortas . . . . Cassel
Kundry . . . . Välkki

March 17
DON GIOVANNI (Mozart)
Same cast as January 29 except:
Donna Anna . . . . Bjoner
Donna Elvira . . . . Lorengar
Zerlina . . . . Scovotti
Don Ottavio . . . . Kraus
Commendatore . . . . Diaz
Leporello . . . . Corena

March 18 (matinee)
154th Metropolitan Opera Guild
Student Performance
LA FANCIULLA DEL WEST
(Puccini)
Same cast as February 8 except:
Dick Johnson . . . . Nagy
Jack Rance . . . . Bardelli
Jake Wallace . . . . Diaz
José Castro . . . . Sgarro

March 18
LA FANCIULLA DEL WEST
(Puccini)
Same cast as December 1 except:
Conductor: Behr
Jake Wallace . . . . Diaz

March 19 (matinee)
IL BARBIERE DI SIVIGLIA
(Rossini)
Same cast as February 25 except:
Don Basilio . . . . Siepi

March 19
TANNHAUSER (Wagner)
Conductor: Rosenstock
Hermann . . . . Macurdy
Tannhäuser . . . . Nuotio
Wolfram . . . . Stewart
Walther . . . . Sergi
Biterolf . . . . Goodloe
Heinrich . . . . Franke
Reinmar . . . . Scott
Elisabeth . . . . Nilsson
Venus . . . . Nilsson
Shepherd . . . . Pracht
Pages . . . . Fercana, Lansché
Eure, Munson

March 21 (matinee)
155th Metropolitan Opera Guild
Student Performance
LA FANCIULLA DEL WEST
(Puccini)
Same cast as February 8 except:
Jake Wallace . . . . Diaz
José Castro . . . . Sgarro

March 21
L'ELISIR D'AMORE (Donizetti)
Same cast as November 12 except:
Adina . . . . Scovotti
Nemorino . . . . Bergonzi
Belcore . . . . Guarrera
Giannetta . . . . Di Franco

March 22
ANDREA CHENIER (Giordano)
Same cast as January 30 except:
Conductor: Molinari-Pradelli
Maddalena . . . . Farrell
Carlo Gérard . . . . Merrill
Madelon . . . . Pospinov
Mathieu . . . . Esparza

March 23
TANNHAUSER (Wagner)
Same cast as March 19

March 24
FALSTAFF (Verdi)
Same cast as October 29 except:
Sir John Falstaff . . . . Colzani
Fenton . . . . Alva
Dr. Caius . . . . Caruso
Mistress Ford . . . . . . Kabaivanska
Dame Quickly . . . . . . Chookasian
Mistress Page . . . . Baldwin

March 25
UN BALLO IN MASCHERA (Verdi)
Same cast as February 7 except:
Anckarström . . . . Milnes
Amelia . . . . Crespin
Ulrica . . . . Pospinov
Oscar . . . . Scovotti
Count de Horn . . . . Alvary

March 26 (matinee)
TANNHAUSER (Wagner)
Same cast as March 19

March 26
IL BARBIERE DI SIVIGLIA
(Rossini)
Same cast as February 25 except:
Almaviva . . . . Alva
Dr. Bartolo . . . . Esparza
Figaro . . . . Guarrera

March 27
BALLET EVENING
CONCERNING ORACLES (Ibert)
World Premiere
Conductor: Lombard
Teller of Fortunes . . . . Paaz
Gypsies . . . . Mahler, Mickens
Sololists: Aschieri, Brayley,
Emanuel, Grinvald, Jerell,
Jorgenson, Martin, Morse,
O'Connell; Allen, Davis,
Friedman, Gregory, Maloney,
D. Milnes, Sayette, Westergard,
Yezer
Singers: Baldwin, Casei,
Ordassy, Pracht
ECHOING OF TRUMPETS (Martinu)
American Premiere
Conductor: Strasfogel
Soloists: Aschieri, Brayley,
Grinvald, Heyes, Jerell, Marritt,
Paaz; Allen, Eddington, Gregory,
Mahler, Maloney, Meister,
Sayette, Yezer
LA VENTANA (Lumbye)
Conductor: Strasfogel
Señorita . . . . Heyes
Young Man . . . . Meister
Soloists: Aragno, Brayley, Knitzer,
Levy, Marritt; Allen, Davis,
Eddington, Mahler, Maloney,
Milnes, Sayette

March 28 (matinee)
156th Metropolitan Opera Guild
Student Performance
LA FANCIULLA DEL WEST
(Puccini)
Same cast as February 8 except:
Minnie . . . . Bower
Jack Rance . . . . Bardelli

March 28
RIGOLETTO (Verdi)
Same cast as February 16 except:
Duke . . . . Alexander
Rigoletto . . . . Colzani
Sparafucile . . . . Diaz
Maddalena . . . . Casei
Page . . . . A. Jones

March 29
TANNHAUSER (Wagner)
Same cast as March 19 except:
Hermann . . . . Hines

March 30
TOSCA (Puccini)
Same cast as December 21 except:
Tosca . . . . Crespin
Cavaradossi . . . . Corelli
Scarpia . . . . Cassel
Angelotti . . . . Scott
Spoletta . . . . Schmorr

March 31
IL BARBIERE DI SIVIGLIA
(Rossini)
Same cast as February 25 except:
Dr. Bartolo . . . . Vinay
Rosina . . . . Peters
Figaro . . . . Guarrera

April 1
FIDELIO (Beethoven)
Same cast as January 8 except:
Conductor: Rosenstock
Don Fernando . . . . Flagello
Don Pizarro . . . . Meredith
Florestan . . . . Vickers
Leonore . . . . Rysanek
Rocco . . . . Wiemann

April 2 (matinee)
PARSIFAL (Wagner)
Same cast as March 10 except:
Amfortas . . . . Cassel
First Knight . . . . Carelli

April 2
TOSCA (Puccini)
Same cast as December 21 except:
Tosca . . . . Nilsson
Cavaradossi . . . . Tucker
Scarpia . . . . Colzani
Angelotti . . . . Scott
Spoletta . . . . Schmorr

April 4
TANNHAUSER (Wagner)
Same cast as March 19 except:
Hermann . . . . Hines
Wolfram . . . . Cassel
Elisabeth . . . . Rysanek
Venus . . . . Välkki

April 5
MADAMA BUTTERFLY (Puccini)
Same cast as October 13 except:
Cio-Cio-San . . . . Tucci
Suzuki . . . . Baldwin

April 6
UN BALLO IN MASCHERA (Verdi)
Same cast as February 7 except:
Gustav III . . . . Tucker
Anckarström . . . . Milnes
Amelia . . . . Crespin
Ulrica . . . . Pospinov
Oscar . . . . Scovotti
Count de Horn . . . . Alvary

April 7
FIDELIO (Beethoven)
Same cast as January 8 except:
Conductor: Rosenstock
Don Pizarro ....Meredith
Florestan ....Vickers
Rocco ....Wiemann
Jacquino ....Schmorr

April 8 (matinee)
PARSIFAL (Wagner)
Same cast as March 10 except:
Amfortas ....Cassel
Kundry ....Välkki
First Knight ....Carelli
Third Esquire ....Franke

April 8
IL BARBIERE DI SIVIGLIA
(Rossini)
Same cast as February 25 except:
Rosina ....Peters
Figaro ....Guarrera

April 9 (matinee)
FAUST (Gounod)
Same cast as September 27 except:
Marguerite ....Fenn
Valentin ....Walker

April 9
RIGOLETTO (Verdi)
Same cast as February 16 except:
Duke (Acts 1 & 2) ......Morell
Duke (Acts 3 & 4) ...Alexander
Rigoletto ....Colzani
Gilda ....Scovotti
Sparafucile ....Diaz
Maddalena ....Cernei
Page ....A. Jones

April 11 (matinee)
157th Metropolitan Opera Guild
Student Performance
LA FANCIULLA DEL WEST
(Puccini)
Same cast as February 8 except:
Minnie ....Bower
Jack Rance ....Bardelli
[Editor's note: This performance
took place in the new Metropolitan
Opera House at Lincoln Center.]

April 11
TOSCA (Puccini)
Same cast as December 21 except:
Tosca ....Crespin
Cavaradossi ....Corelli
Scarpia ....Cassel
Angelotti ....Scott
Spoletta ....Schmorr
Sciarrone ....Walker

April 12
FIDELIO (Beethoven)
Same cast as January 18 except:
Conductor: Rosenstock
Don Fernando ....Flagello
Don Pizarro ....Meredith
Florestan ....Vickers
Leonore ....Rysanek
Rocco ....Wiemann
Second Prisoner ....Goodloe

April 13
ANDREA CHENIER (Giordano)
Same cast as January 30 except:
Conductor: Molinari-Pradelli
Andrea Chénier ....Tucker
Maddalena ....Milanov
Mathieu ....Alvary
Dumas ....Goodloe

April 14
AIDA (Verdi)
Same cast as December 29 except:
Conductor: Varviso
Amneris ....Cernei
Aida ....Price
Radames ....Konya
Amonasro ....Guarrera
Ramfis ....Diaz
Messenger ....Franke

April 15
TANNHAUSER (Wagner)
Same cast as March 19 except:
Hermann ....Wiemann
Elisabeth ....Rysanek
Venus ....Välkki

April 16 (matinee)
LA BOHEME (Puccini)
Same cast as September 29 except:
Conductor: Schick
Rodolfo ....Tucker
Marcello ....Sereni
Colline ....Hines
Mimi ....Tucci
Benoit ....Corena
Alcindoro ....Alvary

April 16
GALA FAREWELL
National Anthem
Entrance of the Guests
(Tannhäuser)
Conductor: Stokowski
Presentation of Honored Guests:
Mmes. Anderson, Bampton, Case,
Georgiou, Glaz, Guilford, Jepson,
Lawrence, Lehmann, Lipton,
Mason, Miller, Morgana, Munsel,
Petina, Pons, Rethberg, Roman,
Sayão, Stevens; Messrs. Bambos-
chek, Bonelli, Brownlee, Chamlee,
Conley, Crooks, Jagel, Jobin,
Kipnis, Kullman, Martinelli; Mas-
ter of ceremonies Hawkins.
Sextet: "Chi mi frena"
(Lucia di Lammermoor)
Moffo, Ordassy, Sergi, Anthony,
Diaz, Walker
"Eri tu" (Un Ballo in Maschera)
Merrill
"Sì, pel ciel" (Otello)
McCracken, Colzani
"Ella giammai m'amò!"
Siepi (Don Carlo)
Conductor: Molinari-Pradelli
"Depuis le jour" (Louise)
Kirsten
Quintet: "Nous avons en tête une
affaire" (Carmen)
Resnik, Votipka, Baldwin,
Franke, Cehanovsky

"Un bel dì" (Madama Butterfly)
Albanese
Conductor: Rudolf
"Winterstürme" (Die Walküre)
Vickers
"Heil diesem Hause"
(Der Barbier von Bagdad)
Corena
Conductor: Schick
"Una voce poco fà"
(Il Barbiere di Siviglia)
Peters
Trio: "Non imprecare"
(La Forza del Destino)
Rigal, Peerce, Tozzi
Conductor: Varviso
"L'amo come il fulgor del creato!"
(La Gioconda)
Crespin, Cvejic
"D'amor sull'ali rosee"
(Il Trovatore)
Price
"Vieni! Colle tue braccia stringi
Manon" (Manon Lescaut)
Tebaldi, Corelli
Conductor: Cleva
"Morgenlich leuchtend"
(Die Meistersinger)
Konya
Immolation: "Starke Scheite"
(Götterdämmerung)
Nilsson
Conductor: Rosenstock
AIDA (Verdi) (Act II, Scene 2)
Conductor: Mehta
King ....Macurdy
Amneris ....Madeira
Aida ....Curtis-Verna
Radames ....Baum
Amonasro ....Sereni
Ramfis ....Scott
Trio: "Are they gone?"
(Così Fan Tutte)
Stratas, Miller, Guarrera
Quintet: "Three spirits young and
wise" (The Magic Flute)
Pracht, Grillo, Kriese, Shirley,
Uppman
Conductor: Leinsdorf
Quintet: "To leave, to break"
(Vanessa)
Steber, Dunn, Thebom,
Alexander, Harvuot
Conductor: Adler
Trio: "Hab' mir's gelobt"
(Der Rosenkavalier)
Raskin, Caballé, Elias
"Vicino a te" (Andrea Chénier)
Milanov, Tucker
Trio: "Alerte! Alerte!" (Faust)
Tucci, Gedda, Hines
Conductor: Prêtre

[Editor's note: The entire company returned to the stage to join
the audience in singing "Auld lang
syne" as a musical farewell to the
old Metropolitan Opera House.]

EXCERPTS FROM PRESS REVIEWS

NEW PRODUCTION of Gounod's *Faust,* September 27, 1965

Everybody agrees that the main problem with French opera at the Met is the lack of French singers. . . . What elevates the new *Faust,* however, is the way a Swedish-Italian-American cast has been anchored into its responsibility by three solid pillars of the French manner. [Jean-Louis] Barrault, as the director, has had the biggest job, but his conception is beautifully integrated with the visual setting by Jacques Dupont and the swift, terse and mercurial musical leadership of Georges Prêtre.

Mr. Dupont flirts a little dangerously with one of the most tiresome of modern stage gimmicks, sometimes known as Raiding the Louvre. His Kermesse scene is pure Brueghel. . . . But he always manages to stop short of obsessiveness. . . .

Mr. Barrault . . . moves his principals and choristers in strong, dynamic patterns. His staging of the Faust-Valentin duel is especially brilliant in its stark angularity, with Méphistophélès . . . kibitzing brilliantly and the glint of swords marvelously emphasized. The final apotheosis, which can be embarrassing in the usual picture-postcard settings, is similarly stark and simple.

Musically, there is also much to admire. Nicolai Gedda's . . . acting may be rudimentary, but his clean, light voice curls itself wonderfully around lyric lines. . . . Gabriella Tucci's Marguerite, new to the house, is also a beautiful achievement in most respects. . . . Robert Merrill, Marcia Baldwin and Gladys Kriese gave solidly of their best qualities in other roles. In a sense, however, it was the Méphistophélès himself, Cesare Siepi, who dominated the proceedings. . . . Mr. Barrault's conception of the part brought out new facets of the singer's art which the older *Faust* had somehow kept under wraps. Mercurial, witty, ardent . . . and menacing, Mr. Siepi gave of himself to an extent that eclipsed everything he has hitherto accomplished.

The opera, by the way, is being given virtually uncut: only the aria for Siébel which Gounod added later has been left out. The scene between Siébel and Marguerite before the Cathedral Scene . . . has been restored, along with the ballet music. If you can't have too much of *Faust,* that should be good news indeed.—Alan Rich, *New York Herald Tribune*

NEW PRODUCTION of Tchaikovsky's *Queen of Spades,* September 28, 1965

As the last new production to be presented by the Metropolitan Opera in its present home, Tchaikovsky's *Pique Dame* could be the summation of many things—experience, judgment, taste, even quality. It turns out, however, to be the summation of what has been at fault with a number of works as unfamiliar to the recent repertory as this one: no central authority from which a style flows, taking in not only conductor Thomas Schippers, designer Robert O'Hearn and stage director Henry Butler but almost all the performers save the regal Regina Resnik as the Countess, from whom the present version takes its title of *Queen of Spades.*

This was to be regretted, for *Pique Dame,* which has not been performed at the Metropolitan in decades, is a more stimulating work than the better-known *Eugene Onegin.* . . . It chanced to be written immediately after what many considered [Tchaikovsky's] finest work in any form, the *Sleeping Beauty* ballet score, and [he] carried over into *Pique Dame* many of the same melodic impulses, orchestral resources and gifts of characterization. . . .

Not too much of this emerged from the musical outline drawn by Schippers or in the vocalizing of Jon Vickers as the unhappy hero Gherman, Teresa Stratas as the irresolute heroine Lisa or any of the others save the redoubtable Resnik. Even the version that was used was open to question, for it eliminated a cheerful chorus of children in the first act and another interlude in Act II which also makes for a touch of lightness amid the prevailing gloom.

Whether this also affected the scenic conception of O'Hearn is hard to say, but it probably did. Altering the first scene from its proper place "in a park" prompted him to create, instead, a pavilion whose pillars and arches provided a frame for all that followed. With some scenes it worked fairly well; with others, such as the barracks and the embankment of the Neva, it was plainly out of place. —Irving Kolodin, *Saturday Review*

DEBUTS OF MIRELLA FRENI and GIANNI RAIMONDI in *La Bohème,* September 29, 1965

Miss Freni, who is small, beautiful, a good actress, and certainly an ideal Mimi, has an appealing lyric voice of considerable power and range, and a personality—evident in both voice and stage bearing—that can instantly charm any audience. . . . Mr. Raimondi is one of the most welcome Italian tenors to have turned up in years. His voice is a lovely lyric instrument that reaches high C's with no perceptible effort. He and Miss Freni made an unusually intimate pair, perhaps partly because they have sung the roles opposite each other many times before.—Winthrop Sargeant, *The New Yorker*

DEBUT OF GRACE BUMBRY as Princess Eboli in *Don Carlo,* October 7, 1965

Her voice is that of a real contralto with a phenomenal upper range, rather than the made-over sopranos who have sung this role in recent years. It is a big voice, but flexible and beautifully focused. And she uses it for genuine dramatic, as well as musical, purposes. An exciting, magnetic, dynamic singer, Miss Bumbry.— Alan Rich, *New York Herald Tribune*

DEBUT OF RENATA SCOTTO, as Cio-Cio-San in *Madama Butterfly,* October 13, 1965

Her strength is dramatic inflection. She conveys more of the meaning of the text than usual. . . . Her performance may have had its share of Italian mannerism, but it also reflected the Oriental background of the story. In short, she is an excellent actress, capable of imbuing feeling in a role. Vocally, Miss Scotto excels in pianissimos, which are quite beguiling. Her voice sometimes went reedy in the upper register . . . but she has a strong top that can catch the fancy of a crowd.—Miles Kastendieck, *New York Journal-American*

DEBUT OF NICOLAI GHIAUROV as Méphistophélès in *Faust,* November 8, 1965

Out of Bulgaria has come Nicolai Ghiaurov. He is a basso, thirty-six years old, he has been receiving the kind of adulation all over the world normally reserved for sopranos and tenors. . . .

He not only has a remarkable voice, but he is also big in every way. A good actor, though somewhat of the old school, he simply dominated the stage. He has presence, the kind that Pinza and Chaliapin had, the kind that jumps over the footlights and seizes the listener in a palpable embrace.

If the voice has any defect it is in the lower range, where it sounds just a shade thin and even uncomfortable. But around a C it takes on strength, and from there it is a thing of glory.—Harold C. Schonberg, *New York Times*

DEBUTS OF MONTSERRAT CABALLÉ and SHERRILL MILNES in *Faust,* December 22, 1965

There was speculation that the soprano, who had made her success here in obscure Donizetti operas, might be miscast as Marguerite, although she has a repertory of wide range. As it turned out, it was not an ideal role for her, but when she was at her best on this occasion, singing as superlatively as she had before, there was no doubt that she belonged on the Met's stage.

There is more to the soprano's singing than just gorgeous sounds. She is a musicianly singer and, instinctively at least, a sincere and tasteful actress, and she combined these qualities in an appealing portrait of Marguerite. She is a plump woman, and her looks were not helped by an unflattering blond wig, but she moved through her role with a becoming simplicity and an honest expression of her emotional awareness of the character she played.

Mr. Milnes's debut had its satisfactions, too. The twenty-nine-year-old baritone handled himself with aplomb, although Valentin is not a role that allows much characterization. More to the point was the rich, fresh sound of his voice, which rang out reassuringly in his aria in the Kermesse Scene.—Raymond Ericson, *New York Times*

DEBUT OF ZUBIN MEHTA, conducting *Aida,* December 29, 1965

An outstanding debut by Zubin Mehta gives the Met a first-class conductor. That he is sorely needed makes him the more welcome. He has positive ideas, which he asserts impressively. . . .

A nice sense of timing, of clarity and of orchestral detail distinguished his direction. He moves apace, perhaps too fast here and too slowly there, but always forward. In contrasting the lyric with the dramatic moments, he may cultivate too much contrast; yet the results created intensity of interest as well as of performance.—Miles Kastendieck, *New York Journal American*

DEBUT OF JAMES KING as Florestan in *Fidelio,* January 8, 1966

King arrived unheralded, but from the sound of things, he will not remain so. . . . Born in Dodge City, Kansas, and a student of Martial Singher . . . King has a magnificent rich tenor voice, beautiful in quality and easy in production. Such a challenging debut brought with it at some points a tentativeness, but the collective nugget shone through: sensitive artistry, musicianship, imposing stage presence, histrionic conviction and, above all, a voice of remarkable sheen.—Harriett Johnson, *New York Post*

DEBUT OF FRANCESCO MOLINARI-PRADELLI, conducting *Un Ballo in Maschera,* February 7, 1966

[Maestro Molinari-Pradelli's] revelation of this magnificent, iridescent score was complete and overwhelming. The ensemble balance (crucial in this work) was beautifully worked out, and the details in Verdi's remarkable scoring were equally well planned and played off against each other. His pacing was considerate, not only of the time-scale of the drama itself but also of the interaction between the musical flow and the requirements of the human voice.—Alan Rich, *New York Herald Tribune*

DEBUT OF PILAR LORENGAR as Donna Elvira in *Don Giovanni,* February 11, 1966

Miss Lorengar is attractive, sensibly built for the stage and seemingly comfortable on it. . . . Her voice is not heavy but of . . . operatic amplitude. . . . There was a . . . tremolo that affected her singing from the top to the bottom of the vocal register in recitatives and arias. This did not make Miss Lorengar's vocal performance ineffective, but it did weaken its impact. She may be able to bring the weakness under better control free from the strain of a . . . debut.—Allen Hughes, *New York Times*

DEBUTS OF ALFREDO KRAUS and RUZA POSPINOV in *Rigoletto,* February 16, 1966

Mr. Kraus is good-looking, slim (as tenors go) and handsome, and he made his entrance with the aplomb of one to whom entrances are no novelty. But he has not been blessed with a voice that is going to make a lasting impression in vocal history. It is of decent size and good texture, up to the bridge notes. Starting above the staff it is produced in a constricted manner, and the very high notes are really squeezed out.

Miss Pospinov, a sexy-looking Maddalena who filled out her bodice to the taste of any Duke, sang her few phrases in a rather attractively husky mezzo.—Harold C. Schonberg, *New York Times*

DEBUT OF RERI GRIST, as Rosina in *Il Barbiere di Siviglia,* February 25, 1966

Lively, pretty, petite and blessed with a bright coloratura voice, Reri Grist won the hearts and hands of all who caught her Metropolitan debut last night. Along with a cameo beauty of face and figure and a vivacious acting style, the new Rosina had what counted most, a well-placed coloratura voice which dispenses pearls instead of tones.—Louis Biancolli, *New York World-Telegram and Sun*

DEBUT OF THOMAS STEWART as Ford in *Falstaff,* March 9, 1966

To stand up and trade note for note and gesture for gesture with Tito Gobbi at his best, and still not be outshadowed, calls for a superior singing actor. Thomas Stewart, an American baritone known better in Europe than at home, was exactly that last night in his debut. . . . His voice was big in volume, satisfying in quality and intelligently handled. His action grew naturally out of the music. The second-act scene between Mr. Stewart and Mr. Gobbi . . . was a high point.—Theodore Strongin, *New York Times*

FAREWELL OF ZINKA MILANOV as Maddalena di Coigny in *Andrea Chénier,* April 13, 1966

After having made 451 appearances with the Metropolitan Opera, 297 of them in New York, where she made her debut in December 1937 as Leonora in *Il Trovatore,*

Zinka Milanov sang her last complete performance at the Broadway house last night. . . . On Saturday night, Mme. Milanov will join with her colleagues in their musical farewell to the old Met, but last night was her night and an occasion for a bulging houseful of cheering, applauding and weeping admirers to let the illustrious Yugoslavian soprano know what she has meant to them through the past twenty-eight years. . . .

She received a series of showstopping ovations, culminating with a seven-minute outpouring of affection following her third-act aria . . . which has had few parallels in the history of the house. Despite the obvious emotional demands of the evening, Mme. Milanov performed as she has always performed here, with the grandeur and authority reserved for the phenomenally gifted few, and it wasn't sentiment alone which told everyone present that they will never hear or see anyone quite like her again.

Before the start of the last act, there were presentations of a silver tray from the Metropolitan Opera Association by Lowell Wadmond, vice-chairman of the Board of Directors, and of a Steuben glass cup from the Met management by general manager Rudolf Bing. "You are a supremely great singer," said Mr. Bing, "and I have never known you to arrive late or unprepared, which shows your great sense of responsibility to your art, your public and to yourself."

Mme. Milanov replied briefly, with the first show of personal emotion of the evening. "I just want to say goodbye," she said. "I love you all with all my heart, and I will carry you with me as long as I live."—Louis Snyder, *New York Herald Tribune*

FAREWELL to the Metropolitan Opera House, April 16, 1966

At 1:17 yesterday morning the gold curtain at the Metropolitan Opera rose to reveal a stage full of $100,000 worth of operatic talent. The audience stood, applauded, cheered and waved. The singers waved back. It looked a little like a steamship departure. Then everybody on both sides of the footlights linked arms and sang "Auld Lang Syne," and the curtain came down, ending life as we have known it at the grand old house on Thirty-ninth and Broadway.

Thus ended one of the most spectacular events in the annals of operatic performance, the gala staged by the Metropolitan Opera Company to bid its old home a fond, loud and melodious farewell. The evening didn't cost the management the $100,000 mentioned above, because the performers donated their services, so that the ticket sales for the evening (nearly $300,000, with a $200 top) can go for bigger and better operas in the new house at Lincoln Center that will open on September 16.

The gala had been advertised, talked about and sold out for months, and the statistics were awesome: fifty-nine top-ranking singers, eleven conductors, chorus and ballet corps in arias and scenes from twenty-four operas. What nobody seemed to discuss, however, was the bare possibility that the whole thing just might turn out to be some sort of musical triumph as well. To everybody's enormous surprise, this is exactly what happened. It will take weeks to sort out recollections of everything that happened during those five hours at the Met, but they are sure to involve some sublime musical experiences.

The whole event had been shrewdly designed to blend history and hopes. History was present in the galaxy of honored guests who sat onstage during the first part, forming a living backdrop for the performers. When Robert Merrill sang "Eri tu" from *Un Ballo in Maschera*, he had to contend with the presence in that backdrop of Richard Bonelli, the great baritone of the 1930's. Licia Albanese's "Un bel dì" was roundly applauded by Elisabeth Rethberg, one of the most beloved of Cio-Cio-Sans.

If this was unnerving, it didn't show. The Met's roster paraded its wares onstage as if everyone's career depended on giving his absolute best. It was amazing how much drama there was, considering that most of the excerpts were sung in evening dress. James McCracken seemed to grow out of himself into the snarling Otello before one's eyes (and ears); Birgit Nilsson—stock still, in a black gown bearing a wreath that an unrelated Nilsson (Christine) had worn at the house's opening —brought down the ultimate dramatic glory of Wagner's Immolation Scene purely through her vocal magic.

There was history, as well, in the living art. Thelma Votipka,

beloved for thirty years for her work in small parts which came to be known as "Tippy's Bits," came out of the shadows to mug and wallow and charm us all in the *Carmen* Quintet. Delia Rigal, who had made her debut on Rudolf Bing's first Metropolitan night (November 6, 1950), stepped in for an ailing Lucine Amara to fill out the *Forza* trio.

Zinka Milanov ended her Met career with a duet from *Chénier* with Richard Tucker that really stopped the show. Eleanor Steber, Kurt Baum, George Cehanovsky, —veterans all, and not very active these days—came to sing, not as relics but as vivid artists somehow made youthful again by the event. Miss Albanese's aria was stunning, and moving also was her gesture of blowing kisses to the venerable stage floor. She has served it well, and did so again on Saturday.

History there was, and also promise. Leontyne Price sang a *Trovatore* aria with a legato far better controlled than in many of her past performances. Montserrat Caballé's brief contribution to a *Rosenkavalier* trio made one hanker mightily to hear her in the whole opera. Régine Crespin's searing contribution to a scene from *Gioconda* aroused hopes that this opera is on her agenda. Franco Corelli sounded like the great musician he still can become in a scene from *Manon Lescaut* with a radiant Renata Tebaldi. Fernando Corena's brief, hilarious aria from Cornelius' *Barber of Bagdad* served as reminder of another opera well worth reviving.

So there you are. There were brief speeches from Mr. Bing and from Lauder Greenway, chairman of the board. There was another, unscheduled speech from Leopold Stokowski, who ended his brief podium appearance with an appeal to save the house—somewhat subversive, in terms of the management's current mood, but stirring. Others in the elegant, jampacked audience shouted "Save the Met!" often during the evening, and these cries were mixed with loud shrieks from the various fan clubs.

It was an evening of shrieks, cries and cheers. Threaded through it, however, was an homage to the power of the human voice in music so majestic as to beggar description. If the gala proved anything, it is that the Metropolitan Opera Company is an artistic unit far beyond any identity as a building.—Alan Rich, *New York Herald Tribune*

FINAL CURTAIN AT THE GALA FAREWELL, APRIL 16, 1966
(Tucci, Sergi, Harvuot, Elias, Hines, Milanov, Uppman,
Tucker, Dunlap, Carelli, Miller, Díaz, Mehta, Madeira)

LIST OF DEBUTS

Artist's Name, Voice Range,
Debut Role and Number of Seasons

This list includes singers, actors and conductors who performed with the resident company at the old Metropolitan Opera House, 1883-1966. It excludes silent roles (i.e., Trouble in *Madama Butterfly*, the Countess of Aremberg in *Don Carlo*, etc.) except in cases where the artist later assumed a singing or speaking role (i.e., Cyril Ritchard as Ambrogio in *Il Barbiere di Siviglia*). The parenthesis following an artist's name indicates his specialty: (s)-soprano; (m)-mezzo-soprano or contralto; (t)-tenor; (b)-baritone; (ba)-boy alto; (bs)-bass; (sp)-speaking role; (cond)-conductor. Where it has been impossible to determine a specialty, the parenthesis has been left blank. Opera titles are listed under the work's first word with the exceptions of *Andrea Chénier* (*Chénier*); *Les Contes d'Hoffmann* (*Hoffmann*); *Der Fliegende Holländer* (*Holländer*); *Gianni Schicchi* (*Schicchi*); *Madama Butterfly* (*Butterfly*); *The Magic Flute*—also given as *Die Zauberflöte* and *Il Flauto Magico* —(*Flute*); *Simon Boccanegra* (*Boccanegra*); and *Guglielmo/Guillaume/William Tell* (*Tell*). The figure in parenthesis at the end of each entry indicates the number of seasons an artist performed at the Metropolitan. Artists who appeared only in concert are omitted from the list; on the other hand, those who participated in staged opera are also credited for concert seasons.

Because of the myriad inconsistencies by which the names of artists are remembered and used, a special system of alphabetization has been evolved for this list. Names prefixed by the articles D', Da, Dal, De, Del, Della, De Los or Di are filed in strict letter order under the letter D. The prefixes L', La and Le are similarly found under the letter L. "Mac" is also filed in strict letter order (after Mab, before Mad), as is Mc (after Maz, before Mea). The same rule applies for the prefixes Van and Von, found in the V section.

Abarbanell, Lina (s) Hänsel, Nov. 25, 1905 (1)
Abott, Bessie (s) Mimi *Bohème* Jan. 20, 1906 (3)
Abramoff, Signor (bs) Melchthal *Tell* Nov. 21, 1894 (2)
Ackté, Aino (s) Marguerite *Faust* Feb. 20, 1904 (2)
Adaberto, Ester (s) Leonora *Trovatore* Mar. 10, 1909 (1)
Adams, Suzanne (s) Juliette *Roméo* Jan. 4, 1899 (5)
Adler, Kurt (cond) *Flute* Jan. 12, 1951 (17)
Agostini, Giuseppe (t) Rodolfo *Bohème* Nov. 27, 1903 (1)
Aimaro, Lina (s) Lucia, Feb. 2, 1939 (1)
Alarie, Pierrette (s) Oscar *Ballo* Dec. 8, 1945 (3)
Albanese, Licia (s) Cio-Cio-San *Butterfly* Feb. 9, 1940 (26)
Albani, Emma (s) Gilda *Rigoletto* Dec. 23, 1891 (1)
Albers, Henri (b) Wolfram *Tannhäuser* Nov. 29, 1898 (1)
Alberti, Mme. (s) Confidante *Huguenots* Mar. 19, 1884 (1)
Alberti, Werner (b) Esquire *Parsifal* Nov. 24, 1904 (2)
Alcock, Merle (m) Beppe *Amico Fritz* Nov. 15, 1923 (7)
Alda, Frances (s) Gilda *Rigoletto* Dec. 7, 1908 (21)
Aldenhoff, Bernd (t) Tannhäuser, Feb. 25, 1955 (1)
Aldrich, Mariska (m) Azucena *Trovatore* Mar. 26, 1910 (2)
Aldridge, Erbert (t) Leopold *Rosenkavalier* Nov. 19, 1962 (3)
Alexander, John (t) Ferrando *Così* Dec. 19, 1961 (5)
Alexy, Herr (b) Herald *Lohengrin* Nov. 23, 1885 (1)
Allen, Mildred (s) Papagena *Flute* Mar. 1, 1957 (6)
Allers, Franz (cond) *Fledermaus* Nov. 30, 1963 (2)
Allyn, Miss (s) Dewman *Hänsel* Dec. 25, 1907 (1)
Alperstein, Max (t) Villager *Pagliacci* Nov. 10, 1958 (2)
Alsen, Herbert (bs) Marke *Tristan* Jan. 16, 1939 (1)
Alten, Bella (s) Cherubino *Nozze* Nov. 30, 1904 (9)
Altglass, Max (t) Missail *Boris* Nov. 6, 1924 (16)
Althouse, Paul (t) Grigori *Boris* Mar. 19, 1913 (16)
Altman, Thelma (m) Fyodor *Boris* Nov. 22, 1943 (7)
Altmann, Freida (m) Flower Maiden *Parsifal* Feb. 22, 1907 (1)
Alva, Luigi (t) Fenton *Falstaff* Mar. 6, 1964 (3)
Alvarez, Albert (t) Roméo, Dec. 18, 1899 (4)
Alvary, Lorenzo (bs) Zuniga *Carmen* Nov. 26, 1942 (23)
Alvary, Max (t) José *Carmen* Nov. 25, 1885 (4)
Amara, Lucine (s) Voice *Don Carlo* Nov. 6, 1950 (16)
Amato, Pasquale (b) Germont *Traviata* Nov. 20, 1908 (13)
Ames, Suzanne (sp) Ida *Fledermaus* Apr. 5, 1951 (6)
Amparán, Belén (m) Giulietta *Hoffmann* Nov. 29, 1956 (4)

Ananian, Paolo (bs) Registrar *Butterfly* Nov. 19, 1908 (23)
Ancona, Mario (b) Tonio *Pagliacci* Dec. 11, 1893 (4)
Anderson, Arthur (bs) Donner *Rheingold* Feb. 26, 1932 (4)
Anderson, Marian (m) Ulrica *Ballo* Jan. 7, 1955 (2)
Andresen, Ivar (bs) Daland *Holländer* Nov. 1, 1930 (2)
Andreva, Stella (s) Olympia *Hoffmann* Jan. 14, 1937 (3)
Anlauf, Herr (bs) Foltz *Meistersinger* Jan. 4, 1886 (1)
Ansermet, Ernest (cond) *Pelléas* Nov. 30, 1962 (1)
Anthes, Georg (t) Lohengrin, Nov. 28, 1902 (2)
Anthony, Charles (t) Simpleton *Boris* Mar. 6, 1954 (13)
Anthony, Grace (s) Page *Lohengrin* Nov. 16, 1921 (6)
Antoine, Josephine (s) Philine *Mignon* Jan. 4, 1936 (13)
Antonicelli, Giuseppe (cond) *Ballo* Nov. 10, 1947 (3)
Arden, Cecil (m) Vannard *Lodoletta* Jan. 12, 1918 (8)
Arden, Joseph (b) Baal Hanan *Königin* Dec. 2, 1889 (1)
Arditi, Luigi (cond) *Marta* Apr. 2, 1892 (1)
Arimondi, Vittorio (bs) Ferrando *Trovatore* Dec. 7, 1895 (1)
Arnaud, Anna (s) Carmen, Jan. 7, 1905 (1)
Arnoldson, Sigrid (s) Baucis *Philémon* Nov. 29, 1893 (1)
Arroyo, Martina (s) Voice *Don Carlo* Mar. 14, 1959 (5)
Arthur, Henry (t) Slave *Flute* Feb. 23, 1956 (3)
Attwood, Martha (s) Liù *Turandot* Nov. 16, 1926 (4)
Audisio, Pietro (t) Roderigo *Otello* Nov. 17, 1909 (15)
Augier, Achille (bs) Raimondo *Lucia* Oct. 24, 1883 (1)
Auspitz, Miss ( ) Flower Maiden *Parsifal* Jan. 11, 1906 (1)
Aves, Dreda (s) Leonora *Trovatore* Apr. 6, 1929 (4)
Axman, Gladys (s) Joy of Understanding *Oiseau Bleu* Dec. 27, 1919 (3)

Baccaloni, Salvatore (bs) Bartolo *Nozze* Dec. 7, 1940 (22)
Bach, Johanna (m) Rossweisse *Walküre* Jan. 9, 1896 (2)
Backgren, Arthur (bs) Noble *Lohengrin* Dec. 26, 1958 (2)
Bacquier, Gabriel (b) High Priest *Samson* Oct. 17, 1964 (2)
Bada, Angelo (t) Messenger *Aida* Nov. 16, 1908 (30)
Baillard, Monsieur (bs) Guard *Flute* Jan. 11, 1904 (3)
Baker, John (b) Morales *Carmen* Nov. 29, 1943 (8)
Baker, Susanne (m) Flower Maiden *Parsifal* Nov. 24, 1904 (1)
Baldwin, Marcia (m) Javotte *Manon* Oct. 17, 1963 (3)
Balestrieri, Anthony (t) Khrushchov *Boris* Oct. 27; 1960 (2)
Ballester, Vincente (b) Alfio *Cavalleria* Dec. 29, 1924 (1)

Bamboschek, Giuseppe (cond) *Faust* Dec. 20, 1919 (13)
Bampton, Rose (m/s) Laura *Gioconda* Nov. 28, 1932 (17)
Baracchi, Aristide (bs) Quinault *Adriana* Nov. 18, 1907 (2)
Barates, Georges (sp) Apprentice *Louise* Jan. 15, 1921 (2)
Barbato, Elisabetta (s) Tosca, Nov. 26, 1949 (1)
Barberis, Signor (t) Giuseppe *Traviata* Nov. 5, 1883 (1)
Barbieri, Fedora (m) Eboli *Don Carlo* Nov. 6, 1950 (5)
Barbini, Ernesto (cond) *Cavalleria* Mar. 4, 1952 (1)
Barbusci, Nicola (bs) Steersman *Gioconda* Dec. 26, 1960 (2)
Bardelli, Cesare (b) Alfio *Cavalleria* Apr. 6, 1957 (10)
Bardini, Gaetano (t) Johnson *Fanciulla* Jan. 17, 1966 (1)
Barioni, Daniele (t) Cavaradossi *Tosca* Feb. 20, 1956 (7)
Baromeo, Chase (bs) Ramfis *Aida* Dec. 20, 1935 (3)
Barrientos, Maria (s) Lucia, Jan. 31, 1916 (5)
Bars, Jacques (t) Watchman *Meistersinger* Nov. 18, 1896 (10)
Bartels, Heinrich (t) Moser *Meistersinger* Mar. 7, 1890 (2)
Barton, Sophie (m) Orphan *Rosenkavalier* Jan. 26, 1916 (2)
Basch, Wilhelm (b) Oberthal *Prophète* Nov. 17, 1886 (1)
Basiola, Mario (b) Amonasro *Aida* Nov. 11, 1925 (7)
Bassi, Amedeo (t) Johnson *Fanciulla* Mar. 2, 1911 (1)
Bastianini, Ettore (b) Germont *Traviata* Dec. 5, 1953 (7)
Bauermeister, Mathilde (s) Gertrude *Roméo* Dec. 14, 1891 (13)
Baum, Kurt (t) Singer *Rosenkavalier* Nov. 27, 1941 (22)
Baumann, Bella (s) Ortlinde *Walküre* Feb. 6, 1891 (1)
Baumann, Carl (t) Thoret *Huguenots* Nov. 21, 1884 (1)
Bavagnoli, Gaetano (cond) *Bohème* Nov. 19, 1915 (1)
Bayer, Julius (t) Knight *Parsifal* Dec. 24, 1903 (14)
Beale, Kitty (s) Aspirant Sister *Suor Angelica* Dec. 14, 1918 (3)
Beattie, Douglas (bs) King *Aida* Feb. 11, 1939 (2)
Beck, Joseph (b) Herald *Lohengrin* Nov. 30, 1888 (2)
Bedeschi, Umberto (t) Normanno *Lucia* Jan. 28, 1909 (1)
Beecham, Thomas (cond) *Phoebus* Jan. 15, 1942 (3)
Beeth, Lola (s) Elsa *Lohengrin* Dec. 2, 1895 (1)
Bégué, Bernard (b) Herald *Otello* Nov. 24, 1902 (15)
Behr, Jan (cond) *Traviata* Feb. 13, 1962 (4)
Behrens, Conrad (bs) High Priest *Königin* Nov. 29, 1889 (2)
Belina, Maria (s) Stefano *Roméo* Nov. 23, 1896 (1)
Belkin, Beatrice (s) Dewman *Hänsel*, Oct. 30, 1930 (1)
Belleri, Lamberto (t) Rider *Fanciulla* Dec. 10, 1910 (11)
Belleri, Marguerite (m) Ludwig *Saint Elizabeth* Jan. 3, 1918 (3)
Belletti, Mme. (m) Lucia *Cavalleria* Dec. 26, 1903 (1)
Bellezza, Vincenzo (cond) *Gioielli* Nov. 4, 1926 (10)
Belton, Signor (t) Eisslinger *Meistersinger* Nov. 18, 1896 (1)
Bely, Hermine (s) Zerlina *Don Giovanni* Dec. 10, 1884 (1)
Bender, Paul (b) Ochs *Rosenkavalier* Nov. 17, 1922 (5)
Bendix, Max (cond) *Alessandro Stradella* Feb. 4, 1910 (1)
Bensaude, Maurizio (b) Amonasro *Aida* Nov. 23, 1894 (2)
Bentonelli, Joseph (t) Des Grieux *Manon* Jan. 10, 1936 (2)
Benzell, Mimi (s) Queen of the Night *Flute* Jan. 5, 1945 (4)
Bérat, Louise (m) Berta *Barbiere* Nov. 27, 1919 (3)
Berger, Erna (s) Sophie *Rosenkavalier* Nov. 21, 1949 (2)
Berger, Rudolph (t) Siegmund *Walküre* Feb. 5, 1914 (2)
Berglund, Joel (b) Sachs *Meistersinger* Jan. 9, 1946 (4)
Bergonzi, Carlo (t) Radames *Aida* Nov. 13, 1956 (10)
Berini, Mario (t) Faust, Nov. 28, 1946 (2)
Berlin, Patricia (m) Waltraute *Walküre* Mar. 24, 1965 (1)
Berl-Resky, Gustavo (b) Enrico *Lucia* Dec. 2, 1905 (1)
Berndorff, Miss ( ) Flower Maiden *Parsifal* Dec. 24, 1903 (1)
Bernstein, Leonard (cond) *Falstaff* Mar. 6, 1964 (1)
Bertinetti, Signor (t) Eisslinger *Meistersinger* Jan. 24, 1900 (2)
Bertram, Theodore (b) Dutchman *Holländer* Jan. 6, 1900 (2)
Besanzoni, Gabriella (m) Amneris *Aida* Nov. 19, 1919 (1)
Besuner, Pearl (s) Siébel *Faust* Dec. 1, 1928 (10)
Bettaque, Katti. See Senger-Bettaque, Katherine
Better, Leonore (s) Helmwige *Walküre* Nov. 10, 1886 (1)
Bevignani, Enrico (cond) *Philémon* Nov. 29, 1893 (6)
Bighinelli, Signor (t) Eisslinger *Meistersinger* Jan. 24, 1902 (2)
Biondo, Santa (s) Nedda *Pagliacci* Dec. 6, 1929 (3)
Birlenbach, Erich (t) Pali *Gypsy Baron* Nov. 25, 1959 (3)
Bispham, David (b) Beckmesser *Meistersinger* Nov. 18, 1896 (5)
Bitterl, Constanze (s) Elizabeth *Saint Elizabeth* Jan. 3, 1918 (1)
Bjoerling, Jussi (t) Rodolfo *Bohème* Nov. 24, 1938 (15)
Bjoerling, Sigurd (b) Telramund *Lohengrin* Nov. 15, 1952 (1)
Bjoner, Ingrid (s) Elsa *Lohengrin* Oct. 28, 1961 (5)
Blair, Lynn (s) Estrella *Perichole* Nov. 25, 1961 (4)
Blass, Robert (bs) Hermann *Tannhäuser* Dec. 24, 1900 (12)
Blatt, Josef (cond) *Fledermaus* Dec. 10, 1951 (1)
Bloch, Max (t) Major-domo *Rosenkavalier* Nov. 20, 1914 (12)

Blum, Alois (b) Pizarro *Fidelio* Nov. 29, 1884 (1)
Bodanskaya [Bodanya], Natalie (s) Micaela *Carmen* May 11, 1936 (7)
Bodanzky, Artur (cond) *Götterdämmerung* Nov. 18, 1915 (24)
Boehm, Karl (cond) *Don Giovanni* Oct. 31, 1957 (7)
Boehme, Kurt (bs) Pogner *Meistersinger* Nov. 11, 1954 (2)
Bogdan, Mr. (t) Eisslinger *Meistersinger* Feb. 2, 1906 (1)
Bohnen, Michael (bs) Francesco/Tourist *Mona Lisa* Mar. 1, 1923 (10)
Bok, Rosa (s) Queen of the Night *Flute* Dec. 11, 1941 (1)
Bollinger, Anne (s) Frasquita *Carmen* Jan. 1, 1949 (5)
Bonci, Alessandro (t) Duke *Rigoletto* Nov. 22, 1907 (3)
Bonelli, Richard (b) Germont *Traviata* Dec. 1, 1932 (12)
Bonetti, Mary (m) Page *Lohengrin* Nov. 10, 1924 (7)
Boninsegna, Celestina (s) Aida, Dec. 21, 1906 (1)
Borg, Kim (b) Almaviva *Nozze* Oct. 30, 1959 (3)
Borgioli, Armando (b) Carlo *Forza* Jan. 22, 1932 (4)
Borgioli, Dino (t) Rodolfo *Bohème* Dec. 31, 1934 (1)
Bori, Lucrezia (s) Manon *Manon Lescaut* Nov. 11, 1912 (19)
Borin, Arturo (b) Nachtigall *Meistersinger* Jan. 24, 1900 (5)
Borkh, Inge (s) Salome, Jan. 24, 1958 (2)
Borniggia, Emma (m) Page *Rigoletto* Nov. 28, 1908 (8)
Borso, Umberto (t) Enzo *Gioconda* Apr. 16, 1962 (2)
Botta, Luca (t) Rodolfo *Bohème* Nov. 21, 1914 (3)
Boucher, Gene (b) Master of Ceremonies *Queen of Spades* Sept. 28, 1965 (1)
Bourgeois, Georges (bs) Yakuside *Butterfly* Nov. 19, 1909 (3)
Bourskaya, Ina (m) Carmen, Mar. 2, 1923 (15)
Bouton, Isabelle (m) Siegrune *Walküre* Jan. 5, 1900 (5)
Bovy, Samuel (cond) *Roméo* Nov. 26, 1906 (2)
Bovy, Vina (s) Violetta *Traviata* Dec. 24, 1936 (2)
Bowe, Morton (t) Noble *Lohengrin* Dec. 20, 1944 (1)
Bower, Beverly (s) Ortlinde *Walküre* Feb. 22, 1965 (2)
Bowman, Audrey (s) Queen of the Night *Flute* Jan. 22, 1944 (1)
Bozzano, Enzo (bs) Schaunard *Bohème* Nov. 21, 1908 (1)
Bradley, Grace (m) Page *Lohengrin* Nov. 16, 1921 (4)
Braendle, Paula (m) Esquire *Parsifal* Dec. 24, 1903 (4)
Brandl, Helena (m) Giovanna *Rigoletto* Jan. 2, 1885 (2)
Brandt, Marianne (m) Leonore *Fidelio* Nov. 19, 1884 (4)
Branzell, Karin (m) Fricka *Walküre* Feb. 6, 1924 (22)
Braslau, Sophie (m) Fyodor *Boris* Nov. 28, 1913 (7)
Braun, Carl (bs) Marke *Tristan* Feb. 8, 1913 (5)
Braun, Helena (s) Brünnhilde *Walküre* Dec. 21, 1949 (1)
Brazis, Algerd (b) D'Obigny *Traviata* Nov. 24, 1951 (3)
Breisach, Paul (cond) *Aida* Dec. 12, 1941 (5)
Brema, Marie (m) Brangäne *Tristan* Nov. 27, 1895 (3)
Breuer, Hans (t) Steersman *Holländer* Jan. 6, 1900 (1)
Bréval, Lucienne (s) Chimène *Cid* Jan. 16, 1901 (2)
Brewer, Nadyne (s) Orphan *Rosenkavalier* Dec. 14, 1962 (2)
Bridewell, Carrie (m) Third Lady *Flute* Mar. 30, 1900 (4)
Broadfoot, Eleanor (Eleanora de Cisneros) (m) Rosweisse *Walküre* Jan. 5, 1900 (1)
Broch, Jennie (s) Marguerite *Huguenots* Dec. 3, 1890 (1)
Browning, Lucielle (m) Kathinka *Bartered Bride* May 15, 1936 (16)
Brownlee, John (b) Rigoletto, Feb. 17, 1937 (21)
Bruni, Frau (m) Waltraute *Walküre* Mar. 5, 1886 (1)
Brysac, Ada (s) Page *Tannhäuser* Dec. 17, 1960 (1)
Bucha, Herr (bs) Hermann *Tannhäuser* Dec. 12, 1895 (1)
Buckreus, Stefan (bs) Old Prisoner *Lobetanz* Nov. 18, 1911 (3)
Budney, Arthur (b) Herald *Lohengrin* Nov. 15, 1952 (5)
Buers, Willy (b) Sachs *Meistersinger* Feb. 13, 1913 (1)
Bumbry, Grace (m) Eboli *Don Carlo* Oct. 7, 1965 (1)
Burger, Julius (cond) *Trovatore* Mar. 24, 1961 (1)
Burgstaller, Alois (t) Siegmund *Walküre* Feb. 12, 1903 (7)
Burgstaller, Ludwig (t) Muff *Bartered Bride* Feb. 19, 1909 (23)
Burke, Edmund (b) King *Aida* Nov. 22, 1922 (3)
Burke, Hilda (s) Micaela *Carmen* Dec. 27, 1935 (8)
Burke, Peter (ba) Shepherd *Tosca* Feb. 28, 1958 (2)
Burrian, Carl (t) Tannhäuser, Nov. 30, 1906 (7)
Busch, Fritz (cond) *Lohengrin* Nov. 26, 1945 (4)
Byrum, Rose (s) Ninetta *Perichole* Dec. 21, 1956 (1)

Caballé, Montserrat (s) Marguerite *Faust* Dec. 22, 1965 (1)
Cajatti, Ida (s) Musetta *Bohème* Nov. 19, 1915 (1)
Calabrese, Ada (s) Orphan *Rosenkavalier* Nov. 19, 1962 (2)
Call, Lucy Lee (s) Flower Maiden *Parsifal* Nov. 24, 1904 (3)

Callas, Maria Meneghini (s) Norma, Oct. 29, 1956 (3)
Calusio, Ferruccio (cond) Trovatore Dec. 12, 1940 (1)
Calvé, Emma (s) Santuzza Cavalleria Nov. 29, 1893 (6)
Camera, Eduardo (b) Di Luna Trovatore Dec. 16, 1891 (1)
Campanari, Giuseppe (b) Di Luna Trovatore Nov. 30, 1894 (14)
Campanini, Cleofonte (cond) Mignon Nov. 3, 1883 (1)
Campanini, Italo (t) Faust, Oct. 22, 1883 (3)
Campora, Giuseppe (t) Rodolfo Bohème Jan. 20, 1955 (7)
Caniglia, Maria (s) Desdemona Otello Nov. 21, 1938 (1)
Capecchi, Renato (b) Germont Traviata Nov. 24, 1951 (3)
Capoul, Victor (t) Faust, Oct. 27, 1883 (3)
Cappuccilli, Piero (b) Germont Traviata Mar. 26, 1960 (1)
Carbone, Agostino (bs) Tristram Marta Jan. 2, 1892 (4)
Cardozo, Miss (   ) Flower Maiden Parsifal Feb. 22, 1907 (1)
Carelli, Gabor (t) Curzio Nozze Nov. 17, 1951 (15)
Carpi, Fernando (t) Alfredo Traviata Nov. 29, 1916 (3)
Carroll, Christina (s) Musetta Bohème Dec. 20, 1943 (3)
Carroll, Jane (m) Da-ud Ägyptische Helena Nov. 6, 1928 (2)
Carron, Arthur (t) Canio Pagliacci May 29, 1936 (11)
Carter, John (t) Singer Rosenkavalier Dec. 4, 1939 (5)
Caruso, Enrico (t) Duke Rigoletto Nov. 23, 1903 (18)
Caruso, Mariano (t) Spy Chénier Dec. 17, 1962 (4)
Case, Anna (s) Page Lohengrin Nov. 20, 1909 (8)
Casei, Nedda (m) Maddalena Rigoletto Oct. 14, 1964 (2)
Cassel, Walter (b) Brétigny Manon Dec. 12, 1942 (15)
Castagna, Bruna (m) Amneris Aida Mar. 2, 1936 (10)
Castellano, Laura (s) Curra Forza Nov. 10, 1952 (1)
Castelmary, Armand (bs) Vulcan Philémon Nov. 29, 1893 (4)
Castino, Frank (sp) Gherardino Schicchi Jan. 19, 1934 (2)
Cathelat, Georges (t) Pelléas, Mar. 7, 1940 (1)
Caupolican, Chief (b) Mathis Polish Jew Mar. 9, 1921 (2)
Cavalieri, Lina (s) Fedora, Dec. 5, 1906 (2)
Cehanovsky, George (b) Kothner Meistersinger Nov. 13, 1926 (40)
Cellini, Renato (cond) Don Carlo Apr. 9, 1952 (3)
Ceppi, Antonio (t) Radames Aida Nov. 28, 1896 (2)
Cernei, Elena (m) Dalila Samson Mar. 17, 1965 (2)
Cernusco, Signor (bs) Gypsy Trovatore Dec. 16, 1891 (12)
Cerri, Francesco (bs) Yakuside Butterfly Nov. 19, 1910 (11)
Chabay, Leslie (t) Curzio Nozze Nov. 13, 1946 (5)
Chalia, Rosalia (s) Santuzza Cavalleria Dec. 17, 1898 (1)
Chaliapin, Fyodor (bs) Mefistofele, Nov. 20, 1907 (9)
Chalmers, Thomas (b) Valentin Faust Nov. 17, 1917 (5)
Chalmin, Victor (bs) Brander Damnation Dec. 7, 1906 (1)
Chambers, Madelaine (s) Second Lady Flute Feb. 23, 1956 (4)
Chamlee, Mario (t) Cavaradossi Tosca Nov. 22, 1920 (12)
Charles-Cahier, Sara (m) Azucena Trovatore Apr. 3, 1912 (2)
Chase, Cora (s) Gilda Rigoletto Feb. 4, 1921 (3)
Chistiakov, Vladimir (bs) Gardener Traviata Nov. 24, 1961 (4)
Chookasian, Lili (m) Cieca Gioconda Mar. 9, 1962 (5)
Christopher, Russell (b) D'Obigny Traviata Dec. 14, 1963 (4)
Ciaparelli, Gina (s) Mimi Bohème Jan. 4, 1910 (1)
Cibelli, Eduardo (b) Morales Carmen Dec. 3, 1908 (1)
Cigna, Gina (s) Aida, Feb. 6, 1937 (2)
Cimara, Pietro (cond) Lucia Mar. 11, 1932 (23)
Cingolani, Flora (s) Maid Marta Dec. 14, 1923 (7)
Claessens, Maria (m) Cieca Gioconda Nov. 23, 1910 (3)
Clare, Miss (   ) Flower Maiden Parsifal Dec. 24, 1903 (1)
Clark, Charleen (s) Peasant Nozze Dec. 10, 1959 (2)
Clark, Elizabeth (m) Page Lohengrin Dec. 18, 1909 (1)
Clark, Lillian (s) Priestess Aida Dec. 30, 1933 (2)
Claus, Signor (t) Eisslinger Meistersinger Mar. 3, 1892 (1)
Claussen, Julia (m) Dalila Samson Nov. 23, 1917 (1)
Clemens, Hans (t) Steersman Holländer Nov. 1, 1930 (8)
Clément, Edmond (t) Des Grieux Manon Dec. 6, 1909 (2)
Clements, Joy (s) Countess Rigoletto Oct. 23, 1963 (3)
Cleva, Fausto (cond) Barbiere Feb. 14, 1942 (20)
Clevenger, Jessie (s) Flower Maiden Parsifal Dec. 24, 1903 (2)
Colombati, Virginia (s) Euridice Orfeo Dec. 11, 1893 (1)
Colzani, Anselmo (b) Simon Boccanegra, Apr. 7, 1960 (7)
Conde, Signor (t) Zorn Meistersinger Feb. 20, 1903 (1)
Conley, Eugene (t) Faust, Jan. 25, 1950 (7)
Conner, Nadine (s) Pamina Flute Dec. 22, 1941 (18)
Constantino, Florencio (t) Duke Rigoletto Nov. 24, 1910 (2)
Conti, Luigi (t) Jailer Tosca Mar. 19, 1914 (1)
Contini, Ludovico (bs) Wagner Faust Oct. 22, 1883 (1)
Cook, Herr (t) Vogelgesang Meistersinger Nov. 4, 1887 (2)
Cook, Miss (   ) Flower Maiden Parsifal Feb. 22, 1907 (1)

Cooke, Charles (t) Parpignol Bohème Oct. 28, 1960 (3)
Cooke, Thomas (ba) Child Wozzeck Mar. 10, 1961 (1)
Cooper, Emil (cond) Pelléas Jan. 26, 1944 (7)
Corani, Ida (s) Enrichetta Puritani Oct. 29, 1883 (1)
Cordon, Norman (bs) Monterone Rigoletto May 13, 1936 (11)
Corelli, Franco (t) Manrico Trovatore Jan. 27, 1961 (6)
Corena, Fernando (bs) Leporello Don Giovanni Feb. 6, 1954 (13)
Cornubert, Pierre (t) Vasco Africaine Feb. 24, 1900 (1)
Corona, Leonora (s) Leonora Trovatore Nov. 24, 1927 (8)
Corsi, Igenio (t) Vogelgesang Meistersinger Nov. 18, 1896 (1)
Corsini, Baldassare (bs) Laerte Mignon Oct. 31, 1883 (1)
Coscia, Carlo (bs) Major-domo Chénier Dec. 27, 1929 (12)
Costa, Mary (s) Violetta Traviata Jan. 6, 1964 (3)
Cotlow, Marilyn (s) Philine Mignon Dec. 4, 1948 (1)
Cottino, Giuseppe (bs) Peters Germania Feb. 1, 1911 (4)
Coulter, Dorothy (s) Musetta Bohème Apr. 10, 1961 (2)
Couzinou, Robert (b) High Priest Samson Nov. 11, 1918 (2)
Cox, Louise (s) Page Tannhäuser Nov. 13, 1912 (4)
Crain, Jon (t) Alfred Fledermaus Mar. 10, 1954 (3)
Cremonini, Giuseppe (t) Fernando Favorita Nov. 29, 1895 (3)
Crespin, Régine (s) Marschallin Rosenkavalier Nov. 19, 1962 (4)
Crimi, Giulio (t) Radames Aida Nov. 13, 1918 (4)
Cristalli, Italo (t) Edgardo Lucia Nov. 26, 1913 (1)
Crooks, Richard (t) Des Grieux Manon Feb. 25, 1933 (11)
Cundari, Emilia (s) Milliner Rosenkavalier Feb. 6, 1956 (4)
Curtin, Phyllis (s) Fiordiligi Così Nov. 4, 1961 (1)
Curtis, Miss (   ) Flower Maiden Parsifal Dec. 24, 1903 (1)
Curtis, Vera (s) First Lady Flute Nov. 23, 1912 (8)
Curtis-Verna, Mary (s) Leonora Trovatore Feb. 13, 1957 (10)
Cvejic, Biserka (m) Amneris Aida Apr. 14, 1961 (5)
Czerwenka, Oskar (bs) Ochs Rosenkavalier Dec. 26, 1959 (1)

Da Costa, Albert (t) Sailor's Voice Tristan Mar. 3, 1955 (8)
D'Addozzio, Tony (ba) Shepherd Tosca Dec. 19, 1942 (1)
Dalis, Irene (m) Eboli Don Carlo Mar. 16, 1957 (9)
Dal Monte, Toti (s) Lucia, Dec. 5, 1924 (1)
Dalossy, Ellen (m) Flower Maiden Parsifal Dec. 10, 1920 (15)
Damacco, Giacomo (t) Almaviva Barbiere Nov. 25, 1915 (1)
Dame, Donald (t) Laerte Mignon Dec. 4, 1943 (2)
Damrosch, Leopold (cond) Tannhäuser Nov. 17, 1884 (1)
Damrosch, Walter (cond) Tannhäuser Feb. 11, 1885 (10)
D'Angelo, Gianna (s) Gilda Rigoletto Apr. 5, 1961 (6)
D'Angelo, Louis (b) Wagner Faust Nov. 17, 1917 (30)
Dani, Carlo (t) Duke Rigoletto Dec. 5, 1902 (1)
Danise, Giuseppe (b) Amonasro Aida Nov. 17, 1920 (12)
Darcy, Emery (t) Messenger Samson Dec. 6, 1940 (13)
D'Arle, Yvonne (s) Musetta Bohème Dec. 1, 1921 (5)
Darwin, Glenn (b) Burr Man Without a Country, Feb. 17, 1938 (1)
D'Aubigné, Lloyd (t) Tybalt Roméo Apr. 20, 1895 (3)
Daum, Margaret (s) Musetta Bohème May 5, 1937 (1)
Davidson, Lawrence (bs) Jailer Tosca Nov. 15, 1947 (18)
Davis, Agnes (s) Elsa Lohengrin May 19, 1937 (1)
Davy, Gloria (s) Aida, Feb. 12, 1958 (4)
De Abravanel, Maurice (cond) Samson Dec. 26, 1936 (2)
De Cesare, Luigi (t) Registrar Butterfly Nov. 1, 1958 (2)
De Cisneros, Eleanora. See Broadfoot, Eleanor
Declery, Maurice (b) Zuniga Carmen Dec. 30, 1901 (2)
De Florio, Evangeline (s) Maid Marta Feb. 25, 1961 (1)
Defrère, Désiré (b) Morales Carmen Nov. 19, 1914 (4)
De Gromzeski, Victor (b) Silvio Pagliacci Dec. 11, 1893 (2)
De Hidalgo, Elvira (s) Rosina Barbiere Mar. 7, 1910 (3)
Delasco, Signor (b) Kothner Meistersinger Mar. 3, 1892 (1)
Delaunois, Raymonde (m) Fyodor Boris Nov. 28, 1914 (12)
Del Corso, Carlo (t) Radames Aida Jan. 18, 1934 (1)
Del Ferro, Leonard (t) José Carmen Nov. 30, 1960 (1)
D'Elia, Frank (t) Parpignol Bohème Apr. 6, 1951 (9)
De Lievin, Lucette (s) Servant Manon Dec. 6, 1909 (1)
Della Casa, Lisa (s) Countess Nozze Nov. 20, 1953 (13)
Del Monaco, Mario (t) Des Grieux Manon Lescaut Nov. 27, 1950 (7)
Delna, Marie (m) Orfeo, Mar. 5, 1910 (1)
De Longprez, Monsieur (b) Morales Carmen Nov. 20, 1895 (1)
De Loor, Gustaaf (t) Siegfried Götterdämmerung Nov. 24, 1932 (1)
De Los Angeles, Victoria (s) Marguerite Faust Mar. 17, 1951 (10)

Del Puente, Giuseppe (b) Valentin *Faust* Oct. 22, 1883 (3)
Delsarta, Mme. (s) Shepherd *Tannhäuser* Dec. 4, 1903 (1)
De Luca, Giuseppe (b) Figaro *Barbiere* Nov. 25, 1915 (22)
De Lucia, Fernando (t) Canio *Pagliacci* Dec. 11, 1893 (1)
De Lussan, Zélie (s) Carmen, Nov. 26, 1894 (3)
Delwary, Stephen (t) Zorn *Meistersinger* Nov. 30, 1907 (2)
De Macchi, Maria (s) Lucrezia Borgia, Dec. 5, 1904 (1)
De Marchi, Emilio (t) Cavaradossi *Tosca* Jan. 3, 1902 (2)
De Marion, Biro (s) Venus *Tannhäuser* Nov. 7, 1887 (1)
Dembaugh, William (t) Noble *Lohengrin* Nov. 29, 1961 (4)
Demers, James (sp) Gherardino *Schicchi* Jan. 7, 1938 (3)
De Mette, Stella (m) Page *Tannhäuser* Nov. 13, 1912 (1)
De Paola, Paul (bs) Singer *Gioconda* Dec. 26, 1960 (6)
De Paolis, Alessio (t) Cassio *Otello* Dec. 3, 1938 (26)
De Pasquali, Bernice (s) Violetta *Traviata* Jan. 2, 1909 (6)
De Reszke, Edouard (bs) Laurent *Roméo* Dec. 14, 1891 (10)
De Reszke, Jean (t) Roméo, Dec. 14, 1891 (7)
Dereyne, Fely (s) Musetta *Bohème* Nov. 23, 1907 (1)
De Salvo, Dina (m) Peasant *Gypsy Baron* Nov. 25, 1959 (6)
De Segurola, Andrés (bs) King *Aida* Mar. 3, 1902 (12)
Destinn, Emmy (s) Aida, Nov. 16, 1908 (10)
De Vaschetti, Antonio (bs) Gregorio *Roméo* Dec. 14, 1891 (5)
Devaux, Leo (t) Yamadori *Butterfly* Nov. 19, 1909 (1)
De Vere, Clementine (s) Ophélie *Hamlet* Jan. 1, 1897 (4)
De Vigne, Jane (m) Stephano *Roméo* Dec. 14, 1891 (2)
Devriès, Herman (bs) Vulcan *Philémon* Dec. 17, 1898 (2)
De Vries, Maurice (b), Mercutio *Roméo* Nov. 18, 1895 (2)
Diakov, Anton (bs) Colline *Bohème* Oct. 16, 1963 (1)
Díaz, Justino (bs) Monterone *Rigoletto* Oct. 23, 1963 (3)
Diaz, Rafaelo (t) Nicias *Thais* Jan. 5, 1918 (12)
Dickenson, Jean (s) Philine *Mignon* Jan. 26, 1940 (3)
Dickey, Annamary (s) Shade *Orfeo* Nov. 29, 1939 (5)
Dickie, Murray (t) David *Meistersinger* Oct. 18, 1962 (3)
Dickson, Donald (b) Valentin *Faust* May 3, 1937 (2)
Dickson, Muriel (s) Marie *Bartered Bride* May 15, 1936 (5)
Didur, Adamo (bs) Ramfis *Aida* Nov. 16, 1908 (25)
Didur, Olga (m) Preziosilla *Forza* Nov. 21, 1930 (1)
Di Franco, Loretta (s) Peasant *Nozze* Jan. 11, 1962 (4)
Dilthey, Minnie (s) Marzelline *Fidelio* Nov. 5, 1887 (1)
Dippel, Andreas (t) Asrael, Nov. 26, 1890 (12)
Di Stefano, Giuseppe (t) Duke *Rigoletto* Feb. 25, 1948 (7)
Ditello, Raimondo (t) Major-domo *Rosenkavalier* Dec. 22, 1923 (4)
Divine, Grace (m) Musician *Manon Lescaut* Nov. 1, 1928 (7)
Djanel, Lily (s) Carmen, Jan. 24, 1942 (5)
Djella, Mme. (s) Stephano *Roméo* Dec. 2, 1898 (1)
Dobbs, Mattiwilda (s) Gilda *Rigoletto* Nov. 9, 1956 (8)
Doe, Doris (m) Brangäne *Tristan* Feb. 3, 1932 (16)
Doench, Karl (b) Beckmesser *Meistersinger* Jan. 22, 1959 (4)
Doerfler, Max (b) Ortel *Meistersinger* Jan. 4, 1886 (5)
Domenech, Consuelo (m) Gertrude *Hamlet* Dec. 6, 1893 (1)
Doninelli, Aida (s) Priestess *Aida* Nov. 2, 1928 (5)
Dooley, William (b) Eugene Onegin, Feb. 15, 1964 (3)
Doré, Jean (b) Noble *Lohengrin* Dec. 15, 1886 (4)
Doree, Doris (s) Third Norn *Götterdämmerung* Nov. 25, 1942 (2)
Dosia, Elen (s) Tosca, Nov. 15, 1947 (2)
Dragoni, Signor (bs) Sergeant *Bohème* Nov. 28, 1906 (2)
Drog, Libia (s) Mathilde *Tell* Nov. 21, 1894 (1)
Dua, Octave (t) Simpleton *Boris* Nov. 24, 1919 (2)
Duchène, Maria (m) Cieca *Gioconda* Mar. 16, 1912 (5)
Dudley, John (t) Philistine *Samson* Dec. 6, 1940 (4)
Dufriche, Eugène (b) Alfio *Cavalleria* Nov. 29, 1893 (11)
Dunlap, John Robert (b) Sharpless *Butterfly* Oct. 13, 1965 (1)
Dunlap, Margaret ( ) Flower Maiden *Parsifal* Feb. 22, 1907 (1)
Dunn, Mignon (m) Nurse *Boris* Nov. 20, 1958 (8)
Dutilloy, Henry (b) Lescaut *Manon* Dec. 6, 1909 (1)
Dvorakova, Ludmila (s) Leonore *Fidelio* Jan. 12, 1966 (1)
Dworsky, Herr (t) Noble *Lohengrin* Nov. 23, 1885 (1)

Eames, Emma (s) Juliette *Roméo* Dec. 14, 1891 (13)
Easton, Florence (s) Santuzza *Cavalleria* Dec. 7, 1917 (13)
Echols, Mr. (bs) Schwarz *Meistersinger* Feb. 10, 1906 (1)
Ecklemann, C. W. (t) Prisoner *Fidelio* Dec. 26, 1890 (1)
Edelmann, Otto (b) Sachs *Meistersinger* Nov. 11, 1954 (10)
Edvina, Louise (s) Tosca, Nov. 27, 1915 (1)
Egener, Minnie (s) Flower Maiden *Parsifal* Dec. 24, 1903 (21)
Egenor, Frau (m) Siegrune *Walküre* Feb. 15, 1889 (1)

Egenor, Herr (t) Noble *Lohengrin* Nov. 30, 1887 (2)
Eiserbeck, Herr (bs) Schwarz *Meistersinger* Jan. 8, 1886 (5)
Eisler, Helen (sp) Hermione *Ägyptische Helena* Nov. 6, 1928(1)
Eisler, Paul (cond) *Fidelio* Dec. 20, 1916 (10)
Eisler, Paul, Jr. (sp) Gherardino *Schicchi* Mar. 21, 1928 (1)
Eisler, Stefan (sp) Gherardino *Schicchi* Feb. 6, 1926 (2)
Elias, Rosalind (m) Grimgerde *Walküre* Feb. 23, 1954 (13)
Elliott, Mildred (s) Flower Maiden *Parsifal* Dec. 24, 1903 (3)
Ellis, Mary (s) Genovieffa *Suor Angelica* Dec. 14, 1918 (4)
Elmblad, Johannes (bs) Pogner *Meistersinger* Nov. 4, 1887 (2)
Elmo, Cloe (m) Azucena *Trovatore* Nov. 19, 1947 (2)
Emanuel, Dawin (bs) Noble *Lohengrin* Feb. 11, 1959 (1)
Engel, Lotte (s) Child *Königskinder* Dec. 28, 1910 (1)
Engelman, Wilfred (b) Morales *Carmen* May 11, 1936 (8)
Engle, Marie (s) Micaela *Carmen* Nov. 23, 1895 (3)
Epstein, Adeline (s) Gerhilde *Walküre* Feb. 6, 1891 (1)
Erede, Alberto (cond) *Traviata* Nov. 11, 1950 (5)
Ernster, Dezso (bs) Marke *Tristan* Nov. 20, 1946 (14)
Errolle, Ralph (t) Roméo, Nov. 8, 1924 (2)
Eschenbach, H. (s) Ortlinde *Walküre* Nov. 30, 1885 (1)
Escobar, Marie (s) Aida, May 6, 1921 (1)
Escott, Frau (m) Rossweisse *Walküre* Nov. 10, 1886 (2)
Esparza, Elfego (bs) Sacristan *Tosca* Nov. 19, 1964 (2)
Eubank, Lillian (m) Second Lady *Flute* Nov. 19, 1913 (1)
Eure, Ella (m) Madrigal Singer *Manon Lescaut* Jan. 20, 1966(1)
Evans, Geraint (b) Falstaff, Mar. 25, 1964 (3)
Eversman, Alice (s) Second Lady *Flute* Nov. 20, 1916 (1)
Ezekiel, Wellington (bs) High Priest *Flute* Dec. 1, 1945 (1)

Fabbri, Guerrina (m) Nancy *Marta* Apr. 2, 1892 (2)
Falco, Philine (s) Curra *Forza* Nov. 4, 1927 (8)
Fanelli, Signor (bs) Foltz *Meistersinger* Jan. 24, 1902 (5)
Fanoni, Sophie (s) Flower Maiden *Parsifal* Feb. 22, 1907 (1)
Farell, Marita (s) Forest Bird *Siegfried* Dec. 3, 1937 (10)
Farnam, Margaret (s) Joy of Being Just *Oiseau Bleu* Dec. 27, 1919 (2)
Farrar, Geraldine (s) Juliette *Roméo* Nov. 26, 1906 (16)
Farrell, Eileen (s) Alcestis, Dec. 6, 1960 (5)
Farruggio, Matthew (t) Djura *Arabella* Feb. 10, 1955 (1)
Favero, Mafalda (s) Mimi *Bohème* Nov. 24, 1938 (1)
Fay, Maude (s) Sieglinde *Walküre* Feb. 28, 1916 (2)
Feiersinger, Sebastian (t) Walther *Meistersinger* Jan.22, 1959 (1)
Feinhals, Fritz (b) Wotan *Walküre* Nov. 18, 1908 (1)
Fenn, Jean (s) Musetta *Bohème* Nov. 21, 1953 (7)
Fercana, Mary (s) Milliner *Rosenkavalier* Dec. 26, 1959 (6)
Ferenczy, T. (t) David *Meistersinger* Nov. 4, 1887 (1)
Fernandi, Eugenio (t) Pinkerton *Butterfly* Feb. 19, 1958 (5)
Ferrari, Rodolfo (cond) *Adriana* Nov. 18, 1907 (1)
Ferrari-Fontana, Edoardo (t) Avito *Amore dei Tre Re* Jan. 2, 1914 (2)
Ferrin, Agostino (bs) Lodovico *Otello* Mar. 21, 1964 (2)
Fields, Anna (m) Grimgerde *Walküre* Feb. 6, 1891 (1)
Filip, Emil (t) Parpignol *Bohème* Oct. 16, 1963 (3)
Finkelstein, Gary (ba) Child *Wozzeck* Feb. 19, 1965 (1)
Fischer, Alan (ba) Shepherd *Tosca* Oct. 27, 1961 (1)
Fischer, Emil (bs) Heinrich *Lohengrin* Nov. 23, 1885 (7)
Fischer, Ernst (b) Telramund *Lohengrin* May 19, 1937 (1)
Fischer, Stuart (ba) Shepherd *Tosca* Oct. 23, 1964 (2)
Fisher, Susanne (s) Cio-Cio-San *Butterfly* Dec. 26, 1935 (4)
Fisher, William (bs) Yakuside *Butterfly* June 3, 1936 (3)
Fitziu, Anna (s) Rosario *Goyescas* Jan. 28, 1916 (1)
Flagello, Ezio (bs) Jailer *Tosca* Nov. 9, 1957 (9)
Flagstad, Kirsten (s) Sieglinde *Walküre* Feb. 2, 1935 (9)
Flahaut, Marianne (m) Amneris *Aida* Jan. 8, 1909 (3)
Fleischer, Editha (s) First Lady *Flute* Nov. 6, 1926 (10)
Fleischer-Edel, Katherine (s) Elisabeth *Tannhäuser* Nov. 30, 1906 (1)
Fleming-Hinrichs, Mme. (m) Schwertleite *Walküre* Dec. 14, 1898 (1)
Flesch, Ella (s) Salome, Jan. 6, 1944 (4)
Fleta, Miguel (t) Cavaradossi *Tosca* Nov. 8, 1923 (2)
Fletcher, Miss ( ) Flower Maiden *Parsifal* Feb. 22, 1907 (1)
Flexer, Dorothea (m) Madelon *Chénier* Mar. 5, 1926 (11)
Fliether, Herbert (b) Pizarro *Fidelio* Feb. 15, 1963 (1)
Flon, Philippe (cond) *Aida* Dec. 22, 1900 (3)
Florence, Miss (s) Child *Oiseau Bleu* Dec. 27, 1919 (2)
Foerster, Elsa (s) Child *Königskinder* Dec. 14, 1911 (2)
Foglia, Signor (bs) Page *Rigoletto* Nov. 24, 1905 (1)

Fohström, Alma (s) Marguerite *Huguenots* Nov. 28, 1888 (1)
Folmer, Joseph (t) Moser *Meistersinger* Jan. 10, 1953 (8)
Forero, Luis (bs) Lackey *Rosenkavalier* Nov. 12, 1964 (2)
Formichini, Dino (t) Nemorino *Elisir* Nov. 25, 1960 (4)
Fornaris, Vincenzo (t) Arturo *Lucia* Oct. 24, 1883 (1)
Fornia, Rita (s/m) Geisha *Iris* Dec. 6, 1907 (15)
Förnsen, Mme. (s) Page *Rigoletto* Nov. 23, 1903 (1)
Forsell, John (b) Telramund *Lohengrin* Nov. 20, 1909 (1)
Forti, Imogene (s) Alisa *Lucia* Oct. 24, 1883 (1)
Fourestier, Louis (cond) *Lakmé* Nov. 11, 1946 (2)
Franconi, Sylvia (m) Waltraute *Walküre* Nov. 10, 1886 (1)
Frank, Herr (   ) Fisherman *Masaniello* Feb. 16, 1887 (1)
Frank, Betty (s) Zerlina *Don Giovanni* Dec. 4, 1889 (1)
Franke, Paul (t) Youth *Amore dei Tre Re* Dec. 1, 1948 (18)
Franke, Tony (b) Reinmar *Tannhäuser* Nov. 25, 1905 (1)
Franklin, Miss (   ) Flower Maiden *Parsifal* Dec. 24, 1903 (2)
Franko, Nahan (cond) *Nozze* Nov. 30, 1904 (5)
Frantz, Ferdinand (b) Wotan *Walküre* Dec. 12, 1949 (3)
Freitag, Otto (bs) Foltz *Meistersinger* Feb. 2, 1906 (1)
Fremstad, Olive (s) Sieglinde *Walküre* Nov. 25, 1903 (11)
Freni, Mirella (s) Mimi *Bohème* Sept. 29, 1965 (1)
Freund, Jane (m) Flower Maiden *Parsifal* Nov. 24, 1904 (2)
Frick, Gottlob (bs) Fafner *Rheingold* Dec. 27, 1961 (1)
Friedberg, Mr. (b) Ortel *Meistersinger* Nov. 23, 1907 (1)
Friedrichs, Fritz (bs) Beckmesser *Meistersinger* Jan. 24, 1900 (1)
Frigerio, Claudio (b) Di Luna *Trovatore* Nov. 15, 1930 (3)
Froelich, Herr (b) Ortel *Meistersinger* Feb. 20, 1901 (1)
Frydel, John (bs) Slave *Flute* Feb. 23, 1956 (6)
Fuhrmann, Adolf (bs) Noble *Lohengrin* Nov. 28, 1910 (4)
Fullin, Vittorio (t) Radames *Aida* Nov. 19, 1925 (2)
Fursch-Madi, Emmy (s) Ortrud *Lohengrin* Nov. 7, 1883 (2)
Furst, Signor (t) Moser *Meistersinger* Mar. 3, 1892 (1)

Gabor, Arnold (b) Watchman *Meistersinger* Nov. 9, 1923 (18)
Gadski, Johanna (s) Senta *Holländer* Jan. 6, 1900 (17)
Galeffi, Carlo (b) Germont *Traviata* Nov. 29, 1910 (1)
Galli-Curci, Amelita (s) Violetta *Traviata* Nov. 14, 1921 (9)
Gandolfi, Alfredo (b) Sergeant *Manon Lescaut* Oct. 28, 1929 (7)
Gardelli, Lamberto (cond) *Chénier* Jan. 30, 1966 (1)
Garden, Charles (t) Eisslinger *Meistersinger* Mar. 12, 1915 (3)
Gari, Giulio (t) Pinkerton *Butterfly* Jan. 6, 1953 (8)
Garris, John (t) Esquire *Parsifal* Feb. 27, 1942 (8)
Garrison, Mabel [Greiner, Martha] (s) Flower Maiden *Parsifal*
    Nov. 26, 1914 (8)
Gary, Elwood (t) Singer *Rosenkavalier* Jan. 8, 1943 (1)
Gascoigne, Cleo (s) Child *Königskinder* Nov. 15, 1911 (2)
Gaudini, Signor (   ) Monk *Huguenots* Mar. 19, 1884 (1)
Gauld, Carlton (bs) Hunding *Walküre* Nov. 14, 1931 (2)
Gay, Maria (m) Carmen, Dec. 3, 1908 (1)
Gedda, Nicolai (t) Faust, Nov. 1, 1957 (9)
Geleng, Miss (   ) Flower Maiden *Parsifal* Dec. 24, 1903 (3)
Genetti, Mme. (s) Countess *Rigoletto* Nov. 16, 1883 (1)
Gentile, Stella (s) Page *Rigoletto* Apr. 20, 1946 (1)
Gentle, Alice (m) Preziosilla *Forza* Nov. 15, 1918 (1)
Georgiou, Vilma (s) Yniold *Pelléas* Nov. 27, 1953 (3)
Gérard, Jacques (t) Gérald *Lakmé* Dec. 2, 1943 (2)
Gerber, Oscar (b) Ortel *Meistersinger* Jan. 14, 1891 (1)
Gerhäuser, Emil (t) Tannhäuser, Dec. 1, 1902 (1)
Gerold, Mr. (bs) Gabriel *Dame Blanche* Feb. 13, 1904 (1)
Ghazal, Edward (bs) Sergeant *Bohème* Mar. 25, 1959 (8)
Ghiaurov, Nicolai (bs) Méphistophélès *Faust* Nov. 8, 1965 (1)
Ghitti, Franco (t) Beppe *Pagliacci* Mar. 11, 1964 (1)
Ghiuselev, Nicola (bs) Ramfis *Aida* Dec. 29, 1965 (1)
Giaccone, Signor (t) Poet *Messaline* Jan. 22, 1902 (2)
Giaconia, Giuseppina (m) Suzuki *Butterfly* Feb. 18, 1911 (1)
Giaiotti, Bonaldo (bs) High Priest *Nabucco* Oct. 24, 1960 (6)
Gianini, Signor (t) Elvino *Sonnambula* Dec. 21, 1891 (1)
Giannini, Dusolina (s) Aida, Feb. 12, 1936 (6)
Gianoli-Galletti, Fernando (bs) Alcindoro *Bohème* Nov. 20,
    1909 (1)
Giffin, Norman (t) Townsman *Wozzeck* Feb. 19, 1965 (1)
Gifford, Electa (s) Marguerite *Huguenots* Jan. 24, 1903 (1)
Gigli, Beniamino (t) Faust *Mefistofele* Nov. 26, 1920 (13)
Gilford, Jack (sp) Frosch *Fledermaus* Dec. 20, 1950 (4)
Gili, Mario (bs) Yakuside *Butterfly* Dec. 26, 1935 (1)
Gili, Signor (bs) Sergeant *Bohème* Dec. 16, 1904 (2)
Gilibert, Charles (b) Duke of Verona *Roméo* Dec. 18, 1900 (3)
Gilly, Dinh (b) Alfio *Cavalleria* Nov. 24, 1909 (5)

Giordani, Signor (t) Messenger *Aida* Nov. 21, 1904 (1)
Giordano, Adele (s) Page *Tannhäuser* Dec. 12, 1913 (1)
Giordano, Anna (s) Page *Lohengrin* Nov. 21, 1913 (1)
Giraldoni, Eugenio (b) Barnaba *Gioconda* Nov. 28, 1904 (1)
Girerd, Anne (m) Marthe *Faust* Nov. 20, 1907 (1)
Glanville, Roberta (s) Flower Maiden *Parsifal* Dec. 1, 1904 (3)
Glaz, Hertha (m) Amneris *Aida* Dec. 25, 1942 (14)
Gleason, Helen (s) Bersi *Chénier* Nov. 25, 1932 (4)
Gluck, Alma (s) Shade *Orfeo* Dec. 23, 1909 (7)
Gobbi, Tito (b) Scarpia *Tosca* Jan. 13, 1956 (6)
Godlsberg, Miss (   ) Flower Maiden *Parsifal* Feb. 22, 1907 (1)
Gogny, Jules (t) Tannhäuser, Nov. 20, 1896 (1)
Gola, Gina (s) Servant *Manon* Dec. 22, 1928 (12)
Golding, Herr (b) Citizen *Prophète* Dec. 17, 1884 (1)
Goldini, Mme. (s) Page *Rigoletto* Nov. 16, 1883 (1)
Goldsticker, Carrie (m) Mercédès *Carmen* Nov. 25, 1885 (1)
Gollner, Nana (sp) Ida *Fledermaus* Dec. 20, 1950 (1)
Goltz, Christel (s) Salome, Dec. 15, 1954 (1)
Goodloe, Robert (b) Philistine *Samson* Oct. 17, 1964 (2)
Gordon, Jeanne (m) Azucena *Trovatore* Nov. 22, 1919 (9)
Gorin, Igor (b) Germont *Traviata* Feb. 10, 1964 (1)
Goritz, Otto (b) Klingsor *Parsifal* Dec. 24, 1903 (14)
Gorr, Rita (m) Amneris *Aida* Oct. 17, 1962 (4)
Gorski, Natalie (m) First Norn *Götterdämmerung* Dec. 18,
    1908 (1)
Gorski, Nicolai (t) David *Meistersinger* Mar. 7, 1890 (1)
Göttich, Hans (t) Eisslinger *Meistersinger* Nov. 4, 1887 (4)
Göttich, Lena (m) Marthe *Faust* Dec. 9, 1887 (3)
Gracia, Carmen (s) Rosina *Barbiere* Jan. 29, 1948 (2)
Graham, Arthur (t) Borsa *Rigoletto* Oct. 23, 1963 (2)
Gramm, Donald (bs) Truffaldin *Ariadne* Jan. 10, 1964 (3)
Grassi, Rinaldo (t) Pinkerton *Butterfly* Feb. 6, 1909 (1)
Grassi, Virginia (s) Page *Rigoletto* Jan. 26, 1923 (2)
Gravina, Giovanni (bs) Sparafucile *Rigoletto* Mar. 2, 1908 (1)
Gray, Maria (s) Musetta *Bohème* Oct. 16, 1963 (1)
Grazzi, Amadeo (t) Normanno *Lucia* Oct. 24, 1883 (1)
Greco, Norina (s) Leonora *Trovatore* Dec. 12, 1940 (2)
Greder, Emil (bs) Reinmar *Tannhäuser* Nov. 26, 1904 (2)
Greene, Ethel (m) Page *Tannhäuser* Dec. 17, 1960 (2)
Greenwood, Bessie (s) Flower Maiden *Parsifal* Nov. 24, 1904 (2)
Greer, Frances (s) Musetta *Bohème* Nov. 30, 1942 (8)
Greindl, Josef (bs) Heinrich *Lohengrin* Nov. 15, 1952 (1)
Greiner, Martha. See Garrison, Mabel
Gress, Miss (   ) Flower Maiden *Parsifal* Feb. 22, 1907 (1)
Grienauer, Alois (b) Nevers *Huguenots* Nov. 28, 1888 (1)
Grillo, Joann (m) Rosette *Manon* Oct. 17, 1963 (3)
Grindell, Miss (   ) Flower Maiden *Parsifal* Feb. 22, 1907 (1)
Grist, Reri (s) Rosina *Barbiere* Feb. 25, 1966 (1)
Griswold, Putnam (bs) Hagen *Götterdämmerung* Nov. 23, 1911
    (3)
Grossi, Signor (t) Bois Rosé *Huguenots* Dec. 18, 1891 (1)
Guadagnini, Luigi (b) Rigoletto, Nov. 16, 1883 (1)
Guardabassi, Mario (b) Silvio *Pagliacci* Dec. 9, 1903 (1)
Guarrera, Frank (b) Escamillo *Carmen* Dec. 14, 1948 (18)
Gudehus, Heinrich (t) Tannhäuser, Nov. 28, 1890 (1)
Gueden, Hilde (s) Gilda *Rigoletto* Nov. 15, 1951 (9)
Guercia, Olimpia (m) Siébel *Faust* Nov. 27, 1893 (1)
Guetary, Pedro (t) Beppe *Pagliacci* Dec. 11, 1893 (1)
Guilford, Nannette (s) Countess *Rigoletto* Nov. 10, 1923 (9)
Guille, Alfred (t) Turiddu *Cavalleria* Apr. 24, 1894 (2)
Gunther, Frederick (bs) Reinmar *Tannhäuser* Nov. 30, 1906 (5)
Gurney, John (bs) Sparafucile *Rigoletto* May 13, 1936 (10)
Gustafson, William (bs) Titurel *Parsifal* Dec. 10, 1920 (11)
Gutjar, Anna (s) Countess *Rigoletto* Jan. 2, 1885 (1)
Gynrod, Frederic (b) Kurvenal *Tristan* Feb. 3, 1945 (2)

Habich, Eduard (b) Peter *Hänsel* Dec. 20, 1935 (2)
Hackett, Charles (t) Almaviva *Barbiere* Jan. 31, 1919 (9)
Hadley, Henry (cond) *Cleopatra's Night* Mar. 3, 1920 (2)
Hageman, Richard (cond) *Faust* Apr. 9, 1912 (12)
Hager, Carl (b) Gatekeeper *Königskinder* Feb. 15, 1912 (3)
Hall, Glenn (t) Noble *Lohengrin* Nov. 20, 1909 (2)
Haller, Gustav (t) Noble *Lohengrin* Jan. 19, 1910 (1)
Halstead, Margaret (s) Venus *Tannhäuser* Nov. 26, 1932 (5)
Hänseler, Max (sp) Frosch *Fledermaus* Feb. 16, 1905 (1)
Harbour, Denis (bs) Jailer *Tosca* Nov. 26, 1949 (1)
Harden, Willy. See Haupt, Willy

113

Hardy, Emily (s) Gilda *Rigoletto* May 13, 1936 (1)

Hargrave, William (b) Noble *Lohengrin* Dec. 20, 1944 (3)

Hargreaves, Charles (t) Alvise *Donne Curiose* Jan. 3, 1912 (1)

Harper, Elinor (s) Frasquinella *Perichole* Jan. 16, 1962 (2)

Harrell, Mack (b) Biterolf *Tannhäuser* Dec. 16, 1939 (12)

Harris, Daniel (b) Officer/Midshipman *Man Without a Country* May 12, 1937 (3)

Harris, Elsa (s) Flower Maiden *Parsifal* Dec. 24, 1903 (1)

Harrold, Orville (t) Léopold *Juive* Nov. 22, 1919 (5)

Harshaw, Margaret (m/s) Second Norn *Götterdämmerung* Nov. 25, 1942 (21)

Hartmann, Carl (t) Siegfried, Dec. 3, 1937 (3)

Hartmann, Nina (m) Grimgerde *Walküre* Feb. 15, 1889 (2)

Harvard, Sue (s) Priestess *Aida* Dec. 18, 1920 (1)

Harvuot, Clifford (b) Guard *Flute* Nov. 14, 1947 (19)

Hasselmans, Louis (cond) *Faust* Jan. 20, 1922 (15)

Hatfield, Lansing (bs) Monterone *Rigoletto* Dec. 29, 1941 (3)

Hauk, Minnie (s) Selika *Africaine* Feb. 10, 1891 (1)

Hauke, Miss ( ) Flower Maiden *Parsifal* Dec. 24, 1903 (1)

Haupt [Harden], Willy (t) Esquire *Parsifal* Dec. 24, 1903 (3)

Hawkins, Osie (b) Donner *Rheingold* Jan. 22, 1942 (23)

Hayward, Thomas (t) Tybalt *Roméo* Nov. 23, 1945 (12)

Hecht, Joshua (bs) Dutchman *Holländer* Mar. 18, 1965 (1)

Heidelbach, Lillian (s) Gerhilde *Walküre* Nov. 25, 1903 (1)

Heidenreich, Bernhard (bs) Schwarz *Meistersinger* Mar. 15, 1911 (3)

Heim, Konrad (bs) Foltz *Meistersinger* Mar. 7, 1890 (2)

Heinrich, Julia (s) Gutrune *Götterdämmerung* Nov. 18, 1915 (1)

Heinrich, Max (b) Baal Hanan *Königin* Nov. 8, 1886 (2)

Heliane, Christine (s) Poussette *Manon* Dec. 6, 1909 (1)

Heller, Mira (s) Mignon, Dec. 10, 1894 (1)

Hemmerly, Walter (bs) Noble *Lohengrin* Dec. 26, 1958 (5)

Hempel, Frieda (s) Marguerite *Huguenots* Dec. 27, 1912 (7)

Henders, Harriet (s) Sophie *Rosenkavalier* Dec. 29, 1939 (1)

Henderson, Mary (s) Micaela *Carmen* Mar. 30, 1946 (2)

Henniges, Mme. (m) Waltraute *Walküre* Nov. 30, 1885 (1)

Hensel, Heinrich (t) Lohengrin, Dec. 22, 1911 (1)

Herbert, Ralph (b) Waldner *Arabella* Feb. 10, 1955 (8)

Herbert-Förster, Therese (s) Konigin von Saba, Nov. 8, 1886 (2)

Herlea, Nicolae (b) Rodrigo *Don Carlo* Mar. 7, 1964 (3)

Herlick, Edith (s) Page *Rigoletto* Dec. 25, 1939 (4)

Hertz, Alfred (cond) *Lohengrin* Nov. 28, 1902 (13)

Herzog, Emilie (s) Flower Maiden *Parsifal* Nov. 24, 1904 (1)

Hill, Lucille (s) Mathilde *Tell* Dec. 29, 1894 (1)

Hinckley, Allen (bs) Hunding *Walküre* Nov. 18, 1908 (4)

Hindemeyer, Harvey (t) Zorn *Meistersinger* Nov. 23, 1907 (1)

Hines, Jerome (bs) Sergeant *Boris* Nov. 21, 1946 (20)

Hinrichs, Gustav (cond) *Cavalleria* Feb. 12, 1904 (1)

Hinshaw, William (b) Biterolf *Tannhäuser* Nov. 16, 1910 (3)

Hober, Beal (s) Helmwige *Walküre* Dec. 2, 1944 (2)

Hoengen, Elisabeth (m) Herodias *Salome* Jan. 10, 1952 (1)

Hoffman, Grace (m) Brangäne *Tristan* Mar. 27, 1958 (1)

Hoffmann, Miss ( ) Flower Maiden *Parsifal* Dec. 24, 1903 (1)

Hofmann, Ludwig (bs) Hagen *Götterdämmerung* Nov, 24, 1932 (6)

Holiday, Elizabeth (m) Companion *Boris* Feb. 10, 1954 (1)

Holland, Florence (s) Frasquinella *Perichole* Dec. 21, 1956 (2)

Holm, Richard (t) David *Meistersinger* Mar. 15, 1952 (2)

Homer, Louise (m) Amneris *Aida* Dec. 22, 1900 (21)

Hopf, Hans (t) Walther *Meistersinger* Mar. 15, 1952 (6)

Hoppe, Herr (t) Zorn *Meistersinger* Jan. 4, 1886 (4)

Hotter, Hans (b) Dutchman *Holländer* Nov. 9, 1950 (4)

Hoveman, Hermann (bs) Pedro *Africaine* Jan. 21, 1891 (1)

Howard, Kathleen (m) Third Lady *Flute* Nov. 20, 1916 (12)

Huehn, Julius (b) Herald *Lohengrin* Dec. 21, 1935 (10)

Hughes, Austin (t) Eisslinger *Meistersinger* Dec. 6, 1912 (1)

Huhn, Charlotte (m) Mary *Holländer* Nov. 27, 1889 (2)

Hundley, Richard (t) Giuseppe *Traviata* Mar. 13, 1962 (1)

Hunt, Clara (s) Stephano *Roméo* Nov. 18, 1895 (1)

Hunt, Lois (s) Milliner *Rosenkavalier* Nov. 21, 1949 (3)

Hunter, Louise (s) Orphan *Rosenkavalier* Nov. 17, 1923 (4)

Hurley, Laurel (s) Oscar *Ballo* Feb. 8, 1955 (11)

Hussa, Maria (s) Marschallin *Rosenkavalier* Dec. 7, 1940 (1)

Hyde, Walter (t) Siegmund *Walküre* Mar. 28, 1910 (1)

Ibles, Anita (s) Mercédès *Carmen* Dec. 20, 1893 (1)

Ilitsch, Daniza (s) Desdemona *Otello* Mar. 12, 1947 (2)

Illy, Monsieur (b) Mercutio *Roméo* Dec. 18, 1899 (1)

Imai, Kunie (s) Cio-Cio-San *Butterfly* Nov. 15, 1958 (1)

Imbart de la Tour, Georges (t) Radames *Aida* Dec. 22, 1900 (1)

Ingram, Frances (m) Suzuki *Butterfly* Nov. 29, 1919 (2)

Islar, Olga (s) Shepherd *Tannhäuser* Nov. 28, 1890 (1)

Jacobo, Clara (s) Leonora *Trovatore* Nov. 8, 1928 (4)

Jacoby, Josephine (m) Rossweisse *Walküre* Nov. 25, 1903 (5)

Jadlowker, Herman (t) Faust, Jan. 22, 1910 (3)

Jagel, Frederick (t) Radames *Aida* Nov. 8, 1927 (23)

Jahn, Marie (s) Nefta *Asrael* Nov. 26, 1890 (1)

Jansen, Jacques (t) Pelléas, Feb. 16, 1949 (1)

Janssen, Herbert (b) Wolfram *Tannhäuser* Jan. 28, 1939 (14)

Jepson, Helen (s) Helene *In the Pasha's Garden* Jan. 24, 1935 (9)

Jeritza, Maria (s) Marietta *Tote Stadt* Nov. 19, 1921 (11)

Jessner, Irene (s) Ortlinde *Walküre* Dec. 21, 1936 (16)

Jobin, Raoul (t) Des Grieux *Manon* Feb. 19, 1940 (10)

Johnson, Christine (m) Erda *Rheingold* Feb. 8, 1944 (1)

Johnson, Edward (t) Avito *Amore dei Tre Re* Nov. 16, 1922 (13)

Jomelli, Jeanne (s) Elisabeth *Tannhäuser* Nov. 25, 1905 (1)

Jones, Alexandra [Lexi] (m) Orphan *Rosenkavalier* Dec. 26, 1959 (6)

Jones, Junetta (s) Voice *Don Carlo* Oct. 31, 1963 (2)

Jordan, Irene (m/s) Mallika *Lakmé* Nov. 1, 1946 (3)

Jörn, Carl (t) Walther *Meistersinger* Jan. 22, 1909 (6)

Journet, Marcel (bs) Ramfis *Aida* Dec. 22, 1900 (8)

Judels, Jules ( ) Councilor *Messaline* Jan. 22, 1902 (1)

Jungmann, Mary (m) Schwertleite *Walküre* Feb. 8, 1912 (1)

Kabaivanska, Raina (s) Nedda *Pagliacci* Oct. 27, 1962 (4)

Kailer, Lucille (s) Flower Maiden *Parsifal* Mar. 22, 1961 (2)

Kalil, Margaret (s) Voice *Don Carlo* Oct. 7, 1965 (1)

Kalisch, Paul (t) Tannhäuser, Jan. 30, 1889 (3)

Kanders, Helene (s) Barbarina *Nozze* Dec. 22, 1917 (1)

Kandt, Elizabeth (s) Aennchen *Freischütz* Jan. 22, 1926 (1)

Kappel, Gertrude (s) Isolde *Tristan* Jan. 16, 1928 (9)

Kaschmann, Giuseppe (b) Enrico *Lucia* Oct. 24, 1883 (2)

Kaschowska, Félicie (s) Urbain *Huguenots* Nov. 28, 1888 (4)

Kaskas, Anna (m) Maddalena *Rigoletto* May 13, 1936 (11)

Kaufmann, Carl (b) Noble *Lohengrin* Nov. 23, 1885 (1)

Keene, Hannah (s) Flower Maiden *Parsifal* Jan. 11, 1906 (1)

Keener, Suzanne (s) Page *Lohengrin* Nov. 16, 1921 (2)

Keith, George (ba) Shepherd *Tosca* Nov. 15, 1956 (2)

Kelley, Norman (t) Mime *Rheingold* Jan. 18, 1957 (3)

Kellogg, Edna (s) Kate *Butterfly* Nov. 29, 1919 (2)

Kemlitz, Frau (m) Grimgerde *Walküre* Jan. 30, 1885 (4)

Kemlitz, Otto (t) Heinrich *Tannhäuser* Nov. 17, 1884 (5)

Kemp, Barbara (s) Mona Fiordalisa/Wife *Mona Lisa* Mar. 1, 1923 (2)

Kempe, Rudolf (cond) *Tannhäuser* Jan. 26, 1955 (2)

Kennedy, Katherine (s) Child *Oiseau Bleu* Dec. 27, 1919 (2)

Kenney, Mary (m) Flower Maiden *Parsifal* Jan. 11, 1906 (1)

Kent, Arthur (b) Philistine *Samson* Dec. 6, 1940 (1)

Kessler, Kurt (t) Animal Vender *Rosenkavalier* Dec. 26, 1959 (3)

Kiepura, Jan (t) Rodolfo *Bohème* Feb. 10, 1938 (3)

King, James (t) Florestan *Fidelio* Jan. 8, 1966 (1)

Kingsbury, Miss (s) Flower Maiden *Parsifal* Dec. 8, 1907 (1)

Kingston, Morgan (t) Manrico *Trovatore* Dec. 1, 1917 (7)

Kinsman, Philip (bs) Herald *Otello* Nov. 16, 1946 (4)

Kipnis, Alexander (bs) Gurnemanz *Parsifal* Jan. 5, 1940 (7)

Kirchhoff, Walter (t) Loge *Rheingold* Jan. 28, 1927 (5)

Kirk, Florence (s) Donna Anna *Don Giovanni* Nov. 29, 1944 (4)

Kirkby-Lunn, Louise (m) Brangäne *Tristan* Jan. 7, 1903 (3)

Kirschberg, Arnold (t) Noble *Lohengrin* Oct. 28, 1961 (2)

Kirsten, Dorothy (s) Mimi *Bohème* Dec. 1, 1945 (18)

Kirwan, Jane (s) Orphan *Rosenkavalier* Dec. 26, 1959 (1)

Kitzu, Aurelia (m) Lola *Cavalleria* Dec. 7, 1895 (1)

Klaus, Herr (t) Eisslinger *Meistersinger* Jan. 4, 1886 (2)

Klein, Ida (s) Shepherd *Tannhäuser* Dec. 11, 1885 (6)

Klein, Peter (t) Valzacchi *Rosenkavalier* Nov. 21, 1949 (2)

Kloepfer, Victor (bs) Marke *Tristan* Jan. 9, 1904 (1)

Knight, Arnold (t) Noble *Lohengrin* Dec. 26, 1958 (1)

Knight, Felix (t) Almaviva *Barbiere* Nov. 30, 1946 (4)

Knote, Heinrich (t) Walther *Meistersinger* Dec. 3, 1904 (3)

Koch, Walter (t) Zorn *Meistersinger* Feb. 2, 1906 (4)

Koch-Böhm, Clara (m) Schwertleite *Walküre* Nov. 26, 1910 (1)

Kögel, Joseph (bs) Hermann *Tannhäuser* Nov. 17, 1884 (1)
Konetzni, Anny (s) Brünnhilde *Walküre* Dec. 26, 1934 (1)
Kónya, Sándor (t) Lohengrin, Oct. 28, 1961 (5)
Koreh, Endre (bs) Ochs *Rosenkavalier* Jan. 22, 1953 (1)
Kört-Kronold, Selma (s) Helmwige *Walküre* Feb. 6, 1891 (3)
Kouba, Maria (s) Salome, Feb. 12, 1965 (2)
Kozma, Tibor (cond) *Fledermaus* Jan. 4, 1951 (7)
Krall, Heidi (s) Frasquita *Carmen* Dec 12, 1953 (10)
Krämer, Felix (t) David *Meistersinger* Jan. 4, 1886 (1)
Krämer-Wiedl, Marie (s) Königin von Saba, Dec. 2, 1885 (1)
Krantz, Miss ( ) Flower Maiden *Parsifal* Feb. 22, 1907 (1)
Kraus, Alfredo (t) Duke *Rigoletto* Feb. 16, 1966 (1)
Kraus, Auguste. See Seidl-Kraus, Auguste
Kraus, Ernst (t) Siegmund *Walküre* Nov. 25, 1903 (1)
Kreatsoulas, Michael (ba) Shepherd *Tosca* Dec. 18, 1941 (1)
Kreidler, Louis (b) Priest *Flute* Nov. 23, 1912 (1)
Krenn, Fritz (bs) Ochs *Rosenkavalier* Jan. 5, 1951 (1)
Kriese, Gladys (m) Mother's Voice *Hoffmann* Dec. 22, 1961 (5)
Kritz, Karl (cond) *Nozze* Feb. 10, 1949 (3)
Kuchta, Gladys (s) Chrysothemis *Elektra* Mar. 4, 1961 (5)
Kuen, Paul (t) Mime *Rheingold* Dec. 16, 1961 (1)
Kuestner, Charles (t) Djura *Arabella* Jan. 7, 1957 (9)
Kuhlmann, Mme. (s) Page *Rigoletto* Jan. 2, 1885 (1)
Kullman, Charles (t) Faust, Dec. 19, 1935 (25)
Kunz, Erich (b) Leporello *Don Giovanni* Nov. 26, 1952 (2)
Kurt, Melanie (s) Isolde *Tristan* Feb. 1, 1915 (3)

Lablache, Emily (m) Flora *Traviata* Nov. 5, 1883 (2)
Lablache, Louise (m) Marthe *Faust* Oct. 22, 1883 (1)
Labò, Flaviano (t) Alvaro *Forza* Nov. 29, 1957 (5)
Laholm, Eyvind (t) Siegmund *Walküre* Dec. 6, 1939 (1)
La Mance, Eleanor (m) Musician *Manon Lescaut* Oct. 28, 1929 (1)
La Marchina, Robert (cond) *Last Savage* Dec. 31, 1964 (1)
Lammers, Gerda (s) Elektra, Mar. 16, 1962 (1)
Landi, Bruno (t) Duke *Rigoletto* Jan. 12, 1938 (7)
Langdon, Michael (bs) Ochs *Rosenkavalier* Nov. 2, 1964 (1)
Lange, Emil (t) Vassal *Götterdämmerung* May 12, 1939 (1)
Lange, Paul (b) Cappadocian *Salome* Jan. 22, 1907 (2)
Langendorff, Frieda (s) Ortrud *Lohengrin* Dec. 7, 1907 (2)
Langer, Herr (t) Moser *Meistersinger* Jan. 4, 1886 (1)
Lankow, Edward (bs) Sarastro *Flute* Nov. 23, 1912 (1)
Lansché, Ruth (s) Peasant *Nozze* Feb. 23, 1962 (2)
Lansing, Gladys (m) Manuelita *Perichole* Dec. 21, 1956 (3)
Lapini, Signor (t) Eisslinger *Meistersinger* Dec. 3, 1904 (1)
Larsen-Todsen, Nanny (s) Brünnhilde *Götterdämmerung* Jan. 31, 1925 (3)
Lassalle, Jean (b) Nelusko *Africaine* Jan. 15, 1892 (3)
Laubenthal, Rudolf (t) Walther *Meistersinger* Nov. 9, 1923 (10)
Laufer, Armin (bs) Servant *Madeleine* Jan. 24, 1914 (1)
Laufkötter, Karl (t) Shepherd *Tristan* Dec. 23, 1936 (10)
Laurenti, Mario (b) Innkeeper *Manon Lescaut* Jan. 6, 1916 (7)
Lauri-Volpi, Giacomo (t) Duke *Rigoletto* Jan. 26, 1923 (11)
Lawrence, Lucille (s) Flower Maiden *Parsifal* Dec. 22, 1904 (3)
Lawrence, Marjorie (s) Brünnhilde *Walküre* Dec. 18, 1935 (8)
Lawson, Mr. (t) Zorn *Meistersinger* Jan. 24, 1902 (1)
Lazaro, Hipolito (t) Duke *Rigoletto* Jan. 31, 1918 (3)
Lazzari, Carolina (m) Amneris *Aida* Dec. 25, 1920 (1)
Lazzari, Virgilio (bs) Pedro *Africaine* Dec. 28, 1933 (14)
Lechner, Frederick (bs) Calatrava *Forza* Nov. 27, 1943 (5)
Lecomte, Armando (b) Silvio *Pagliacci* Jan. 15, 1909 (2)
Leffler-Burckhard, Martha (s) Brünnhilde *Walküre* Mar. 4, 1908 (1)
Le Fontenay, Odette (s) Genie *Flute* Nov. 20, 1916 (1)
Legrand, Antoinette (sp) Servant *Manon* Feb. 20, 1909 (1)
Lehmann, Lilli (s) Carmen, Nov. 25, 1885 (7)
Lehmann, Lotte (s) Sieglinde *Walküre* Jan. 11, 1934 (12)
Lehmler, Phillip (bs) Zuniga *Carmen* Nov. 25, 1885 (1)
Leider, Frida (s) Isolde *Tristan* Jan. 16, 1933 (2)
Leinsdorf, Erich (cond) *Walküre* Jan. 21, 1938 (14)
Lellman, Adam (t) Guillot *Eugene Onegin* Mar. 24, 1920 (2)
Lellman, Phillip (t) Zorn *Meistersinger* Jan. 14, 1891 (1)
Lemon, Marguerite (s) Forest Bird *Siegfried* Jan. 18, 1904 (2)
Lenchner, Paula (s) Genie *Flute* Dec. 3, 1947 (6)
Leonard, Myrtle (m) Cieca *Gioconda* Mar. 23, 1935 (2)
Leone, Maria (s) Peasant *Nozze* Nov. 20, 1953 (4)
Leonhardt, Robert (b) Peter *Hänsel* Dec. 26, 1913 (8)

Lerch, Louise (s) Countess *Rigoletto* Nov. 10, 1926 (6)
Leskaya, Anna (s) Santuzza *Cavalleria* June 6, 1936 (1)
Leveroni, Elvira (m) Wowkle *Fanciulla* Feb. 4, 1911 (2)
Lewis, Brenda (s) Musetta *Bohème* Feb. 26, 1952 (8)
Lewis, Mary (s) Mimi *Bohème* Jan. 28, 1926 (5)
Lewis, William (t) Narraboth *Salome* Mar. 1, 1958 (2)
L'Huillier, Isabelle (s) Nuri *Tiefland* Nov. 23, 1908 (1)
Liebl, Karl (t) Lohengrin, Feb. 11, 1959 (8)
Liebling, Estelle (s) Marguerite *Huguenots* Feb. 24, 1902 (2)
Lind, Gloria (s) Helmwige *Walküre* Jan. 22, 1957 (6)
Lipkowska, Lydia (s) Violetta *Traviata* Nov. 18, 1909 (2)
Lipparini, Raffaele (t) Animal Vender *Rosenkavalier* Nov. 17, 1922 (8)
Lipton, Martha (m) Siébel *Faust* Nov. 27, 1944 (17)
Lisitsian, Pavel (b) Amonasro *Aida* Mar. 3, 1960 (1)
List, Emanuel (bs) Hermann *Tannhäuser* Dec. 27, 1933 (16)
Litvinne, Félia (s) Valentine *Huguenots* Nov. 25, 1896 (1)
Livermann, John August (b) Biterolf *Tannhäuser* Dec. 12, 1895 (1)
Ljungberg, Göta (s) Sieglinde *Walküre* Jan. 20, 1932 (4)
London, George (b) Amonasro *Aida* Nov. 13, 1951 (15)
Lorengar, Pilar (s) Elvira *Don Giovanni* Feb. 11, 1966 (1)
Lorenz, Max (t) Walther *Meistersinger* Nov. 12, 1931 (5)
Lötzsch, Otto (bs) Schwarz *Meistersinger* Dec. 3, 1904 (2)
Love, Shirley (m) Second Lady *Flute* Nov. 30, 1963 (2)
Lubert, Albert (t) José *Carmen* Nov. 20, 1895 (1)
Lucas, George (t) Abbé *Adriana* Nov. 18, 1907 (1)
Ludikar, Pavel (bs) Timur *Turandot* Nov. 16, 1926 (6)
Ludwig, Anton (b) Noble *Lohengrin* Nov. 20, 1909 (1)
Ludwig, Christa (m) Cherubino *Nozze* Dec. 10, 1959 (2)
Luise, Melchiorre (bs) Innkeeper *Manon* Nov. 12, 1947 (3)
Lund, John (cond) *Tannhäuser* Feb. 19, 1885 (1)
Lurgenstein, Bruno (bs) Lucifer *Asrael* Nov. 26, 1890 (1)
Luria, Juan (b) Nevers *Huguenots* Dec. 3, 1890 (1)

Maazel, Lorin (cond) *Don Giovanni* Nov. 1, 1962 (1)
Mabilli, Reno ( ) Bird Food Vender *Louise* Jan. 20, 1940 (2)
MacIntyre, Marguerite (s) Margherita/Elena *Mefistofele* Jan. 14, 1901 (1)
MacKenzie, Mary (m) Serving Woman *Elektra* Feb. 13, 1961 (2)
MacNeil, Cornell (b) Rigoletto, Mar. 21, 1959 (8)
Macnez, Umberto (t) Almaviva *Barbiere* Jan. 1, 1913 (1)
Macpherson, Joseph (bs) Rigel *Ballo* Dec. 30, 1926 (6)
Macurdy, John (bs) Tom *Ballo* Dec. 8, 1962 (4)
MacWatters, Virginia (s) Adele *Fledermaus* Jan. 10, 1953 (4)
Madeira, Jean [Browning] (m) First Norn *Götterdämmerung* Dec. 2, 1948 (17)
Maestri, Catullo (t) Moser *Meistersinger* Jan. 8, 1894 (9)
Magini-Coletti, Antonio (b) Capulet *Roméo* Dec. 14, 1891 (1)
Mahler, Gustav (cond) *Tristan* Jan. 1, 1908 (3)
Maison, René (t) Walther *Meistersinger* Feb. 3, 1936 (8)
Malagrida, Luisa (s) Leonora *Trovatore* Dec. 26, 1963 (1)
Malaspina, Nazzarena (s) Servant *Marta* Dec. 11, 1915 (5)
Malatesta, Mario (sp) Gherardino *Schicchi* Dec. 14, 1918 (2)
Malatesta, Pompilio (bs) Bartolo *Barbiere* Nov. 25, 1915 (24)
Mancinelli, Luigi (cond) *Faust* Nov. 27, 1893 (7)
Mandelli, Sante (t) Gypsy *Lakmé* Mar. 24, 1917 (7)
Mandile, Frank (t) Noble *Lohengrin* Feb. 11, 1959 (2)
Manetti, Eugenie (s) Child *Oiseau Bleu* Dec. 27, 1919 (2)
Manghi, Enrico (bs) Policeman *Marouf* May 21, 1937 (1)
Mann, Jack (sp) Frosch *Fledermaus* Nov. 30, 1951 (5)
Manning, Richard (t) Messenger *Aida* Nov. 30, 1944 (2)
Manski, Dorothee (s) Witch *Hänsel* Nov. 5, 1927 (14)
Manski, Inge (s) Inez *Trovatore* Nov. 19, 1947 (3)
Mantel, Anna (m) Rossweisse *Walküre* Feb. 6, 1891 (1)
Mantelli, Eugenia (m) Amneris *Aida* Nov. 23, 1894 (6)
Mantonio, Giaco (sp) Gherardino *Schicchi* Jan. 3, 1920 (1)
Mapleson, Helen (m) Leuconoe *Messaline* Jan. 22, 1902 (13)
Maran, Ernst (b) Gate-Keeper *Königskinder* Dec. 28, 1910 (1)
Marcella, Lou (t) Giuseppe *Traviata* Nov. 2, 1958 (8)
Mardones, Jose (bs) Ramfis *Aida* Nov. 12, 1917 (9)
Marek, Dan (t) Arturo *Lucia* Sept. 30, 1965 (1)
Maresi, Giulio (bs) Officer *Bohème* Mar. 25, 1910 (1)
Mariani, Alfonso (bs) King *Aida* Nov. 23, 1894 (1)
Mariani, Leopoldo (t) Officer *Boris* Mar. 19, 1913 (3)
Marinelli, G. (t) Parpignol *Bohème* Nov. 29, 1924 (2)
Mario, Queena (s) Micaela *Carmen* Nov. 30, 1922 (17)

115

Mark, Peter (ba) Shepherd *Tosca* Dec. 8, 1955 (1)
Markan, Maria (s) Countess *Nozze* Jan. 7, 1942 (1)
Märkl, Margarete (m) Orphan *Rosenkavalier* Dec. 14, 1914 (2)
Marko, Paul (bs) Jankel *Arabella* Feb. 10, 1955 (2)
Marlowe, Anthony (t) Sailor's Voice *Tristan* Jan. 1, 1940 (6)
Marsano, Signor (b) Kothner *Meistersinger* Jan. 16, 1891 (1)
Marsh, Calvin (b) Nachtigall *Meistersinger* Nov. 11, 1954 (12)
Marsh, Helena (m) Musician *Manon Lescaut* Feb. 8, 1919 (2)
Marsh, Lucie Isabelle (s) Flower Maiden *Parsifal* Nov. 24, 1904 (1)
Marshall, Everett (b) Herald *Lohengrin* Nov. 12, 1927 (4)
Martapoura, Jean (b) Mercutio *Roméo* Dec. 14, 1891 (2)
Martin, Frieda (s) Milliner *Rosenkavalier* Nov. 20, 1914 (2)
Martin, Gaston (b) Nachtigall *Meistersinger* Jan. 20, 1911 (3)
Martin, Janis (m) Flora *Traviata* Dec. 19, 1962 (3)
Martin, Riccardo (t) Faust *Mefistofele* Nov. 20, 1907 (9)
Martin, Wolfgang (cond) *Tristan* Jan. 30, 1947 (2)
Martinelli, Giovanni (t) Rodolfo *Bohème* Nov. 20, 1913 (32)
Martinez, Isadora (m) Urbain *Huguenots* Nov. 21, 1884 (1)
Martini, Nino (t) Duke *Rigoletto* Dec. 28, 1933 (13)
Martino, Giovanni (bs) Ramfis *Aida* Nov. 19, 1919 (8)
Marwick, Dudley (bs) Herald *Juive* Jan. 11, 1936 (1)
Marylli, Marguerite (s) Siegrune *Walküre* Jan. 5, 1901 (3)
Mascherini, Enzo (b) Marcello *Bohème* Dec. 7, 1949 (1)
Mascotti, Signor (t) Priest *Huguenots* Mar. 19, 1884 (1)
Masiero, Aristide (t) Benvolio *Roméo* Dec. 18, 1900 (2)
Masini, Galliano (t) Edgardo *Lucia* Dec. 14, 1938 (1)
Mason, Edith (s) Sophie *Rosenkavalier* Nov. 20, 1915 (3)
Massue, Nicholas (t) Duke *Rigoletto* May 16, 1936 (6)
Mastorff, P. (b) Peasant *Asrael* Nov. 26, 1890 (1)
Mastrobuono, N. (t) Arturo *Lucia* Dec. 4, 1893 (1)
Materna, Amalia (s) Elisabeth *Tannhäuser* Jan. 5, 1885 (1)
Mattfeld, Marie (s/m) Siegrune *Walküre* Apr. 29, 1901 (21)
Mátyás, Mária (m) American Girl *Man Without a Country* May 12, 1937 (1)
Matzenauer, Margarete (m/s) Amneris *Aida* Nov. 13, 1911 (19)
Maubourg, Jeanne (m) Lola *Cavalleria* Dec. 31, 1909 (5)
Mauguière, Georges (t) Philémon, Nov. 29, 1893 (3)
Maurel, Victor (b) Iago *Otello* Dec. 3, 1894 (3)
Maurer, Marie (m) Magdalene *Meistersinger* Jan. 24, 1902 (2)
Mayer, Wilhelmine (m) Schwertleite *Walküre* Nov. 10, 1886 (1)
Mayr, Richard (bs) Pogner *Meistersinger* Nov. 2, 1927 (3)
Mayreder, Rudolf (bs) Leopold *Rosenkavalier* Jan. 22, 1953 (10)
Mazella, Renée (s) Marguerite *Faust* Nov. 16, 1946 (1)
Mazza, Giuseppina (m) Peasant *Nozze* Jan. 1, 1917 (2)
Mazzanti, Amedo (bs) Policeman *Marouf* May 21, 1937 (1)
McArthur, Edwin (cond) *Tristan* Feb. 17, 1941 (1)
McCord, Nancy (s) Princess *Marouf* May 21, 1937 (1)
McCormack, John (t) Alfredo *Traviata* Nov. 29, 1910 (5)
McCracken, James (t) Parpignol *Bohème* Nov. 21, 1953 (8)
McFerrin, Robert (b) Amonasro *Aida* Jan. 27, 1955 (3)
McIlhenny, Helen (s) Madrigal Singer *Manon Lescaut* Jan. 20, 1966 (1)
McKinley, Andrew (t) Shuiski *Boris* Mar. 6, 1953 (1)
Meader, George (t) Victorin *Tote Stadt* Nov. 19, 1921 (10)
Meffert, Hans (t) Heinrich *Tannhäuser* Nov. 29, 1898 (1)
Mehta, Zubin (cond) *Aida* Dec. 29, 1965 (1)
Meisle, Kathryn (m) Amneris *Aida* Feb. 28, 1935 (4)
Meisslinger, Louise (m) Brangäne *Tristan* Nov. 21, 1887 (4)
Meitschik, Anna (m) Cieca *Gioconda* Nov. 15, 1909 (1)
Melatti, Jean (s) Frasquinella *Perichole* Jan. 11, 1957 (2)
Melba, Nellie (s) Lucia, Dec. 4, 1893 (8)
Melchior, Lauritz (t) Tannhäuser, Feb. 17, 1926 (24)
Mellish, Mary (s) Xenia *Boris* Nov. 25, 1918 (6)
Melton, James (t) Tamino *Flute* Dec. 7, 1942 (8)
Meneguzzer, Jolanda (s) Musetta *Bohème* Nov. 23, 1963 (1)
Mercer, Ruby (s) Marguerite *Faust* May 8, 1937 (2)
Meredith, Maud (s) Flower Maiden *Parsifal* Dec. 24, 1903 (2)
Meredith, Morley (b) Lindorf/Coppélius/Dappertutto/Miracle *Hoffmann* Jan. 3, 1962 (5)
Merli, Francesco (t) Radames *Aida* Mar. 2, 1932 (1)
Merrill, Robert (b) Germont *Traviata* Dec. 15, 1945 (21)
Mertens, William (b) Kurvenal *Tristan* Jan. 30, 1897 (1)
Metternich, Josef (b) Carlo *Forza* Nov. 21, 1953 (3)
Meux, Theodore (b) Reinmar *Tannhäuser* Nov. 29, 1898 (2)
Meyer, Julius (t) Noble *Lohengrin* Dec. 15, 1886 (1)
Meyer, Kerstin (m) Carmen, Oct. 29, 1960 (3)
Michaelis, Else (s) Katchen *Werther* Feb. 28, 1910 (1)
Michalski, Raymond (bs) King *Aida* Dec. 29, 1965 (1)

Middleton, Arthur (bs) Herald *Lohengrin* Nov. 18, 1914 (2)
Mielke, Antonia (s) Elisabeth *Tannhäuser* Nov. 28, 1890 (1)
Milanov, Zinka (s) Leonora *Trovatore* Dec. 17, 1937 (25)
Miles, Roland G. (t) Villager *Pagliacci* Dec. 5, 1959 (2)
Miller, Joseph (bs) Biterolf *Tannhäuser* Nov. 17, 1884 (1)
Miller, Mildred (m) Cherubino *Nozze* Nov. 17, 1951 (15)
Miller, Ruth (s) Musetta *Bohème* Nov. 16, 1917 (1)
Milnes, Sherrill (b) Valentin *Faust* Dec. 22, 1965 (1)
Minges, Jessie (m) Flower Maiden *Parsifal* Jan. 11, 1906 (1)
Mira, Signor (bs) Foltz *Meistersinger* Mar. 3. 1892 (1)
Mirabella, Giovanni (bs) Giorgio *Puritani* Oct. 29, 1883 (1)
Miramar, Julia (s) Poussette *Manon* Feb. 9, 1895 (1)
Miriam, Alice (s) Child *Oiseau Bleu* Dec. 27, 1920 (2)
Miron, Emmy (m) Rosswiesse *Walküre* Jan. 18, 1888 (3)
Mirsalis, Otto (t) Shepherd *Tristan* Nov. 27, 1895 (1)
Missiano, Eduardo (t) Jailer *Tosca* Nov. 21, 1908 (4)
Mitropoulos, Dimitri (cond) *Salome* Dec. 15, 1954 (6)
Mittelhauser, Albert (t) Bois Rosé *Huguenots* Nov. 28, 1888 (2)
Mittelmann, Norman (b) Herald *Lohengrin* Oct. 28, 1961 (4)
Mödl, Martha (s) Brünnhilde *Siegfried* Jan. 30, 1957 (3)
Mödlinger, Ludwig (bs) St. Bris *Huguenots* Nov. 28, 1888 (1)
Moffo, Anna (s) Violetta *Traviata* Nov. 14, 1959 (7)
Molinari-Pradelli, Francesco (cond) *Ballo* Feb. 7, 1966 (2)
Molka-Kellog, Minnie (m) Grimgerde *Walküre* Dec. 14, 1898 (3)
Moll, Mariquita (s) Waltraute *Walküre* Feb. 4, 1954 (3)
Mollica, Giulio (t) Noble *Lohengrin* Dec. 26, 1958 (2)
Monroe, Lucy (s) Musetta *Bohème* May 10, 1937 (1)
Montariol, Sebastian (t) Wilhelm *Mignon* Jan. 8, 1892 (1)
Montemezzi, Italo (cond) *Amore dei Tre Re* Feb. 7, 1941 (1)
Montesanto, Luigi (b) Marcello *Bohème* Nov. 27, 1918 (1)
Monteux, Pierre (cond) *Faust* Nov. 17, 1917 (5)
Monti, Augusto (t) Major-domo *Rosenkavalier* Nov. 17, 1922 (1)
Monti, Signor (t) Jonas *Prophète* Jan. 1, 1892 (1)
Moore, Agnes (s) Servant *Marta* Dec. 19, 1925 (4)
Moore, Grace (s) Mimi *Bohème* Feb. 7, 1928 (15)
Moran, Karl (t) Florestan *Fidelio* Dec. 31, 1888 (1)
Moran, Katherine (s) Esquire *Parsifal* Dec. 24, 1903 (5)
Moran-Olden, Fanny (s) Valentine *Huguenots* Nov. 28, 1888 (2)
Moranzoni, Roberto (cond) *Aida* Nov. 12, 1917 (7)
Morel, Jean (cond) *Perichole* Dec. 21, 1956 (6)
Morel, Marisa (s) Musetta *Bohème* Nov. 24, 1938 (1)
Morell, Barry (t) Pinkerton *Butterfly* Nov. 1, 1958 (8)
Morelli, Carlo (b) Marcello *Bohème* Dec. 21, 1935 (5)
Morena, Berta (s) Sieglinde *Walküre* Mar. 4, 1908 (5)
Morgana, Nina (s) Gilda *Rigoletto* Nov. 27, 1920 (16)
Morgenstern, Hans (cond) *Hänsel* Mar. 7, 1912 (3)
Morse, Carrie (m) Lady *Huguenots* Nov. 21, 1884 (1)
Moscona, Nicola (bs) Ramfis *Aida* Dec. 13, 1937 (25)
Mottl, Felix (cond) *Walküre* Nov. 25, 1903 (1)
Mühe, Karl (bs) Zacharias *Prophet* Jan. 9, 1889 (1)
Mühlmann, Adolph (b) Biterolf *Tannhäuser* Nov. 29, 1898 (12)
Mulford, Florence (m) Flower Maiden *Parsifal* Dec. 24, 1903 (7)
Müller, Edmund (t) Walther *Tannhäuser* Nov. 28, 1890 (1)
Müller, Maria (s) Sieglinde *Walküre* Jan. 21, 1925 (11)
Munsel, Patrice (s) Philine *Mignon* Dec. 4, 1943 (15)
Munson, Pamela (m) Page *Tannhäuser* Dec. 17, 1960 (5)
Murphy, Lambert (t) Joe *Fanciulla* Nov. 16, 1911 (3)
Murray, Frank (t) Jew *Salome* Feb. 24, 1949 (1)
Muzio, Claudia (s) Tosca, Dec. 4, 1916 (7)

Nache, Maria (s) Micaela *Carmen* Oct. 31, 1959 (1)
Nagy, Robert (t) Giuseppe *Traviata* Nov. 2, 1957 (9)
Navál, Fran (t) Georges Brown *Dame Blanche* Feb. 13, 1904 (1)
Navarini, Vittorio (bs) Officer *Bohème* Nov. 28, 1906 (2)
Nelli, Herva (s) Aida, Jan. 23, 1953 (6)
Nepoti, Lodovico (t) Körner *Germania* Jan. 22, 1910 (1)
Neuendorff, Georgine [von Januschowsky] (s) Ortlinde *Walküre* Nov. 10, 1886 (4)
Newcombe, Miss ( ) Flower Maiden *Parsifal* Jan. 11, 1906 (1)
Nicholson, Robert (b) Wagner *Faust* May 3, 1937 (1)
Nicolini, Signor (bs) Pistol *Falstaff* Feb. 4, 1895 (1)
Nielsen, Alice (s) Mimi *Bohème* Nov. 20, 1909 (4)
Niemann, Albert (t) Siegmund *Walküre* Nov. 10, 1886 (2)
Nikolaidi, Elena (m) Amneris *Aida* Nov. 13, 1951 (5)
Nikolov, Nikola (t) José *Carmen* Nov. 7, 1960 (1)
Nilsson, Birgit (s) Isolde *Tristan* Dec. 18, 1959 (7)
Nilsson, Christine (s) Marguerite *Faust* Oct. 22, 1883 (1)

Nilsson, Sven (bs) Daland *Holländer* Nov. 9, 1950 (1)
Nissen, Hans Hermann (b) Wotan *Walküre* Nov. 23, 1938 (1)
Noldi, Helene (s) Leonora *Trovatore* Jan. 19, 1906 (1)
Nordica, Lillian (s) Valentine *Huguenots* Dec. 18, 1891 (11)
Nordmo-Lövberg, Aase (s) Elsa *Lohengrin* Feb. 11, 1959 (2)
Norelli, Jenny (s) Gilda *Rigoletto* Jan. 9, 1904 (1)
Noréna, Eidé (s) Mimi *Bohème* Feb. 9, 1933 (6)
Noria, Jane (s) Nedda *Pagliacci* Nov. 24, 1909 (1)
Noté, Jean (b) Escamillo *Carmen* Dec. 3, 1908 (1)
Nouvelli, Ottavio (t) Wilhelm *Mignon* Dec. 10, 1894 (1)
Novara, Franco (bs) Méphistophélès *Faust* Oct. 22, 1883 (2)
Novotna, Jarmila (s) Mimi *Bohème* Jan. 5, 1940 (16)
Nuibo, Francisco (t) Turiddu *Cavalleria* Feb. 21, 1905 (1)
Nuotio, Pekka (t) Tannhäuser, Mar. 19, 1966 (1)

Ober, Margarete (m) Ortrud *Lohengrin* Nov. 21, 1913 (4)
Occellier, Victor (b) Valentin *Faust* Jan. 27, 1900 (1)
Occhiolini, Anita (s) Musetta *Bohème* Dec. 26, 1900 (1)
Oehman, Martin (t) Laca *Jenufa* Dec. 6, 1924 (1)
Oerner, Inga (s) Servant *Marta* Feb. 9, 1906 (3)
Ohms, Elisabeth (s) Brünnhilde *Götterdämmerung* Jan. 17, 1930 (3)
Olheim, Helen (m) Siébel *Faust* Dec. 19, 1935 (9)
Olitzka, Rosa (m) Siébel *Faust* Nov. 30, 1895 (4)
Olitzki, Walter (b) Beckmesser *Meistersinger* Dec. 2, 1939 (8)
Oliviero, Lodovico (t) Remendado *Carmen* May 11, 1936 (12)
Olszewska, Maria (m) Brangäne *Tristan* Jan. 16, 1933 (3)
Oltrabella, Augusta (s) Musetta *Bohème* Nov. 18, 1929 (1)
Olvis, William (t) Priest *Flute* Nov. 18, 1958 (5)
Onegin, Sigrid (m) Amneris *Aida* Nov. 22, 1922 (2)
Onofrei, Dimitri (t) Lohengrin, May 19, 1937 (1)
Oppicelli, Aurelio (b) Carlo *Forza* Apr. 13, 1960 (1)
Ordassy, Carlotta (s) Gerhilde *Walküre* Jan. 22, 1957 (10)
Ordognez, Augusto (b) Schaunard *Bohème* May 6, 1922 (1)
Orlandi, Edmondo (t) Parpignol *Bohème* Mar. 31, 1909 (1)
Ormandy, Eugene (cond) *Fledermaus* Dec. 20, 1950 (2)
Orner, Miss (   ) Flower Maiden *Parsifal* Jan. 11, 1906 (2)
Orridge, Theodora (m) Cieca *Gioconda* Nov. 29, 1911 (1)
Ortica, Mario (t) Radames *Aida* Nov. 19, 1955 (2)
Osborn-Hannah, Jane (s) Elisabeth *Tannhäuser* Jan. 5, 1910 (2)
Ottein, Angeles (s) Rosina *Barbiere* Mar. 10, 1922 (1)
Otto, Wilhelm (t) Noble *Lohengrin* Nov. 20, 1909 (1)
Owen, Lynn (s) Marianne *Rosenkavalier* Oct. 13, 1964 (2)

Pache, Martin (b) Captain *Prophète* Dec. 17, 1884 (3)
Palmer, Jeanne (s) Waltraute *Walküre* Dec. 2, 1944 (7)
Paltrinieri, Giordano (t) Trabucco *Forza* Nov. 15, 1918 (22)
Pandiscio, Rocco (b) Amonasro *Aida* May 26, 1937 (1)
Panizza, Ettore (cond) *Aida* Dec. 22, 1934 (8)
Panni, Nicoletta (s) Mimi *Bohème* Nov. 9, 1963 (3)
Papi, Gennaro (cond) *Manon Lescaut* Nov. 16, 1916 (16)
Parada, Claudia (s) Amelia *Ballo* Feb. 27, 1962 (2)
Paris, Signor (t) Eisslinger *Meistersinger* Apr. 22, 1895 (2)
Parisette, Mildred (s) Bice *Violanta* Nov. 5, 1927 (4)
Parks, Ethel (s) Queen of the Night *Flute* Nov. 23, 1912 (1)
Parnelle, Miss (   ) Flower Maiden *Parsifal* Feb. 22, 1906 (1)
Paroli, Giovanni (t) Isepo *Gioconda* Nov. 20, 1905 (2)
Parsons, Meredith (s) Madrigal Singer *Manon Lescaut* Oct. 25, 1960 (2)
Parvis, Taurino (b) Enrico *Lucia* Nov. 23, 1904 (2)
Pasero, Tancredi (bs) Alvise *Gioconda* Nov. 1, 1929 (4)
Paskalis, Kostas (b) Carlo *Forza* Feb. 17, 1965 (1)
Paterna, Concetto (bs) Yakuside *Butterfly* Nov. 19, 1908 (1)
Patterson, Robert (b) Kothner *Meistersinger* Jan. 14, 1963 (3)
Patti, Adelina (s) Harriet *Marta* Apr. 2, 1892 (1)
Patton, Fred (bs) Donner *Rheingold* Feb. 24, 1920 (2)
Paulee, Mona (m) Giannetta *Elisir* Nov. 28, 1941 (5)
Pauli, Miss (`) Flower Maiden *Parsifal* Dec. 24, 1903 (1)
Paull, Jarna (m) Page *Rigoletto* May 13, 1936 (2)
Pauly, Rose (s) Elektra, Jan. 7, 1938 (3)
Paur, Emil (cond) *Lohengrin* Dec. 23, 1899 (1)
Pavek, Janet (s) Musetta *Bohème* Nov. 9, 1963 (1)
Pechner, Gerhard (bs) Notary *Rosenkavalier* Nov. 27, 1941 (24)
Peerce, Jan (t) Alfredo *Traviata* Nov. 29, 1941 (25)
Pellaton, Alberto (bs) Foltz *Meistersinger* Mar. 12, 1915 (1)
Pelletier, Wilfrid (cond) *King's Henchman* Apr. 14, 1928 (28)
Pengelly, Jeanne (s) Euridice *Orfeo* May 22, 1936 (1)
Penno, Gino (t) Alvaro *Forza* Feb. 17, 1954 (2)

Peralta, Frances (s) Elena *Mefistofele* Dec. 25, 1920 (10)
Perini, Flora (m) Lola *Cavalleria* Dec. 2, 1915 (9)
Perlea, Jonel (cond) *Tristan* Dec. 1, 1949 (1)
Pernerstorfer, Alois (bs) Sparafucile *Rigoletto* Nov. 15, 1951 (1)
Perotti, Julius (t) Raoul *Huguenots* Nov. 28, 1888 (3)
Pertile, Aureliano (t) Cavaradossi *Tosca* Dec. 1, 1921 (1)
Peters, Roberta (s) Zerlina *Don Giovanni* Nov. 17, 1950 (15)
Peterson, May (s) Micaela *Carmen* Nov. 29, 1917 (4)
Petina, Irra (m) Schwertleite *Walküre* Dec. 29, 1933 (13)
Petrova, Faina (m) Azucena *Trovatore* Nov. 15, 1930 (3)
Pettigiani, Maria (s) Marguerite *Huguenots* Dec. 18, 1891 (2)
Pevny, Olga (s) Venus *Tannhäuser* Jan. 29, 1894 (3)
Pfeiffer, Selma (s) Flower Maiden *Parsifal* Nov. 24, 1904 (1)
Philo, Viola (s) Priestess *Aida* Nov. 26, 1921 (1)
Piazza, Marguerite (s) Rosalinda *Fledermaus* Jan. 4, 1951 (1)
Picchi, Italo (b) Grenvil *Traviata* Nov. 30, 1922 (2)
Picco, Millo (b) Manfredo *Amore dei Tre Re* Apr. 7, 1919 (18)
Pilarczyk, Helga (s) Marie *Wozzeck* Feb. 19, 1965 (1)
Pini-Corsi, Antonio (bs) Bartolo *Barbiere* Dec. 25, 1899 (7)
Pinza, Claudia (s) Micaela *Carmen* Nov. 18, 1947 (1)
Pinza, Ezio (bs) Pontifex *Vestale* Nov. 1, 1926 (22)
Piroia, Monsieur (t) Remendado *Carmen* Dec. 21, 1898 (1)
Piso, Ion (t) Edgardo *Lucia* Sept. 30, 1965 (1)
Plançon, Pol (bs) Jupiter *Philémon* Nov. 29, 1893 (12)
Plotkin, Alice (s) Child *Wozzeck* Mar. 5, 1959 (1)
Pobbè, Marcella (s) Mimi *Bohème* Mar. 8, 1958 (1)
Podesti, Vittorio (cond) *Traviata* Nov. 18, 1909 (3)
Poehlmann, Johanna (m) Grimgerde *Walküre* Nov. 25, 1903 (3)
Poggi, Gianni (t) Duke *Rigoletto* Dec. 14, 1955 (2)
Polacco, Giorgio (cond) *Manon Lescaut* Nov. 11, 1912 (5)
Polese, Giovanni (b) Germont *Traviata* Jan. 6, 1912 (1)
Pons, Lily (s) Lucia, Jan. 3, 1931 (28)
Ponselle, Carmela (m) Amneris *Aida* Dec. 5, 1925 (9)
Ponselle, Rosa (s) Leonora *Forza* Nov. 15, 1918 (19)
Pospinov, Ruza (m) Maddalena *Rigoletto* Feb. 16, 1966 (1)
Powell, Thomas (bs) Mityukh *Boris* Oct. 29, 1958 (2)
Pracht, Mary Ellen (s) Annina *Traviata* Nov. 24, 1961 (5)
Prandelli, Giacinto (t) Alfredo *Traviata* Nov. 24, 1951 (3)
Prêtre, Georges (cond) *Samson* Oct. 17, 1964 (2)
Prevedi, Bruno (t) Cavaradossi *Tosca* Mar. 6, 1965 (2)
Prey, Hermann (b) Wolfram *Tannhäuser* Dec. 17, 1960 (2)
Price, Leontyne (s) Leonora *Trovatore* Jan. 27, 1961 (6)
Pringle, Lampriere (b) Hermann *Tannhäuser* Dec. 3, 1898 (1)
Puglioli, Lavinia (s) Servant *Marta* Dec. 25, 1916 (10)

Quartararo, Florence (s) Micaela *Carmen* Jan. 18, 1946 (4)
Quarti, Ariodante (t) Rodolfo *Bohème* Nov. 21, 1908 (1)
Quesnel, Albert (t) Zorn *Meistersinger* Feb. 20, 1901 (5)
Queyla, Mr. (t) Remendado *Carmen* Dec. 20, 1899 (1)
Quintina, Paolo (bs) Yakuside *Butterfly* Nov. 24, 1921 (14)

Rabenstein, Ida (m) Flower Maiden *Parsifal* Dec. 24, 1903 (2)
Raidich, Hubert (bs) Wagner *Faust* Dec. 19, 1935 (1)
Raimondi, Gianni (t) Rodolfo *Bohème* Sept. 29, 1965 (1)
Raimondi, Primo (t) Borsa *Rigoletto* Feb. 27, 1907 (3)
Rains, Leon (bs) Hagen *Götterdämmerung* Feb. 24, 1909 (1)
Rakowska, Elena (s) Rachel *Juive* Dec. 23, 1927 (3)
Ralf, Torsten (t) Lohengrin, Nov. 26, 1945 (3)
Ralph, Paula (s) Ortlinde *Walküre* Nov. 25, 1903 (4)
Rand, Lloyd (t) Vogelgesang *Meistersinger* Dec. 3, 1904 (2)
Randall, Miss (s) Genie *Flute* Jan. 27, 1902 (1)
Rankin, Nell (m) Amneris *Aida* Nov. 22, 1951 (15)
Ransome, Edward (t) Manrico *Trovatore* Dec. 14, 1929 (3)
Ranzenberg, Mary (m) Rosweisse *Walküre* Nov. 18, 1908 (2)
Ranzow, Maria (m) Erda *Siegfried* Mar. 6, 1931 (1)
Rappold, Marie (s) Sulamith *Königin* Nov. 22, 1905 (14)
Rasely, George (t) Wenzel *Bartered Bride* May 15, 1936 (8)
Raskin, Judith (s) Susanna *Nozze* Feb. 23, 1962 (5)
Ravogli, Giulia (m) Azucena *Trovatore* Dec. 16, 1891 (1)
Ravogli, Sophia (s) Euridice *Orfeo* Dec. 30, 1891 (1)
Raymondi, Lillian (s) Papagena *Flute* Nov. 27, 1942 (9)
Rayner, Florence (s) Flower Maiden *Parsifal* Feb. 22, 1907 (1)
Rayner, Sydney (t) José *Carmen* May 23, 1936 (3)
Reardon, John (b) Tomsky *Queen of Spades* Sept. 28, 1965 (1)
Reep, Nancy (s) Peasant *Gypsy Baron* Nov. 25, 1959 (2)
Reggiani, Hilde (s) Gilda *Rigoletto* Dec. 7, 1939 (4)
Régis, Georges (t) Brétigny *Manon* Dec. 6, 1909 (1)
Rehkopf, Adolf (b) Narumov *Queen of Spades* Mar. 17, 1910 (1)

Reichmann, Theodore (b) Dutchman *Holländer* Nov. 27, 1889 (2)

Reid, Margaret (s) Ophélie *Hamlet* Feb. 10, 1892 (1)

Reil, Hedwig (m) Lady *Huguenots* Nov. 28, 1888 (2)

Reiner, Fritz (cond) *Salome* Feb. 4, 1949 (5)

Reiner, Marcel (bs) Noble *Lohengrin* Nov. 20, 1909 (5)

Reinhardt, Delia (s) Sieglinde *Walküre* Jan. 27, 1923 (2)

Reiss, Albert (t) Shepherd/Steersman *Tristan* Dec. 23, 1901 (19)

Reitan, Roald (b) Gypsy *Trovatore* Oct. 26, 1959 (4)

Remi, Mme. (m) Schwertleite *Walküre* Jan. 5, 1901 (1)

Renaud, Maurice (b) ·Rigoletto, Nov. 24, 1910 (2)

Reschiglian, Vincenzo (b) Montano *Otello* Nov. 17, 1909 (20)

Resnik, Regina (s/m) Leonora *Trovatore* Dec. 6, 1944 (21)

Rethberg, Elisabeth (s) Aida, Nov. 22, 1922 (20)

Reuss-Belce, Luise (s) Brünnhilde *Walküre* Feb. 11, 1902 (2)

Rhodes, Jane (s) Carmen, Nov. 15, 1960 (2)

Ribla, Gertrude (s) Aida, Jan. 8, 1949 (2)

Ricci, Signor (bs) Brahmin *Africaine* Jan. 25, 1892 (1)

Rich, Martin (cond) *Manon* Jan. 25, 1955 (11)

Ricker, Mr. (t) Eisslinger *Meistersinger* Nov. 23, 1907 (1)

Riedel, Herr (b) Melot *Tristan* Nov. 27, 1895 (2)

Riedel, Karl (cond) *Lohengrin* Nov. 20, 1929 (13)

Rigal, Delia (s) Elisabeth *Don Carlo* Nov. 6, 1950 (7)

Righi, Vezio (b) Policeman *Louise* Nov. 21, 1921 (2)

Rinaldini, Signor (t) Benvolio *Roméo* Dec. 14, 1891 (4)

Ringland, Earl (t) Soldier *Wozzeck* Mar. 5, 1959 (2)

Risley, Greta (m) Mercédès *Carmen* Mar. 4, 1892 (2)

Risse, Max (bs) Samiel *Freischütz* Nov. 24, 1884 (1)

Ritchard, Cyril (b) Ambrogio *Barbiere* Feb. 19, 1954 (5)

Ritchie, Miss ( ) Flower Maiden *Parsifal* Dec. 24, 1903 (4)

Ritter-Götze, Marie (m) Loretta *Asrael* Nov. 26, 1890 (1)

Rivera, Graciela (s) Lucia, Feb. 4, 1952 (1)

Rivière, Pierre (t) José *Carmen* Feb. 6, 1904 (1)

Roberti, Margherita (s) Tosca, Jan. 27, 1962 (1)

Roberto, Francesca (s) Cio-Cio-San *Butterfly* Jan. 5, 1966 (1)

Roberts, Hal (s) Slave *Flute* Feb. 23, 1956 (9)

Robertson, Laura (s) Young Woman *Amore dei Tre Re* Nov. 16, 1922 (4)

Robeson, Lila (m) Witch *Königskinder* Nov. 18, 1912 (8)

Robinson, Adolf (b) Wolfram *Tannhäuser* Nov. 17, 1884 (5)

Robinson, Anna (s) Valentine *Huguenots* Nov. 21, 1884 (1)

Rockwell, Mabel (s) Flower Maiden *Parsifal* Nov. 24 1904 (1)

Rodeschi, Signor (bs) Ortel *Meistersinger* Feb. 20, 1903 (1)

Roggero, Margaret (m) Annina *Traviata* Nov. 11, 1950 (13)

Rolla, Kati (s) Elvira *Don Giovanni* Dec. 27, 1893 (1)

Romaine, Margaret (s) Musetta *Bohème* Nov. 27, 1918 (4)

Roman, Stella (s) Aida, Jan. 1, 1941 (10)

Romolo, Giulio (b) Commissioner *Butterfly* Nov. 20, 1911 (4)

Röseler, Marcella (s) Marianne *Rosenkavalier* Nov. 17, 1923 (4)

Roselle, Anne (s) Musetta *Bohème* Dec. 4, 1920 (2)

Rosenstock, Joseph (cond) *Meistersinger* Oct. 30, 1929 (7)

Roslyn, Juliette (m) Tsilla *Messaline* Jan. 22, 1902 (1)

Rossi, Anafesto (t) Di Luna *Trovatore* Mar. 13, 1913 (1)

Rossi, Arcangelo (bs) Schaunard *Bohème* Nov. 27, 1903 (4)

Rossi, Giulio (bs) King *Aida* Nov. 16, 1908 (11)

Rossi-Lemeni, Nicola (bs) Méphistophélès *Faust* Nov. 16, 1953 (1)

Rothe, Hannah (m) Lady *Huguenots* Dec. 3, 1890 (1)

Rothenberger, Anneliese (s) Zdenka *Arabella* Nov. 18, 1960 (6)

Rothier, Léon (bs) Méphistophélès *Faust* Dec. 10, 1910 (29)

Rothmüller, Marko (b) Kothner *Meistersinger* Jan. 21, 1959 (4)

Roudez, Maud (m) Flora *Traviata* Dec. 5, 1898 (2)

Rousselière, Charles (t) Roméo, Nov. 26, 1906 (1)

Royer, Joseph (b) Escamillo *Carmen* May 16, 1936 (2)

Rozsa, Louis (b) Telramund *Lohengrin* Jan. 30, 1922 (1)

Rudolf, Max (cond) *Rosenkavalier* Mar. 2, 1946 (12)

Rudolfi, Signor (t) Moser *Meistersinger* Dec. 3, 1904 (1)

Ruenger, Gertrud (s) Brünnhilde *Walküre* Feb. 3, 1937 (1)

Ruffo, Titta (b) Figaro *Barbiere* Jan. 19, 1922 (8)

Russitano, Giuseppe (t) Duke *Rigoletto* Dec. 7, 1894 (2)

Ruth, Joan (s) Frasquita *Carmen* Nov. 26, 1924 (2)

Ruysdael, Basil Millspaugh (bs) Hunding *Walküre* Nov. 18, 1910 (8)

Ruzdak, Vladimir (b) Amonasro *Aida* Nov. 20, 1962 (2)

Ryan, Miss (s) Hedwig *Tell* Nov. 21, 1894 (1)

Ryan, Charlotte (s) Gerhilde *Walküre* Nov. 23, 1922 (10)

Ryan, George (ba) Shepherd *Tosca* Oct. 29, 1959 (1)

Rysanek, Leonie (s) Lady Macbeth *Macbeth* Feb. 5, 1959 (8)

Saar, Louis (cond) *Aida* Dec. 28, 1891 (5)

Sabanιeeva, Thalia (s) Cio-Cio-San *Butterfly* Feb. 24, 1923 (13)

Sachs, Evelyn (m) Marguerite *Louise* Dec. 12, 1947 (1)

St. Leger, Frank (cond) *Fille* Dec. 19, 1941 (3)

Salazar, Manuel (t) Alvaro *Forza* Dec. 31, 1921 (2)

Saléza, Albert (t) Roméo, Dec. 2, 1898 (4)

Salignac, Thomas (t) José *Carmen* Dec. 11, 1896 (6)

Salzberg, Herr (b) Priest *Flûte* Jan. 11, 1904 (1)

Sanderson, Sibyl (s) Manon, Jan. 16, 1895 (2)

Sanford, Alice ( ) Flower Maiden *Parsifal* Nov. 24, 1904 (1)

Sänger, Emil (bs) Noble *Lohengrin* Nov. 23, 1885 (3)

Sannee, Oscar (bs) Hangman *Lobetanz* Nov. 18, 1911 (1)

Santi, Nello (cond) *Ballo* Jan. 25, 1962 (4)

Santini, Nerina (s) Gilda *Rigoletto* Mar. 11, 1961 (1)

Santoro, Joseph (t) Shepherd *Amore dei Tre Re* Jan. 4, 1940 (2)

Sapio, Maurice (bs) Cavalier *Cyrano* Feb. 27, 1913 (1)

Sappio, Alfred (t) Animal Vender *Rosenkavalier* Dec. 9, 1913 (4)

Sarto, Andre (b) Silvio *Pagliacci* Jan. 4, 1908 (1)

Savage, Maria (s/m) Duchess *Fille* Dec. 17, 1917 (17)

Savage, May (m) Servant *Manon* Jan. 10, 1941 (7)

Saville, Frances (s) Juliette *Roméo* Nov. 18, 1895 (2)

Sayão, Bidù (s) Manon, Feb. 13, 1937 (16)

Scalchi, Sofia (m) Siébel *Faust* Oct. 22, 1883 (5)

Schaaf, Myrtle (m) Page *Lohengrin* Nov. 16, 1921 (2)

Schaffer, Josephine (s) Priestess *Aida* Nov. 30, 1903 (2)

Schalk, Franz (cond) *Walküre* Dec. 14, 1898 (1)

Schech, Marianne (s) Sieglinde *Walküre* Jan. 22, 1957 (2)

Scheff, Fritzi (s) Marzelline *Fidelio* Dec. 28, 1900 (3)

Schick, George (cond) *Rigoletto* Feb. 18, 1959 (8)

Schilling, Mina (s) Forest Bird *Siegfried* Jan. 11, 1897 (1)

Schipa, Tito (t) Nemorino *Elisir* Nov. 23, 1932 (4)

Schippers, Thomas (cond) *Don Pasquale* Dec. 23, 1955 (10)

Schlegel, Carl (b) Priest *Flute* Nov. 19, 1913 (13)

Schlömann, Edward (bs) Baal Hanan *Königin* Nov. 29, 1889 (1)

Schlueter, Erna (s) Isolde *Tristan* Nov. 26, 1947 (1)

Schmedes, Erik (t) Siegmund *Walküre* Nov. 18, 1908 (1)

Schmorr, Robert (t) Goro *Butterfly* Oct. 13, 1965 (1)

Schoeffler, Paul (b) Jochanaan *Salome* Jan. 26, 1950 (9)

Scholl, Albert (b) Priest *Flute* Feb. 3, 1917 (1)

Schölfer-Haag, Pauline (s) Valentine *Huguenots* Dec. 3, 1890 (1)

Schon, Kenneth (b) Pizarro *Fidelio* Mar. 17, 1945 (7)

Schorr, Friedrich (b) Sachs *Meistersinger* Feb. 23, 1924 (20)

Schott, Anton (t) Tannhäuser, Nov. 17, 1884 (2)

Schramm, Ada (m) Flower Maiden *Parsifal* Dec. 24, 1903 (3)

Schröder-Hanfstängl, Marie (s) Marguerite *Huguenots* Nov. 21, 1884 (2)

Schubel, Anton (bs) Sergeant *Bohème* Apr. 7, 1944 (1)

Schubert, Erik (bs) Nachtigall *Meistersinger* Jan. 22, 1909 (1)

Schueler, Mme. (m) Rossweisse *Walküre* Apr. 20, 1904 (1)

Schueller, Herr (t) Alphonso *Masaniello* Jan. 3, 1885 (1)

Schumann, Elisabeth (s) Sophie *Rosenkavalier* Nov. 20, 1914 (1)

Schumann-Heink, Ernestine (m) Ortrud *Lohengrin* Jan. 9, 1899 (14)

Schuster, Wilhelm (bs) Watchman *Huguenots* Dec. 3, 1890 (1)

Schützendorf, Gustav (b) Faninal *Rosenkavalier* Nov. 17, 1922 (13)

Schwarzkopf, Elisabeth (s) Marschallin *Rosenkavalier* Oct. 13, 1964 (2)

Schymberg, Hjördis (s) Susanna *Nozze* Feb. 15, 1947 (1)

Scotney, Evelyn (s) Princess *Juive* Nov. 22, 1919 (2)

Scott, Henri (bs) Ramfis *Aida* Nov. 20, 1915 (4)

Scott, Norman (bs) Monterone *Rigoletto* Nov. 15, 1951 (15)

Scotti, Antonio (b) Don Giovanni, Dec. 27, 1899 (34)

Scotto, Renata (s) Cio-Cio-San *Butterfly* Oct. 13, 1965 (1)

Scovotti, Jeanette (s) Adele *Fledermaus* Nov. 15, 1962 (4)

Sedlmayer, Frau (s) Gerhilde *Walküre* Feb. 23, 1889 (1)

Sedlmayer, Wilhelm (t) Cosse *Huguenots* Nov. 28, 1888 (2)

Seefried, Irmgard (s) Susanna *Nozze* Nov. 20, 1953 (1)

Seidl, Anton (cond) *Lohengrin* Nov. 23, 1885 (11)

Seidl-Kraus, Auguste (s) Elisabeth *Tannhäuser* Nov. 17, 1884 (3)

Seitz, Herr (b) Herald *Lohengrin* Apr. 15, 1896 (1)

Sembach, Johannes (t) Parsifal, Nov. 26, 1914 (5)

Sembrich, Marcella (s) Lucia, Oct. 24, 1883 (11)

Senger-Bettaque, Katherine (s) Elsa *Lohengrin* Nov. 30, 1888 (2)

Seppilli, Armando (cond) *Trovatore* Dec. 7, 1895 (2)

Serafin, Tullio (cond) *Aida* Nov. 3, 1924 (10)

Serbolini, Enrico (bs) St. Bris *Huguenots* Dec. 18, 1891 (1)

Sereni, Mario (b) Gérard *Chénier* Nov. 9, 1957 (9)
Sergi, Arturo (t) Grigori *Boris* Mar. 25, 1963 (4)
Setti, Giulio (cond) *Barbiere* Feb. 12, 1922 (16)
Seygard, Camille (s) Grimgerde *Walküre* Jan. 13, 1902 (3)
Sgarro, Louis (bs) Major-domo *Chénier* Nov. 16, 1954 (12)
Sharlow, Myrna (s) Nedda *Pagliacci* Nov. 27, 1930 (1)
Shawn, Dorothy (m) Orphan *Rosenkavalier* Feb. 21, 1953 (11)
Sherman, Alice (s) Page *Lohengrin* Mar. 17, 1913 (1)
Sherman [Shearman], Estelle (s) Flower Maiden *Parsifal* Nov. 24, 1904 (3)
Shirley, George (t) Ferrando *Così* Oct. 24, 1961 (5)
Sieglitz, Georg (bs) Hunding *Walküre* Nov. 10, 1886 (1)
Siepi, Cesare (bs) Philip *Don Carlo* Nov. 6, 1950 (16)
Siersdorfer, Miss ( ) Flower Maiden *Parsifal* Dec. 24, 1903 (1)
Silveri, Paolo (b) Don Giovanni, Nov. 20, 1950 (3)
Simard, Monsieur (b) Mercutio *Roméo* Nov. 26, 1906 (1)
Simeoli, Lina (s) Alisa *Lucia* Dec. 22, 1906 (1)
Simionato, Giulietta (m) Azucena *Trovatore* Oct. 26, 1959 (3)
Simoneau, Léopold (t) Ottavio *Don Giovanni* Oct. 18, 1963 (1)
Sims, Lilias (s) Farmer's Wife *Marta* Jan. 26, 1961 (5)
Singher, Martial (b) Dappertutto *Hoffmann* Dec. 10, 1943 (12)
Sizes, Eugène (b) Mercutio *Roméo* Dec. 18, 1900 (1)
Slach, Anna (s) Venus *Tannhäuser* Nov. 17, 1884 (2)
Slezak, Leo (t) Otello, Nov. 17, 1909 (4)
Slezak, Walter (bs) Szupán *Gypsy Baron* Nov. 25, 1959 (1)
Sliker, Peter (bs) Noble *Lohengrin* Dec. 11, 1961 (5)
Smirnoff, Dmitri (t) Duke *Rigoletto* Dec. 30, 1910 (2)
Smith, Kenneth (bs) High Priest *Flute* Dec. 16, 1963 (1)
Snelling, Lillia (m) Peasant *Nozze* Jan. 13, 1909 (4)
Sodero, Cesare (cond) *Aida* Nov. 28, 1942 (5)
Soederstroem, Elisabeth (s) Susanna *Nozze* Oct. 30, 1959 (4)
Solti, Georg (cond) *Tannhäuser* Dec. 17, 1960 (3)
Somigli, Franca (s) Cio-Cio-San *Butterfly* Mar. 8, 1937 (1)
Sonntag-Uhl, Emmy (m) Elvira *Don Giovanni* Dec. 4, 1889 (1)
Soomer, Walter (b) Wolfram *Tannhäuser* Feb. 18, 1909 (3)
Sordello, Enzo (b) Marcello *Bohème* Nov. 3, 1956 (1)
Soubeyran, Fernand (t) Roméo, Dec. 1, 1906 (1)
Souzay, Gérard (b) Almaviva *Nozze* Jan. 21, 1965 (1)
Sparkes, Lenora (s) Priestess *Aida* Nov. 16, 1908 (16)
Spetrino, Francesco (cond) *Traviata* Nov. 20, 1908 (1)
Stabe, Miss (s) Child *Oiseau Bleu* Dec. 27, 1919 (1)
Staber, Anna (s) Servant *Marta* Dec. 14, 1923 (2)
Stagi, Signor (t) Rambaldo *Robert le Diable* Nov. 19, 1883 (1)
Stagno, Roberto (t) Manrico *Trovatore* Oct. 26, 1883 (1)
Stanz, William (t) Noble *Lohengrin* Feb. 11, 1959 (6)
Starling, William (bs) Villager *Pagliacci* Nov. 7, 1958 (2)
Statile, Anthony (sp) Gherardino *Schicchi* Jan. 6, 1944 (1)
Staudigl, Joseph (b) Fernando *Fidelio* Nov. 19, 1884 (2)
Steber, Eleanor (s) Sophie *Rosenkavalier* Dec. 7, 1940 (22)
Steger, Emil (b) Telramund *Lohengrin* Jan. 23, 1888 (1)
Stein, Herr (b) Noble *Lohengrin* Nov. 30, 1887 (2)
Steinberg, William (cond) *Aida* Jan. 2, 1965 (1)
Stella, Antonietta (s) Aida, Nov. 13, 1956 (4)
Stellmach, Herr (bs) Foltz *Meistersinger* Jan. 9, 1905 (1)
Stellman, Maxine (s) Amor *Orfeo* May 22, 1936 (15)
Stern, Anna (s) Shepherd *Tannhäuser* Nov. 17, 1884 (1)
Sternberg, Harold (bs) Servant *Macbeth* Feb. 5, 1959 (3)
Sternberg, Sam (bs) Officer *Bohème* Nov. 8, 1958 (1)
Sterzini, Giuseppe (b) Policeman *Louise* Jan. 15, 1921 (2)
Stevens, Risë (m) Mignon, Dec. 17, 1938 (23)
Stewart, Thomas (b) Ford *Falstaff* Mar. 9, 1966 (1)
Stich-Randall, Teresa (s) Fiordiligi *Così* Oct. 24, 1961 (4)
Stiedry, Fritz (cond) *Siegfried* Nov. 15, 1946 (12)
Stiner, Franz (b) Nazarene *Salome* Jan. 22, 1907 (1)
Stokowski, Leopold (cond) *Turandot* Feb. 24, 1961 (3)
Stoska, Polyna (s) Elvira *Don Giovanni* Nov. 7, 1947 (3)
Stracciari, Riccardo (b) Germont *Traviata* Dec. 1, 1906 (2)
Strang, Lloyd (bs) Noble *Lohengrin* Feb. 11, 1959 (8)
Strasfogel, Andrew (sp) Gherardino *Schicchi* Jan. 24, 1958 (1)
Strasfogel, Ignace (cond) *Eugene Onegin* Jan. 26, 1959 (8)
Stratas, Teresa (s) Poussette *Manon* Oct. 28, 1959 (7)
Strebel, Miss ( ) Flower Maiden *Parsifal* Dec. 24, 1903 (1)
Stritt, Albert (t) Lohengrin, Nov. 23, 1885 (1)
Strong, Susan (s) Elsa *Lohengrin* Jan. 27, 1897 (3)
Stückgold, Grete (s) Eva *Meistersinger* Nov. 2, 1927 (7)
Sturani, Giuseppe (cond) *Faust* Nov. 22, 1911 (4)
Sturznegger, Miss ( ) Flower Maiden *Parsifal* Feb. 22, 1907 (1)
Sukis, Lilian (s) Flower Maiden *Parsifal* Mar. 10, 1966 (1)

Sullivan, Brian (t) Peter Grimes, Feb. 23, 1948 (12)
Sullivan, John (ba) Shepherd *Tosca* Feb. 3, 1944 (1)
Sumner, Miss ( ) Flower Maiden *Parsifal* Feb. 22, 1907 (1)
Sundelius, Marie (s) Priestess *Iphigénie* Nov. 25, 1916 (11)
Sundermann, Josef (t) Moser *Meistersinger* Jan. 22, 1909 (1)
Sutherland, Joan (s) Lucia, Nov. 26, 1961 (4)
Svanholm, Set (t) Siegfried, Nov. 15, 1946 (10)
Sved, Alexander (b) Renato *Ballo* Dec. 2, 1940 (8)
Swarthout, Gladys (m) Cieca *Gioconda* Nov. 15, 1929 (13)
Sylva, Eloi (t) Jean *Prophète* Nov. 27, 1885 (1)
Symonette, Randolph (b) Telramund *Lohengrin* Nov. 17, 1961 (1)
Symons, Charlotte (s) Gerhilde *Walküre* Dec. 18, 1935 (4)
Szánthó, Enid (m) Fricka *Walküre* Feb. 17, 1938 (1)
Székely, Mihály (bs) Hunding *Walküre* Jan. 17, 1947 (3)
Szell, George (cond) *Salome* Dec. 9, 1942 (5)

Tagliabue, Carlo (b) Amonasro *Aida* Dec. 2, 1937 (2)
Tagliavini, Ferruccio (t) Rodolfo *Bohème* Jan. 10, 1947 (9)
Tajo, Italo (bs) Basilio *Barbiere* Dec. 28, 1948 (2)
Talley, Marion (s) Gilda *Rigoletto* Feb. 17, 1926 (4)
Talma, Cecile (s) Nedda *Pagliacci* Feb. 21, 1905 (1)
Tamagno, Francesco (t) Arnoldo *Tell* Nov. 21, 1894 (1)
Tango, Egisto (cond) *Tosca* Nov. 22, 1909 (1)
Tappolet, Siegfried (bs) Hagen *Götterdämmerung* Mar. 14, 1930 (4)
Tassinari, Pia (s) Tosca, Dec. 26, 1947 (1)
Taucher, Curt (t) Siegmund *Walküre* Nov. 23, 1922 (5)
Taussig, Walter (cond) *Don Giovanni* Apr. 7, 1960 (3)
Tavary, Marie (s) Carmen, Mar. 4, 1892 (1)
Tavecchia, Signor (bs) Don Pasquale, Dec. 27, 1901 (1)
Taylor, Myron (t) Nolan *Man Without a Country* May 28, 1937 (1)
Tebaldi, Renata (s) Desdemona *Otello* Jan. 31, 1955 (10)
Tecchi, Giuseppe (t) Wagner/Nereus *Mefistofele* Nov. 20, 1907 (3)
Tedesco, Alfio (t) Léopold *Juive* Nov. 12, 1926 (9)
Tegani, Riccardo (b) Schaunard *Bohème* Nov. 21, 1914 (3)
Telva, Marion (m) Musician *Manon Lescaut* Dec. 31, 1920 (12)
Tentoni, Rosa (s) Santuzza *Cavalleria* May 22, 1936 (2)
Ternina, Milka (s) Elisabeth *Tannhäuser* Jan. 27, 1900 (4)
Testi, Lorenzo (b) Marcello *Bohème* Oct. 28, 1960 (3)
Tetrazzini, Luisa (s) Lucia, Dec. 27, 1911 (1)
Thebom, Blanche (m) Fricka *Walküre* Dec. 14, 1944 (21)
Thill, Georges (t) Roméo, Mar. 20, 1931 (2)
Thomas, Adeline (s) Flower Maiden *Parsifal* Nov. 24, 1904 (1)
Thomas, Jess (t) Walther *Meistersinger* Dec. 11, 1962 (4)
Thomas, John Charles (b) Germont *Traviata* Feb. 2, 1934 (9)
Thomas, Thomas L. (b) Silvio *Pagliacci* May 15, 1937 (1)
Thomaz, Neyde (s) Zerlina *Don Giovanni* Oct. 18, 1963 (1)
Thompson, Fanchon (m) Lola *Cavalleria* Jan. 15, 1904 (1)
Thompson, Hugh (b) Schaunard *Bohème* Dec. 1, 1944 (6)
Thorborg, Kerstin (m) Fricka *Walküre* Dec. 21, 1936 (13)
Tibbett, Lawrence (b) Lovitsky *Boris* Nov. 24, 1923 (27)
Tiferro, Emil (t) Walther *Tannhäuser* Nov. 17, 1884 (1)
Tiffany, Marie (s) Milliner *Rosenkavalier* Nov. 17, 1916 (13)
Tindal, Muriel (s) Milliner *Rosenkavalier* Nov. 17, 1922 (2)
Tokatyan, Armand (t) Lucio *Anima Allegra* Feb. 14, 1923 (20)
Tomanelli, Carlo (bs) Sergeant *Bohème* Mar. 10, 1951 (12)
Tomasini, Gaetano (t) Radames *Aida* May 6, 1921 (1)
Tomisani, Paolina (s) Page *Rigoletto* Nov. 15, 1924 (12)
Tonry, Eugene (sp) Gherardino *Schicchi* Jan. 10, 1952 (1)
Tonry, Reginald Jr. (sp) Gherardino *Schicchi* Feb. 4, 1949 (2)
Töpper, Hertha (m) Octavian *Rosenkavalier* Nov. 19, 1962 (1)
Tortolero, Francisco (t) Parpignol *Bohème* Apr. 20, 1946 (1)
Toscanini, Arturo (cond) *Aida* Nov. 16, 1908 (7)
Totzech, Emil (bs) De Retz *Huguenots* Nov. 21, 1884 (1)
Tourel, Jennie (m) Mignon, May 15, 1937 (4)
Tozier, Louise (m) Servant *Marta* Dec. 7, 1918 (2)
Tozzi, Giorgio (bs) Alvise *Gioconda* Mar. 9, 1955 (12)
Tracy, Minnie (s) Aida, Dec. 22, 1900 (1)
Trantoul, Antonin (t) Faust, Feb. 13, 1930 (1)
Traubel, Helen (s) Mary *Man Without a Country* May 12, 1937 (16)
Traubmann, Sophie (s) Helmwige *Walküre* Jan. 18, 1888 (7)
Trebelli, Zelia (m) Azucena *Trovatore* Oct. 26, 1883 (1)
Trehy, John (bs) Gardener *Traviata* Nov. 2, 1958 (8)
Treptow, Günther (t) Siegmund *Walküre* Feb. 1, 1951 (1)

119

Tretti, Alessandro (b) Ceprano *Rigoletto* Nov. 28, 1908 (1)
Triebner, Arthur (bs) Ortel *Meistersinger* Jan. 22, 1909 (2)
Troxell, Barbara (s) Inez *Trovatore* Dec. 28, 1950 (1)
Trucco, Victor (cond) *Traviata* Mar. 2, 1962 (1)
Tucci, Gabriella (s) Cio-Cio-San *Butterfly* Oct. 29, 1960 (6)
Tucker, Richard (t) Enzo *Gioconda* Jan. 25, 1945 (21)
Tuminia, Josephine (s) Gilda *Rigoletto* Feb. 8, 1941 (2)
Turner, Claramae (m) Marthe *Faust* Nov. 16, 1946 (4)
Tyers, John (b) Falke *Fledermaus* Mar. 8, 1952 (1)
Tyroler, Willy [William] (bs/cond) Nachtigall *Meistersinger* Feb. 25, 1911 (4)

Udvardy, Anton (t) Raoul *Huguenots* Nov. 21, 1884 (1)
Uhde, Hermann (b) Telramund *Lohengrin* Nov. 18, 1955 (6)
Uppman, Theodor (b) Pelléas, Nov. 27, 1953 (12)
Urlus, Jacques (t) Tristan, Feb. 8, 1913 (5)
Uzunov, Dimiter (t) José *Carmen* Dec. 10, 1958 (3)

Vaghi, Giacomo (bs) Colline *Bohème* Feb. 18, 1946 (3)
Vail, Edith (s) Flower Maiden *Parsifal* Nov. 24, 1904 (4)
Vajda, Frederick (bs) Nachtigall *Meistersinger* Nov. 28, 1925 (4)
Valdengo, Giuseppe (b) Tonio *Pagliacci* Dec. 19, 1947 (7)
Valentino, Frank [Francesco] (b) Enrico *Lucia* Dec. 9, 1940 (21)
Valero, Fernando (t) Turiddu *Cavalleria* Dec. 30, 1891 (1)
Välkki, Anita (s) Brünnhilde *Walküre* Jan. 23, 1962 (3)
Valleria, Alwina (s) Leonora *Trovatore* Oct. 26, 1883 (1)
Valletti, Cesare (t) Ottavio *Don Giovanni* Dec. 10, 1953 (7)
Van Cauteren, Marie (s) Mercédès *Carmen* Nov. 26, 1894 (7)
Van Delden, Maria (s) Helmwige *Walküre* Dec. 6, 1941 (1)
Van der Zee, Miss (m) Flower Maiden *Parsifal* Feb. 22, 1907 (2)
Van Dresser, Marcia (m) Siegrune *Walküre* Nov. 25, 1903 (1)
Van Dyck, Ernest (t) Tannhäuser, Nov. 29, 1898 (4)
Van Dyck, Rosina (s) Ortlinde *Walküre* Nov. 18, 1908 (9)
Van Gordon, Cyrena (m) Amneris *Aida* Jan. 18, 1934 (1)
Van Kirk, Mary (m) Grimgerde *Walküre* Dec. 6, 1941 (2)
Van Niessen-Stone, Matja (m) Grimgerde *Walküre* Nov. 18, 1908 (2)
Vanni, Helen (m) Page *Rigoletto* Nov. 9, 1956 (8)
Vanni, Roberto (t) Fisherman *Tell* Nov. 21, 1894 (7)
Van Rooy, Anton (b) Wotan *Walküre* Dec. 14, 1898 (9)
Van Zandt, Marie (s) Amina *Sonnambula* Dec. 21, 1891 (1)
Varnay, Astrid (s) Sieglinde *Walküre* Dec. 6, 1941 (15)
Vartenissian, Shakeh (s) Poussette *Manon* Dec. 3, 1954 (2)
Varviso, Silvio (cond) *Lucia* Nov. 26, 1961 (5)
Velis, Andrea (t) Joe *Fanciulla* Oct. 23, 1961 (5)
Venturini, Emilio (t) Cassio *Otello* Apr. 14, 1911 (1)
Verchi, Nino (cond) *Cavalleria* Oct. 31, 1959 (3)
Verreau, Richard (t) Faust, Nov. 28, 1963 (2)
Verworner, Herr (t) Moser *Meistersinger* Jan. 21, 1887 (2)
Vettori, Elda (s) Santuzza *Cavalleria* Nov. 20, 1926 (11)
Vianesi, Auguste (cond) *Faust* Oct. 22, 1883 (2)
Vichey, Luben [Vichegonov, Lubomir] (bs) Sparafucile *Rigoletto* Dec. 4, 1948 (10)
Vicini, Cleopatra (s) Musetta *Bohème* Nov. 27, 1903 (1)
Vickers, Jon (t) Canio *Pagliacci* Jan. 17, 1960 (6)
Vicos, Athena (s) Maid *Boccanegra* Mar. 1, 1960 (1)
Vigna, Arturo (cond) *Rigoletto* Nov. 23, 1903 (4)
Vignas, Francesco (t) Turiddu *Cavalleria* Nov. 29, 1893 (1)
Villani, Luisa (s) Cio-Cio-San *Butterfly* Dec. 11, 1915 (1)
Vinay, Ramon (t/b) José *Carmen* Feb. 22, 1946 (17)
Vinche, Jules (bs) Laurent *Roméo* Dec. 22, 1891 (1)
Vishnevskaya, Galina (s) Aida, Nov. 6, 1961 (1)
Viviani, Lodovico (bs) Duke of Verona *Roméo* Dec. 14, 1891 (8)
Vogel, Adolf (bs) Alberich *Siegfried* Dec. 3, 1937 (2)
Vogl, Heinrich (t) Lohengrin, Jan. 1, 1890 (1)
Von Bandrowski, Alexander (t) Manru, Feb. 14, 1902 (1)
Von Bitterl, Carl (bs) Noble *Lohengrin* Nov. 18, 1914 (3)
Von Doenhoff, Helene (s) Gerhilde *Walküre* Feb. 15, 1889 (1)
Von Essen, Marie (m) Magdalene *Meistersinger* Nov. 12, 1931 (1)
Von Hübbbell, Adolph (t) Heinrich *Tannhäuser* Nov. 28, 1890 (3)
Von Januschowsky, Georgine. See Neuendorff, Georgine
Von Milde, Rudolph (b) Mathiesen *Prophète* Nov. 17, 1886 (2)
Von Schuch, Ernst (cond) *Lohengrin* Apr. 7, 1900 (1)
Vosari, Adeline (s) Xenia *Boris* Nov. 24, 1919 (1)
Votipka, Thelma (s) Flora *Traviata* Dec. 16, 1935 (29)

Wächter, Eberhard (b) Wolfram *Tannhäuser* Jan. 25, 1961 (1)
Waeffing, Miss ( ) Flower Maiden *Parsifal* Feb. 22, 1907 (1)

Waelchli, India (m) Flower Maiden *Parsifal* Nov. 24, 1904 (2)
Wakefield, Henriette (m) Flower Maiden *Parsifal* Feb. 22, 1907 (20)
Walker, Edyth (m) Amneris *Aida* Nov. 30, 1903 (3)
Walker, William (b) Commissioner *Butterfly* Oct. 16, 1962 (4)
Wall, Joan (m) Rosette *Manon* Oct. 28, 1959 (3)
Wallnöfer, Adolph (t) Tannhäuser, Dec. 12, 1895 (1)
Walsingham, Frances (m) Stella *Hoffmann* Jan. 14, 1937 (1)
Walter, Bruno (cond) *Fidelio* Feb. 14, 1941 (10)
Walter, Edna (s) Child *Königskinder* Dec. 28, 1910 (1)
Walther, Herr (bs) Steersman *Tristan* Jan. 3, 1903 (5)
Ward, David (bs) Sarastro *Flute* Jan. 3, 1964 (3)
Warfield, Sandra (m) Peasant *Nozze* Nov. 20, 1953 (4)
Warner, Genevieve (s) Genie *Flute* Nov. 25, 1950 (4)
Warren, Leonard (b) Paolo *Boccanegra* Jan. 13, 1939 (22)
Warrum, Helen (s) Gerhilde *Walküre* Dec. 16, 1915 (1)
Warwick, Veni (s) Page *Tannhäuser* Nov. 13, 1912 (5)
Waterous, Herbert (bs) Schwarz *Meistersinger* Nov. 23, 1907 (2)
Weathers, Felicia (s) Lisa *Queen of Spades* Oct. 21, 1965 (1)
Weber, Hermann (bs) Citizen *Prophète* Dec. 17, 1884 (2)
Weber, Otto (bs) Schwarz *Meistersinger* Apr. 4, 1886 (3)
Webster Powell, Alma (s) Gilda *Rigoletto* Dec. 31, 1904 (1)
Weed, Marion (s) Brünnhilde *Walküre* Nov. 28, 1903 (5)
Weede, Robert (b) Tonio *Pagliacci* May 15, 1937 (10)
Wegner, Walburga (s) Chrysothemis *Elektra* Feb. 18, 1952 (1)
Weidt, Lucy (s) Brünnhilde *Walküre* Nov. 18, 1910 (1)
Weil, Hermann (b) Kurvenal *Tristan* Nov. 17, 1911 (6)
Weisberg, Aaron (t) Moser *Meistersinger* Jan. 7, 1928 (2)
Weiss, Eugene (bs) Maurevert *Huguenots* Nov. 28, 1888 (1)
Welitsch, Ljuba (s) Salome, Feb. 4, 1949 (4)
Wells, Phradie (s) Priestess *Aida* Nov. 7, 1923 (12)
Werner, August (bs) Foltz *Meistersinger* Dec. 3, 1904 (1)
Werrenrath, Reinald (b) Silvio *Pagliacci* Feb. 19, 1919 (3)
Wespi, Louis (b) Ortel *Meistersinger* Jan. 20, 1911 (1)
Wettengren, Gertrud (m) Amneris *Aida* Dec. 20, 1935 (3)
White, Miss ( ) Flower Maiden *Parsifal* Dec. 24, 1903 (2)
White, Phyllis (s) Page *Lohengrin* Dec. 1, 1916 (5)
Whitehill, Clarence (b) Amfortas *Parsifal* Nov. 25, 1909 (19)
Whitfield, Philip (b) King *Aida* Nov. 30, 1944 (1)
Wickham, Florence (m) Emilia *Otello* Nov. 17, 1909 (3)
Wiemann, Ernst (bs) Heinrich *Lohengrin* Nov. 17, 1961 (5)
Wiener, Otto (b) Sachs *Meistersinger* Oct. 18, 1962 (1)
Wiesner, Sophie (s) Senta *Holländer* Nov. 27, 1889 (1)
Wilde, Mathilde (s) Valentine *Huguenots* Dec. 12, 1884 (1)
Wildermann, William (bs) Guardiano *Forza* Jan. 8, 1958 (7)
Wilkes, Benjamin (t) Zorn *Meistersinger* Dec. 11, 1954 (2)
Wilkins, Marie (s) Lakmé, Dec. 2, 1942 (1)
Wilson, Dolores (s) Lucia, Feb. 8, 1954 (6)
Windgassen, Wolfgang (t) Siegmund *Walküre* Jan. 22, 1957 (1)
Windheim, Marek (t) Lamplighter *Manon Lescaut* Nov. 1, 1928 (8)
Witherspoon, Herbert (bs) Titurel *Parsifal* Nov. 26, 1908 (8)
Witt, Herr (b) Peasant *Prophète* Dec. 17, 1884 (2)
Witte, Erich (t) Walther *Tannhäuser* Dec. 1, 1938 (1)
Wittig, Miss ( ) Flower Maiden *Parsifal* Dec. 24, 1903 (1)
Woehning, Paula (m) Schwertleite *Walküre* Mar. 1, 1907 (5)
Wolf, Ludwig (bs) Reinmar *Tannhäuser* Nov. 17, 1884 (1)
Wolfe, James (bs) King *Aida* Nov. 7, 1923 (17)
Wolff, Albert (cond) *Faust* Nov. 21, 1919 (3)
Wulman, Paolo (bs) Bonze *Butterfly* Nov. 19, 1909 (1)

Yauger, Maria (m) Maid *Boccanegra* Mar. 25, 1960 (2)
Yaw, Ellen Beach (s) Lucia, Mar. 21, 1908 (1)
Yeend, Frances (s) Chrysothemis *Elektra* Feb. 13, 1961 (3)
York, Blanche (m) Flower Maiden *Parsifal* Dec. 24, 1903 (2)
Yurka, Blanche (s) Flower Maiden *Parsifal* Dec. 24, 1903 (2)

Zadek, Hilde (s) Donna Anna *Don Giovanni* Nov. 26, 1952 (1)
Zakariesen, William (t) Giuseppe *Traviata* Jan. 6, 1962 (5)
Zambruno, Primo (t) Turiddu *Cavalleria* Nov. 7, 1958 (1)
Zampieri, Giuseppe (t) Cavaradossi *Tosca* Nov. 20, 1961 (1)
Zanasi, Mario (b) Germont *Traviata* Feb. 6, 1958 (3)
Zanelli, Renato (b) Amonasro *Aida* Nov. 19, 1919 (4)
Zarska, Erma (s) Elsa *Lohengrin* Nov. 26, 1915 (1)
Zebranska, Elsa (s) Venus *Tannhäuser* Jan. 17, 1941 (1)
Zecchi, Signor (t) Parpignol *Bohème* Jan. 4, 1905 (1)
Zeiher, Gladys (m) Giovanna *Rigoletto* Apr. 20, 1946 (1)
Ziegler, Helen (s) Page *Lohengrin* Dec. 22, 1911 (1)
Zobel, Carl (t) Radames *Aida* Nov. 12, 1886 (1)

LIST OF ERRATA

This list corrects errors and omissions in
METROPOLITAN OPERA ANNALS: FIRST SUPPLEMENT
and covers the seasons 1947-1957.

p7   February 19, *add* Blanche . . . Altman
p24   January 20, *should read* Magdalene was sung by Harshaw in Acts I and II
      and by Glaz in Act III.
p35   January 25 (matinee), *should read* Donner . . . Hawkins
p37   March 9, *add* Conductor: Kozma
p37   March 10 (matinee), *should read* Same cast as March 6 except: Florestan
      . . . Svanholm
p38   March 24, *add* Conductor: Kozma
p43   *Add* date, December 29, over AIDA in third column
p61   March 18, *should read* Same cast as March 13 except:
p65   *Delete* Di Giacomo, Constance, from Personnel list
p70   March 10, *delete* Famous Dancer . . . Ames
p71   March 15, *delete* 2nd Companion . . . Di Giacomo
p71   March 25, *delete* Famous Dancer . . . Ames
p71   March 27, *should read* LA FORZA DEL DESTINO: Overture (Verdi) Con-
      ductor: Stiedry
p72   March 27, *add* IL BARBIERE DI SIVIGLIA: Overture (Rossini) Conductor:
      Erede
p72   March 27, *add* Eugene Slavin as soloist in SAMSON ET DALILA: (Bacchanale)
p78   December 30, *delete* Second Jew . . . McCracken
p90   March 10, *delete* Khrushchov . . . Carelli
p97   December 21, "Minetta" *should read* Ninetta
p99   February 6, *add* Circus Ballerina . . . Moylan

LIST OF OMISSIONS

This is a list of omissions in
METROPOLITAN OPERA ANNALS: SECOND SUPPLEMENT
and covers the seasons 1957-1966.

p11   *Ballet Soloists, add* Devon, Hlenka; Edwards, Joyce
p14   January 7, *add* Maids . . . Devon, Edwards
p21   *Male Artists, add* Sternberg, Harold
p25   January 28, *add* Captain of Guard . . . Sternberg
p51   March 28, *add* First Executioner . . . Farrington
p51   March 30 (matinee), *add* Gastone . . . Velis
p52   April 18, *add* Wowkle . . . Wall
p52   April 21 (matinee), *add* Conductor: Strasfogel
p59   *Male Artists, add* Sternberg, Harold
p63   December 29 (matinee), *add* Same cast as November 30 except:
p64   January 26 (matinee), *add* Captain of Guard . . . Sternberg
p66   March 21, *add* Brangäne . . . Dunn
p79   March 27, *add* In Memory of John F. Kennedy
p83   *Male Artists, add* Uppman, Theodor

INDEX

To Artists, Operas, Composers, and Critics

This index is by SEASONS rather than pages insofar as it applies to performances of operas and participation of artists. (However, page numbers are given for reviews and portraits.) To trace the performances of an opera, or the appearances of an artist, consult the inclusive seasons indicated.

Adams, Wally 1960-61
Adler, Kurt 1957-66; rev p82
Adriana Lecouvreur (Cilèa) 1962-63; rev p70
Aida (Verdi) 1957-66; rev p 10, 42, 53, 68, 80, 94, 106
Albanese, Licia 1957-63, 1964-66; rev p 107
Alcestis (Gluck) 1960-61; rev p41
Aldridge, Erbert 1962-65
Alexander, John 1961-66; rev p53, 94
Allen, Ivan 1964-66
Allen, Mildred 1957-62
Allers, Franz 1963-64, 1965-66
Alperstein, Max 1958-59, 1962-63
Alva, Luigi 1963-66; rev p82
Alvary, Lorenzo 1957-61, 1962-66; rev p42
Amara, Lucine 1957-66; rev p9, 19, 107
Ames, Suzanne 1957-60, 1961-64
Amparan, Belen 1957-60
Andrea Chénier (Giordano) 1957-58, 1959-60, 1962-63, 1965-66; rev p 106, 107
Andrew, Thomas 1957-63
Ansermet, Ernest 1962-63; rev p69
Anthony, Charles 1957-66; rev p 19, 20, 42, 52, 69
Aoyama, Yoshio rev p 10, 19, 42
Arabella (Richard Strauss) 1960-61, 1965-66; rev p41
Aragno, Anna 1965-66
Ariadne auf Naxos (Richard Strauss) 1962-64; rev p69, 81
Armistead, Horace rev p31
Arroyo, Martina 1958-59, 1960-62, 1964-66
Arthur, Henry 1958-59
Aschieri, Susana 1965-66

Baccaloni, Salvatore 1957-62
Backgren, Arthur 1958-59, 1960-61
Bacquier, Gabriel 1964-66; rev p93
Baldwin, Marcia 1963-66; rev p 105
Balestrieri, Anthony 1960-62
Ballo in Maschera (Verdi) 1958-59, 1961-63, 1965-66; rev p54, 106, 107
Barber, Samuel. See *Vanessa*
Barber of Bagdad (Cornelius) rev p 107

Barbiere di Siviglia (Rossini) 1957-58, 1962-63, 1965-66; rev p 106
Barbusci, Nicola 1960-62
Bardelli, Cesare 1957-66
Bardin, Micheline 1957-58
Bardini, Gaetano 1965-66
Barioni, Daniele 1957-60, 1961-63
Barrault, Jean-Louis rev p 105
Bastianini, Ettore 1959-60, 1964-66
Baum, Kurt 1957-62, 1964-66; rev p 10, 20, 107
Bausch, Pina 1960-61
Beaton, Cecil rev p9, 42
Beethoven, Ludwig van. See *Fidelio*
Behr, Jan 1961-62, 1963-66
Bellini, Vincenzo. See *Sonnambula*
Berg, Alban. See *Wozzeck*
Bergonzi, Carlo 1957-66; rev p20, 54, 81
Berlin, Patricia 1964-65
Berman, Eugene rev p9, 70
Bernheimer, Martin p94
Bernstein, Leonard 1963-64; rev p82
Biancolli, Louis p9, 20, 31, 42, 52, 106
Bing, Rudolf 1957-66; rev p9, 19, 42, 81, 107
Birlenbach, Erich 1959-61, 1965-66
Bishop, Robert 1960-61
Bizet, Georges. See *Carmen*
Bjoerling, Jussi 1959-60
Bjoner, Ingrid 1961-66; rev p52, 68
Black, Margaret 1957-58
Blair, Lynn 1961-65
Blecker, Ingrid 1961-62
Boehm, Karl 1957-61, 1962-63, 1964-66; rev p9, 20, 30, 31, 70, 94
Bohème (Puccini) 1957-59, 1960-62, 1963-64, 1965-66; rev p 105
Bonelli, Richard p 107
Bonynge, Richard p70
Borg, Kim 1959-62; rev p29
Boris Godunov (Mussorgsky) 1958-59, 1960-61, 1962-63
Borkh, Inge 1957-58, 1960-61; rev p 10, 42
Borso, Umberto 1961-63
Boucher, Gene 1965-66
Bower, Beverly 1964-66
Brayley, Sally 1963-66

Brewer, Nadyne 1962-63, 1964-65
Brook, Peter rev p9
Brysac, Ada 1960-61
Bumbry, Grace 1965-66; rev p 105
Burdick, William 1959-63, 1964-66
Burger, Julius 1960-61; rev p9
Burke, Peter 1957-59
Butler, Henry rev p52, 70, 105

Caballé, Montserrat 1965-66; rev p 106, 107
Calabrese, Ada 1962-63, 1964-65
Callas, Maria (Meneghini) 1957-58, 1964-65; rev p 10, 19, 93, 94
Campora, Giuseppe 1957-59, 1963-65
Cappuccilli, Piero 1959-60
Carelli, Gabor 1957-66; por p 108
Carmen (Bizet) 1957-61
Caruso, Mariano 1962-66
Casei, Nedda 1964-66
Cassel, Walter 1957-66; rev p30, 41, 69
Cavalleria Rusticana (Mascagni) 1958-60, 1962-64; rev p 19
Cehanovsky, George 1957-66; rev p 107
Cernei, Elena 1964-66
Chaliapin, Fyodor p 106
Chambers, Madelaine 1957-59
Chazin, Judith 1961-63
Chistiakov, Vladimir 1961-64, 1965-66
Chookasian, Lili 1961-66; rev p54, 82
Chopin, Frédéric François. See *Sylphides* (ballet)
Christopher, Russell 1963-66
Cilèa, Francesco. See *Adriana Lecouvreur*
Cimara, Pietro 1957-58
Clark, Charleen 1959-61
Clements, Joy 1963-66
Cleva, Fausto 1957-66; rev p29, 41, 52
Coleman, Robert p 10, 29, 53
Collins, Eugene 1963-64
Colonnello, Attilio rev p93
Colzani, Anselmo 1959-66; rev p31, 52, 70, 82; por p56
Conner, Nadine 1957-58, 1959-60
Contes d'Hoffmann (Offenbach) 1958-59, 1961-62, 1964-65; rev p54
Cooke, Charles 1960-62, 1963-64
Cooke, Thomas 1960-61

Corelli, Franco 1960-66; rev p42, 70, 107; por p57
Corena, Fernando 1957-66; rev p9, 41, 107
Così Fan Tutte (Mozart) 1961-62, 1964-65; rev p52, 53
Costa, Mary 1963-66; rev p81
Coulter, Dorothy 1960-62
Crain, Jon 1957-58
Crespin, Régine 1962-66; rev p69, 107; por p58
Crosson, Craig 1960-65
Cundari, Emilia 1957-59
Curtin, Phyllis 1961-62; rev p52
Curtis-Verna, Mary 1957-66
Cvejic, Biserka 1960-61, 1962-66; rev p42
Czerwenka, Oskar 1959-60

Da Costa, Albert 1957-62
Dalis, Irene 1957-58, 1959-66; rev p30, 70, 81, 94
D'Amboise, Jacques 1958-59
D'Angelo, Gianna 1960-66; rev p42, 69
Davidson, Lawrence 1957-62, 1963-66
Davis, Robert 1965-66
Davy, Gloria 1957-61; rev p 10
Debussy, Claude. See *Pelléas et Mélisande*
De Cesare, Luigi 1958-60
De Florio, Evangeline 1960-61
De Lavallade, Carmen 1957-58
Del Ferro, Leonard 1960-61
D'Elia, Frank 1958-59, 1960-66
Della Casa, Lisa 1957-66; rev p9, 30
Del Monaco, Mario 1957-59; rev p 19
De Los Angeles, Victoria 1957-61; rev p42
Dembaugh, William 1961-65
De Paola, Paul 1960-66
De Paolis, Alessio 1957-64; rev p20, 42
De Salvo, Dina 1959-63, 1964-66
Devon, Hlenka 1958-59
Diakov, Anton 1963-64
Diaz, Justino 1963-66; por p 108
Dickie, Murray 1962-65; rev p68
Di Franco, Loretta 1960-63, 1964-66
Di Stefano, Giuseppe 1964-65
Dobbs, Mattiwilda 1957-64
Doench, Karl 1958-59, 1962-65; rev p 19, 20, 68
Don Carlo (Verdi) 1958-59, 1960-61, 1963-64, 1965-66; rev p82, 105
Don Giovanni (Mozart) 1957-61, 1962-64, 1965-66; rev p9, 69, 81, 106
Donizetti, Gaetano. See *Don Pasquale; Elisir d'Amore; Lucia di Lammermoor*
Don Pasquale (Donizetti) 1964-65
Dooley, William 1963-66; rev p82, 94
Douglas, Scott 1958-60

Dunlap, John Robert 1965-66; por p 108
Dunn, Mignon 1958-66
Dupont, Jacques rev p 105
Dvorakova, Ludmila 1965-66

Ebert, Carl rev p20, 41, 69
Eddington, Lawrence 1962-63, 1964-66
Edelmann, Otto 1957-59, 1961-66
Edwards, Joyce 1958-59
Ehrenberg, Miriam 1963-65
Elektra (Richard Strauss) 1960-62; rev p42, 54
Elias, Rosalind 1957-66; rev p 10, 41, 42, 82; por p 108
Elisir d'Amore (Donizetti) 1960-62, 1965-66; rev p41
Elson, Charles rev p 10
Emanuel, Dawin 1958-59
Emanuel, Nicolyn 1965-66
Enckell, Thomas 1962-63, 1964-65
Ericson, Raymond p53, 54, 69, 82, 93, 106
Ernani (Verdi) 1962-63, 1964-65
Ernster, Dezso 1957-58, 1959-60, 1963-64
Esparza, Elfego 1964-66
Etgen, Ann 1957-59
Eugene Onegin (Tchaikovsky) 1957-59, 1963-64; rev p9, 82
Eure, Ella 1965-66
Evans, Geraint 1963-66; rev p82; por p58
Eyer, Ronald p42, 53, 68

Falstaff (Verdi) 1963-66; rev p82, 106
Fanciulla del West (Puccini) 1961-62, 1965-66; rev p52, 53
Farrell, Eileen 1960-64, 1965-66; rev p41; por p56
Farrington, Hubert 1957-58, 1959-63
Faust (Gounod) 1957-58, 1959-60, 1963-64, 1965-66; rev p9, 105, 106
Feiersinger, Sebastian 1958-59; rev p 19
Fenn, Jean 1958-59, 1963-66
Fercana, Mary 1959-63, 1964-66
Fernandi, Eugenio 1957-62; rev p 10, 41
Ferraro, Edilio 1960-63
Ferrin, Agostino 1963-65
Fidelio (Beethoven) 1959-60, 1962-63, 1965-66; rev p31, 106
Filip, Emil 1963-66
Finkelstein, Gary 1964-65
Fischer, Alan 1961-62
Fischer, Stuart 1963-65
Flagello, Ezio 1957-66; rev p20, 31, 68, 69, 82; por p56
Flagstad, Kirsten p20, 30, 41
Fledermaus (Johann Strauss) 1958-59, 1962-64; rev p69
Fliegende Holländer (Wagner) 1959-60, 1962-63, 1964-65; rev p30
Fliether, Herbert 1962-63
Flotow, Friedrich von. See *Martha*

Fokine, Michel. See *Sylphides*
Folmer, Joseph 1958-61, 1962-66
Forero, Luis 1964-66
Formichini, Dino 1960-64; rev p41
Forza del Destino (Verdi) 1957-58, 1959-60, 1961-62, 1964-65; rev p9
Fox, Frederick rev p31
Franke, Paul 1957-66; rev p20, 69, 70
Freni, Mirella 1965-66; rev p 105; por p58
Frick, Gottlob 1961-62; rev p53
Friedman, Martin 1965-66
Frydel, John 1958-59, 1960-62, 1963-64

Gardelli, Lamberto 1965-66
Garden, Mary p81
Gari, Giulio 1957-59, 1960-61
Gavers, Mattlyn rev p70
Gedda, Nicolai 1957-66; rev p9, 10, 30, 41, 70, 81, 82, 105; por p55
Gérard, Rolf rev p9, 19, 30, 70, 93
Ghazal, Edward 1958-66
Ghiaurov, Nicolai 1965-66; rev p 105; por p58
Ghitti, Franco 1963-64
Ghiuselev, Nicola 1965-66
Giaiotti, Bonaldo 1960-66
Gianni Schicchi (Puccini) 1957-58
Giffin, Norman 1964-65
Gilford, Jack 1958-59, 1962-64
Gioconda (Ponchielli) 1958-59, 1960-62; rev p54, 107
Giordano, Umberto. See *Andrea Chénier*
Gluck, Christoph Willibald. See *Alcestis; Orfeo ed Euridice*
Gniewek, Raymond 1958-59
Gobbi, Tito 1958-59, 1963-66; rev p 19, 106
Goodloe, Robert 1964-66
Gorin, Igor 1963-64
Gorr, Rita 1962-66; rev p68, 93
Götterdämmerung (Wagner) 1961-62, 1963-64
Gounod, Charles. See *Faust*
Graf, Herbert rev p9, 20, 29, 30, 31, 70
Graham, Arthur 1963-65
Gramm, Donald 1963-66; rev p81
Gray, Maria 1963-64
Greene, Ethel 1960-62
Gregory, Josef 1965-66
Grillo, Joann 1963-66
Grinvald, Sylvia 1965-66
Grishin, Natalie 1957-58
Grist, Reri 1965-66; rev p 106
Gruen, John p54, 69
Guarrera, Frank 1957-66; rev p41, 42
Gueden, Hilde 1957-60
Gutierrez, Jose 1958-59
Gutman, John rev p69
Gypsy Baron (Johann Strauss) 1959-60; rev p30

INDEX

Hagen, Walter 1957-58
Harper, Elinor 1961-63
Harrell, Mack 1957-58
Harrison, Jay S. p30
Harshaw, Margaret 1957-62, 1963-64
Harvuot, Clifford 1957-66; por p 108
Hawkins, Osie 1957-63, 1964-65
Hayden, Melissa 1957-58
Hecht, Joshua 1964-65
Heinrich, Rudolf rev p94
Hemmerly, Walter 1958-62, 1963-64
Herbert, Ralph 1957-58, 1959-63
Herlea, Nicolae 1963-66; rev p82
Heyes, Patricia 1962-66
Hillyer, Jane 1962-63
Hines, Jerome 1957-66; rev p20, 30; por p 108
Hirschl, Ilona 1959-60
Hoffman, Grace 1957-58
Holder, Geoffrey 1957-58
Holland, Florence 1957-58
Hopf, Hans 1960-62, 1963-64
Horne, Katharyn [Horn, Catherine] 1959-65
Hughes, Allen p41, 106
Hundley, Richard 1961-62
Hurley, Laurel 1957-65; rev p69

Imai, Kunie 1958-59

Jerell, Edith 1957-61, 1962-66
Johnson, Harriett p 19, 31, 54, 70, 82, 106
Jones, Alexandra [Lexi] 1959-63, 1964-66
Jones, Harry 1959-60, 1961-63, 1964-66
Jones, Junetta 1963-65
Jorgenson, Rhodie 1963-66
Jurinac, Sena p 10

Kabaivanska, Raina 1962-66; rev p69
Kailer, Lucille 1960-61, 1965-66
Kalil, Margaret 1965-66
Kapilow, Gloria 1962-63
Kastendieck, Miles p 10, 30, 41, 42, 54, 69, 70, 81, 105, 106
Kaye, Nora 1958-59
Keane, Audrey 1957-63
Keith, George 1957-58
Kelley, Norman 1957-58, 1960-61
Kessler, Kurt 1959-62
King, James 1965-66; rev p 106
King, Nancy 1957-63
Kirschberg, Arnold 1961-62, 1963-64
Kirsten, Dorothy 1959-66; rev p53
Kirwan, Jane 1959-60
Knight, Arnold 1958-59
Knitzer, Pauline 1965-66
Kolodin, Irving p 10, 19, 31, 41, 42, 53, 54, 69, 70, 81, 82, 93, 105
Kónya, Sándor 1961-66; rev p52, 68; por p57
Kouba, Maria 1964-66

Krall, Heidi 1957-62, 1965-66
Kraus, Alfredo 1965-66; rev p 106
Kriese, Gladys 1961-66; rev p69, 105
Kroon, Carole 1960-64
Kuchta, Gladys 1960-65; rev p42
Kuen, Paul 1961-62; rev p53
Kuestner, Charles 1958-66
Kullman, Charles 1957-61

Labò, Flaviano 1957-58, 1962-66; rev p9
La Marchina, Robert 1964-65
Lammers, Gerda 1961-62; rev p54
Lang, Paul Henry p 10, 20, 30, 42, 52, 54
Langdon, Michael 1964-65
Lansché, Ruth 1961-62, 1965-66
Lansing, Gladys 1957-58, 1959-60
Last Savage (Menotti) 1963-65; rev p81
Lee, Ming Cho rev p 10
Lee, Sondra 1958-59
Leinsdorf, Erich 1957-62, 1965-66; rev p 19, 20, 29, 30, 41
Leoncavallo, Ruggiero. See Pagliacci
Levy, Diana 1965-66
Lewis, Brenda 1957-59, 1960-62, 1964-65
Lewis, William 1957-59
Liebl, Karl 1958-66; rev p20, 30, 31, 94
Lind, Gloria 1957-62
Linn, Bambi 1958-59
Lipton, Martha 1957-61
Lisitsian, Pavel 1959-60
Loevberg, Aase Nordmo 1958-60; rev p20, 31
Lohengrin (Wagner) 1958-59, 1961-62, 1963-64; rev p20, 52, 53
Lombard, Alain 1965-66
London, George 1957-66; rev p9, 31, 82
Lorengar, Pilar 1965-66; rev p 106
Love, Shirley 1963-64, 1965-66
Lucia di Lammermoor (Donizetti) 1957-59, 1961-62, 1964-66; rev p53, 92
Ludwig, Christa 1959-61; rev p30
Lyall, Christopher 1964-65

Maazel, Lorin 1962-63; rev p69
Macbeth (Verdi) 1958-60, 1961-62, 1963-64; rev p 19
MacKenzie, Mary 1960-62
MacLarnon, Fern 1964-66
MacNeil, Cornell 1958-66; rev p20, 41; por p55
Macurdy, John 1962-66; rev p93
Madama Butterfly (Puccini) 1957-63, 1964-66; rev p 10, 19, 41, 105
Madeira, Jean 1957-64, 1965-66; rev p54; por p 108
Magic Flute (Mozart) 1958-59, 1963-64; rev p81
Mahler, Donald 1961-66
Malagrida, Luisa 1963-64
Maloney, William 1964-66

Mandile, Frank 1958-59, 1961-62
Manon (Massenet) 1959-60, 1963-65; rev p81
Manon Lescaut (Puccini) 1958-59, 1960-61, 1965-66; rev p 107
Manuel, Michael rev p41
Marcella, Lou 1958-66
Marek, Dan 1965-66
Markova, Alicia 1957-58; rev p81, 93
Marks, Bruce 1957-61
Marritt, Naomi 1963-66
Marsh, Calvin 1957-66; rev p20
Martha (Flotow) 1960-61; rev p41
Martin, Carolyn 1962-66
Martin, Donald 1957-60
Martin, Janis 1962-65
Mascagni, Pietro. See Cavalleria Rusticana
Massenet, Jules. See Manon
Maule, Michael 1957-58
Maximowna, Ita rev p54
Mayreder, Rudolf 1957-58, 1959-63
McCracken, James 1962-66; rev p70, 107; por p57
McIlhenny, Helen 1965-66
McLuckey, William 1963-65
Mehta, Zubin 1965-66; rev p 106; por p 108
Meister, Hans 1962-66
Meistersinger (Wagner) 1958-59, 1962-65; rev p 19, 68, 69
Melatti, Jean 1957-58
Meneguzzer, Jolanda 1963-64
Menotti, Gian Carlo. See Last Savage; Vanessa
Meredith, Morley 1961-66; rev p54, 69, 82
Merrill, Nathaniel rev p41, 42, 70, 80, 93
Merrill, Robert 1957-66; rev p54, 70, 105, 107
Messel, Oliver rev p29, 69
Meyer, Kerstin 1960-63; rev p69
Michalski, Raymond 1965-66
Mickens, Jan 1964-66
Mihalic, Melanija 1963-64
Milanov, Zinka 1957-66; rev p 19, 106, 107; por p 108
Miles, Roland 1959-61
Miller, Mildred 1957-66; por p 108
Milnes, David 1965-66
Milnes, Sherrill 1965-66; rev p 106
Mitchell, Arthur 1961-62
Mitropoulos, Dimitri 1957-60; rev p9, 19, 20, 31
Mittelmann, Norman 1961-65; rev p52, 68
Moedl, Martha 1957-58, 1959-60
Moffo, Anna 1959-66; rev p30, 42, 81; por p55
Molinari-Pradelli, Francesco 1965-66; rev p 106
Moll, Mariquita 1957-58
Mollica, Giulio 1958-60
Montresor, Beni rev p82
Morel, Jean 1957-62

Morell, Barry 1958-66; rev p 19; por p55
Morse, Janet 1965-66
Moscona, Nicola 1957-62
Motley rev p29, 31
Mozart, Wolfgang Amadeus. See *Così Fan Tutte; Don Giovanni; Magic Flute; Nozze di Figaro*
Munsel, Patrice 1957-58
Munson, Pamela 1960-63, 1964-66
Murray, Ron 1958-60
Mussorgsky, Modeste. See *Boris Godunov*

Nabucco (Verdi) 1960-61; rev p40
Nache, Maria 1959-60
Nagasaka, Motohiro rev p 10
Nagy, Robert 1957-66; rev p42
Neher, Caspar rev p20
Nelli, Herva 1959-61
Nikolov, Nikola 1960-61
Nilsson, Birgit 1959-66; rev p30, 42, 81, 94, 107; por p56
Nilsson, Christine p 107
Nordmo-Lövberg, Aase. See Loev-berg, Aase Nordmo
Nozze di Figaro (Mozart) 1957-58, 1959-62, 1964-65; rev p29, 30, 54
Nuotio, Pekka 1965-66

O'Connell, Sharon 1965-66
Offenbach, Jacques. See *Contes d'Hoffmann; Perichole*
O'Hearn, Robert rev p41, 68, 80, 93, 105
Oliver, Jess 1963-64
Olvis, William 1958-63; rev p20, 31
Oppicelli, Aurelio 1959-60
Ordassy, Carlotta 1957-66; rev p20
Orfeo ed Euridice (Gluck) 1957-58, 1961-62
Otello (Verdi) 1957-59, 1962-65; rev p 19, 70
Otto, Teo rev p30
Owen, Lynn 1964-66

Paaz, Nira 1964-66
Pagliacci (Leoncavallo) 1958-60, 1962-64; rev p 19, 31, 69
Panni, Nicoletta 1963-64
Parada, Claudia 1961-63
Parmenter, Ross p 10
Parsifal (Wagner) 1957-58, 1959-61, 1965-66
Parsons, Meredith 1960-62
Paskalis, Kostas 1964-65
Patterson, Robert 1962-65
Pavek, Janet 1963-64
Pechner, Gerhard 1957-65
Peerce, Jan 1957-66
Pelléas et Mélisande (Debussy) 1959-60, 1962-63; rev p69
Perichole (Offenbach) 1957-58, 1961-62, 1965-66
Perkins, Francis D. p53
Peters, Roberta 1957-66; rev p9, 82

Pilarczyk, Helga 1964-65
Pinza, Ezio p 106
Piper, Frank 1959-60
Pique Dame. See *Queen of Spades*
Piso, Ion 1965-66
Plotkin, Alice 1958-59
Pobbe, Marcella 1957-58
Ponchielli, Amilcare. See *Gioconda*
Pons, Lily 1957-58, 1960-61
Ponselle, Rosa p54
Pospinov, Ruza 1965-66; rev p 106
Pourfarrokh, Ali 1963-64
Powell, Thomas 1958-59, 1960-61
Pracht, Mary Ellen 1961-66
Prêtre, Georges 1964-66; rev p93, 105
Prevedi, Bruno 1964-66; rev p94
Prey, Hermann 1960-61, 1964-65
Price, Leontyne 1960-66; rev p42, 52, 107; por p57
Puccini, Giacomo. See *Bohème; Fanciulla del West; Gianni Schicchi; Madama Butterfly; Manon Lescaut; Tosca; Turandot*

Queen of Spades (Tchaikovsky) 1965-66; rev p 105
Quintero, José rev p 19

Raimondi, Gianni 1965-66; rev p 105
Rankin, Nell 1957-66
Raskin, Judith 1961-66; rev p54, 82; por p57
Reardon, John 1965-66
Reep, Nancy 1959-61
Reiner, Fritz p30
Reitan, Roald 1959-63
Rennert, Günther rev p81, 94
Resnik, Regina 1957-66; rev p 10, 30, 82, 105
Rethberg, Elisabeth p 107
Rheingold (Wagner) 1961-62; rev p53
Rhodes, Jane 1960-62
Rich, Alan p53, 81. 82, 93. 94, 105, 106, 107
Rich, Martin 1958-66
Rigal, Delia 1965-66; rev p 107
Rigoletto (Verdi) 1958-59, 1960-62, 1963-66; rev p20, 42, 106
Ringland, Earl 1958-59, 1960-61; rev p20
Ritchard, Cyril 1957-58, 1961-62, 1965-66; rev p29, 30
Roberti, Margherita 1961-62; rev p54
Roberto, Francesca 1965-66
Roberts, Hal 1958-59, 1960-66
Roggero, Margaret 1957-63; rev p20
Rosenkavalier (Richard Strauss) 1957-58, 1959-60, 1962-63, 1964-65; rev p69, 93, 107
Rosenstock, Joseph 1960-66; rev p68
Rossini, Gioacchino. See *Barbiere di Siviglia*

Rothenberger, Anneliese 1960-66; rev p41, 54
Rothmuller, Marko 1958-61, 1964-65; rev p 19
Rudolf, Max 1957-58, 1965-66
Russell, Thomas 1960-62
Ruzdak, Vladimir 1962-64
Ryan, George 1959-60
Rysanek, Leonie 1958-66; rev p 19, 31, 40, 54, 69; por p55

Saint-Saëns, Charles Camille. See *Samson et Dalila*
Salome (Richard Strauss) 1957-58, 1961-62, 1964-66; rev p 10, 94
Salzman, Eric p20, 42, 54, 81
Samson et Dalila (Saint-Saëns) 1957-58, 1964-66; rev p93
San Miguel, Lolita 1957-63
Santi, Nello 1961-65; rev p54
Santiago, Anthony 1965-66
Santini, Nerina 1960-61
Sargeant, Winthrop p9, 19, 31, 41, 54, 69, 70, 82, 105
Savage, May 1959-60
Sayette, Howard 1960-66
Schech, Marianne 1957-58
Schick, George 1958-66
Schippers, Thomas 1957-61, 1962-66; rev p30, 41, 81, 82, 105
Schmorr, Robert 1965-66
Schoch, Jean Lee 1957-58
Schoeffler, Paul 1962-65
Schonberg, Harold C. p 19, 30, 41, 52, 68, 69, 81, 94, 106
Schwarzkopf, Elisabeth 1964-66; rev p93; por p58
Scott, Norman 1957-66
Scotto, Renata 1965-66; rev p 105
Scovotti, Jeanette 1962-66; rev p69
Sequoio, Ron 1960-63
Sereni, Mario 1957-66; rev p 19, 81, 82
Sergi, Arturo 1962-66; por p 108
Serrano, Lupe 1958-59
Sgarro, Louis 1957-66
Shawn, Dorothy 1957-58, 1959-66
Shirley, George 1961-66; rev p52
Sibley, Louellen 1958-60, 1961-62
Siegfried (Wagner) 1961-62; rev p53
Siepi, Cesare 1957-66; rev p9, 41, 81, 105
Simionato, Giulietta 1959-61, 1962-63; rev p29; por p55
Simon Boccanegra (Verdi) 1959-61, 1964-65; rev p31
Simoneau, Leopold 1963-64; rev p81
Simonson, Lee rev p53
Sims, Lilias 1960-63, 1964-66
Singher, Martial 1957-59
Slezak, Walter 1959-60; rev p30
Sliker, Peter 1961-66
Smith, Kenneth 1963-64
Smith, Oliver rev p42
Snyder, Louis p94, 107
Soederstroem, Elisabeth 1959-61, 1962-64; rev p29, 41
Solov, Zachary 1957-58; rev p9, 93

Solti, Georg 1960-61, 1962-64; rev p70, 81
Sonnambula (Bellini) 1962-64; rev p70
Souzay, Gérard 1964-65
Stanz, William 1958-60, 1962-66
Starling, William 1958-60
Steber, Eleanor 1957-61, 1962-63, 1965-66; rev p9, 10, 20, 107
Steinberg, William 1964-65; rev p94
Stella, Antonietta 1957-60; rev p 10
Sternberg, Harold 1958-60, 1962-63
Sternberg, Sam 1958-59
Stevens, Risë 1957-61
Stewart, Thomas 1965-66; rev p 106
Stich-Randall, Teresa 1961-64, 1965-66; rev p52
Stiedry, Fritz 1957-58
Stokowski, Leopold 1960-62, 1965-66; rev p42, 107
Strang, Lloyd 1958-66
Strasfogel, Andrew 1957-58
Strasfogel, Ignace 1958-66
Stratas, Teresa 1959-66; rev p82, 105
Strauss, Johann. See Fledermaus; Gypsy Baron
Strauss, Richard. See Arabella; Ariadne auf Naxos; Elektra; Rosenkavalier; Salome
Strongin, Theodore p 106
Sukis, Lilian 1965-66
Sullivan, Brian 1958-59, 1960-61
Sutherland, Joan 1961-65; rev p53, 70, 93; por p57
Sylphides (Chopin) (ballet) 1964-65; rev p93
Symonette, Randolph 1961-62; rev p53

Tagliavini, Ferruccio 1961-62
Tannhäuser (Wagner) 1960-61, 1965-66
Taubman, Howard p9, 19, 20, 29
Taussig, Walter 1958-61
Tchaikovsky, Peter Ilich. See Eugene Onegin; Queen of Spades
Tebaldi, Renata 1958-61, 1962-66; rev p 19, 70, 107
Terry, Walter p94
Testi, Lorenzo 1960-63
Teyte, Maggie p81
Thebom, Blanche 1957-59, 1960-66

Thomas, Jess 1962-66; rev p69, 93; por p58
Thomaz, Neyde 1963-64; rev p81
Tibbett, Lawrence p31
Tol Padu, Khemfoia 1963-64
Tomanelli, Carlo 1958-66
Töpper, Hertha 1962-63; rev p69
Tosca (Puccini) 1957-60, 1961-62, 1963-66; rev p54, 94
Tozzi, Giorgio 1957-66; rev p9, 10, 31, 42, 70, 81
Traviata (Verdi) 1957-60, 1961-64; rev p 10, 30, 81
Trehy, John 1958-66
Tristan und Isolde (Wagner) 1957-58, 1959-61, 1962-63; rev p30
Trovatore (Verdi) 1959-61, 1963-64, 1965-66; rev p29, 42, 107
Trucco, Victor 1961-62
Tucci, Gabriella 1960-66; rev p41, 70, 82, 105; por p56, 108
Tucker, Richard 1957-66; rev p9, 31, 42, 52, 107; por p 108
Tudor, Antony rev p41
Turandot (Puccini) 1960-63, 1964-65; rev p42

Uhde, Hermann 1958-61, 1963-64; rev p20, 31
Uppman, Theodor 1957-66; rev p9, 69; por p 108
Uzunov, Dimiter 1958-60, 1964-65

Valentino, Frank 1957-61
Välkki, Anita 1961-62, 1964-66; rev p54
Valletti, Cesare 1957-60; rev p9, 41
Vanessa (Barber) 1957-59, 1964-65; rev p9
Vanni, Helen 1957-63, 1964-65; rev p68
Varviso, Silvio 1961-66; rev p53, 70
Velis, Andrea 1961-66; rev p69
Verchi, Nino 1959-62
Verdi, Giuseppe. See Aida; Ballo in Maschera; Don Carlo; Ernani; Falstaff; Forza del Destino; Macbeth; Nabucco; Otello; Rigoletto; Simon Boccanegra; Traviata; Trovatore
Verdy, Violette 1959-60, 1961-62
Verreau, Richard 1963-65
Vichey, Luben 1961-63, 1965-66
Vickers, Jon 1959-63, 1964-66; rev p31, 105; por p56

Vicos, Athena 1959-62, 1963-65
Vinay, Ramon 1957-58, 1959-62, 1965-66
Vishnevskaya, Galina 1961-62; rev p53
Votipka, Thelma 1957-63, 1965-66; rev p 107

Wächter, Eberhard 1960-61
Wagner, Richard. See Fliegende Holländer; Götterdämmerung; Lohengrin; Meistersinger; Parsifal; Rheingold; Siegfried; Tannhäuser; Tristan und Isolde; Walküre
Walker, William 1962-66
Walküre (Wagner) 1957-58, 1959-60, 1961-62, 1964-65; rev p54
Wall, Joan 1959-62
Wallmann, Margherita rev p93
Walter, Bruno 1958-59
Ward, David 1963-66; rev p81
Warren, Leonard 1957-60; rev p 10, 19, 20, 30, 31
Warren, Marsha 1957-58, 1959-60, 1962-65
Watt, Douglas p9, 42, 52, 81
Weathers, Felicia 1965-66
Webster, Margaret rev p31
Welitsch, Ljuba p94
Westergard, Lance 1965-66
Wiemann, Ernst 1961-66; rev p53
Wiener, Otto 1962-63; rev p68
Wiland, Steve 1957-58
Wilder, Joan 1961-63
Wilder, Kenlin 1962-63
Wilderman, William 1957-64
Wilson, Dolores 1957-59
Wilson, Lee 1965-66
Wozzeck (Berg) 1958-59, 1960-61, 1964-65; rev p20

Yauger, Maria 1959-61
Yeend, Frances 1960-62, 1963-64; rev p42
Yezer, Franklin 1965-66
Youskevitch, Igor 1962-63

Zakariasen, William 1961-66
Zambruno, Primo 1958-59; rev p 19
Zampieri, Giuseppe 1961-62
Zanasi, Mario 1957-60; rev p 10
Zauberflöte. See Magic Flute
Zeffirelli, Franco rev p82
Zelens, Richard 1961-62, 1964-65
Zybine, Alek 1958-59

(2797)